KEY TEXTS

Printed and bound by
Antony Rowe Ltd., Chippenham, Wiltshire

KEY TEXTS
Classic Studies in the History of Ideas

THE REASONABLENESS OF CHRISTIANITY AS DELIVERED IN THE SCRIPTURES

John Locke

With a new Introduction by
Victor Nuovo
Middlebury College, Vermont

 THOEMMES
PRESS

This edition published by Thoemmes Press, 1997

Thoemmes Press
11 Great George Street
Bristol BS1 5RR, England

US office: Distribution and Marketing
22883 Quicksilver Drive
Dulles, Virginia 20166, USA

ISBN 1 85506 522 3

This reprint is taken from the 1794 Edition
of the *Works of John Locke*

Publisher's Note

The publisher has gone to great lengths to ensure the
quality of this reprint but points out that some
imperfections in the original book may be apparent.

#37807010

INTRODUCTION

The Reasonableness of Christianity as delivered in the Scriptures (TRC) is a theological work by one of the greatest modern philosophers, John Locke (1632–1704). It was published anonymously in August 1695. Like his other principal writings, *An Essay concerning Human Understanding* (1689/90), *Epistola de Tolerantia* (1689), *Two Treatises on Government* (1689) and *Some Thoughts concerning Education* (1693), it is a work of originality and genius. It was a staple of theological education during the eighteenth century, but since then it has suffered from disrepute and neglect.[1] Its fortunes have not appreciably changed despite the remarkable revival of Locke studies of the past few decades. There is reason to believe, however, that its time of neglect is over, for the religious motivation in Locke's thought is now well established, and this will no doubt give rise to renewed attention to his main theological work and assessments of its place in his philosophical programme.[2] *A Vindication of the Reasonableness of*

---

[1] Richard Watson gave it first place in his popular *Collection of Theological Tracts*, 6 vols. (London: J. Edwards, 1785). For a critical account of recent theological assessments of Locke and *TRC*, see Stephen N. Williams, *Revelation and Reconciliation* (Cambridge University Press, 1995).

[2] For important discussions of the religious motivation in Locke's thought, see Richard Ashcraft, 'Faith and Knowledge in Locke's Philosophy', in John Yolton (ed.), *John Locke: Problems and Perspectives* (Cambridge University Press, 1969); John Dunn, *The Political Thought of John Locke* (Cambridge University Press, 1969); John Marshall, *John Locke*, (Cambridge University Press, 1994); G. A. J. Rogers, Introduction to

Christianity and *A Second Vindication of the Reasonableness of Christianity* are works of a different kind from the one that they were written to defend and should, therefore, be approached differently. How they differ will be clarified later on after an account of the context and content of *TRC* has been given.

1

On Locke's account, he began *TRC* during the winter of 1694/95.[3] He wrote it at Oates in Essex, the residence of Sir Francis and Lady Damaris Masham, where he lived during the last decade of his life. There he had comfortable rooms, an ample library of his own and intellectual companionship.[4] Locke also gives us clear statements of his reasons or motives for writing the book. In the preface to *TRC*, he mentions the failure of 'most of the systems of divinity' known to him to satisfy religious concerns as one reason. The religious concerns in question were of the greatest importance, namely, eternal life and the form and content of faith in Christ that was requisite for receiving it. The authors of these unsatisfactory systems failed to provide clear answers to these questions such as would satisfy the anxious

---

Locke's Philosophy (Oxford: Clarendon Press, 1993); W. M. Spellman, *John Locke and the Problem of Depravity* (Oxford: Clarendon Press, 1988).

[3] Locke to Philip van Limborch, 10 May 1695, in *The Correspondence of John Locke*, ed. E. S. de Beer (Oxford University Press, 1979–89), vol. 5, no. 1901.

[4] On Locke's library at Oates, see John Harrison and Peter Laslett, *The Library of John Locke* (Oxford University Press, 1965). Damaris Masham was the daughter of Ralph Cudworth, the Cambridge Platonist. She is undoubtedly the 'other person', his interlocutor, who, Locke attests, shared in the progress of the work from start to finish. See below, *The Second Vindication*, p. 189. See also Sarah Hutton, 'Between Platonism and Enlightenment: Damaris Cudworth, Lady Masham', *British Journal for the History of Philosophy*, vol. 1 (1993), pp. 29–54.

concerns of ordinary unschooled Christians and thus a new attempt based on an 'attentive and unbiased' reading of Scripture was called for.

Locke gives a more personal account of his motives in his correspondence. In a letter to Philip van Limborch written in London and dated 11 December 1694, he comments on two events that relate to his project: his receipt of Limborch's *Theologia Christiana* and the death of John Tillotson, the late Archbishop of Canterbury who was Locke's friend and counsellor.

> As soon as I find leisure I shall examine your *Theologia Christiana* diligently, for I think that I ought now to give my mind for the most part to such studies, and I wish so much the more that I were with you because, now that that great and candid searcher after truth, to say nothing of his other virtues, has been taken from us, I have scarcely anyone whom I can freely consult about theological uncertainties.[5]

Locke does not say why he thinks he 'ought now' to engage in theological studies. The two events he mentions are not reasons, but they may, nonetheless, have been causes of his engagement. Yet, in a subsequent letter, he writes that he delayed reading Limborch's *Theologia* and other systems of divinity until *after* he had completed his own inquiry, so that the standard by which he judged most systems of divinity deficient was his own system. It should come as no surprise, however, that Limborch's system of divinity was not among those that Locke found wanting.

---

[5] E. S. de Beer (ed.), *op. cit.*, vol. 5, no. 1826. The English translation of the correspondence between Locke and Limborch is de Beer's. Locke is referring to the second edition of Limborch's *Theologia Christiana*. The first edition was published in 1686, when Locke was in the Netherlands. He was, therefore, already familiar with the work.

I must now thank you again for your *Theologia Christiana*, not because it has enriched [my] library with a volume but because it has enriched me with knowledge. For this winter, considering diligently wherein the Christian faith consists, I thought that it ought to be drawn from the very fountains of Holy Writ, the opinions and orthodoxies of sects and systems, whatever they may be, being set aside. From an intent and careful reading of the New Testament the conditions of the New Covenant and the teaching of the Gospel became clearer to me, as it seemed to me, than the noontide light, and I am fully convinced that a sincere reader of the Gospel cannot be in doubt as to what the Christian faith is. I therefore set down my thoughts on paper, thereby the better to survey, tranquilly and at leisure, the agreement of the parts with one another, their harmony, and the foundations on which they rested. When everything in this creed of mine seemed everywhere sound and conformable to the word of God I thought that the theologians (that is, the Reformed) ought to be consulted, so that I might see what they thought about the faith. I went to Calvin, Turrettini and others, who I am compelled to admit, have treated that subject in such a way that I can by no means grasp what they say or what they mean; so discordant does everything in them seem to me with the sense and simplicity of the Gospel that I am unable to understand their writings, much less to reconcile them with Holy Writ. At last, with better hopes I took in hand your *Theologia* and not without very great joy read book V, chapter VIII, from which I perceived that one theologian was to be found for whom I am not a heretic. I have not yet obtained enough free time to go further with the reading of your book. Nothing could be more desirable for me now possessed the leisure and experience to pursue them. The sustaining and guiding friendships of Limborch, who was far away, and of Damaris Masham, who was close by, the senseless controversy among the dissenters and its demonic and divisive consequences, which might as well be called the Calvinist Crisis as the Crisis of Deism, altogether provided the occasion, the motive and the issue of his own theological project. Finally, the satisfying result of his research, which had all the marks of a discovery of truth, and finding confirmation of it in the independent judgement of another, provided a motive to publish. Although he was made bold to publish his book, he was not so bold as to put his name on it.

Whether this is a true account of the origin of Locke's work depends upon how ingenuous he was in telling about it and how perceptive he was of his own reasons and motives. Even if it is not true, it is plausible and it is Locke's own account and hence the one which every critical interpreter must first consider even if only to use it as an object on which to cast suspicion. In this introductory account, I shall treat it as though it were true.

2

The title is crafted to assert a single simple proposition: Christianity as delivered in the Scriptures is reasonable. The subject of this sentence is the Gospel of Jesus Christ, delivered in the New Testament in the preaching of Jesus and the Apostles, and it is to be distinguished from other less reasonable if not downright irrational varieties of the Christian religion whose modes of delivery hide its simple truth. To assert that pure Christianity is reasonable is not to claim that it can be discovered by rational inquiry or demonstrated by argument. 'Reasonable' here means 'advantageous'. To all who are concerned about their moral duty and the possibility of eternal bliss, which are the great concerns of life, Christianity as delivered in the Scriptures offers assurance and direction that surpasses every other religious doctrine.

Notwithstanding the precision of its title and the simplicity of its theme, *TRC* is a richly textured work. Through a series of digressions that punctuate the main discourse with increasing frequency the reader is led into much broader and more complex themes: human frailty and depravity, natural law and human obligation, faith and reason, internal evidence for the authenticity of the gospel revelation, the meaning of the Messianic titles, the Messianic secret, the wisdom and justice and goodness of God as manifest in the plan of salvation, the meaning of history and the end of existence.

Moreover, the work in its entirety exemplifies a method of biblical interpretation which is historical rather than dogmatic. The principal content of Scripture is not doctrine but a narrative, not one that originated in the collective imagination of the first Christians, but a narrative of true events to which they testified and which can be objectively constructed from their testimony. The entire work can be taken as an exposition of the Pauline dictum that as in Adam all die, so in Christ all shall be made alive [I Cor. 15:22]. Adam and Christ, the two 'Sons of God', who were such because they had no human father, encompass the whole of history. The doctrine of redemption presupposes Adam's fall and its consequences. By disobeying the divine commandment, Adam fell from perfect obedience, and the consequences of his fall – the loss of immortality and of bliss – were extended to all his posterity. In this narrative, Adam appears in the role of our ancestor, but not our representative.[12] God was not unjust in depriving mankind of immortal bliss, for no creature has an inherent right to it. Besides, mortal existence is better than no existence at all. Unlike Hobbes, Locke did not believe that life even if lived in a state of nature was 'solitary, poor, nasty, brutish and short'. Being mortal, therefore, is not a just ground of complaint against God. Moreover, any mortal being capable of understanding a law can gain the *right* to immortal bliss by perfect obedience to the Law of Nature, otherwise called the Law of Works, and the first outcome of the work of redemption in Christ is to make this right viable. In Christ all shall be made alive. This is the first consequence of Christ's obedient death and resurrection. Christ will come again and all shall be raised and judged, although not all shall be saved. At the last judgement anyone who can justly claim perfect obedience to the Law of Nature will be rewarded. Those who cannot will be returned to death.

But, since all have sinned, our redemption from death, from the first death, would be futile unless God provided another way of being judged righteous. This other way is the Law of Faith, which involves the acceptance of God's new covenant and trust that God will keep his promises. What, then, does this law require? It requires acceptance of the one great proposition, that Jesus is the Messiah. The Law of Faith also requires repentance and obedience to the Law of Nature, to which it is identical as a moral law , but it does not require perfect obedience. Faith in Jesus as the Messiah substitutes as righteousness. The advantage of the Christian Law of Faith over the Law of Nature and the Law of Works

---

[12] As his natural progeny, we inherit his natural mortality but not his guilt. On this distinction see Ian Harris, 'The Politics of Christianity', in G. A. J. Rogers, *op. cit.*

derives from its milder and more likely attainable standard. And, since its source is revelation, it offers also an unshakeable assurance. The surety of the truth that Jesus the Messiah has restored life and righteousness derives from God himself, and the authenticity of God's revelation is discernible in the narrative itself.

3

Immortal bliss and the Law of Nature are themes that are basic to the philosophical project to found morality that was an original motive of Locke's major work, *An Essay concerning Human Understanding.* Hence, *TRC*, being Locke's last major new work published during his lifetime, should cast light on the welfare of that project. In a recent discussion of 'the contexts of *The Reasonableness of Christianity*', one that represents a growing consensus, it is claimed that Locke's accounts in *TRC* of belief in immortality and the knowability of the Law of Nature show that his project ended in failure, since belief in immortality is a necessary motive to moral obedience and knowledge of the Law of Nature a condition of right action.[13] But this judgement seems both precipitous and false.

It is, indeed, quite clear that Locke believed that Scripture teaches that human nature is mortal after the Fall.

This is so clear in these cited places [Rom. v. 12; I Cor. xv. 22], and so much the current of the New

[13] John Marshall, *op. cit.*, chap. 5, esp. p. 388. See also *TRC*, pp. 138–51. Marshall's characterization of Locke is a variation on the theme of Locke as a tragic figure which originates with John Dunn. See his *Locke* (Oxford University Press, 1984). The plausibility of this view of Locke is significantly diminished if, as I argue here, Locke managed in *TRC* to formulate a theory of morality that is grounded both on reason and revelation.

Testament, that nobody can deny, but that the doctrine of the gospel is, that death came on all men by Adam's sin; only they differ about the signification of the word death.... (p. 6)[14]

[Gen iii. 17–19] shows that paradise was a place of bliss, as well as immortality... But when man was turned out, he was exposed to the toil, anxiety, and frailties of this mortal life, which should end in the dust, out of which he was made, and to which he should return; *and then have no more life or sense, than the dust had, out of which he was made.* (p. 7)[15]

One could not ask for a more unambiguous assertion of the complete mortality of the human soul. But if the soul is mortal, then any demonstration of its immortality is impossible. The certainty of immortality must rest on some other basis than human nature. But, as already noted, Locke also believed that Adam's Fall did not abrogate the right to immortality of any rational being who maintained perfect obedience to the Law of Nature. What was needed was not proof of immortality, but assurance that this right would be fulfilled. The knowledge of this hypothetical right is an important part of Locke's account of the Law of Nature and of the Christian narrative of redemption. Knowledge of the

[14] Locke then remarks in mock seriousness that 'some' interpret the word 'death' to mean an inherited state of guilt and the prospect of eternal torment in Hell.

[15] Italics mine. It would be precipitous, however, to read this final clause as intimating materialism. It is, however, a clear expression of the mortality of the soul. Locke's point is that when death occurs the soul is just as lifeless, which is to say, senseless, as dust. In Locke's notes inscribed in his interleaved personal copy of the first edition of *TRC* (p. 15, n. 2), he notes that death, or the first death, is equivalent to the cessation of perception and activity. He makes no mention of the destruction of the soul. This copy, which also contains Locke's revisions for the 2d edition, is deposited in the Houghton Library, Harvard University.

Law of Nature, of the divine will that we keep it, and of
the divine justice by which any who obey it perfectly
may claim the right to immortality and bliss, is a presup-
position of the gospel and is, in principle, rationally
discoverable. If this is so, then it is clear, that Locke did
not abandon his moral program but remained
committed to it, all the more now because his account
of Christianity required it.

It was not the knowledge of the Law of Nature but the
rigour of it that posed a problem for Locke. Having
noted that all have sinned and that accordingly no one
has gained a right to immortality, and anticipating the
objection that he was sure would follow, Locke asks
why God would require such a rigorous standard that
has turned out to be so impractical that no one has
satisfied it. After a preliminary answer that the purity
of God's nature requires it, Locke observes, in a manner
that anticipates Kant, that the rigour of the law follows
from the fact that God has made us rational beings.
Rational beings must live by a law of reason and as such
they cannot fail to know this, so that any of them who
violates this law must do so knowingly, and since
whatever reason demands is what God requires, and
since this also is something we cannot fail to know to
some degree, it follows that anyone who violates the
Law of Nature rebels against God (p. 11).

Locke's commitment to the Law of Nature and its
knowability, then, is no less active in *TRC* than in
anything he wrote before it. It is not diminished by the
fact that the Law of Faith, which is also a divine law,
establishes a different and easier way to gain
immortality and bliss, one that is more in keeping with
the anxiety, frailty and fallibility of the human
condition, for Locke states emphatically that the Law of

Nature remains an eternal and immutable obligation (pp. 13f, 157).

Yet, towards the close of his book, he writes of the universal ignorance of the Law of Nature and of the incapacity of reason to discover its content and even more its foundation. As though addressing himself he writes: '...it is too hard a task for unassisted reason to establish morality in all its parts upon its true foundation, with a clear and convincing light' (p. 139). But Locke's actual position in the very part of his book where this pronouncement is made is more subtly dialectical. Reasons of space require that I merely state his argument barely and without elaboration or defence.

The Law of Nature is the whole system of morality. It exists eternally and immutably. It can be known in two ways: by reason or by revelation. Before Christ, no one succeeded in discovering the whole Law of Nature. Yet, this ignorance was not complete. Parts of this law were known, as prescriptions of civil law or recommendations of philosophers, and since we cannot have knowledge without knowing it to be such, these parts would have had to have been sufficiently grounded to count as knowledge. Necessity was the cause of these portions of moral knowledge, for the Law of Nature is a law of convenience, which is to say, its principles can be founded, although imperfectly, on utility. Moreover, their praiseworthiness and their agreeableness lend support to their acceptance (pp. 142, 144).[16] So, there is knowledge of the Law of Nature, albeit incomplete

---

[16] Locke anticipates two leading eighteenth-century moral theories: the moral sentiment theory of Francis Hutcheson and Jeremy Bentham's utilitarianism. The true heir of Locke's moral theory as it is presented in *TRC* is William Paley who distinguished modern moral philosophy from its ancient varieties just because it is based on reason enhanced and made certain by revelation. See his *Moral and Political Philosophy* (London: R. Faulder, 1785).

and imperfect, but Christ has made it known perfectly and completely. In that respect, revelation restores reason.[17]

Locke draws a further distinction between ways in which moral knowledge is appropriated. It is either discovered, which is rare, or it is taught. Either way, it must be adequately founded. Knowledge, however acquired, is one's own possession and as such familiar. On account of this familiarity, it is easy to imagine that one could have as well have discovered it as learned it. This is an illusion, for the discovery of moral knowledge is in fact difficult. Ever since Christ and because of him, moral knowledge has become common knowledge, which is just one more advantage of Christianity. Thus, '...many [viz. deists] are beholden to revelation, who do not acknowledge it' (p. 145).

Christ the lawgiver, then, not only delivers the whole Law of Nature, but restores it to rationality, and yet, it must be noted, it is rationality historicized. If this is a correct account of what Locke meant to say in *TRC* about revelation and the moral law, then it also may be concluded that the philosophical project that Locke began when he and some friends gathered in his rooms in London during the winter of 1670/71 'to explore questions of "morality and revealed religion"', was not abandoned in this work but completed in a way that was not fully anticipated in his previous works.[18] Hence its originality must be reconsidered.

4

Nevertheless, the Law of Faith, which is the heart of the

[17] Compare this account of the Law of Nature with bk 1, chap. 2 of Locke's *Essay*.

[18] On the origin of Locke's *Essay*, see G. A. J. Rogers, Introduction, *op. cit.*, p. 2.

doctrine of justification, is not a principle discoverable by reason, but established by historical revelation. This law prescribes a necessary, although not sufficient condition of justification.[19] Its content is the acceptance of Jesus as the Messiah and all that this involves: that he is the divine king and lawgiver announced by the prophets, that although innocent he died, was resurrected and will return as King and Judge. Locke attempts to prove this complex article of Christianity by recounting in considerable detail and comprehensiveness the narrative of Jesus's words and deeds and of the apostolic preaching, setting these in the context of Hebrew prophecy and Jewish Messianic expectation, thereby using historical methods to discover Scripture's own principle.[20] The presentation of this evidence fills more than half the book (pp. 17–101), and, unless one is repeatedly reminded of Locke's intentions, it may seem repetitive and boring.

Locke's purpose, however, is not, or is not only, to overwhelm the reader with evidence. Besides showing that the content of saving faith is the one great proposition that Jesus is the Messiah, he wants to prove also the authenticity of the gospel as revelation, which makes his presentation more complex than it first seems. In his *Essay*, Locke defines revelation as a kind of testimony that carries 'Assurance beyond Doubt, Evidence beyond Exception', just because it comes from

---

[19] In general and in brief, the Law of Faith 'is for every one to believe what God requires him to believe, as a condition of the covenant he makes with him' (p. 16). The other conditions are repentance and a sincere effort to obey the moral law.

[20] For Locke's own account of his exegetical principles see his Preface to *A Paraphrase and Notes on the Epistles of St. Paul*, ed. Arthur W. Wainwright (Oxford: Clarendon Press, 1987), vol. 1, pp. 103–16.

xxii Introduction

God who does not deceive and cannot be deceived.[21]
But before this assurance can properly take hold of the
mind, it must be rightly understood and its authenticity
assured. This is reason's task. Understanding comes
from reading Scripture impartially according to
historical principles. Authentication involves the same
procedure, and a good example of how Locke employs
it to this end is given here.

The heart of Locke's proof is his long account of the
Messianic secret (pp. 35–100). It begins with a paradox:
'This concealment of himself must seem strange, in one
who was come to bring light into the world....' Locke
had previously observed that Jesus, and subsequently the
Apostles, used three means to announce his Messianic
mission: miracles, 'plain and direct words', and circumlocutions, that is, parables and other indirect expressions
that only intimate his identity.[22] Jesus's frequent use of
indirect means and his stern prohibition to any who
might recognize him not to disclose his identity is

---

[21] *An Essay Concerning Human Understanding*, bk 4, chap. 16, sect. 14, ed.
Peter Nidditch (Oxford: Clarendon Press, 1975), p. 667:

> ...there is one sort of Propositions that challenge the highest Degree of
> our Assent, upon bare Testimony, whether the thing proposed, agree or
> disagree with common experience, and the ordinary course of Things, or
> no. The Reason whereof is, because the Testimony is of such an one, as
> cannot deceive nor be deceived, and that is of God himself. This carries
> with it Assurance beyond Doubt, Evidence beyond Exception. This is
> called by a peculiar Name, *Revelation*, and our Assent to it, *Faith:* which
> as absolutely determines our Minds, and as perfectly excludes all
> wavering as our Knowledge it self; and we may as well doubt of our own
> Being, as we can, whether any Revelation from GOD be true.... Only we
> must be sure, that it be a divine Revelation, and that we understand it
> right: else we shall expose our selves to all the Extravagancy of
> Enthusiasm, and all the Error of wrong Principles, if we have Faith and
> Assurance in what is not divine Revelation.

[22] It should be noted that Locke does not claim here that miracles count as
general evidence of revelation. In his brief discussion of them, he relates
their evidential efficacy to historical context. A messiah was expected in
Palestine at the beginning of the common era, and it was also expected that

perplexing only so long as one ignores the context of his ministry. The political situation in Judaea, the Roman occupation, partisan conflict within the Jewish community and the expectation that the Messiah would establish the Kingdom of God on earth through miraculous deeds required that Jesus proceed cautiously lest his mission be aborted or wrongly exploited, and also so that he might 'fill out the time foretold in his ministry', that the prophecies concerning him might be fulfilled and the universal, and non-political significance of his mission might be more effectively revealed.[23] And since Jesus would depart after his resurrection and leave it to his disciples to publish the news of his new kingdom abroad, a slow and patient disclosure of his identity and purpose was required to prepare them. His selection of humble and uncultivated men was to ensure their docility but also to forestall any charge that they invented the gospel themselves. Thus, Locke supposes that Jesus moves deliberately and with foresight in the

'with an extraordinary and divine power, and miracles, [the messiah] should evidence his mission, and work their deliverance' (p. 32). In this context miracles are 'properly evidential'.

[23] Locke understands Jesus's Messianic office is apolitical only with respect to secular politics. He regards it as cosmically or apocalyptically political. According to Scripture, Jesus the Messiah is 'head and chieftain in opposition to "the prince of this world, the prince of the power of the air"...'. He rules now and will come again to judge the world (pp. 135, 151). Thus, Locke carries over the doctrine of the two kingdoms that he develops in *A Letter concerning Toleration*. See John Locke, *Political Writings*, ed. David Wootton (London: Penguin Books, 1993), p. 396. One can imagine existing in another possible world a different introduction than this one to a counterpart of this edition, whose principal focus is the complementarity of Locke's first *Letter* and *TRC*. Locke must have foreseen that the policy of toleration which he advocated in the former work along with his views on the constitution of churches as voluntary societies that prescribe rules of faith and practice for their members would lead to further division among Christians. *TRC* offers a means to counteract this tendency by showing that Scripture provides a rule of faith that permits a latitude of faith among Christians.

historical situation in which he was destined to
introduce the new covenant. The conclusion that he
draws from this detailed exposition of the narrative
texts is that they are reliable witnesses to an authentic
revelation. Jesus's authenticity is vouchsafed by the
ingenious strategy that he followed in disclosing his
identity and mission; the reliability of the testimony of
the gospels derives from the ingenuousness of the
disciples who were witnesses of the words and deeds of
Jesus.

5

The Reasonableness of Christianity is an Olympian
essay of the same type as *An Essay concerning Human
Understanding* and *Epistola de Tolerantia*.[24]   It was
written from an attitude of disengagement from partisan
conflicts. Although its author, Locke, was not unaware
of them, he was not constrained by them and therefore
was free to reflect philosophically on his theme, which
is to say, to consider it impartially and with a concern
for truth. The *Vindications*, in contrast, are contro-
versial writings. Because, as defences of *TRC*, they
cover much the same ground, they may be used,
although with care, to clarify its author's original
intentions. But to use them only in this way would be
to miss their significance. They are defences and, as
such, are primarily and self-referentially about an author
and his book and, only secondarily, about the truth that
the author hoped to represent. Although set in the very
same context as *TRC*, that context has become a hostile

---

[24] I have borrowed this expression from Mark Goldie who applies it to
Locke's *Epistola de Tolerantia* to distinguish it from its successors. See
Goldie, 'John Locke, Jonas Proast and Religious Toleration 1688–1692',
in John Walsh et al. (eds.), *The Church of England c. 1689–c. 1833*
(Cambridge University Press, 1993), p. 143.

world in which *TRC*, now made public, appears as an odious object.

The *Vindications* are responses to a charge made by John Edwards (1637–1716), an Anglican divine, a moderate Calvinist, but an intemperate man who accused the author of *TRC*, whom he suspected might be Locke, of having Socinian intentions, of being 'all over Socinianized'.[25] Edwards does not allege that the author of *TRC* has openly advocated Socinianism, rather he makes the more serious charge of deceitful insinuation of a doctrine that not only is heretical but that tends also towards atheism. He plays the part of Locke's accuser and of his unmasker as well, hoping, perhaps, also to be his unmaker. Edwards' public accusation brought near the noise and heat of another set of controversies that, with the exception of the first, are unmentioned by Locke in *TRC*: about Original Sin, Satisfaction, and the Trinity.[26]

Edwards supports this allegation with the following evidence: that the author of *TRC* advocated a minimalist creed that reduced the Christian faith to a single article, that Jesus is the Messiah, and that he gave assurances that Christians need not believe anything more than this; that he denied that guilt and depravity are universal

[25] John Edwards, *Some Thoughts concerning the Several Causes and occasions of Atheism* (London: J. Robinson, 1695), pp. 104–22; *Socinianism Unmask'd* (London: J. Robinson, 1696) [these were bound together and reprinted, New York: Garland Publishing, 1984. For extracts from these works see my *John Locke and Christianity*]; *The Socinian Creed* (London: J. Robinson, 1697); *A Brief Vindication of the Fundamental Articles of the Christian Faith* (London: J. Robinson, 1697). Edwards had earlier written favourably on Locke's *Some Thoughts concerning Education* and the *Essay*, and he mentions both favourably in the first of the above works.

[26] For a concise account of the Trinitarian Controversy see Toulmin, *op. cit.*, pp. 172–87, reprinted with other pertinent documents in *John Locke and Christianity*.

human inheritances resulting from Adam's first sin; that he failed to assert Jesus's divine nature and that the death of the Messiah was necessary to satisfy divine justice; that he ignored or willfully misinterpreted biblical texts that assert these doctrines; that for the same reason he limited his inquiry to the Gospels and Acts and ignored the New Testament Epistles; that he was a mob-pleaser who fashioned a version of Christianity within the limits of vulgar understanding.

Locke's initial response to these charges in the first *Vindication* is ambiguous. He claims that these doctrines, even if true, are not essential to the faith that makes one a Christian, that is, to the evangelical faith evoked by the preaching of the Gospel. As to his being a Socinian: he seems to deny it, but does not do so directly. He observes that Edwards' charge lacks positive evidence. It is a charge based on a suspicion about what the author of *TRC* believes, based not on what the author says but on what he fails to say. Such a suspicion or surmise can be refuted by a simple denial. However, Locke offers not a simple denial, but a hypothetical one: 'But what if I should say, I set down as much as my argument requires, and yet am no Socinian?' (p. 163). Further on, he denies that there is any 'word of socinianism in [my book]' (p. 167), and later asserts that he consulted no Socinian ('racovian') sources when preparing his work (171).[27] These evasive answers kindle anew the suspicion not so much that Locke set out to write a Socinian book, but that in writing it he reached Socinian conclusions which now he

---

[27] The term 'Racovian' derives from the Polish city of Racow, where during the late sixteenth and early seventeenth century a community of Socinians had established a theological academy. It is the name also of a Socinian catechism, published in Polish in 1609 and later translated into Latin and English.

preferred to keep to himself. And this is the general opinion today among Locke scholars.[28] But this judgement is insensitive to the subtleties of Locke's thought and expression and of the situation in which he was writing, and it is arguably false.

In the first place, the first *Vindication* is written in an ironic mode that barely conceals its authors rage and contempt for his accuser. Locke describes Edwards as someone who 'has got the faculty to heighten every thing that displeases him, into the capital crime of atheism; and breathes against those, who come in his way, a pestilential air, whereby every the least distemper is turned into the plague, and becomes mortal' (p. 161), a reference most likely to Edwards' father, Thomas Edwards, a puritan divine whose malignant wit compared the beliefs and practices of independent divines to gangrene.[29] In such a rhetorical setting a forthright denial or admission would seem out of place.

Furthermore, Locke is correct in his claim that Edwards misrepresents his work so egregiously that it is incumbent on him first of all to demonstrate Edwards' misreadings, to restate and defend his intentions clearly, and not to confuse them with anything else. This task

---

[28] Maurice Cranston, *John Locke* (New York: Macmillan, 1957), p. 390: 'The Reasonableness of Christianity is a Unitarian or Socinian book in everything but name...'; J. R. Milton, 'Locke at Oxford', in G. A. J. Rogers, *op. cit.*, p. 44, writes that by 1690 Locke had become, among other things, a 'secret Unitarian'. In *John Locke, Resistance, Religion and Responsibility* (Cambridge University Press, 1994), John Marshall claims to have shown Locke's development from orthodox Anglican to a secret Unitarian. However, Arthur Wainwright, rightly, I believe, shows the difficulty of classifying Locke's theological opinions. See his Introduction to Locke's *A Paraphrase and Notes on the Epistles of St. Paul* (Oxford: Clarendon Press, 1987), vol. 1, p. 38.

[29] Thomas Edwards (1599–1647), *Gangræna: or A Catalogue and Discovery of many of the Errours, Heresies, Blasphemies and pernicious Practices of the Sectaries of this Time* (London: Ralph Smith, 1646).

is carried out in the *Second Vindication*. His method is to respond seriatim to Edwards' misreadings, but the key to his defence is his doctrine of fundamentals. This doctrine is treated very briefly almost as an epilogue to *TRC* (pp. 155–8), but it is considered at length in this last defence. Briefly, fundamentals are those doctrines that must be believed by anyone who would become a Christian and would reap the benefits and advantages of the Christian Gospel. Thus, they are evangelical doctrines that make up the preaching of the Gospel to an unbelieving world. They do not constitute the whole of Christian truth, nor the whole of Scripture doctrine, nor the whole of what Christians are obliged to believe who, as they ought, regularly study Scripture and apply its doctrine to life. It seems fitting that this doctrine should be clear and simple, and that theologians should be obliged to preserve its character and content and not to make it obscure by encumbering it with uncertain considerations however profound or with disputes over confessional differences like those that embroiled Calvinists and deists, Trinitarians and Unitarians.

In this light, Locke's relief in finding himself 'not a heretic' in his letter to Limborch appears not as a claim of orthodoxy, but as a claim of consistency with it. What Locke meant was that evangelical Christianity as delivered in the Scriptures does not address issues of the divine nature of Christ or of the atoning significance of his death. This concedes nothing more to Unitarians than it does to Trinitarians, rather it extends to both the right to be considered Christians. It is a subtle position, but interpreters of Locke should attempt at least to be as subtle as Locke even though they must fall short of his originality.

Theological controversy and the suspicion which it produced, which Locke proved unable to dispel, should not be allowed to obscure what he accomplished in these works. He produced a cogent and morally attractive account of the Christian religion based upon its sources, one that conjoins the simplicity and clarity of the Gospel with a respectful awareness of its metaphysical and moral depth; a modern, that is, historical realist understanding of the sources of Christianity, one that respects the integrity of the texts and proceeds in interpreting them on the proper assumption that their meaning is, in part, a function of their context;[30] the completion of his philosophical programme so far as it was directed towards moral and religious ends. In doing these things, Locke showed himself to be a Christian philosopher. This last claim is undeniable if one takes *TRC* seriously as a product of Locke's philosophical endeavour. Its meaning is less certain. To any who suppose that the Christian religion is true, *TRC* provides a view of Christianity as a religion of universal significance; to any who hold a contrary opinion, taking *TRC* seriously requires at the very least a reconsideration of received views of the relation of religion and modernity and of the Enlightenment project concerning the foundation of morality.

A NOTE ON THE TEXT: *The Reasonableness of Christianity as delivered in the Scriptures* was published in August 1695. *A Vindication of the Reasonableness of Christianity*, the first *Vindication,* appeared in October of the same year. A second edition of *TRC* was

---

[30] Postmodernism, it seems to me, does not and should not contradict modern historical realism. By bringing to light the various levels of construction involved in the consciousness of events and the historical representation of them, it rather complicates the task of historical inquiry, but it does not end it. To suppose that it does is to reduce postmodernism to a hopeless and viciously circular self-referential idealism. In this respect, Locke's constructivism may be illuminating for the postmodernist project (see his account of mixed modes and the complex idea of substances: *Essay*, bk 2, chaps. xxii, xxiii, bk 3, chaps. v, vi.

published together with the first *Vindication* in 1696. *A Second Vindication of the Reasonableness of Christianity* was published in March 1697. No further edition of either of these works appeared during Locke's lifetime. The present volume contains an unabridged text of *TRC* and its *Vindications* as they appeared in the ninth edition (1794) of Locke's collected works. The ninth edition was a resetting in octavo of the eighth quarto edition (1777) edited by Edmund Law, Bishop of Carlisle, who was an influential promoter of Locke's philosophy during the eighteenth century. Law promised a corrected text but not a critical one. What is offered here, then, is a corrected and slightly modernized version of the second edition of *TRC* according to eighteenth-century conventions (viz. reduction of capitals and other minor changes in spelling; substitution of quotation marks for italics).[31]

Victor Nuovo
Middlebury College,
Vermont, 1997[32]

---

[31] See Law's preface to the eighth edition of *The Works of John Locke*, vol. 1 (London, 1777; reprinted in vol. 5 of *The Collected Works of Edmund Law*, Bristol: Thoemmes Press, 1997).

[32] This introduction was largely written while I was in residence at the Center of Theological Inquiry in Princeton. I am grateful to the directors, Wallace Alston and William Lazareth, for their support and encouragement. I am also grateful to friends, who offered useful commentary and advice on earlier drafts of the Introduction or provided useful information: Jan Albers, George Hunsinger, W. J. Torrance Kirby, Andrew Pyle, Peter Scott, Maurice Wiles and Avihu Zakai. I am especially indebted to William Harris, Archivist and Curator of Special Collections of Speer Library of Princeton Seminary, for making available the rich collection of documents which he oversees with such competence and care, and to the curators of the Bodleian and Houghton Libraries for permission to use manuscript materials.

THE

REASONABLENESS

OF

CHRISTIANITY,

AS DELIVERED IN THE

SCRIPTURES.

THE

PREFACE.

THE little fatisfaction and confiftency that is to be found, in moft of the fyftems of divinity I have met with, made me betake myfelf to the fole reading of the Scriptures (to which they all appeal) for the underftanding the Chriftian Religion. What from thence, by an attentive and unbiaffed fearch, I have received, Reader, I here deliver to thee. If by this my labour thou receiveft any light, or confirmation in the truth, join with me in thanks to the Father of lights, for his condefcenfion to our underftandings. If, upon a fair and unprejudiced examination, thou findeft I have miftaken the fenfe and tenour of the Gofpel, I befeech thee, as a true Chriftian, in the fpirit of the Gofpel, (which is that of charity) and in the words of fobriety, fet me right, in the doctrine of falvation.

THE

THE

REASONABLENESS

OF

CHRISTIANITY,

AS DELIVERED IN THE

SCRIPTURES.

IT is obvious to any one, who reads the New Testament, that the doctrine of redemption, and consequently of the gospel, is founded upon the supposition of Adam's fall. To understand therefore, what we are restored to by Jesus Christ, we must consider what the scriptures show we lost by Adam. This I thought worthy of a diligent and unbiassed search: since I found the two extremes, that men run into on this point, either on the one hand shook the foundations of all religion, or, on the other, made christianity almost nothing: for while some men would have all Adam's posterity doomed to eternal, infinite punishment, for the transgression of Adam, whom millions had never heard of, and no one had authorised to transact for him, or be his representative; this seemed to others so little consistent with the justice or goodness of the great

and

and infinite God, that they thought there was no re-demption neceffary, and confequently, that there was none; rather than admit of it upon a fuppofition fo derogatory to the honour and attributes of that infinite Being; and fo made Jefus Chrift nothing but the re-ftorer and preacher of pure natural religion; thereby doing violence to the whole tenour of the New Teftament. And, indeed, both fides will be fufpected to have tref-paffed this way, againft the written word of God, by any one, who does but take it to be a collection of writings, defigned by God, for the inftruction of the illiterate bulk of mankind, in the way to falvation; and therefore, generally, and in neceffary points, to be underftood in the plain direct meaning of the words and phrafes: fuch as they may be fuppofed to have had in the mouths of the fpeakers, who ufed them accord-ing to the language of that time and country wherein they lived; without fuch learned, artificial, and forced fenfes of them, as are fought out, and put upon them, in moft of the fyftems of divinity, according to the notions that each one has been bred up in.

To one that, thus unbiaffed, reads the fcriptures, what Adam fell from (is vifible), was the ftate of per-fect obedience, which is called juftice in the New Tef-tament; though the word, which in the original fig-nifies juftice, be tranflated righteoufnefs: and, by this fall he loft paradife, wherein was tranquillity and the tree of life; i. e. he loft blifs and immortality. The penalty annexed to the breach of the law, with the fen-tence pronounced by God upon it, fhow this. The penalty ftands thus, Gen. ii. 17. " In the day, that " thou eateft thereof, thou fhalt furely die." How was this executed? He did eat: but, in the day he did eat, he did not actually die; but was turned out of pa-radife from the tree of life, and fhut out for ever from it, left he fhould take thereof, and live for ever. This fhows, that the ftate of paradife was a ftate of immor-tality, of life without end; which he loft that very day that he eat: his life began from thence to fhorten, and wafte, and to have an end; and from thence, to his ac-tual death, was but like the time of a prifoner, between the sentence passed and the execution, which was in view and certain. Death then entered, and showed his face, which before was shut out, and not known. So St. Paul, Rom. v. 12. "By one man sin entered into "the world, and death by sin;" i. e. a state of death and mortality: and, 1 Cor. xv. 22. "In Adam all die;" i. e. by reason of his transgression, all men are mortal, and come to die.

This is so clear in these cited places, and so much the current of the New Testament, that nobody can deny, but that the doctrine of the gospel is, that death came on all men by Adam's sin; only they differ about the signification of the word death: for some will have it to be a state of guilt, wherein not only he, but all his posterity was so involved, that every one descended of him deserved endless torment, in hell-fire. I shall say nothing more here, how far, in the apprehensions of men, this consists with the justice and goodness of God, having mentioned it above: but it seems a strange way of understanding a law, which requires the plainest and directest words, that by death should be meant eternal life in misery. Could any one be supposed, by a law, that says, "For felony thou shalt die," not that he should lose his life; but be kept alive in perpetual, exquisite torments? And would any one think himself fairly dealt with, that was so used?

To this, they would have it be also a state of necessary sinning, and provoking God in every action that men do: a yet harder sense of the word death than the other. God says, that "in the day that thou eatest of the for- "bidden fruit, thou shalt die;" i. e. thou and thy posterity shall be, ever after, incapable of doing any thing, but what shall be sinful and provoking to me, and shall justly deserve my wrath and indignation. Could a worthy man be supposed to put such terms upon the obedience of his subjects? Much less can the righteous God be supposed, as a punishment of one sin, wherewith he is displeased, to put man under the necessity of sinning continually, and so multiplying the provocation. The reason of this strange interpretation, we shall perhaps find, in some mistaken places of the

New

New Teftament. I muft confefs, by death here, I can underftand nothing but a ceafing to be, the lofing of all actions of life and fenfe. Such a death came on Adam, and all his pofterity, by his firft difobedience in paradife; under which death they fhould have lain for ever, had it not been for the redemption by Jefus Chrift. If by death, threatened to Adam, were meant the corruption of human nature in his pofterity, 'tis ftrange, that the New Teftament fhould not any where take notice of it, and tell us, that corruption feized on all, becaufe of Adam's tranfgreffion, as well as it tells us fo of death. But, as I remember, every one's fin is charged upon himfelf only.

Another part of the fentence was, " Curfed is the " ground for thy fake : in forrow fhalt thou eat of it " all the days of thy life; in the fweat of thy face fhalt " thou eat bread, till thou return unto the ground : for " out of it waft thou taken; duft thou art, and to duft " fhalt thou return," Gen. iii. 17.—19. This fhows, that paradife was a place of blifs, as well as immortality; without drudgery, and without forrow. But, when man was turned out, he was expofed to the toil, anxiety, and frailties of this mortal life, which fhould end in the duft, out of which he was made, and to which he fhould return; and then have no more life or fenfe, than the duft had, out of which he was made.

As Adam was turned out of paradife, fo all his pofterity were born out of it, out of the reach of the tree of life; all, like their father Adam, in a ftate of mortality, void of the tranquillity and blifs of paradife. Rom. v. 12. " By one man fin entered into the world, " and death by fin." But here will occur the common objection, that fo many ftumble at: " How doth it " confift with the juftnefs and goodnefs of God, that " the pofterity of Adam fhould fuffer for his fin ; the " innocent be punifhed for the guilty ?" Very well, if keeping one from what he has no right to, be called a punifhment; the ftate of immortality, in paradife, is not due to the pofterity of Adam, more than to any other creature. Nay, if God afford them a temporary, mortal life, 'tis his gift; they owe it to his bounty ; they could not claim it as their right, nor does

he

he injure them when he takes it from them. Had he taken from mankind any thing that was their right, or did he put men in a ſtate of miſery, worſe than not being, without any fault, or demerit of their own; this, indeed, would be hard to reconcile with the notion we have of juſtice; and much more with the goodneſs, and other attributes of the ſupreme Being, which he has declared of himſelf; and reaſon, as well as revelation, muſt acknowledge to be in him; unleſs we will confound good and evil, God and Satan. That ſuch a ſtate of extreme, irremediable torment is worſe than no being at all; if every one's own ſenſe did not determine againſt the vain philoſophy, and fooliſh metaphyſics of ſome men; yet our Saviour's peremptory deciſion, Matt. xxvi. 24, has put it paſt doubt, that one may be in ſuch an eſtate, that it had been better for him not to have been born. But that ſuch a temporary life, as we now have, with all its frailties and ordinary miſeries, is better than no being, is evident, by the high value we put upon it ourſelves. And therefore, though all die in Adam, yet none are truly puniſhed, but for their own deeds. Rom. ii. 6. " God will render to " every one," How? " According to his deeds. To " thoſe that obey unrighteouſneſs, indignation and " wrath, tribulation and anguiſh, upon every ſoul of " man that doth evil." ver. 9. 2 Cor. v. 10. " We " muſt appear before the judgment ſeat of Chriſt, that " every one may receive the things done in his body, " according to that he has done, whether it be good or " bad." And Chriſt himſelf, who knew for what he ſhould condemn men at the laſt day, aſſures us, in the two places, where he deſcribes his proceeding at the great judgment, that the ſentence of condemnation paſſes only upon the workers of iniquity, ſuch as neglected to fulfil the law in acts of charity, Matt. vii. 23. Luke xiii. 27. Matt. xxv. 41, 42, &c. " And " again, John v. 29, our Saviour tells the jews, that " all ſhall come forth of their graves, they that have " done good, to the reſurrection of life; and they that " have done evil, unto the reſurrection of damnation." But here is no condemnation of any one, for what his

fore-

fore-father Adam had done; which it is not likely fhould have been omitted, if that fhould have been a caufe, why any one was adjudged to the fire, with the devil and his angels. And he tells his difciples, that when he comes again with his angels, in the glory of his Father, that then he will render to every one according to his works, Matt. xvi. 27.

Adam being thus turned out of paradife, and all his pofterity born out of it, the confequence of it was, that all men fhould die, and remain under death for ever, and fo be utterly loft.

From this eftate of death, Jefus Chrift reftores all mankind to life; 1 Cor. xv. 22. "As in Adam all die, "fo in Chrift fhall all be made alive." How this fhall be, the fame apoftle tells us in the foregoing ver. 21. "By man death came, by man alfo came the refurrec- "tion from the dead." Whereby it appears, that the life, which Jefus Chrift reftores to all men, is that life, which they receive again at the refurrection. Then they recover from death, which otherwife all mankind fhould have continued under, loft for ever; as appears by St. Paul's arguing, 1 Cor. xv. concerning the refurrection.

And thus men are, by the fecond Adam, reftored to life again; that fo by Adam's fin they may none of them lofe any thing, which by their own righteoufnefs they might have a title to: for righteoufnefs, or an exact obedience to the law, feems, by the fcripture, to have a claim of right to eternal life, Rom. iv. 4. "To him "that worketh," i. e. does the works of the law, "is "the reward not reckoned of grace, but OF DEBT." And Rev. xxii. 14. "Bleffed are they who do his com- "mandments, that they may HAVE RIGHT to the tree "of life, which is in the paradife of God." If any of the pofterity of Adam were juft, they fhall not lofe the reward of it, eternal life and blifs, by being his mortal iffue: Chrift will bring them all to life again; and then they fhall be put every one upon his own trial, and receive judgment, as he is found to be righteous, or not. And the righteous, as our Saviour fays, Matth. xxv. 46. fhall go into eternal life. Nor fhall any one mifs it, who has done, what our Saviour directed the lawyer, who

afked,

afked, Luke x. 25. What he fhould do to inherit eternal
life? " Do this," i. e. what is required by the law,
" and thou fhalt live."

On the other fide, it feems the unalterable purpofe of
the divine juftice, that no unrighteous perfon, no one
that is guilty of any breach of the law, fhould be in paradife : but that the wages of fin fhould be to every
man, as it was to Adam, an exclufion of him out of
that happy ftate of immortality, and bring death upon
him. And this is fo conformable to the eternal and
eftablifhed law of right and wrong, that it is fpoken of
too, as if it could not be otherwife. St. James fays,
chap. i. 15, " Sin, when it is finifhed, bringeth forth
" death," as it were, by a natural and neceffary pro--
duction. " Sin entered into the world, and death by
" fin," fays St. Paul, Rom. v. 12: and vi. 23, " The
" wages of fin is death." Death is the purchafe of
any, of every fin. Gal. iii. 10. " Curfed is every one,
" who continueth not in all things, which are written
" in the book of the law to do them." And of this St.
James gives a reafon, chap. ii. 10, 11. " Whofoever
" fhall keep the whole law, and yet offend in one
" point, he is guilty of all : for he that faid, Do not
" commit adultery, faid alfo, Do not kill :" i. e. he
that offends in any one point, fins againft the authority
which eftablifhed the law.

Here then we have the ftanding and fixed meafures
of life and death. Immortality and blifs belong to the
righteous ; thofe who have lived in an exact conformity
to the law of God, are out of the reach of death ; but
an exclufion from paradife and lofs of immortality is
the portion of finners ; of all thofe, who have any way
broke that law, and failed of a complete obedience to it,
by the guilt of any one tranfgreffion. And thus mankind by the law, are put upon the iffues of life or death,
as they are righteous or unrighteous, juft or unjuft ;
i. e. exact performers or tranfgreffors of the law.

But yet, " all having finned," Rom. iii. 23. " and
" come fhort of the glory of God," i. e. the kingdom
" of God in heaven, (which is often called his glory)
" both Jews and Gentiles ;" ver. 22. fo that, " by the
                                                " deeds

" deeds of the law," no one could be juftified, ver. 20. it follows, that no one could then have eternal life and blifs.

Perhaps, it will be demanded, " Why did God give " fo hard a law to mankind, that to the apoftle's time, " no one of Adam's iffue had kept it? As appears by " Rom. iii. and Gal. iii. 21, 22."

Anfw. It was fuch a law as the purity of God's na- ture required, and muft be the law of fuch a creature as man; unlefs God would have made him a rational creature, and not required him to have lived by the law of reafon; but would have countenanced in him irregularity and difobedience to that light which he had, and that rule which was fuitable to his nature; which would have been to have authorifed diforder, confu- fion, and wickednefs in his creatures: for that this law was the law of reafon, or, as it is called, of nature; we fhall fee by and by: and if rational creatures will not live up to the rule of their reafon, who fhall ex- cufe them? If you will admit them to forfake reafon in one point, why not in another? Where will you ftop? To difobey God in any part of his commands, (and 'tis he that commands what reafon does) is direct rebel- lion; which, if difpenfed with in any point, govern- ment and order are at an end; and there can be no bounds fet to the lawlefs exorbitancy of unconfined man. The law therefore was, as St. Paul tells us, Rom. vii. 12, " holy, juft, and good," and fuch as it ought, and could not otherwife be.

This then being the cafe, that whoever is guilty of any fin fhould certainly die, and ceafe to be; the be- nefit of life, reftored by Chrift at the refurrection, would have been no great advantage, (for as much as, here again, death muft have feized upon all mankind, be- caufe all had finned; for the wages of fin is every where death, as well after as before the refurrection) if God had not found out a way to juftify fome, i. e. fo many as obeyed another law, which God gave; which in the New Teftament is called " the law of faith," Rom. iii. 27. and is oppofed to " the law of works." And therefore the punifhment of thofe, who would not fol-

low

low him, was to lose their souls, i. e. their lives, Mark viii. 35—38. as is plain, considering the occasion it was spoke on.

The better to understand the law of faith, it will be convenient, in the first place, to consider the law of works. The law of works then, in short, is that law which requires perfect obedience, without any remission or abatement; so that, by that law, a man cannot be just, or justified, without an exact performance of every tittle. Such a perfect obedience, in the New Testament, is termed δικαιοσύνη, which we translate righteousness.

The language of this law is, "Do this and live, "transgress and die." Lev. xviii. 5. "Ye shall keep "my statutes and my judgments, which if a man do, "he shall live in them." Ezek. xx. 11. "I gave "them my statutes, and showed them my judgments, "which if a man do, he shall even live in them. "Moses, says St. Paul, Rom. x. 5, describeth the "righteousness, which is of the law, that the man, "which doth those things, shall live in them." Gal. iii. 12. "The law is not of faith; but that man, that "doth them, shall live in them." On the other side, transgress and die; no dispensation, no atonement. ver. 10. "Cursed is every one that continueth not in "all things, which are written in the book of the law "to do them."

Where this law of works was to be found, the New Testament tells us, viz. in the law delivered by Moses. John i. 17. "The law was given by Moses, but grace "and truth came by Jesus Christ." Chap. vii. 19. "Did not Moses give you the law?" says our Saviour, "and yet none of you keep the law." And this is the law, which he speaks of, where he asks the lawyer, Luke x. 26, "What is written in the law? How readest "thou? ver. 28. This do, and thou shalt live." This is that which St. Paul so often styles the law, without any other distinction, Rom. ii. 13. "Not the hearers "of the law are just before God, but the doers of the "law are justified." 'Tis needless to quote any more places;

places; his epiftles are full of it, efpecially this of the Romans.

" But the law given by Mofes, being not given to " all mankind, how are all men finners; fince, with- " out a law, there is no tranfgreffion?" To this the apoftle, ver. 14, anfwers, " For when the Gentiles, " which have not the law, do, (i. e. find it reafonable " to do) by nature the things contained in the law; " thefe, having not the law, are a law unto themfelves: " which fhow the work of the law written in their " hearts; their confciences alfo bearing witnefs, and " amongft themfelves their thoughts accufing or ex- " cufing one another." By which, and other places in the following chapter, 'tis plain, that under the law of works, is comprehended alfo the law of nature, knowable by reafon, as well as the law given by Mofes. For, fays St. Paul, Rom. iii. 9, 23. " We have proved " both jews and gentiles, that they are all under fin : " For all have finned, and come fhort of the glory of " God:" which they could not do without a law.

Nay, whatever God requires any where to be done, without making any allowance for faith, that is a part of the law of works : fo that forbidding Adam to eat of the tree of knowledge was part of the law of works. Only we muft take notice here, that fome of God's pofitive commands, being for peculiar ends, and fuited to particular circumftances of times, places, and per- fons ; have a limited and only temporary obligation, by virtue of God's pofitive injunction; fuch as was that part of Mofes's law, which concerned the outward worfhip, or political conftitution of the jews ; and is called the ceremonial and judicial law, in contradi- ftinction to the moral part of it ; which being conform- able to the eternal law of right, is of eternal obligation ; and therefore remains in force ftill, under the gofpel; nor is abrogated by the law of faith, as St. Paul found fome ready to infer, Rom. iii. 31. " Do we then " make void the law, through faith ? God forbid ; yea, " we eftablifh the law."

Nor can it be otherwife: for, were there no law of works, there could be no law of faith. For there
could

could be no need of faith, which should be counted to men for righteousness; if there were no law, to be the rule and measure of righteousness, which men failed in their obedience to.   Where there is no law, there is no sin; all are righteous equally, with or without faith.

The rule, therefore, of right, is the same that ever it was; the obligation to observe it is also the same: the difference between the law of works, and the law of faith, is only this: that the law of works makes no allowance for failing on any occasion.   Those that obey are righteous; those that in any part disobey, are unrighteous, and must not expect life, the reward of righteousness.   But, by the law of faith, faith is allowed to supply the defect of full obedience; and so the believers are admitted to life and immortality, as if they were righteous.   Only here we must take notice, that when St. Paul says, that the gospel establishes the law, he means the moral part of the law of Moses; for that he could not mean the ceremonial, or political part of it, is evident, by what I quoted out of him just now, where he says, That the gentiles do, by nature, the things contained in the law, their consciences bearing witness.   For the gentiles neither did, nor thought of, the judicial or ceremonial institutions of Moses; 'twas only the moral part their consciences were concerned in.   As for the rest, St. Paul tells the galatians, chap. iv. they are not under that part of the law, which ver. 3, he calls elements of the world; and, ver. 9, weak and beggarly elements. And our Saviour himself, in his gospel sermon on the mount, tells them, Matt. v. 17. That, whatever they might think, he was not come to dissolve the law, but to make it more full and strict: for that that is meant by πληρῶσαι, is evident from the following part of that chapter, where he gives the precepts in a stricter sense, than they were received in before.   But they are all precepts of the moral law, which he re-inforces.   What should become of the ritual law, he tells the woman of Samaria, in these words, John iv. 21, 23. " The hour " cometh, when you shall, neither in this mountain,
                                            " nor

" nor yet at Jerufalem, worfhip the Father. But the
" true worfhippers fhall worfhip the Father in fpirit
" and in truth; for the Father feeketh fuch to worfhip
" him."

Thus then, as to the law, in fhort: the civil and
ritual part of the law, delivered by Mofes, obliges not
chriftians, though, to the jews, it were a part of the
law of works; it being a part of the law of nature, that
man ought to obey every pofitive law of God, whenever
he fhall pleafe to make any fuch addition to the law
of his nature. But the moral part of Mofes's law, or
the moral law, (which is every where the fame, the
eternal rule of right) obliges chriftians, and all men,
every where, and is to all men the ftanding law of
works. But chriftian believers have the privilege to be
under the law of faith too; which is that law, whereby
God juftifies a man for believing, though by his works
he be not juft or righteous, i. e. though he come fhort
of perfect obedience to the law of works. God alone
does or can juftify, or make juft, thofe who by their
works are not fo: which he doth, by counting their
faith for righteoufnefs, i. e. for a complete performance
of the law. Rom. iv. 3. " Abraham believed God,
" and it was counted to him for righteoufnefs." ver.
5. " To him that believeth on him that juftifieth the
" ungodly, his faith is counted for righteoufnefs."
ver. 6. " Even as David alfo defcribeth the bleffednefs
" of the man unto whom God imputeth righteoufnefs
" without works;" i. e. without a full meafure of works,
which is exact obedience. Ver. 7. Saying, " Bleffed
" are they whofe iniquities are forgiven, and whofe
" fins are covered." Ver. 8. " Bleffed is the man, to
" whom the Lord will not impute fin."

This faith, for which God juftified Abraham, what
was it? It was the believing God, when he engaged his
promife in the covenant he made with him. This will
be plain to any one, who confiders thefe places together, Gen. xv. 6. " He believed in the Lord, or be-
" lieved the Lord." For that the Hebrew phrafe,
" believing in," fignifies no more but believing, is
plain from St. Paul's citation of this place, Rom. iv. 3,
where

where he repeats 'it thus: " Abraham believed God,"
which he thus explains, ver. 18—22, " Who against
" hope believed in hope, that he might become the fa-
" ther of many nations: according to that which was
" spoken, So shall thy feed be.   And, being not weak
" in faith, he considered not his own body now dead,
" when he was about an hundred years old, nor yet
" the deadness of Sarah's womb.   He staggered not at
" the promise of God, through unbelief; but was
" strong in faith giving glory to God.   And being fully
" persuaded, that what he had promised he was also
" able to perform.   And therefore it was imputed
" to him for righteousness."   By which it is clear,
that the faith which God counted to Abraham for
righteousness, was nothing but a firm belief of what
God declared to him; and a steadfast relying on him,
for the accomplishment of what he had promised.

    " Now this," says St. Paul, ver. 23, 24, " was not
" writ for his [Abraham's] fake alone, but for us also ;"
teaching us, that as Abraham was justified for his faith,
so also ours shall be accounted to us for righteousness,
if we believe God, as Abraham believed him.   Whereby
it is plain is meant the firmness of our faith, without
staggering, and not the believing the same propositions
that Abraham believed; viz. that though he and Sarah
were old, and past the time and hopes of children, yet
he should have a son by her, and by him become the
father of a great people, which should possess the land
of Canaan.   This was what Abraham believed, and
was counted to him for righteousness.   But nobody, I
think, will say, that any one's believing this now, shall
be imputed to him for righteousness.   The law of faith
then, in short, is for every one to believe what God requires him to believe, as a condition of the covenant he
makes with him : and not to doubt of the performance
of his promises.   This the apostle intimates in the close
here, ver. 24. " But for us also, to whom it shall be
" imputed, if we believe on him that raised up Jesus
" our Lord from the dead."   We must, therefore, examine and fee what God requires us to believe now,
under the revelation of the gospel ; for the belief of one
                                            invisible,

invifible, eternal, omnipotent God, maker of heaven
and earth, &c. was required before, as well as now.

What we are now required to believe to obtain
eternal life, is plainly fet down in the gofpel. St.
John tells us, John iii. 36. " He that believeth on the
" Son, hath eternal life; and he that believeth not the
" Son, fhall not fee life." What this believing on
him is, we are alfo told in the next chapter: " The
" woman faith unto him, I know that the Meffiah
" cometh: when he is come, he will tell us all things.
" Jefus faid unto her, I that fpeak unto thee, am he.
" The woman then went into the city, and faith to the
" men, come fee a man that hath told me all things
" that ever I did: is not this the Meffiah? and many of
" the Samaritans believed on him for the faying of the
" woman, who teftified, he told me all that ever I
" did. So when the Samaritans were come unto him,
" many more believed becaufe of his words, and faid
" to the woman, We believe not any longer, becaufe
" of thy faying; for we have heard ourfelves, and we
" know that this man is truly the Saviour of the world,
" the Meffiah," John iv. 25, 26, 29, 39, 40, 41, 42.

By which place it is plain, that believing on the Son
is the believing that Jefus was the Meffiah; giving
credit to the miracles he did, and the profeffion he
made of himfelf. For thofe who were faid to BELIEVE
ON HIM, for the faying of the woman, ver. 39, tell the
woman that they now believed not any longer, becaufe
of her faying: but that having heard him themfelves, they
knew, i. e. BELIEVED, paft doubt, THAT HE WAS THE
MESSIAH.

This was the great propofition that was then controverted, concerning Jefus of Nazareth, " Whether he
" was the Meffiah or no?" And the affent to that was
that which diftinguifhed believers from unbelievers.
When many of his difciples had forfaken him, upon
his declaring that he was the bread of life, which came
down from heaven, " He faid to his apoftles, Will ye
" alfo go away? Then Simon Peter anfwered him,
" Lord, to whom fhall we go? Thou haft the words of
" eternal life. And we believe, and are fure, that

" thou art the Messiah, the Son of the living God,"
John vi. 69.   This was the faith which distinguished
them from apostates and unbelievers, and was sufficient
to continue them in the rank of apostles: and it was
upon the same proposition, " That Jesus was the Mes-
" siah, the Son of the living God," owned by St. Peter,
that our Saviour said, he would build his church, Matt.
xvi. 16—18.

To convince men of this, he did his miracles: and
their assent to, or not assenting to this, made them
to be, or not to be, of his church; believers, or not
believers: " The jews came round about him, and
" said unto him, How long dost thou make us doubt?
" If thou be the Messiah, tell us plainly.   Jesus an-
" swered them, I told you, and ye believed not: the
" works that I do in my Father's name, they bear
" witness of me.   But ye believe not, because ye are
" not of my sheep," John x. 24—26.   Conformable
hereunto, St. John tells us, that " many deceivers are
" entered into the world, who confess not that Jesus,
" the Messiah, is come in the flesh.   This is a de-
" ceiver, and an antichrist; whosoever abideth not in
" the doctrine of the Messiah, has not God.   He that
" abideth in the doctrine of the Messiah," i. e. that
Jesus is he, " hath both the Father and the Son,"
2 John 7, 9.   That this is the meaning of the place, is
plain from what he says in his foregoing epistle, " Who-
" soever believeth that Jesus is the Messiah, is born
" of God," 1 John v. 1.   And therefore, drawing to a
close of his gospel, and showing the end for which he
writ it, he has these words: " Many other signs truly
" did Jesus in the presence of his disciples, which are
" not written in this book: but these are written that
" ye may believe that Jesus is the Messiah, the Son of
" God; and that, believing, you might have life
" through his name," John xx. 30, 31.   Whereby it
is plain, that the gospel was writ to induce men into a
belief of this proposition, " That Jesus of Nazareth was
" the Messiah;" which if they believed, they should
have life.

Accordingly

Accordingly the great queſtion among the jews was, whether he were the Meſſiah or no? and the great point inſiſted on and promulgated in the goſpel, was, that he was the Meſſiah. The firſt glad tidings of his birth, brought to the ſhepherds by an angel, was in theſe words: " Fear not: for, behold, I bring you " good tidings of great joy, which ſhall be to all " people: for to you is born this day, in the city of " David, a Saviour, who is the Meſſiah, the Lord," Luke ii. 11. Our Saviour diſcourſing with Martha about the means of attaining eternal life, faith to her, John xi. 27. " Whoſoever believeth in me, ſhall never " die. Believeſt thou this? She faith unto him, Yea, " Lord, I believe that thou art the Meſſiah, the Son of " God, which ſhould come into the world." This anſwer of hers ſhoweth, what it is to believe in Jeſus Chriſt, ſo as to have eternal life; viz. to believe that he is the Meſſiah, the Son of God, whoſe coming was foretold by the prophets. And thus Andrew and Philip expreſs it: " Andrew ſays to his brother Simon, " we have found the Meſſiah, which is, being inter- " preted, the Chriſt. Philip faith to Nathanael, we " have found him, of whom Moſes in the law and the " prophets did write, Jeſus of Nazareth, the Son of " Joſeph," John i. 41, 45. According to what the Evangeliſt ſays in this place, I have, for the clearer underſtanding of the ſcripture, all along put Meſſiah for Chriſt: Chriſt being but the Greek name for the Hebrew Meſſiah, and both ſignifying the Anointed.

And that he was the Meſſiah, was the great truth he took pains to convince his diſciples and apoſtles of; appearing to them after his reſurrection: as may be ſeen, Luke xxiv, which we ſhall more particularly con- ſider in another place. There we read what goſpel our Saviour preached to his diſciples and apoſtles ; and that as ſoon as he was riſen from the dead, twice, the very day of his reſurrection.

And, if we may gather what was to be believed by all nations from what was preached unto them, we may certainly know what they were commanded, Matt. ult. to teach all nations, by what they actually did teach

all

all nations. We may obferve, that the preaching of
the apoftles every where in the Acts, tended to this one
point, to prove that Jefus was the Meffiah. Indeed,
now, after his death, his refurrection was alfo commonly
required to be believed, as a neceffary article, and
fometimes folely infifted on: it being a mark and undoubted evidence of his being the Meffiah, and neceffary now to be believed by thofe who would receive
him as the Meffiah. For fince the Meffiah was to be a
Saviour and a king, and to give life and a kingdom to
thofe who received him, as we fhall fee by and by;
there could have been no pretence to have given him out
for the Meffiah, and to require men to believe him to
be fo, who thought him under the power of death, and
corruption of the grave. And therefore thofe who believed him to be the Meffiah, muft believe that he was
rifen from the dead: and thofe who believed him to be
rifen from the dead, could not doubt of his being the
Meffiah. But of this more in another place.

Let us fee therefore, how the apoftles preached Chrift,
and what they propofed to their hearers to believe.
St. Peter at Jerufalem, Acts ii, by his firft fermon, converted three thoufand fouls. What was his word,
which, as we are told, ver. 41, " they gladly received,
" and thereupon were baptized?" That may be feen
from ver. 22 to 36. In fhort, this; which is the conclufion, drawn from all that he had faid, and which he
preffes on them, as the thing they were to believe, viz.
" Therefore let all the houfe of Ifrael know affuredly,
" that God hath made that fame Jefus, whom ye have
" crucified, Lord and Meffiah," ver. 36.

To the fame purpofe was his difcourfe to the jews,
in the temple, Acts iii. the defign whereof you have,
ver. 18. " But thofe things that God before had fhowed,
" by the mouth of all his prophets, that the Meffiah
" fhould fuffer, he hath fo fulfilled."

In the next chapter, Acts iv, Peter and John being
examined, about the miracle on the lame man, profefs
it to have been done in the name of Jefus of Nazareth,
who was the Meffiah, in whom alone there was falvation, ver. 10—12. The fame thing they confirm to
them

them again, Acts v. 29—32. " And daily in the tem-
" ple, and in every houfe, they ceafed not to teach and
" preach Jefus the Meffiah," ver. 42.

What was Stephen's fpeech to the council, Acts vii,
but a reprehenfion to them, that they were the betrayers and murderers of the Juft One? Which is the
title, by which he plainly defigns the Meffiah, whofe
coming was forefhown by the prophets, ver. 51, 52.
And that the Meffiah was to be without fin, (which is
the import of the word Juft) was the opinion of the
jews, appears from John ix. ver. 22, compared with 24.

Acts viii, Philip carries the gofpel to Samaria:
" Then Philip went down to Samaria, and preached to
" them." What was it he preached? You have an
account of it in this one word, " the Meffiah," ver. 5.
This being that alone which was required of them, to
believe that Jefus was the Meffiah: which when they
believed, they were baptized. " And when they be-
" lieved Philip's preaching the gofpel of the kingdom
" of God, and the name of Jefus the Meffiah, they
" were baptized, both men and women," ver. 12.

Philip being fent from thence, by a fpecial call of
the Spirit, to make an eminent convert; out of Ifaiah
preaches to him Jefus, ver. 35. And what it was he
preached concerning Jefus, we may know by the profeffion of faith the eunuch made, upon which he was
admitted to baptifm, ver. 37. " I believe that Jefus
" Chrift is the Son of God:" which is as much as to
fay, I believe that he, whom you call Jefus Chrift, is
really and truly the Meffiah, that was promifed. For,
that believing him to be the Son of God, and to be the
Meffiah, was the fame thing, may appear, by comparing John i. 45, with ver. 49, where Nathanael owns
Jefus to be the Meffiah, in thefe terms: " Thou art
" the Son of God; thou art the king of Ifrael." So
the jews, Luke xxii. 70, afking Chrift, whether he
were the Son of God, plainly demanded of him, whether
he were the Meffiah? Which is evident, by comparing
that with the three preceding verfes. They afk him,
ver. 67, Whether he were the Meffiah? He anfwers,
" If I tell you, you will not believe:" but withal tells

them,

them, that from thenceforth he should be in possession of
the kingdom of the Messiah, expressed in these words,
ver. 69. " Hereafter shall the Son of Man sit on " the
" right hand of the power of God:" which made them
all cry out, " Art thou then the Son of God?" i. e. Dost
thou then own thyself to be the Messiah? To which
he replies, " Ye say that I am." That the Son of God
was the known title of the Messiah at that time,
amongst the jews, we may see also, from what the
jews say to Pilate, John xix. 7. " We have a law, and
" by our law he ought to die, because he made him-
" self THE SON OF GOD;" i. e. by making himself the
Messiah, the prophet which was to come, but falsly;
and therefore he deserves to die by the law, Deut. xviii.
20. That this was the common signification of the
Son of God, is farther evident, from what the chief
priests, mocking him, said, when he was on the
cross, Matt. xxvii. 42. " He saved others, himself he
" cannot save: if he be the king of Israel, let him now
" come down from the cross, and we will believe him.
" He trusted in God, let him deliver him now, if he
" will have him; for he said, I am the SON OF GOD;"
i. e. He said, he was the Messiah: but 'tis plainly
false; for, if he were, God would deliver him: for the
Messiah is to be king of Israel, the Saviour of others;
but this man cannot save himself. The chief priests
mention here the two titles, then in use, whereby the
jews commonly designed the Messiah, viz. " Son of
" God, and king of Israel." That of Son of God was
so familiar a compellation of the Messiah, who was
then so much expected and talked of, that the romans,
it seems, who lived amongst them, had learned it, as
appears from ver. 54. " Now when the centurion, and
" they that were with him, watching Jesus, saw the
" earthquake, and those things that were done, they
" feared greatly, saying, truly this was the SON OF
" GOD;" this was that extraordinary person that was
looked for.

Acts ix. St. Paul, exercising the commission to preach
the gospel, which he had received in a miraculous way,
ver. 20. " Straitway preached Christ in the synagogues,

I   " that

" that he is the Son of God;" i. e. that Jefus was the
the Meffiah: for Chrift, in this place, is evidently a
proper name. And that this was it, which Paul
preached, appears from ver. 22. " Saul increafed the
" more in ftrength, and confounded the jews, who
" dwelt in Damafcus, proving that this is the very
" Chrift," i. e. the Meffiah.

Peter, when he came to Cornelius at Cæfarea, who,
by a vifion, was ordered to fend for him, as St. Peter
on the other fide was by a vifion commanded to go to
him; what does he teach him? His whole difcourfe,
Acts x, tends to fhow what, he fays, God commanded
the apoftles, " To preach unto the people, and to
" teftify, that it is he [Jefus,] which was ordained of
" God to be the judge of the quick and the dead.
" And that it was to him, that all the prophets give
" witnefs, that, through his name, whofoever be-
" lieveth in him fhall have remiffion of fins," ver. 42,
43. " This is the word, which God fent to the chil-
" dren of Ifrael; that WORD, which was publifhed
" throughout all Judea, and began from Galilee, after
" the baptifm which John preached," ver. 36, 37.
And thefe are the words, which had been promifed to
Cornelius, Acts xi. 14. " Whereby he and all his houfe
" fhould be faved:" which words amount only to thus
much: that Jefus was the Meffiah, the Saviour that
was promifed. Upon their receiving of this, (for this
was all was taught them) the Holy Ghoft fell on them,
and they were baptized. 'Tis obfervable here, that the
Holy Ghoft fell on them, before they were baptized,
which, in other places, converts received not 'till after
baptifm. The reafon whereof feems to be this, that
God, by beftowing on them the Holy Ghoft, did thus
declare from heaven, that the gentiles, upon believing
Jefus to be the Meffiah, ought to be admitted into the
church by baptifm, as well as the jews. Whoever
reads St. Peter's defence, Acts xi, when he was accufed
by thofe of the circumcifion, that he had not kept that
diftance, which he ought, with the uncircumcifed, will
be of this opinion; and fee by what he fays, ver. 15, 16,
17, that this was the ground, and an irrefiftible autho-

rity

rity to him for doing fo ftrange a thing, as it appeared
to the jews, (who alone yet were members of the chriftian church) to admit gentiles into their communion,
upon their believing. And therefore St. Peter, in the
foregoing chapter, Acts x, before he would baptize
them, propofes this queftion, " to thofe of the circumcifion, which came with him, and were aftonifhed,
becaufe that on the gentiles alfo was poured out the
gift of the Holy Ghoft: can any one forbid water, that
thefe fhould not be baptized, who have received the
Holy Ghoft as well as we?" ver. 47. And when fome of
the fect of the pharifees, who believed, thought it needful that the converted gentiles fhould be circumcifed
and keep the law of Mofes, Acts xv, " Peter rofe up
and faid unto them, men and brethren, you know that
a good while ago God made choice amongft us, that the
gentiles," viz. Cornelius, and thofe here converted
with him, " by my mouth fhould hear the gofpel, and
believe. And God, who knoweth the hearts, bare
them witnefs, giving them the Holy Ghoft, even as
he did unto us, and put no difference between us and
them, purifying their hearts by faith," v. 7—9. So that
both jews and gentiles, who believed Jefus to be the
Meffiah, received thereupon the feal of baptifm; whereby they were owned to be his, and diftinguifhed from
unbelievers. From what is above faid, we may obferve, that this preaching Jefus to be the Meffiah is
called the Word, and the Word of God; and believing
it, receiving the Word of God. vid. Acts x. 36, 37.
and xi. 1, 19, 20. and the word of the gofpel, Acts xv.
7. And fo likewife in the hiftory of the gofpel, what
Mark, chap. iv. 14, 15, calls fimply the word, St. Luke
calls the word of God, Luke viii. 11. And St. Matthew, chap. xiii. 19, the word of the kingdom; which
were, it feems, in the gofpel-writers fynonymous
terms, and are fo to be underftood by us.

But to go on: Acts xiii, Paul preaches in the fynagogue at Antioch, where he makes it his bufinefs to
convince the jews, that " God, according to his promife, had of the feed of David raifed to Ifrael a Saviour Jefus." v. 24. That he was He of whom the
prophets

prophets writ, v. 25—29, i. e. the Meſſiah: and that, as a demonſtration of his being ſo, God had raiſed him from the dead, v. 30. From whence he argues thus, v. 32, 33. We evangelize to you, or bring you this goſpel, " how that the promiſe which was made to our fathers, God hath fulfilled the ſame unto us, in that he hath raiſed Jeſus again; as it is alſo written in the ſecond pſalm, " Thou art my Son, this day I have begotten thee." And having gone on to prove him to be the Meſſiah, by his reſurrection from the dead, he makes this concluſion, v. 38, 39. " Be it known unto you therefore, men and brethren, that through this man is preached unto you forgiveneſs of ſins; and by him all who believe are juſtified from all things, from which they could not be juſtified by the law of Moſes." This is in this chapter called " the Word of God," over and over again: compare v. 42, with 44, 46, 48, 49, and chap. xii. v. 24.

Acts xvii. 2—4. At Theſſalonica, " Paul, as his manner was, went into the ſynagogue, and three ſabbath days reaſoned with the jews out of the ſcriptures; opening and alleging, that the Meſſiah muſt needs have ſuffered, and riſen again from the dead: and that this Jeſus, whom I preach unto you, is the Meſſiah. And ſome of them believed, and conſorted with Paul and Silas: but the jews which believed not, ſet the city in an uproar." Can there be any thing plainer, than that the aſſenting to this propoſition, that Jeſus was the Meſſiah, was that which diſtinguiſhed the believers from the unbelievers? For this was that alone, which, three ſabbaths, Paul endeavoured to convince them of, as the text tells us in direct words.

From thence he went to Berœa, and preached the ſame thing: and the berœans are commended, v. 11, for ſearching the ſcriptures, whether thoſe things, i. e. which he had ſaid, v. 2, 3, concerning Jeſus's being the Meſſiah, were true or no.

The ſame doctrine we find him preaching at Corinth, Acts xviii. 4—6. " And he reaſoned in the ſynagogue every ſabbath, and perſuaded the jews and the greeks. And when Silas and Timotheus were come from Macedonia,

donia, Paul was preſſed in ſpirit, and teſtified to the
jews, that Jeſus was the Meſſiah.   And when they op-
poſed themſelves, and blaſphemed, he ſhook his rai-
ment, and ſaid unto them, Your blood be upon your
own heads, I am clean; from henceforth I will go unto
the greeks.''

Upon the like occaſion he tells the jews at Antioch,
Acts xiii. 46. '' It was neceſſary that the word of God
ſhould firſt have been ſpoken to you: but ſeeing you put
it off from you, we turn to the gentiles.'' 'Tis plain
here, St. Paul's charging their blood on their own heads,
is for oppoſing this ſingle truth, that Jeſus was the
Meſſiah; that ſalvation or perdition depends upon believing or rejecting this one propoſition.   I mean, this
is all that is required to be believed by thoſe who acknowledge but one eternal and inviſible God, the maker
of heaven and earth, as the jews did.   For that there is
ſomething more required to ſalvation, beſides believing,
we ſhall ſee hereafter.   In the mean time, it is fit here
on this occaſion to take notice, that though the apoſtles
in their preaching to the jews, and the devout, (as we
tranſlate the word σεβόμενοι, who were proſelytes of the
gate, and the worſhippers of one eternal and inviſible
God) ſaid nothing of the believing in this one true God,
the maker of heaven and earth; becauſe it was needleſs
to preſs this to thoſe who believed and profeſſed it already (for to ſuch, 'tis plain, were moſt of their diſcourſes hitherto.)   Yet when they had to do with idolatrous heathens, who were not yet come to the knowledge of the one only true God; they began with that,
as neceſſary to be believed; it being the foundation on
which the other was built, and without which it could
ſignify nothing.

Thus Paul ſpeaking to the idolatrous lyſtrians, who
who would have ſacrificed to him and Barnabas, ſays,
Acts xiv. 15, '' We preach unto you, that ye ſhould turn
from theſe vanities unto the living God, who made
heaven and earth, and the ſea, and all things that are
therein : who in times paſt ſuffered all nations to walk
in their own ways.   Nevertheleſs he left not himſelf
without witneſs, in that he did good, and gave us rain

from heaven, and fruitful feafons, filling our hearts with food and gladnefs."

Thus alfo he proceeded with the idolatrous athenians, Acts xvii, telling them, upon occafion of the altar dedicated to the unknown God, " whom you ignorantly worfhip, him declare I unto you. God who made the world, and all things therein, feeing that he is Lord of heaven and earth, dwelleth not in temples made with hands.—Forafmuch then as we are the offspring of God, we ought not to think that the Godhead is like unto gold, or filver, or ftone, graven by art, or man's device. And the times of this ignorance God winked at; but now commandeth all men every where to repent; becaufe he hath appointed a day in which he will judge the world in righteoufnefs, by that man whom he hath ordained : whereof he hath given affurance unto all men, in that he hath raifed him from the dead." So that we fee, where any thing more was neceffary to be propofed to be believed, as there was to the heathen idolators, there the apoftles were careful not to omit it.

Acts xviii. 4, " Paul at Corinth reafoned in the fynagogue every fabbath-day, and teftified to the jews, that Jefus was the Meffiah." Ver. 11, " And he continued there a year and fix months, teaching the word of God amongft them;" i. e. The good news, that Jefus was the Meffiah; as we have already fhown is meant by " the Word of God."

Apollos, another preacher of the gofpel, when he was inftructed in the way of God more perfectly, what did he teach but this fame doctrine? As we may fee in this account of him, Acts xviii. 27. That " when he was come into Achaia, he helped the brethren much, who had believed through grace. For he mightily convinced the jews, and that publicly, fhowing by the fcriptures that Jefus was the Meffiah."

St. Paul, in the account he gives of himfelf before Feftus and Agrippa, profeffes this alone to be the doctrine he taught after his converfion : for, fays he, Acts xxvi. 22, " Having obtained help of God, I continue unto this day, witneffing both to fmall and great, faying none other things than thofe which the prophets and Mofes

did

did say should come: that the Messiah should suffer, and that he should be the first that should rise from the dead, and should show light unto the people, and to the gentiles." Which was no more than to prove that Jesus was the Messiah. This is that, which, as we have above observed, is called the Word of God; Acts xi. 1. compared with the foregoing chapter, from v. 34. to the end. And xiii. 42. compared with 44, 46, 48, 49. and xvii. 13. compared with v. 11, 13. It is also called, " the Word of the Gospel," Acts xv. 7. And this is that Word of God, and that Gospel, which, wherever their discourses are set down, we find the apostles preached; and was that faith, which made both jews and gentiles believers and members of the church of Christ; purifying their hearts, Acts xv. 9. and carrying with it remission of sins, Acts x. 43. So that all that was to be believed for justification, was no more but this single proposition, that " Jesus of Nazareth was the Christ, or the Messiah." All, I say, that was to be believed for justification: for that it was not all that was required to be done for justification, we shall see hereafter.

Though we have seen above from what our Saviour has pronounced himself, John iii. 36, " that he that believeth on the Son, hath everlasting life; and he that believeth not the Son, shall not see life, but the wrath of God abideth on him;" and are taught from John iv. 39, compared with v. 42, that believing on him, is believing that he is the Messiah, the Saviour of the world; and the confession made by St. Peter, Matt. xvi. 16, that he is "the Messiah, the Son of the living God," being the rock, on which our Saviour has promised to build his church; though this I say, and what else we have already taken notice of, be enough to convince us what it is we are in the gospel required to believe to eternal life, without adding what we have observed from the preaching of the apostles; yet it may not be amiss, for the farther clearing this matter, to observe what the evangelists deliver concerning the same thing, though in different words; which, therefore, perhaps, are not so generally taken notice of to this purpose.

We have above observed, from the words of Andrew and Philip compared, that " the Messiah, and him of
whom

whom Mofes in the law and the prophets did write," fignify the fame thing. We fhall now confider that place, John i. a little farther. Ver. 41, " Andrew fays to Simon, we have found the Mefliah." Philip, on the fame occafion, v. 45, fays to Nathanael, " we have found him of whom Mofes in the law and the prophets did write, Jefus of Nazareth, the fon of Jofeph." Nathanael, who difbelieved this, when, upon Chrift's fpeaking to him, he was convinced of it, declares his affent to it in thefe words: " Rabbi, thou art the Son of God, thou art the king of Ifrael." From which it is evident, that to believe him to be " Him of whom Mofes and " the prophets did write," or to be the " Son of God," or to be " the king of Ifrael," was in effect the fame as to believe him to be the Mefliah: and an affent to that, was what our Saviour received for believing. For, upon Nathanael's making a confeffion in thefe words, " Thou art the Son of God, thou art the king of Ifrael ; " Jefus anfwered and faid to him, Becaufe I faid to " thee I faw thee under the fig-tree, doft thou BELIEVE? " Thou fhall fee greater things than thefe," ver. 51. I defire any one to read the latter part of the firft of John, from ver. 25, with attention, and tell me, whether it be not plain, that this phrafe, The Son of God, is an expreffion ufed for the Mefliah. To which let him add Martha's declaration of her faith, John xi. 27, in thefe words: " I believe that thou are the Mefliah, THE SON OF GOD, who fhould come into the world;" and that paffage of St. John xx. 31, " That ye might believe " that Jefus is the Mefliah, THE SON OF GOD ; and that, " believing, ye might have life through his name:" and then tell me whether he can doubt that Mefliah, the Son of God, were fynonymous terms, at that time, amongft the jews.

The prophecy of Daniel, chap. ix, when he is called " Mefliah the Prince;" and the mention of his government and kingdom, and the deliverance by him, in Ifaiah, Daniel, and other prophecies, underftood of the Mefliah ; were fo well known to the jews, and had fo raifed their hopes of him about this time, which, by their account, was to be the time of his coming, to re-

ftore

ftore the kingdom of Ifrael; that Herod no fooner heard
of the magi's inquiry after " Him that was born king
" of the jews," Matt. ii, but he forthwith " demanded
" of the chief priefts and fcribes, where the Meffiah
" fhould be born," ver. 4.   Not doubting but, if there
were any king born to the jews, it was the Meffiah:
whofe coming was now the general expectation, as appears, Luke iii. 15, " The people being in expectation,
" and all men mufing in their hearts, of John, whether
" he were the Meffiah or not."   And when the priefts
and levites fent to afk him who he was; he, underftanding their meaning, anfwers, John i. 20, " That he was
not the Meffiah;" but he bears witnefs, that Jefus " is
the Son of God," i. e. the Meffiah, ver. 34.

This looking for the Meffiah, at this time, we fee
alfo in Simeon; who is faid to be " waiting for the con-
" folation of Ifrael," Luke ii. 21.   And having the
child Jefus in his arms, he fays, he had " feen the fal-
" vation of the Lord," ver. 30.   And, " Anna coming
" at the fame inftant into the temple, fhe gave thanks
" alfo unto the Lord, and fpake of him to all them
" that looked for redemption in Ifrael," ver. 38.   And
of Jofeph of Arimathea, it is faid, Mark xv. 43, That
" he alfo expected the kingdom of God:" by all which
was meant the coming of the Meffiah; and Luke xix.
11, it is faid, " They thought that the kingdom of God
" fhould immediately appear."

This being premifed, let us fee what it was that John
the Baptift preached, when he firft entered upon his
miniftry.   That St. Matthew tells us, chap. iii. 1, 2,
" In thofe days came John the Baptift preaching in the
" wildernefs of Judea, faying, repent; for the kingdom
" of heaven is at hand."   This was a declaration of the
coming of the Meffiah: the kingdom of heaven, and
the kingdom of God, being the fame, as is clear out of
feveral places of the evangelifts; and both fignifying the
kingdom of the Meffiah.   The profeffion, which John
the Baptift made, when fent to the jews, John i. 19, was,
that " he was not the Meffiah;" but that Jefus was.
This will appear to any one, who will compare ver.

26——

26—34, with John iii. 27, 30. The jews being very inquifitive to know, whether John were the Meffiah; he pofitively denies it; but tells them, he was only his fore-runner; and that there ftood one amongft them, who would follow him, whofe fhoe-latchet he was not worthy to untie. The next day, feeing Jefus, he fays, he was the man; and that his own baptizing in water was only that Jefus might be manifefted to the world; and that he knew him not, till he faw the Holy Ghoft defcend upon him: he that fent him to baptize, having told him, that he on whom he fhould fee the Spirit defcend, and reft upon, he it was that fhould baptize with the Holy Ghoft; and that therefore he witneffed, that " this was the Son of God," ver. 34, i. e. the Meffiah; and, chap. iii. 26, &c. they come to John the Baptift, and tell him, that Jefus baptized, and that all men went to him. John anfwers, He has his authority from heaven; you know I never faid, I was the Meffiah, but that I was fent before him. He muft increafe, but I muft decreafe; for God hath fent him, and he fpeaks the words of God; and God hath given all things into the hands of his Son, " And he that believes on the Son, hath eternal life;" the fame doctrine, and nothing elfe, but what was preached by the apoftles afterwards: as we have feen all through the Acts, v. g. that Jefus was the Meffiah. And thus it was, that John bears witnefs of our Saviour, as Jefus himfelf fays, John v. 33.

This alfo was the declaration given of him at his baptifm, by a voice from heaven: " This is my beloved " Son in whom I am well pleafed," Matt. iii. 17. Which was a declaration of him to be the Meffiah, the Son of God being (as we have fhowed) underftood to fignify the Meffiah. To which we may add the firft mention of him after his conception, in the words of the angel to Jofeph, Matt. i. 21. " Thou fhalt call " his name Jefus," or Saviour; " for he fhall fave " his people from their fins." It was a received doctrine in the jewifh nation, that at the coming of the Meffiah, all their fins fhould be forgiven them. Thefe words, therefore, of the angel, we may look upon as a declaration, that Jefus was the Meffiah; whereof thefe

words,

words, " his people," are a farther mark : which suppose him to have a people, and consequently to be a king.

After his baptism, Jesus himself enters upon his ministry. But, before we examine what it was he proposed to be believed, we must observe, that there is a threefold declaration of the Messiah.

1. By miracles. The spirit of prophecy had now for many ages forsaken the jews: and, though their commonwealth were not quite dissolved, but that they lived under their own laws, yet they were under a foreign dominion, subject to the Romans. In this state, their account of the time being up, they were in expectation of the Messiah, and of deliverance by him in a kingdom he was to set up, according to their ancient prophecies of him: which gave them hopes of an extraordinary man yet to come from God, who, with an extraordinary and divine power, and miracles, should evidence his mission, and work their deliverance. And, of any such extraordinary person, who should have the power of doing miracles, they had no other expectation, but only of their Messiah. One great prophet and worker of miracles, and only one more, they expected; who was to be the Messiah. And therefore we see the people justified their believing in him, i. e. their believing him to be the Messiah, because of the miracles he did ; John vii. 31. " And many of the people believed in him,
" and said, When the Messiah cometh, will he do more
" miracles, than this man hath done?" And when the jews, at the feast of dedication, John x. 24, 25, coming about him, said unto him, "How long dost thou
" make us doubt? If thou be the Messiah, tell us
" plainly; Jesus answered them, I told you, and ye be-
" lieved not ; the works that I do in my Father's
" name, bear witness of me." And, John v. 36, he says, " I have a greater witness than that of John; for
" the works, which the Father hath given me to do,
" the same works that I do, bear witness of me, that
" the Father hath sent me." Where, by the way, we may observe, that his being " sent by the Father," is but another way of expressing the Messiah; which is

2   evident

evident from this place here, John v, compared with
that of John x, laſt quoted. For there he ſays, that his
woiks bear witneſs of him: And what was that witneſs?
viz. That he was "the Meſſiah." Here again he ſays,
that his works bear witneſs of him: And what is that
witneſs? viz. "That the Father ſent him." By which
we are taught, that to be ſent by the Father, and
to be the Meſſiah, was the ſame thing, in his way of
declaring himſelf. And accordingly we find, John iv.
53, and xi. 45, and elſewhere, many hearkened and aſ-
ſented to his teſtimony, and believed on him, ſeeing
the things that he did.

2. Another way of declaring the coming of the Me-
ſiah, was by phraſes and circumlocutions, that did ſignify or intimate his coming; though not in direct
words pointing out the perſon. The moſt uſual of theſe
were, "The kingdom of God, and of heaven;" becauſe it was that which was often ſpoken of the Meſſiah,
in the Old Teſtament, in very plain words: and a kingdom was that which the Jews moſt looked after and
wiſhed for. In that known place, Iſa. ix, "The GO-
" VERNMENT ſhall be upon his ſhoulders; he ſhall be
" called the PRINCE of peace: of the increaſe of his
" GOVERNMENT and peace there ſhall be no end; upon
" the THRONE of David, and upon his KINGDOM, to
" order it, and to eſtabliſh it with judgment, and with•
" juſtice, from henceforth even for ever." Micah v. 2,
" But thou, Bethlehem Ephratah, though thou be lit-
" tle among the thouſands of Judah, yet out of thee
" ſhall he come forth unto me, that is to be the RULER
" in Iſrael." And Daniel, beſides that he calls him,
" Meſſiah the PRINCE," chap. ix. 25, in the account
of his viſion " of the Son of man," chap. vii. 13, 14,
ſays, "There was given him dominion, glory, and a
" KINGDOM, that all people, nations, and languages,
" ſhould ſerve him: his dominion is an everlaſting do-
" minion, which ſhall not paſs away; and his KING-
" DOM that which ſhall not be deſtroyed." So that the
kingdom of God, and the kingdom of heaven, were
common phraſes amongſt the jews, to ſignify the times
of the Meſſiah. Luke xiv. 15, "One of the jews that

" fat at meat with him, said unto him, Blessed is he
" that shall eat bread in the kingdom of God." Chap.
xvii. 20, The pharisees demanded, " when the king-
" dom of God should come?" And St. John Baptist
" came, saying, Repent; for the kingdom of heaven is
" at hand;" a phrase he would not have used in
preaching, had it not been understood.

There are other expressions that signified the Messiah,
and his coming, which we shall take notice of, as they
come in our way.

3. By plain and direct words, declaring the doctrine
of the Messiah, speaking out that Jesus was he; as we
see the apostles did, when they went about preaching
the gospel, after our Saviour's resurrection. This was
the open clear way, and that which one would think
the Messiah himself, when he came, should have taken;
especially, if it were of that moment, that upon men's
believing him to be the Messiah, depended the forgiveness of their sins. And yet we see, that our Saviour
did not: but on the contrary, for the most part, made
no other discovery of himself, at least in Judea, and at
the beginning of his ministry, but in the two former
ways, which were more obscure; not declaring himself
to be the Messiah, any otherwise than as it might be
gathered from the miracles he did, and the conformity
of his life and actions, with the prophecies of the Old
Testament concerning him; and from some general discourses of the kingdom of the Messiah being come, under the name of the " kingdom of God, and of hea-
" ven." Nay, so far was he from publicly owning
himself to be the Messiah, that he forbid the doing of
it: Mark viii. 27—30. " He asked his disciples,
" Whom do men say that I am? And they answered
" John the Baptist; but some say Elias; and others,
" one of the prophets." (So that it is evident, that even
those, who believed him an extraordinary person, knew
not yet who he was, or that he gave himself out for the
Messiah; though this was in the third year of his ministry, and not a year before his death.) " And he saith
" unto them, But whom say ye that I am? And Peter
" answered and said unto him, Thou art the Messiah.
" And

" And he charged them, that they fhould tell no man
" of him," Luke iv. 41. " And devils came out of
" many, crying, Thou art the Meffiah, the Son of God:
" and he, rebuking them, fuffered them not to fpeak,
" that they knew him to be the Meffiah." Mark iii.
11, 12. " Unclean fpirits, when they faw him, fell
" down before him, and cried, faying, Thou art the
" Son of God : and he ftraitly charged them, that they
" fhould not make him known." Here again we may
obferve, from the comparing of the two texts, that
" Thou art the Son of God," or, " Thou art the Mef-
" fiah," were indifferently ufed for the fame thing.
But to return to the matter in hand.

This concealment of himfelf will feem ftrange, in
one who was come to bring light into the world, and
was to fuffer death for the teftimony of the truth. This
refervednefs will be thought to look, as if he had a
mind to conceal himfelf, and not to be known to the
world for the Meffiah, nor to be believed on as fuch.
But we fhall be of another mind, and conclude this proceeding of his according to divine wifdom, and fuited
to a fuller manifeftation and evidence of his being the
Meffiah ; when we confider that he was to fill out the
time foretold of his miniftry ; and after a life illuftrious
in miracles and good works, attended with humility,
meeknefs, patience, and fufferings, and every way conformable to the prophefies of him ; fhould be led as a
fheep to the flaughter, and with all quiet and fubmiffion
be brought to the crofs, though there were no guilt,
nor fault found in him. This could not have been, if,
as foon as he appeared in public, and began to preach,
he had prefently profeffed himfelf to have been the
Meffiah ; the king that owned that kingdom, he publifhed to be at hand. For the fanhedrim would then
have laid hold on it, to have got him into their power,
and thereby have taken away his life ; at leaft they
would have difturbed his miniftry, and hindered the
work he was about. That this made him cautious, and
avoid, as much as he could, the occafions of provoking
them, and falling into their hands, is plain from John
vii. 1. " After thefe things Jefus walked in Galilee ;"

out

out of the way of the chief priests and rulers; "for
"he would not walk in Jewry, because the jews sought
"to kill him." Thus, making good what he foretold
them at Jerusalem, when, at the first passover after his
beginning to preach the gospel, upon his curing the
man at the pool of Bethesda, they sought to kill him,
John v. 16, "Ye have not," says he, ver. 38, "his
"word abiding amongst you; for whom he hath sent,
"him ye believe not." This was spoken more particularly to the jews of Jerusalem, who were the forward
men, zealous to take away his life: and it imports,
that, because of their unbelief and opposition to him,
the word of God, i. e. the preaching of the kingdom of
the Messiah, which is often called, "the word of God,"
did not stay amongst them, he could not stay amongst
them, preach and explain to them the kingdom of the
Messiah.

That the word of God, here, signifies "the word of
"God," that should make Jesus known to them to be
the Messiah, is evident from the context: and this
meaning of this place is made good by the event. For,
after this, we hear no more of Jesus at Jerusalem, 'till
the pentecost come twelve-month; though it is not to
be doubted, but that he was there the next passover,
and other feasts between; but privately. And now at
Jerusalem, at the feast of pentecost, near fifteen months
after, he says little of any thing, and not a word of the
kingdom of heaven being come, or at hand; nor did he
any miracle there. And returning to Jerusalem at the
feast of tabernacles, it is plain, that from this time 'till
then, which was a year and a half, he had not taught
them at Jerusalem.

For, 1, it is said, John vii. 2, 15, That, he teaching in the temple at the feast of tabernacles, "the jews
"marvelled, saying, How knoweth this man letters,
"having never learned?" A sign they had not been
used to his preaching: for, if they had, they would not
now have marvelled.

2. Ver. 19, He says thus to them: "Did not Moses
"give you the law, and yet none of you keep the law?
"Why go ye about to kill me? One work," or miracle,

cle, "I did here amongst you, and ye all marvel.
" Moses therefore gave unto you circumcision, and ye
" on the sabbath-day circumcise a man: if a man on the
" sabbath-day receive circumcision, that the law of
" Moses should not be broken, are ye angry with me,
" because I have made a man every way whole on the
" sabbath-day?" Which is a direct defence of what he
did at Jerusalem, a year and a half before the work he
here speaks of. We find he had not preached to them
there, from that time to this; but had made good what
he had told them, ver. 38, "Ye have not the word of
" God remaining among you, because whom he hath
" sent ye believe not." Whereby, I think, he signifies
his not staying, and being frequent amongst them at
Jerusalem, preaching the gospel of the kingdom; because their great unbelief, opposition, and malice to
him, would not permit it.

This was manifestly so in fact: for the first miracle
he did at Jerusalem, which was at the second passover
after his baptism, brought him in danger of his life.
Hereupon we find he forbore preaching again there,
'till the feast of tabernacles, immediately preceding his
last passover: so that 'till the half a year before his passion, he did but one miracle, and preached but once
publicly at Jerusalem. These trials he made there;
but found their unbelief such, that if he had staid and
persisted to preach the good tidings of the kingdom,
and to show himself by miracles among them, he could
not have had time and freedom to do those works which
his Father had given him to finish, as he says, ver. 36,
of this fifth of St. John.

When, upon the curing of the withered hand on the
sabbath-day, "The pharisees took council with the
" herodians, how they might destroy him, Jesus with-
" drew himself, with his disciples, to the sea: and a
" great multitude from Galilee followed him, and from
" Judea, and from Jerusalem, and from Idumea, and
" from beyond Jordan, and they about Tyre and Sidon,
" a great multitude; when they had heard what great
" things he did, came unto him, and he healed them all,
" and CHARGED THEM, THAT THEY SHOULD NOT MAKE

" HIM

" HIM KNOWN: that it might be fulfilled which was
" spoken by the prophet Isaiah, saying, Behold, my
" servant, whom I have chosen; my beloved, in whom
" my soul is well pleased: I will put my spirit upon
" him, and he shall show judgment to the Gentiles.
" He shall not strive, nor cry, neither shall any man
" hear his voice in the streets, Matt. xii. Mark iii.

And, John xi. 47, upon the news of our Saviour's
raising Lazarus from the dead, "The chief priests and
" pharisees convened the sanhedrim, and said, What
" do we? For this man does many miracles." Ver. 53,
" Then from that day forth they took counsel together
" for to put him to death." Ver. 54, Jesus therefore
" walked no more openly amongst the jews." His
miracles had now so much declared him to be the Messiah, that the jews could no longer bear him, nor he
trust himself amongst them; "But went thence unto a
" country near to the wilderness, into a city called
" Ephraim; and there continued with his disciples."
This was but a little before his last passover, as appears
by the following words, ver. 55. "And the jews pass-
" over was nigh at hand," and he could not, now his
miracles had made him so well known, have been secure, the little time that remained, 'till his hour was
fully come, if he had not, with his wonted and necessary caution, withdrawn; "And walked no more
" openly amongst the jews," 'till his time (at the next
passover) was fully come; and then again he appeared
amongst them openly.

Nor would the romans have suffered him, if he had
gone about preaching, that he was the king whom the
jews expected. Such an accusation would have been
forwardly brought against him by the jews, if they
could have heard it out of his own mouth; and that had
been his public doctrine to his followers, which was
openly preached by the apostles after his death, when he
appeared no more. And of this they were accused,
Acts xvii. 5—9. "But the jews, which believed not,
" moved with envy, took unto them certain lewd fel-
" lows of the baser sort, and gathered a company, and
" set all the city in an uproar, and assaulted the house
" of

" of Jaſon, and fought to bring them out to the people.
" And when they found them [Paul and Silas] not,
" they drew Jaſon, and certain brethren, unto the
" rulers of the city, crying, Theſe that. have turned
" the world upfide down, are come hither alfo ; whom
" Jaſon hath received : and theſe all do contrary to the
" decrees of Cæſar, ſaying, That there is another king,
" one Jeſus. And they troubled the people, and the
" rulers of the city, when they heard theſe things : and
" when they had taken ſecurity of Jaſon and the other,
" they let them go."

Though the magiſtrates of the world had no great regard to the talk of a king who had ſuffered death, and
appeared no longer any where ; yet, if our Saviour had
openly declared this of himſelf in his life-time, with a
train of diſciples and followers every-where owning and
crying him up for their king ; The roman governors
of Judea could not have forborn to have taken notice of
it, and have made uſe of their force againſt him. This
the jews were not miſtaken in ; and therefore made
uſe of it as the ſtrongeſt accuſation, and likelieſt to prevail with Pilate againſt him, for the taking away his
life ; it being treaſon, and an unpardonable offence,
which could not eſcape death from a roman deputy,
without the forfeiture of his own life. Thus then they
accuſe him to Pilate, Luke xxiii. 2. " We found this
" fellow perverting the nation, forbidding to give tri-
" bute to Cæſar, ſaying, that he himſelf is a king;"
or rather " the Meſſiah, the King."

Our Saviour, indeed, now that his time was come,
(and he in cuſtody, and forſaken of all the world, and
ſo out of all danger of raiſing any ſedition or diſ-
turbance) owns himſelf to Pilate to be a king; after
firſt having told Pilate, John xviii. 36, " That his
" kingdom was not of this world;" and, for a kingdom in another world, Pilate knew that his maſter at
Rome concerned not himſelf. But had there been any
the leaſt appearance of truth in the allegations of the
jews, that he had perverted the nation, forbidding to
pay tribute to Cæſar, or drawing the people after him,
as their king; Pilate would not ſo readily have pro-

nounced

nounced him innocent. But we fee what he faid to his
accufers, Luke xxiii. 13, 14.   " Pilate, when he had
" called together the chief priefts and the rulers of the
" people, faid unto them, you have brought this man
" unto me, as one that perverteth the people; and
" behold, I, having examined him before you, have
" found no fault in this man, touching thofe things
" whereof you accufe him : no, nor yet Herod, for I
" fent you to him ; and, lo, nothing worthy of death
" is done by him." And therefore, finding a man of
that mean condition, and innocent life, (no mover of
feditions, or difturber of the publick peace) without a
friend or a follower, he would have difmiffed him, as a
king of no confequence; as an innocent man, falfely
and malicioufly accufed by the jews.

How neceffary this caution was in our Saviour, to
fay or do nothing that might juftly offend, or render
him fufpected to the roman governor ; and how glad
the jews would have been to have had any fuch thing
againft him, we may fee, Luke xx. 20. The chief
priefts and the fcribes " watched him, and fent forth
" fpies, who fhould feign themfelves juft men, that
" might take hold of his words, that fo they might
" deliver him unto the power and authority of the
" governor."   And the very thing wherein they hoped
to entrap him in this place, was paying tribute to
Cæfar ; which they afterwards falfely accufed him of.
And what would they have done, if he had before them
profeffed himfelf to have been the Meffiah, their King
and deliverer ?

And here we may obferve the wonderful providence
of God, who had fo ordered the ftate of the jews, at
the time when his fon was to come into the world, that
though neither their civil conftitution, nor religious worfhip were diffolved, yet the power of life and death was
taken from them ; whereby he had an opportunity to publifh " the kingdom of the Meffiah ;" that is, his own
royalty, under the name of " the kingdom of God, and of
" heaven ;" which the jews well enough underftood,
and would certainly have put him to death for, had the
power been in their own hands.   But this being no mat-
tcr

ter of accufation to the romans, hindered him not from fpeaking of the "kingdom of heaven," as he did, fometimes in reference to his appearing in the world, and being believed on by particular perfons; fometimes in reference to the power fhould be given him by the Father at his refurrection; and fometimes in reference to his coming to judge the world at the laft day, in the full glory and completion of his kingdom. Thefe were ways of declaring himfelf, which the jews could lay no hold on, to bring him in danger with Pontius Pilate, and get him feized and put to death.

Another reafon there was, that hindered him as much as the former, from profeffing himfelf, in exprefs words, to be the Meffiah; and that was, that the whole nation of the jews, expecting at this time their Meffiah, and deliverance by him, from the fubjection they were in to a foreign yoke, the body of the people would certainly, upon his declaring himfelf to be the Meffiah, their king, have rofe up in rebellion, and fet him at the head of them. And indeed, the miracles that he did, fo much difpofed them to think him to be the Meffiah, that, though fhrouded under the obfcurity of a mean condition, and a very private fimple life; though he paffed for a Galilean, (his birth at Bethlehem being then concealed) and affumed not to himfelf any power or authority, or fo much as the name of the Meffiah; yet he could hardly avoid being fet up by a tumult, and proclaimed their king. So John tells us, chap vi. 14, 15, "Then thofe men, when they had "feen the miracles that Jefus did, faid, This is of a "truth that prophet that fhould come into the world. "When therefore Jefus perceived that they would "come to take him by force to make him king, he "departed again into a mountain, himfelf alone." This was upon his feeding of five thoufand with five barley loaves and two fifhes. So hard was it for him, doing thofe miracles which were neceffary to teftify his miffion, and which often drew great multitudes after him, Matt. iv. 25, to keep the heady and hafty multitude from fuch diforder, as would have involved him in it; and have difturbed the courfe, and cut fhort the

the time of his miniftry ; and drawn on him the reputation and death of a turbulent, feditious malefactor :
contrary to the defign of his coming, which was, to be
offered up a lamb blamelefs, and void of offence; his
innocence appearing to all the world, even to him that
delivered him up to be crucified. This it would have
been impoffible to have avoided, if, in his preaching every-where, he had openly affumed to himfelf the
title of their Meffiah ; which was all was, wanting to
fet the people in a flame ; who drawn by his miracles,
and the hopes of finding a Deliverer in fo extraordinary
a man, followed him in great numbers. We read every-
where of multitudes, and in Luke xii. 1, of myriads
that were gathered about him.   This conflux of people,
thus difpofed, would not have failed, upon his declaring
himfelf to be the Meffiah, to have made a commotion,
and with force fet him up for their King.   It is plain,
therefore, from thefe two reafons, why (though he came
to preach the gofpel, and convert the world to a belief
of his being the Meffiah ; and though he fays fo much of
his kingdom, under the title of the kingdom of God,
and the kingdom of heaven) he yet makes it not his bufinefs to perfuade them, that he himfelf is the Meffiah,
nor does, in his publick preaching, declare himfelf to
be him.   He inculcates to the people, on all occafions,
that the kingdom of God is come : he fhows the way of
admittance into this kingdom, viz. repentance and
baptifm ; and teaches the laws of it, viz. good life, according to the ftricteft rules of virtue and morality.
But who the King was of this kingdom, he leaves to his
miracles to point out, to thofe who would confider
what he did, and make the right ufe of it now ; or to
witnefs to thofe who fhould hearken to the apoftles
hereafter, when they preached it in plain words, and
called upon them to believe it, after his refurrection,
when there fhould be no longer room to fear, that it
fhould caufe any difturbance in civil focieties, and the
governments of the world.   But he could not declare
himfelf to be the Meffiah, without manifeft danger of
tumult and fedition : and the miracles he did declared
it fo much, that he was fain often to hide himfelf, and
                                                withdraw

withdraw from the concourfe of the people. The leper
that he cured, Mark i, though forbid to fay any thing,
yet " blazed it fo abroad, that Jefus could no more
" openly enter into the city, but was without in defert
" places," living in retirement, as appears from Luke
v. 16. and there " they came to him from every quar-
" ter." And thus he did more than once.

This being premifed, let us take a view of the promulgation of the gofpel by our Saviour himfelf, and fee
what it was he taught the world, and required men to
believe.

The firft beginning of his miniftry, whereby he
fhowed himfelf, feems to be at Cana in Galilee, foon
after his baptifm; where he turned water into wine: of
which St. John, chap ii. 11, fays thus: " This begin-
" ning of miracles Jefus made, and manifefted his
" glory, and his difciples believed in him." His difciples here believed in him, but we hear not of any
other preaching to them, but by this miracle, whereby
he " manifefted his glory," i. e. of being the Meffiah,
the Prince. So Nathanael, without any other preaching, but only our Saviour's difcovering to him, that he
knew him after an extraordinary manner, prefently acknowledges him to be the Meffiah; crying, " Rabbi,
" thou art the Son of God; thou art the King of
" Ifrael."

From hence, ftaying a few days at Capernaum, he
goes to Jerufalem to 'the paffover, and there he drives
the traders out of the temple, John ii. 12—15, faying,
" Make not my Father's houfe a houfe of merchan-
" dize." Where we fee he ufes a phrafe, which, by
interpretation, fignifies that he was the " Son of God,"
though at that time unregarded. Ver. 16, Hereupon
the Jews demand, " What fign doft thou fhow us, fince
" thou doeft thefe things?" Jefus anfwered, " Deftroy
" ye this temple, and in three days I will raife it
" again." This is an inftance of what way Jefus took
to declare himfelf: for it is plain, by their reply, the
Jews underftood him not, nor his difciples neither; for
it is faid, ver. 22, " When, therefore, he was rifen
from the dead, his difciples remembered, " that he
" faid

" said this to them : and they believed the scripture,
" and the saying of Jesus to them."

This, therefore, we may look on in the beginning, as
a pattern of Christ's preaching, and showing himself to
the jews, which he generally followed afterwards; viz.
such a manifestation of himself, as every one at present
could not understand; but yet carried such an evidence
with it, to those who were well disposed now, or would
reflect on it when the whole course of his ministry was
over, as was sufficient clearly to convince them that he
was the Messiah.

The reason of this method used by our Saviour, the
scripture gives us here, at this his first appearing in
public, after his entrance upon his ministry, to be a
rule and light to us in the whole course of it : for the
next verse taking notice, that many believed on him,
" because of his miracles," (which was all the preaching they had,) it is said, ver. 24, " But Jesus did not
" commit himself unto them, because he knew all
" men;" i. e. he declared not himself so openly to be
the Messiah, their King, as to put himself into the power
of the jews, by laying himself open to their malice ;
who, he knew, would be so ready to lay hold on it to
accuse him; for, as the next verse 25, shows, he knew
well enough what was in them. We may here farther
observe, that " believing in his name" signifies believing him to be the Messiah. Ver. 22, tells us, That
" many at the passover believed in his name, when they
" saw the miracles that he did." What other faith
could these miracles produce in them who saw them,
but that this was he of whom the scripture spoke, who
was to be their Deliverer?

Whilst he was now at Jerusalem, Nicodemus, a ruler
of the jews, comes to him, John iii. 1—21. to whom he
preaches eternal life by faith in the Messiah, ver. 15 and
17, but in general terms, without naming himself to be
that Messiah, though his whole discourse tends to it.
This is all we hear of our Saviour the first year of his
ministry, but only his baptism, fasting, and temptation
in the beginning of it, and spending the rest of it after
the passover, in Judea with his disciples, baptizing
                                                    there.

there. But " when he knew that the pharifees re-
" ported, that he made and baptized more difciples
" than John, he left Judea," and got out of their way
again into Galilee, John iv. 1, 3.

In his way back, by the well of Sichar, he difcourfes
with the famaritan woman; and after having opened to
her the true and fpiritual worfhip which was at hand,
which the woman prefently underftands of the times of
the Meffiah, who was then looked for; thus fhe anfwers,
ver. 25, " I know that the Meffiah cometh: when he
" is come, he will tell us all things." Whereupon our
Saviour, though we hear no fuch thing from him in
Jerufalem or Judea, or to Nicodemus; yet here, to this
famaritan woman, he in plain and direct words owns
and declares, that he himfelf, who talked with her, was
the Meffiah, ver. 26.

This would feem very ftrange, that he fhould be more
free and open to a famaritan, than he was to the jews,
were not the reafon plain, from what we have obferved
above. He was now out of Judea, among a people with
whom the jews had no commerce; ver. 9. who were not
difpofed, out of envy, as the jews were, to feek his life,
or to accufe him to the roman governor, or to make an
infurrection, to fet a jew up for their King. What the
confequence was of his difcourfe with this famaritan woman, we have an account, ver. 28, 39—42. " She left
" her water-pot, and went her way into the city, and
" faith to the men, Come, fee a man who told me all
" things that ever I did: Is not this the Meffiah? And
" many of the famaritans of that city BELIEVED ON HIM
" for the faying of the woman, which teftified, He told
" me all that ever I did. So when the famaritans were
" come unto him, they befought him, that he would
" tarry with them: and he abode there two days. And
" many more believed becaufe of his own word; and
" faid unto the woman, Now we believe not becaufe of
" thy faying: for we have heard him ourfelves; and we
" know," (i. e. are fully perfuaded) " that this is indeed
" the Meffiah, the Saviour of the world." By comparing ver. 39, with 41 and 42, it is plain, that " believ-
" ing

" ing on him" fignifies no more than believing him to
be the Meffiah.

From Sichar Jefus goes to Nazareth, the place he was
bred up in; and there reading in the fynagogue a prophecy concerning the Meffiah, out of the lxi. of Ifaiah,
he tells them, Luke iv. 21, " This day is this fcripture
" fulfilled in your ears."

But being in danger of his life at Nazareth, he leaves
it for Capernaum: and then, as St. Matthew informs
us, chap. iv. 17, " He began to preach and fay, Re-
" pent; for the kingdom of heaven is at hand."   Or,
as St. Mark has it, chap. i. 14, 15, " Preaching the
" gofpel of the kingdom of God, and faying, The
" time is fulfilled, and the kingdom of God is at hand;
" repent ye and believe the gofpel;" i. e. believe this
good news.   This removing to Capernaum, and feating
himfelf there in the borders of Zabulon and Naphtali,
was, as St. Matthew obferves, chap. iv. 13—16, that a
prophecy of Ifaiah might be fulfilled.   Thus the actions and circumftances of his life anfwered the prophecies, and declared him to be the Meffiah.   And by what
St. Mark fays in this place, it is manifeft, that the
gofpel which he preached and required them to believe,
was no other but the good tidings of the coming of the
Meffiah, and of his kingdom, the time being now fulfilled.

In his way to Capernaum, being come to Cana, a
nobleman of Capernaum came to him, ver. 47, " And
" befought him that he would come down and heal his
" fon; for he was at the point of death."   Ver. 48,
" Then faid Jefus unto him, Except ye fee figns and
" wonders, ye will not believe."   Then he returning
homewards, and finding that his fon began to " mend
" at the fame hour which Jefus faid unto him, Thy fon
" liveth; he himfelf believed, and his whole houfe,"
ver. 53.

Here this nobleman is by the apoftles pronounced to
be a believer.   And what does he believe? Even that
which Jefus complains, ver. 48, " they would not BE-
" LIEVE," except they faw figns and wonders; which
could be nothing but what thofe of Samaria in the fame
chapter

chapter believed, viz. that he was the Messiah. For we no where in the gospel hear of any thing else, that had been proposed to be believed by them.

Having done miracles, and cured all their sick at Capernaum, he says, " Let us go to the adjoining towns, " that I may preach there also; for therefore came I " forth," Mark i. 38. Or, as St. Luke has it, chap. iv. 43, he tells the multitude, who would have kept him, that he might not go from them, " I must evangelize," or tell the good tidings of " the kingdom of God to " other cities also; for therefore am I sent." And St. Matthew, chap. iv. 23, tells us how he executed this commission he was sent on: " And Jesus went about all " Galilee, teaching in their synagogues, and preaching " the gospel of the kingdom, and curing all diseases." This then was what he was sent to preach every where, viz. the gospel of the kingdom of the Messiah; and by the miracles and good he did he let them know who was the Messiah.

Hence he goes up to Jerusalem, to the second pass-over, since the beginning of his ministry. And here, discoursing to the jews, who sought to kill him, upon occasion of the man whom he had cured carrying his bed on the sabbath-day, and for making God his Father, he tells them that he wrought these things by the power of God, and that he shall do greater things; for that the dead shall, at his summons, be raised; and that he, by a power committed to him from his Father, shall judge them; and that he is sent by his Father; and that who-ever shall hear his word, and believe in him that sent him, has eternal life. This though a clear description of the Messiah, yet we may observe, that here, to the angry jews, who sought to kill him, he says not a word of his kingdom, nor so much as names the Messiah; but yet that he is the Son of God, and sent from God, he refers them to the testimony of John the Baptist, to the testimony of his own miracles, and of God himself in the voice from heaven, and of the scriptures, and of Moses. He leaves them to learn from these the truth they were to believe, viz. that he was the Messiah sent

from

from God.   This you may read more at large, John v.
1—47.

The next place where we find him preaching, was on
the mount, Matt. v. and Luke vi.   This is by much
the longest sermon we have of his, any where; and, in
all likelihood, to the greatest auditory: for it appears
to have been to the people gathered to him from Galilee, and Judea, and Jerusalem, and from beyond Jordan, and that came out of Idumea, and from Tyre and
Sidon, mentioned Mark iii. 7, 8. and Luke vi. 17.
But in this whole sermon of his, we do not find one
word of believing, and therefore no mention of the
Messiah, or any intimation to the people who himself
was.   The reason whereof we may gather from Matt.
xii. 16, where "Christ forbids them to make him
known;" which supposes them to know already who he
was.   For that this 12th chapter of St. Matthew ought
to precede the sermon in the mount, is plain, by comparing it with Mark ii, beginning at ver. 13, to Mark
iii. 8, and comparing those chapters of St. Mark with
Luke vi.   And I desire my reader, once for all, here to
take notice, that I have all along observed the order of
time in our Saviour's preaching, and have not, as I
think, passed by any of his discourses.   In this sermon,
our Saviour only teaches them what were the laws of his
kingdom, and what they must do who were admitted into
it, of which I shall have occasion to speak more at large
in another place, being at present only inquiring what
our Saviour proposed as matter of faith, to be believed.

After this, John the Baptist sends to him this message,
Luke vii. 19, asking, " Art thou he that should come,
" or do we expect another?" That is, in short, art thou
the Messiah? And if thou art, why dost thou let me, thy
forerunner, languish in prison? Must I expect deliverance from any other? To which Jesus returns this answer, ver. 22, 23, " Tell John what ye have seen and
" heard; the blind see, the lame walk, the lepers are
" cleansed, the deaf hear, the dead are raised, to the
" poor the gospel is preached; and blessed is he who is
" not offended in me." What it is to be " offended,
" or scandalized in him," we may see by comparing
                                                          Matt.

Matt. xiii. 28, and Mark iv. 17, with Luke viii. 13.
For what the two firſt call " ſcandalized," the laſt call
" ſtanding off from, or forſaking," i. e. not receiving
him as the Meſſiah, (vid. Mark vi. 1—6.) or revolting
from him. Here Jeſus refers John, as he did the jews
before, to the teſtimony of his miracles, to know who
he was ; and this was generally his preaching, whereby
he declared himſelf to be the Meſſiah; who was the
only prophet to come, whom the jews had any expectation of; nor did they look for any other perſon to be
ſent to them with the power of miracles, but only the
Meſſiah. His miracles, we ſee by his anſwer to John
the Baptiſt, he thought a ſufficient declaration amongſt
them, that he was the Meſſiah. And therefore, upon
his curing the poſſeſſed of the devil, the dumb, and
blind, Matt. xii, the people, who ſaw the miracles, ſaid,
ver. 23, " Is not this the ſon of David?" As much as
to ſay, Is not this the Meſſiah? Whereat the phariſees
being offended, ſaid, "He caſt out devils by Beelzebub."
Jeſus, ſhowing the falſehood and vanity of their blaſ-
phemy, juſtifies the concluſion the people made from
this miracle, ſaying, ver. 28, That his caſting out devils
by the Spirit of God, was an evidence that the kingdom of the Meſſiah was come.

One thing more there was in the miracles done by
his diſciples, which ſhowed him to be the Meſſiah; that
they were done in his name. " In the name of Jeſus of
" Nazareth, riſe up and walk," ſays St. Peter to the
lame man, whom he cured in the temple, Acts iii. 6.
And how far the power of that name reached, they themſelves ſeem to wonder, Luke x. 17. " And the ſeventy
" returned again with joy, ſaying, Lord, even the devils
" are ſubject to us in thy name."

From this meſſage from John the Baptiſt, he takes
occaſion to tell the people that John was the forerunner
of the Meſſiah ; that from the time of John the Baptiſt
the kingdom of the Meſſiah began; to which time all
the prophets and the law pointed, Luke vii. and Matt.
xi.

Luke viii. 1, " Afterwards he went through every
" city and village, preaching and ſhowing the good tid-

" ings of the kingdom of God." Here we see as every where, what his preaching was, and consequently what was to be believed.

Soon after, he preaches from a boat to the people on the shore. His sermon at large we may read Matt. xiii. Mark iv. and Luke viii. But this is very observable, that this second sermon of his, here, is quite different from his former in the mount: for that was all so plain and intelligible, that nothing could be more so; whereas this is all so involved in parables, that even the apostles themselves did not understand it. If we inquire into the reason of this, we shall possibly have some light, from the different subjects of these two sermons. There he preached to the people only morality; clearing the precepts of the law from the false glosses which were received in those days, and setting forth the duties of a good life, in their full obligation and extent, beyond what the judiciary laws of the Israelites did, or the civil laws of any country could prescribe, or take notice of. But here, in this sermon by the sea-side, he speaks of nothing but the kingdom of the Messiah, which he does all in parables. One reason whereof St. Matthew gives us, chap. xiii. 35, " That it might be fulfilled which was " spoken by the prophet," saying, " I will open my " mouth in parables, I will utter things that have been " kept secret from the foundations of the world." Another reason our Saviour himself gives of it, ver. 11, 12, " Because to you is given to know the mysteries of " the kingdom of heaven, but to them it is not given. " For whosoever hath, to him shall be given, and he " shall have more abundantly; but whosoever hath not," i. e. improves not the talents that he hath, " from him " shall be taken away even that he hath."

One thing it may not be amiss to observe, that our Saviour here, in the explication of the first of these parables to his apostles, calls the preaching of the kingdom of the Messiah, simply, " The word;" and Luke viii. 21, " The word of God:" from whence St. Luke, in the Acts, often mentions it under the name of the " word," and " the word of God," as we have elsewhere observed. To which I shall here add that of Acts viii.

viii. 4. " Therefore they that were fcattered abroad,
" went every where preaching the word ;" which word,
as we have found by examining what they preached all
through their hiftory, was nothing but this, that " Jefus
" was the Meffiah:" I mean, this was all the doctrine
they propofed to be believed : for what they taught, as
well as our Saviour, contained a great deal more; but that
concerned practice, and not belief.   And therefore our
Saviour fays, in the place before quoted, Luke viii. 21,
" they are my mother and my brethren, who hear the
" word of God, and do it :" obeying the law of the
Meffiah their king being no lefs required, than their
believing that Jefus was the Meffiah, the king and deliverer that was promifed them.

Matt. ix. 13, we have an account again of this preaching; what it was, and how: " And Jefus went about all
" the cities and villages, teaching in their fynagogues,
" and preaching the gofpel of the kingdom, and healing
" every ficknefs and every difeafe among the people."
He acquainted them, that the kingdom of the Meffiah
was come, and left it to his miracles to inftruct and convince them, that he was the Meffiah.

Matt. x, when he fent his apoftles abroad, their commiffion to preach we have, ver. 7, 8, in thefe words:
" As ye go, preach faying, The kingdom of heaven is
" at hand: heal the fick," &c.   All that they had to
preach was, that the kingdom of the Meffiah was come.

Whofoever fhould not receive them, the meffengers
of thefe good tidings, nor hearken to their meffage, incurred a heavier doom than Sodom and Gomorrah, at
the day of judgment, ver. 14, 15.   But, ver. 32, " Who-
" foever fhall confefs me before men, I will confefs
" him before my Father who is in heaven."   What
this confeffing of Chrift is, we may fee by comparing John xii. 42. with ix. 22. " Neverthelefs, among
" the chief rulers alfo many believed on him; but be-
" caufe of the pharifees they did not CONFESS HIM, left
" they fhould be put out of the fynagogue."   And
chap. ix. 22. " Thefe words fpake his parents, becaufe
" they feared the jews; for the jews had agreed already,
" that if any man did CONFESS THAT HE WAS THE MES-

E 2   " SIAH,

" SIAH, he should be put out of the synagogue." By
which places it is evident, that to confess him was to
confess that he was the Messiah.   From which, give me
leave to observe also, (what I have cleared from other
places, but cannot be too often remarked, because of the
different sense has been put upon that phrase) viz. " that
" believing on, or in him," (for εἰς αὐτὸν is rendered
either way by the english translation) signifies believing that he was the Messiah.   For many of the rulers
(the text says) " believed on him :" but they durst not
confess what they believed, " for fear they should be
" put out of the synagogue."   Now the offence for
which it was agreed that any one should be put out of
the synagogue, was, if he " did confess, that Jesus was
" the Messiah."   Hence we may have a clear understanding of that passage of St. Paul to the romans, where
he tells them positively, what is the faith he preaches,
Rom. x. 8, 9, " That is the word of faith which we
" preach, that if thou shalt confess with thy mouth the
" Lord Jesus, and believe in thine heart, that God hath
" raised him from the dead, thou shalt be saved ; and
that also of 1 John iv. 14, 15, " We have seen, and do
" testify, that the Father sent the Son to be the Saviour
" of the world : whosoever shall confess, that Jesus is
" the Son of God, God dwelleth in him, and he in
" God."   Where confessing Jesus to be the Son of God,
is the same with confessing him to be the Messiah ; those
two expressions being understood amongst the jews to
signify the same thing, as we have shown already.

How calling him the Son of God, came to signify
that he was the Messiah, would not be hard to show.
But it is enough, that it appears plainly, that it was so
used, and had that import among the jews at that time :
which if any one desires to have further evidenced to
him, he may add Matt. xxvi. 63. John vi. 69. and xi.
27. and xx. 31. to those places before occasionally taken
notice of.

As was the apostles commission, such was their performance ; as we read, Luke xi. 6, " They departed
" and went through the towns, preaching the gospel,
" and healing every-where."   Jesus bid them preach,
" saying,

" faying, The kingdom of heaven is at hand." And St. Luke tells us, they went through the towns preaching the gofpel; a word which in Saxon anfwers well the Greek εὐαγγέλιον, and fignifies, as that does, " good " news." So that what the infpired writers call the gofpel, is nothing but the good tidings, that the Mefliah and his kingdom was come; and fo it is to be underftood in the New Teftament, and fo the angel calls it, " good tidings of great joy," Luke ii. 10, bringing the firft news of our Saviour's birth. And this feems to be all that his difciples were at that time fent to preach.

So, Luke ix. 59, 60, to him that would have excufed his prefent attendance, becaufe of burying his father; " Jefus faid unto him, Let the dead bury their dead, " but go thou and preach the kingdom of God." When I fay, this was all they were to preach, I muft be underftood, that this was the faith they preached; but with it they joined obedience to the Mefliah, whom they received for their king. So likewife, when he fent out the feventy, Luke x, their commiffion was in thefe words, ver. 9, " Heal the fick, and fay unto them, " The kingdom of God is come nigh unto you."

After the return of his apoftles to him, he fits down with them on a mountain; and a great multitude being gathered about them, St. Luke tells us, chap. ix. 11, " The people followed him, and he received them, and " fpake unto them of the kingdom of God, and healed " them that had need of healing." This was his preaching to this affembly, which confifted of five thoufand men, befides women and children: all which great multitude he fed with five loaves and two fifhes, Matt. xiv. 21. And what this miracle wrought upon them, St. John tells us, chap. vi. 14, 15, " Then thefe " men, when they had feen the miracle that Jefus did, " faid, This is of a truth that prophet that fhould " come into the world," i. e. the Mefliah. For the Mefliah was the only perfon that they expected from God, and this the time they looked for him. And h nce John the Baptift, Matt. xi. 3, ftyles him, " He " that fhould come:" as in other places, " come from

　　　　　　　　　　　　　　　　　　" God,"

" God," or " sent from God," are phrases used for the Messiah.

Here we see our Saviour keep to his usual method of preaching: he speaks to them of the kingdom of God, and does miracles; by which they might understand him to be the Messiah, whose kingdom he spake of. And here we have the reason also, why he so much concealed himself, and forbore to own his being the Messiah. For what the consequence was, of the multitude's but thinking him so, when they were got together, St. John tells us in the very next words: " When Jesus then perceived, that they would come " and take him by force to make him a king, he de- " parted again into a mountain himself alone." If they were so ready to set him up for their king, only because they gathered from his miracles, that he was the Messiah, whilst he himself said nothing of it: what would not the people have done, and what would not the scribes and pharisees have had an opportunity to accuse him of, if he had openly professed himself to have been the Messiah, that king they looked for? But this we have taken notice of already.

From hence going to Capernaum, whither he was followed by a great part of the people, whom he had the day before so miraculously fed; he, upon the occasion of their following him for the loaves, bids them seek for the meat that endureth to eternal life: and thereupon, John vi. 22—69, declares to them his being sent from the Father; and that those who believed in him, should be raised to eternal life: but all this very much involved in a mixture of allegorical terms of eating, and of bread; bread of life, which came down from heaven, &c. Which is all comprehended and expounded in these short and plain words, ver. 47 and 54, " Verily, verily, I say unto you, he that believeth " on me, hath everlasting life, and I will raise him up " at the last day." The sum of all which discourse is, that he was the Messiah sent from God; and that those who believed him to be so, should be raised from the dead at the last day, to eternal life. These whom he spoke to here were of those who, the day before, would

by

by force have made him king; and therefore it is no wonder he fhould fpeak to them of himfelf, and his kingdom and fubjects, in obfcure and myftical terms; and fuch as fhould offend thofe who looked for nothing but the grandeur of a temporal kingdom in this world, and the protection and profperity they had promifed themfelves under it. The hopes of fuch a kingdom, now that they had found a man that did miracles, and therefore concluded to be the Deliverer they expected; had the day before almoft drawn them into an open infurrection, and involved our Saviour in it. This he thought fit to put a ftop to; they ftill following him, 'tis like, with the fame defign. And therefore, though he here fpeaks to them of his kingdom, it was in a way that fo plainly baulked their expectation, and fhocked them, that when they found themfelves difappointed of thofe vain hopes, and that he talked of their eating his flefh, and drinking his blood, that they might have life; the Jews faid, ver. 52, " How can this man " give us his flefh to eat? And many, even of his dif- " ciples, faid, It was an hard faying: Who can hear it?" And fo were fcandalized in him, and forfook him, ver. 60, 66. But what the true meaning of this difcourfe of our Saviour was, the confeffion of St. Peter, who underftood it better, and anfwered for the reft of the apoftles, fhows: when Jefus anfwered him, ver. 67, " Will ye " alfo go away? Then Simon Peter anfwered him, " Lord, to whom fhall we go? Thou haft the words of " eternal life:" i. e. thou teacheft us the way to attain eternal life; and accordingly, " we believe, and are " fure, that thou art the Meffiah, the Son of the living " God." This was the eating his flefh and drinking his blood, whereby thofe who did fo had eternal life.

Some time after this, he inquires of his difciples, Mark viii. 27, who the people took him for? They telling him, " for John-the Baptift," or one of the old prophets rifen from the dead; he afked, What they themfelves thought? And here again, Peter anfwers in thefe words, Mark viii. 29, " Thou art the Meffiah." Luke ix. 20, " The Meffiah of God." And, Matt. xvi. 16, " Thou art the Meffiah, the Son of the living

" God;"

" God:" Which expreſſions, we may hence gather, amount to the ſame thing. Whereupon our Saviour tells Peter, Matt. xvi. 17, 18, That this was ſuch a truth " as fleſh and blood could not reveal to him, but " only his Father who was in heaven;" and that this was the foundation, on which he was " to build his " church:" by all the parts of which paſſage it is more than probable, that he had never yet told his apoſtles in direct words, that he was the Meſſiah; but that they had gathered it from his life and miracles. For which we may imagine to ourſelves this probable reaſon; becauſe that, if he had familiarly, and in direct terms, talked to his apoſtles in private, that he was the Meſſiah the Prince, of whoſe kingdom he preached ſo much in public every where; Judas, whom he knew falſe and treacherous, would have been readily made uſe of, to teſtify againſt him, in a matter that would have been really criminal to the roman governor. This, perhaps, may help to clear to us that ſeemingly abrupt reply of our Saviour to his apoſtles, John vi. 70, when they confeſſed him to be the Meſſiah: I will, for the better explaining of it, ſet down the paſſage at large. Peter having ſaid, " We believe " and are ſure that thou art the Meſſiah, the Son of the " living God; Jeſus anſwered them, Have not I choſen " you twelve, and one of you is διάβολ©-?" This is a reply, ſeeming at firſt ſight, nothing to the purpoſe; when yet it is ſure all our Saviour's diſcourſes were wiſe and pertinent. It ſeems therefore to me to carry this ſenſe, to be underſtood afterwards by the eleven (as that of deſtroying the temple, and raiſing it again in three days was) when they ſhould reflect on it, after his being betrayed by Judas: you have confeſſed, and believe the truth concerning me; I am the Meſſiah your king: but do not wonder at it, that I have never openly declared it to you; for amongſt you twelve, whom I have choſen to be with me, there is one who is an informer, or falſe accuſer, (for ſo the greek word ſignifies, and may, poſſibly, here be ſo tranſlated, rather than devil) who, if I had owned myſelf in plain

I   words

words to have been the " Meſſiah, the king of Iſrael,"
would have betrayed me, and informed againſt me.

That he was yet cautious of owning himſelf to his
apoſtles, poſitively, to be the Meſſiah, appears farther
from the manner wherein he tells Peter, ver. 18, that
he will build his church upon that confeſſion of his,
that he was the Meſſiah: I ſay unto thee, " Thou art
" Cephas," or a rock, " and upon this rock I will
" build my church, and the gates of hell ſhall not pre-
" vail againſt it." Words too doubtful to be laid hold
on againſt him, as a teſtimony that he profeſſed himſelf to be the Meſſiah; eſpecially if we join with them the
following words, ver. 19, " And I will give thee the
" keys of the kingdom of heaven, and what thou ſhalt
" bind on earth, ſhall be bound in heaven; and what
" thou ſhalt looſe on earth, ſhall be looſed in heaven."
Which being ſaid perſonally to Peter, render the foregoing words of our Saviour, (wherein he declares the
fundamental article of his church to be the believing
him to be the Meſſiah) the more obſcure and doubtful,
and leſs liable to be made uſe of againſt him; but yet
ſuch as might afterwards be underſtood. And for the
ſame reaſon, he yet, here again, forbids the apoſtles to
ſay that he was the Meſſiah, ver. 20.

From this time (ſay the evangeliſts) " Jeſus began to
ſhow to his diſciples," i. e. his apoſtles, (who are often
called diſciples) " that he muſt go to Jeruſalem, and
" ſuffer many things from the elders, chief prieſts, and
" ſcribes; and be killed, and be raiſed again the third
" day," Matt. xvi. 21. Theſe, though all marks of
the Meſſiah, yet how little underſtood by the apoſtles,
or ſuited to their expectation of the Meſſiah, appears
from Peter's rebuking him for it in the following words,
Matt. xvi. 22. Peter had twice before owned him to
be the Meſſiah, and yet he cannot here bear that he
ſhould ſuffer, and be put to death, and be raiſed again.
Whereby we may perceive, how little yet Jeſus had explained to the apoſtles what perſonally concerned himſelf. They had been a good while witneſſes of his life
and miracles: and thereby being grown into a belief
that he was the Meſſiah, were, in ſome degree, prepared
to

to receive the particulars that were to fill up that character, and answer the prophecies concerning him. This,
from henceforth, he began to open to them (though in
a way which the jews could not form an accusation out
of;) the time of the accomplishment of all, in his sufferings, death, and resurrection, now drawing on. For
this was in the last year of his life; he being to meet
the jews at Jerusalem but once more at the passover,
and then they should have their will upon him: and,
therefore, he might now begin to be a little more open
concerning himself: though yet so, as to keep himself
out of the reach of any accusation, that might appear
just or weighty to the roman deputy.

After his reprimand to Peter, telling him, " That he
" favoured not the things of God, but of man," Mark
viii. 34, he calls the people to him, and prepares those,
who would be his disciples, for suffering, telling them,
ver. 38, " Whosoever shall be ashamed of me and my
" words in this adulterous and sinful generation, of
" him also shall the Son of man be ashamed, when he
" cometh in the glory of his Father, with the holy an-
" gels:" and then subjoins, Matt. xvi. 27, 28, two
great and solemn acts, wherein he would show himself
to be the Messiah, the king: " For the Son of man
" shall come in the glory of his Father, with his an-
" gels; and then he shall render to every man accord-
" ding to his works."   This is evidently meant of the
glorious appearance of his kingdom, when he shall
come to judge the world at the last day; described more
at large, Matt. xxv. " When the Son of man shall come
" in his glory, and all the holy angels with him, then
" shall he sit upon the THRONE of his glory.   Then
" shall the KING say to them on his right hand," &c.

But what follows in the place above quoted, Matt.
xvi. 28, " Verily, verily, there be some standing here,
" who shall not taste of death, till they see the Son of
" man coming in his kingdom;" importing that dominion, which some there should see him exercise over
the nation of the jews; was so covered, by being annexed to the preaching, ver. 27, (where he spoke of the
manifestation and glory of his kingdom, at the day of
judgment)

judgment) that though his plain meaning here in ver. 28, be, that the appearance and vifible exercife of his kingly power in his kingdom was fo near, that fome there fhould live to fee it; yet, if the foregoing words had not caft a fhadow over thefe latter, but they had been left plainly to be underftood, as they plainly fignified; that he fhould be a King, and that it was fo near, that fome there fhould fee him in his kingdom; this might have been laid hold on, and made the matter of a plaufible and feemingly juft accufation againft him, by the jews before Pilate. This feems to be the reafon of our Saviour's inverting here the order of the two folemn manifeftations to the world, of his rule and power; thereby perplexing at prefent his meaning, and fecuring himfelf, as was neceffary, from the malice of the jews, which always lay at catch to intrap him, and accufe him to the roman governor; and would no doubt, have been ready to have alleged thefe words, " Some here fhall not tafte of death, till they fee the " Son of man coming in his kingdom," againft him, as criminal, had not their meaning been, by the former verfe, perplexed, and the fenfe at that time rendered unintelligible, and not applicable by any of his auditors to a fenfe that might have been prejudicial to him before Pontius Pilate. For how well the chief of the jews were difpofed towards him, St. Luke tells us, chap. xi. 54, " Laying wait for him, and feeking to " catch fomething out of his mouth, that they might " accufe him:" which may be a reafon to fatisfy us of the feemingly doubtful and obfcure way of fpeaking, ufed by our Saviour in other places; his circumftances being fuch, that without fuch a prudent carriage and refervednefs, he could not have gone through the work which he came to do; nor have performed all the parts of it, in a way correfpondent to the defcriptions given of the Meffiah; and which would be afterwards fully underftood to belong to him, when he had left the world.

After this, Matt. xvii. 10, &c. he, without faying it in direct words, begins, as it were, to own himfelf to his apoftles to be the Meffiah, by affuring them, that as
the

the scribes, according to the prophecy of Malachi,
chap iv. 5, rightly said, that Elias was to usher in the
Messiah; so indeed Elias was already come, though the
jews knew him not, and treated him ill: whereby
" they understood that he spoke to them of John the
" Baptist," ver. 13. And a little after he somewhat
more plainly intimates, that he is the Messiah, Mark ix.
41, in these words: " Whosover shall give you a cup
" of water to drink in my name, because ye belong to
" the Messiah."   This, as I remember, is the first
place where our Saviour ever mentioned the name of
Messiah; and the first time that he went so far towards
the owning, to any of the jewish nation, himself to be
him.

In his way to Jerusalem, bidding one follow him,
Luke ix. 59, who would first bury his father, ver. 60,
" Jesus said unto him, Let the dead bury their dead;
" but go thou and preach the kingdom of God." And
Luke x. 1, sending out the seventy disciples, he says to
them, ver. 9, " Heal the sick, and say, The kingdom
" of God is come nigh unto you."   He had nothing
else for these, or for his apostles, or any one, it seems,
to preach, but the good news of the coming of the kingdom of the Messiah. And if any city would not receive
them, he bids them, ver. 10, " Go into the streets of
" the same, and say, Even the very dust of your city,
" which cleaveth on us, do we wipe off against you:
" notwithstanding, be ye sure of this, that the king-
" dom of God is come nigh unto you."   This they were
to take notice of, as that which they should dearly answer for; viz. that they had not with faith received the
good tidings of the kingdom of the Messiah.

After this, his brethren say unto him, John vii. 2, 3,
4, (the feast of tabernacles being near) " Depart hence,
" and go into Judea, that thy disciples also may see the
" works that thou doest: for there is no man that does
" any thing in secret, and he himself seeketh to be
" known openly. If thou do these things, show thy-
" self to the world."   Here his brethren, which, the
next verse tells us, " did not believe in him," seem to
upbraid him with the inconsistency of his carriage; as
if

if he defigned to be received for the Meffiah, and yet was afraid to fhow himfelf: to whom he juftified his conduct, (mentioned ver. 1.) in the following verfes, by telling them, " That the world," (meaning the jews efpecially) " hated him, becaufe he teftified of it, that " the works thereof are evil; and that his time was " not yet fully come," wherein to quit his referve, and abandon himfelf freely to their malice and fury. There-fore, though he, "went up unto the feaft," it was " not " openly, but, as it were, in fecret," ver. 10. And here, coming into the temple about the middle of the feaft, he juftifies his being fent from God; and that he had not done any thing againft the law, in curing the man at the pool of Bethefda, John v. 1—16, on the fabbath-day; which, though done above a year and a half before, they made ufe of as a pretence to deftroy him. But what was the true reafon of feeking his life, appears from what we have in this viith chapter, ver. 25—34, " Then faid fome of them at Jerufalem, Is not " this he whom they feek to kill? But lo, he fpeaketh " boldly, and they fay nothing unto him. Do the " rulers know indeed, that this is the very MESSIAH? " Howbeit, we know this man whence he is; but when " the Meffiah cometh, no man knoweth whence he is. " Then cried Jefus in the temple, as he taught, Ye " both know me, and ye know whence I am: and I " am not come of myfelf, but he that fent me is true, " whom ye know not. But I know him; for I am " from him, and he hath fent me. Then they fought " [an occafion] to take him, but no man laid hands on " him, becaufe his hour was not yet come. And many " of the people believed on him, and faid, When the " Meffiah cometh, will he do more miracles than thefe, " which this man hath done? The pharifees heard that " the people murmured fuch things concerning him; " and the pharifees and chief priefts fent officers to take " him. Then faid Jefus unto them, Yet a little while " am I with you, and then I go to him that fent me: " ye fhall feek me, and not find me; and where I am, " there you cannot come. Then faid the jews among " themfelves, Whither will he go, that we fhall not

" find

" find him?"   Here we find that the great fault in our
Saviour, and the great provocation to the jews, was his
being taken for the Messiah; and doing such things as
made the people "believe in him;" i. e. believe that
he was the Messiah.   Here also our Saviour declares, in
words very easy to be understood, at least after his resurrection, that he was the Messiah: for, if he were
" sent from God," and did his miracles by the Spirit
of God, there could be no doubt but he was the Messiah.
But yet this declaration was in a way that the pharisees
and priests could not lay hold on, to make an accusation of, to the disturbance of his ministry, or the
seizure of his person, how much soever they desired it:
for his time was not yet come.   The officers they had
sent to apprehend him, charmed with his discourse, returned without laying hands on him, ver. 45, 46.   And
when the chief priests asked them, " Why they brought
" him not?" They answered, " Never man spake like
" this man."   Whereupon the pharisees reply, " Are
" ye also deceived? Have any of the rulers, or of the
" pharisees, believed on him? But this people, who
" know not the law, are cursed."   This shows what
was meant by " believing on him," viz. believing that
he was the Messiah.   For, say they, have any of the
rulers, who are skilled in the law, or of the devout and
learned pharisees, acknowledged him to be the Messiah?
For as for those, who in the division among the people
concerning him, say, " That he is the Messiah," they
are ignorant and vile wretches, know nothing of the
scripture, and being accursed, are given up by God,
to be deceived by this impostor, and to take him for
the Messiah.   Therefore, notwithstanding their desire
to lay hold on him, he goes on; and ver. 37, 38, " In
" the last and great day of the feast, Jesus stood and
" cried, saying, If any man thirst, let him come unto
" me and drink: he that believeth on me, as the scrip-
" ture hath said, out of his belly shall flow rivers of
" living water."   And thus he here again declares himself to be the Messiah; but in the prophetic style, as
we may see by the next verse of this chapter, and those
                                                          places

places in the Old Teftament, that thefe words of our Saviour refer to.

In the next chapter, John viii, all that he fays concerning himfelf, and what they were to believe, tends to this, viz. that he was fent from God his Father; and that, if they did not believe that he was the Meffiah, they fhould die in their fins: but this, in a way, as St. John obferves, ver. 27, that they did not well underftand. But our Saviour himfelf tells them, ver. 28, " When ye have lift up the Son of man, then fhall ye " know that I am he."

Going from them, he cures the man born blind, whom meeting with again, after the jews had queftioned him, and caft him out, John ix. 35—38, " Jefus faid " to him, Doft thou believe on the Son of God? " He anfwered, Who is he, Lord, that I might be " lieve on him? And Jefus faid unto him, Thou haft " both feen him, and it is he that talketh with thee. " And he faid, Lord, I believe." Here we fee this man is pronounced a believer, when all that was propofed to him to believe, was, that Jefus was " the Son " of God;" which was, as we have already fhown, to believe that he was the Meffiah.

In the next chapter, John x. 1—21, he declares the laying down of his life both for jews and gentiles; but in a parable which they underftood not, ver. 6—20.

As he was going to the feaft of the dedication, the pharifees afk him, Luke xvii. 20, " When the king " dom of God," i. e. of the Meffiah, " fhould come?" He anfwers, That it fhould not come with pomp and obfervation, and great concourfe; but that it was already begun amongft them. If he had ftopt here, the fenfe had been fo plain, that they could hardly have miftaken him; or have doubted, but that he meant, that the Meffiah was already come, and amongft them; and fo might have been prone to infer, that Jefus took upon him to be him. But here, as in the place before taken notice of, fubjoining to this future revelation of himfelf, both in his coming to execute vengeance on the jews, and in his coming to judgment, mixed together,

ther, he so involved his sense, that it was not easy to understand him. And therefore the jews came to him again in the temple, John x. 23, and said, " How long " dost thou make us doubt? If thou be the Christ tell " us plainly. Jesus answered, I told you, and ye BE-" LIEVED not: the works that I do in my Father's " name, they bear witness of me. But ye BELIEVED not, " because ye are not of my sheep, as I told you." The BELIEVING here, which he accuses them of not doing, is plainly their not BELIEVENG him to be the Messiah, as the foregoing words evince; and in the same sense it is evidently meant in the following verses of this chapter.

From hence Jesus going to Bethabara, and thence returning into Bethany; upon Lazarus's death, John xi. 25—27, Jesus said to Martha, " I am the resurrection " and the life; he that believeth in me, though he were " dead, yet shall he live,; and whosoever liveth and " believeth in me shall not die for ever." So I understand ἀποθάνη εἰς τὸν αἰῶνα, answerable to ζήσεται εἰς τὸν αἰῶνα, of the septuagint, Gen. iii. 22, or John vi. 51, which we read right, in our english translation, " live " for ever." But whether this saying of our Saviour here, can with truth be translated, " He that liveth and " believeth in me shall never die," will be apt to be questioned. But to go on, " Believest thou this? She " said unto him, Yea, Lord, I believe that thou art " the Messiah, the Son of God, which should come into " the world." This she gives as a full answer to our Saviour's demands; this being that faith, which whoever had, wanted no more to make them believers.

We may observe farther, in this same story of the raising of Lazarus, what faith it was our Saviour expected, by what he says, ver. 41, 42, " Father I thank " thee, that thou hast heard me; and I know that thou " hearest me always. But because of the people who " stand by, I said it, that they may believe that thou " hast sent me." And what the consequence of it was, we may see, ver. 45, " Then many of the jews who " came to Mary, and had seen the things which Jesus " did, believed on him:" which belief was, that he was " sent from the Father;" which, in other words, was,

that

that he was the Meſſiah. That this is the meaning, in the evangeliſts, of the phraſe of "believing on him," we have a demonſtration in the following words, ver. 47, 48, " Then gathered the chief prieſts and phariſees " a council, and ſaid, What do we? For this man does "' many miracles; and if we let him alone, all men will " BELIEVE ON HIM." Thoſe who here ſay, all men would BELIEVE ON HIM, were the chief prieſts and pha-riſees, his enemies, who ſought his life; and therefore could have no other ſenſe nor thought of this faith in him, which they ſpake of; but only the believing him to be the Meſſiah: and that that was their meaning, the adjoining words ſhow: " If we let him alone, all the " world will believe on him;" i. e. believe him to be the Meſſiah. " And the romans will come and take " away both our place and nation." Which reaſoning of theirs was thus grounded: If we ſtand ſtill, and let the people " believe on him." i.'e. receive him for the Meſſiah: they will thereby take him and ſet him up for their king, and expect deliverance by him; which will draw the roman arms upon us, to the deſtruction of us and our country. The romans could not be thought to be at all concerned in any other belief whatſoever, that the people might have on him. It is therefore plain, that " believing on him," was, by the writers of the goſpel, underſtood to mean the " believing him to be " the Meſſiah." The ſanhedrim therefore, ver. 53, 54, from that day forth conſulted to put him to death. " Jeſus therefore walked not yet" (for ſo the word ἔτι ſignifies, and ſo I think it ought here to be tranſlated) " boldly," or open-faced, " among the jews," i. e. of Jeruſalem. Ἔτι cannot well here be tranſlated "no more," becauſe, within a very ſhort time after, he appeared openly at the paſſover, and by his miracles and ſpeech declared himſelf more freely than ever he had done; and all the week before his paſſion, taught daily in the temple, Matt. xx. 17. Mark x. 32. Luke xviii. 31, &c. The meaning of this place ſeems therefore to be this: that his time being not yet come, he durſt not yet ſhow him-ſelf openly and confidently before the ſcribes and pha-riſees, and thoſe of the ſanhedrim at Jeruſalem, who were full of malice against him, and had resolved his death: " But went thence into a country near the wil-" derness, into a city called Ephraim, and there con-" tinued with his disciples," to keep himself out of the way until the passover, " which was nigh at hand," ver. 55. In his return thither, he takes the twelve aside, and tells them before-hand, what should happen to him at Jerusalem, whither they were now going; and that all things that are written by the prophets, concerning the Son of man, should be accomplished; that he should be betrayed to the chief priests and scribes : and that they should condemn him to death, and deliver him to the gentiles; that he should be mocked, and spit on, and scourged, and put to death ; and the third day he should rise again. But St. Luke tells us, chap. xviii. 34, That the apostles " understood none of these things, and this " saying was hid from them; neither knew they the " things which were spoken." They believed him to be the Son of God, the Messiah sent from the Father; but their notion of the Messiah was the same with the rest of the jews, that he should be a temporal prince and deliverer : accordingly we see, Mark x. 35, that, even in this their last journey with him to Jerusalem, two of them, James and John, coming to him, and falling at his feet, said, " Grant unto us, that we may sit one on " thy right hand, and the other on thy left hand, in thy " glory:" or, as St. Matthew has it, chap. xx. 21, " in " thy kingdom." That which distinguished them from the unbelieving jews, was, that they believed Jesus to be the very Messiah, and so received him as their King and Lord.

And now, the hour being come that the Son of man should be glorified, he, without his usual reserve, makes his public entry into Jerusalem, riding on a young ass! " As it is written, Fear not, daughter of Sion; behold, " thy King cometh, sitting on an ass's colt." But " these things," says St. John, chap. xii. 16, " his dis-" ciples understood not, at the first; but when Jesus " was glorified, then remembered they that these things " were written of him, and that they had done these " things unto him." Though the apostles believed him

him to be the Meſſiah, yet there were many occurrences
of his life, which they underſtood not (at the time when
they happened) to be foretold of the Meſſiah; which,
after his aſcenſion, they found exactly to quadrate. Thus
according to what was foretold of him, he rode into the
city, "all the people crying, Hoſanna, bleſſed is the
" King of Iſrael, that cometh in the name of the Lord."
This was ſo open a declaration of his being the Meſſiah,
that, Luke xix. 39, " Some of the phariſees from among
" the multitude ſaid unto him, Maſter, rebuke thy diſ-
" ciples." But he was ſo far now from ſtopping them,
or diſowning this their acknowledgment of his being the
Meſſiah, that he ſaid unto them, " I tell you, that if
" theſe ſhould hold their peace, the ſtones would im-
" mediately cry out." And again upon the like occaſion of their crying, "Hoſanna to the Son of David," in
the temple, Matt. xxi. 15, 16, " When the chief prieſts
" and ſcribes were ſore diſpleaſed, and ſaid unto him,
" Heareſt thou what they ſay? Jeſus ſaid unto them,
" Yea; Have ye never read, Out of the mouths of babes
" and ſucklings thou haſt perfected praiſe?" And now,
ver. 14, 15, " He cures the blind and the lame openly
" in the temple. And when the chief prieſts and
" ſcribes ſaw the wonderful things that he did, and the
" children crying in the temple, Hoſanna, they were
" enraged." One would not think, that after the multitude of miracles, that our Saviour had now been doing
for above three years together, the curing the lame and
blind ſhould ſo much move them. But we muſt remember, that though his miniſtry had abounded with
miracles, yet the moſt of them had been done about Galilee, and in parts remote from Jeruſalem. There is
but one left on record, hitherto done in that city; and
that had ſo ill a reception, that they ſought his life for
it: as we may read John v. 16. And therefore we hear
not of his being at the next paſſover, becauſe he was
there only privately, as an ordinary jew: the reaſon
whereof we may read, John vii. 1. " After theſe things
" Jeſus walked in Galilee; for he would not walk in
" Jewry, becauſe the jews ſought to kill him."
Hence we may gueſs the reaſon why St. John omitted

the

the mention of his being at Jerusalem, at the third passover after his baptism; probably because he did nothing memorable there. Indeed, when he was at the feast of tabernacles, immediately preceding this his last passover, he cured the man born blind: but it appears not to have been done in Jerusalem itself, but in the way, as he retired to the mount of Olives; for there seems to have been nobody by, when he did it, but his apostles. Compare ver. 2. with ver. 8, 10, of John ix. This, at least, is remarkable, that neither the cure of this blind man, nor that of the other infirm man, at the passover, above a twelve-month before, at Jerusalem, was done in the fight of the scribes, pharisees, chief priests, or rulers. Nor was it without reason, that in the former part of his ministry, he was cautious of showing himself to them to be the Messiah. But now, that he was come to the last scene of his life, and that the passover was come, the appointed time, wherein he was to complete the work he came for, in his death and resurrection, he does many things in Jerusalem itself, before the face of the scribes, pharisees, and whole body of the jewish nation, to manifest himself to be the Messiah. And, as St. Luke says, chap. xix. 47, 48, " He taught daily in the tem- " ple: but the chief priests, and the scribes, and the " chief of the people, sought to destroy him; and " could not find what they might do; for all the people " were very attentive to hear him." What he taught we are left to guess, by what we have found him constantly preaching elsewhere: but St. Luke tells us, chap. xx. 1, " He taught in the temple, and evangelized;" or, as we translate it, " preached the gospel:" which, as we have showed, was the making known to them the good news of the kingdom of the Messiah. And this we shall find he did, in what now remains of his history.

In the first discourse of his, which we find upon record, after this, John xii. 20, &c. he foretels his crucifixion, and the belief of all sorts, both jews and gentiles, on him after that. Whereupon the people say to him, ver. 34, " We have heard out of the law, that the " Messiah abideth for ever: and how sayest thou, that " the Son of man must be lifted up? Who is this Son
" of

" of Man?" In his anfwer, he plainly defigns himfelf under the name of Light; which was what he had declared himfelf to them to be, the laft time that they had feen him in Jerufalem. For then, at the feaft of tabernacles, but fix months before, he tells them in the very place where he now is, viz. in the temple, " I am " the Light of the world; whofoever follows me, fhall " not walk in darknefs, but fhall have the light of life;" as we may read, John viii. 12. And ix. 5, he fays, " As " long as I am in the world, I am the LIGHT of the " world." But neither here, nor any where elfe, does he, even in thefe four or five laft days of his life, (though he knew his hour was come, and was prepared to his death, ver. 27, and fcrupled not to manifeft himfelf to the rulers of the jews to be the Meffiah, by doing miracles before them in the temple) ever once in direct words own himfelf to the jews to be the Meffiah; though by miracles and other ways he did every where make it known unto them, fo that it might be underftood. This could not be without fome reafon; and the prefervation of his life, which he came now to Jerufalem on purpofe to lay down, could not be it. What other could it then be, but the fame which had made him ufe caution in the former part of his miniftry; fo to conduct himfelf, that he might do the work which he came for, and in all parts anfwer the character given of the Meffiah, in the law and the prophets? He had fulfilled the time of his miniftry; and now taught, and did miracles openly in the temple, before the rulers and the people, not fearing to be feized. But he would not be feized for any thing, that might make him a criminal to the government: and therefore he avoided giving thofe, who, in the divifion that was about him, inclined towards him, occafion of tumult for his fake: or to the jews, his enemies, matter of juft accufation againft him, out of his own mouth, by profeffing himfelf to be the Meffiah, the King of Ifrael, in direct words. It was enough, that by words and deeds he declared it fo to them, that they could not but underftand him; which it is plain they did, Luke xx. 16, 19. Matt. xxi. 45. But yet neither his actions, which were only

doing

doing of good; nor words, which were myftical and parabolical (as we may fee, Matt. xxi. and xxii, and the
parallel places of Matthew and Luke;) nor any of his
ways of making himfelf known to be the Meffiah;
could be brought in teftimony, or urged againft him, as
oppofite or dangerous to the government.   This preferved him from being condemned as a malefactor;
and procured him a teftimony from the roman governor, his judge, that he was an innocent man, facrificed
to the envy of the jewifh nation.   So that he avoided
faying, that he was the Meffiah, that to thofe who would
call to mind his life and death, after his refurrection,
he might the more clearly appear to be fo.   It is farther to be remarked, that though he often appeals to
the teftimony of his miracles, who he is, yet he never
tells the jews, that he was born at Bethlehem, to remove the prejudice that lay againft him, whilft he
paffed for a galilean, and which was urged as a proof
that he was not the Meffiah, John vii. 41, 42.   The
healing of the fick, and doing good miraculoufly, could
be no crime in him, nor accufation againft him.   But
the naming of Bethlehem for his birth-place might have
wrought as much upon the mind of Pilate, as it did on
Herod's; and have raifed a fufpicion in Pilate, as
prejudicial to our Saviour's innocence as Herod's was
to the children born there.   His pretending to be born
at Bethlehem, as it was liable to be explained by the
jews, could not have failed to have met with a finifter
interpretation in the roman governor, and have rendered
Jefus fufpected of fome criminal defign againft the government.   And hence we fee, that when Pilate afked
him, John xix. 9, " Whence art thou? Jefus gave him
" no anfwer.".

Whether our Saviour had not an eye to this ftrait-
nefs, this narrow room that was left to his conduct, between the new converts and the captious jews, when he
fays, Luke xii. 50, " I have a baptifm to be baptized
" with, and πῶς συνέχομαι, how I am ftraitened, until it
" be accomplifhed!" I leave to be confidered.   " I
" am come to fend fire on the earth," fays our Saviour,
" and what if it be already kindled?" i. e. There begin

gin already to be divifions about me, John vii. 12, 43, and ix. 16, and x. 19. And I have not the freedom, the latitude, to declare myfelf openly to be the Meffiah; though I am he, that muft not be fpoken on, until after my death. My way to my throne is clofely hedged in on every fide, and much ftraitened; within which I muft keep, until it bring me to my crofs in its due time and manner; fo that it do not cut fhort the time, nor crofs the end of my miniftry.

And therefore, to keep up this inoffenfive character, and not to let it come within the reach of accident or calumny, he withdrew, with his apoftles, out of the town, every evening; and kept himfelf retired out of the way, Luke xxi. 37. "And in the day-time he was " teaching in the temple, and every night he went out " and abode in the mount, that is called the Mount of " Olives," that he might avoid all concourfe to him in the night, and give no occafion of difturbance, or fuf- picion of himfelf, in that great conflux of the whole na- tion of the jews, now aſſembled in Jerufalem at the paffover.

But to return to his preaching in the temple: he bids them, John xii. 36, "To believe in the Light, whilft " they have it." And he tells them, ver. 46, "I am " the Light come into the world, that every one who " believes in me, fhould not remain in darknefs;" which belieҫving in him, was the believing him to be the Meffiah, as I have elfewhere fhowed.

The next day, Matt. xxi, he rebukes them for not having believed John the Baptift, who had teftified that he was the Meffiah. And then, in a parable, declares himfelf to be the "Son of God," whom they fhould de- ftroy; and that for it God would take away the king- dom of the Meffiah from them, and give it to the gen- tiles. That they underftood him thus, is plain from Luke xxi. 16. "And when they heard it, they faid, " God forbid." And ver. 19, "For they knew that " he had fpoken this parable againft them."

Much to the fame purpofe was his next parable, concerning "the kingdom of heaven," Matt. xxi. 1—10. That the jews not accepting of the kingdom the Messiah, to whom it was first offered, other should be brought in.

The scribes and pharisees and chief priests, not able to bear the declaration he made of himself to be the Messiah (by his discourses and miracles before them, ἔμπροσθεν αὐτῶν, John xii. 37, which he had never done before) impatient of his preaching and miracles, and being not able otherwise to stop the increase of his followers, (for, "said the pharisees among themselves, " Perceive ye how ye prevail nothing? Behold, the " world is gone after him,") John xii. 19. So that " the chief priests, and the scribes, and the chief of the " people sought to destroy him," the first day of his entrance into Jerusalem, Luke xix. 47. The next day, again, they were intent upon the same thing, Mark xi. 17, 18, "And he taught in the temple ; and the scribes " and the chief priests heard it, and sought how they " might destroy him ; for they feared him, because all " the people were astonished at his doctrine."

The next day but one, upon his telling them the kingdom of the Messiah should be taken from them, " The chief priests and scribes sought to lay hands on " him the same hour, and they feared the people," Luke xx. 19. If they had so great a desire to lay hold on him, why did they not? They were the chief-priests and the rulers, the men of power. The reason St. Luke plainly tells us in the next verse : "And they watched " him, and sent forth spies, who should feign them- " selves just men, that they might take hold of his " words ; that so they might deliver him unto the " power and authority of the governor." They wanted matter of accusation against him, to the power they were under ; that they watched for, and that they would have been glad of, if they could have "entangled him in his " talk ;" as St. Matthew expresses it, chap. xxii. 15. If they could have laid hold on any word, that had dropt from him, that they might have rendered him guilty, or suspected to the roman governor ; that would have served their turn, to have laid hold upon him, with hopes to destroy him. For their power not answering their malice, they could not put him to death by their

own

own authority, without the permiſſion and aſſiſtance of the governor; as they confeſs, John xviii. 31, "It is "not lawful for us to put any man to death." This made them ſo earneſt for a declaration in direct words, from his own mouth, that he was the Meſſiah. It was not that they would more have believed in him, for ſuch a declaration of himſelf, than they did for his miracles, or other ways of making himſelf known, which it appears they underſtood well enough. But they wanted plain direct words, ſuch as might ſupport an accuſation, and be of weight before an heathen judge. This was the reaſon, why they preſſed him to ſpeak out, John x. 24, "Then came the jews round about him, and ſaid "unto him, How long doſt thou hold us in ſuſpence? "If thou be the Meſſiah, tell us PLAINLY, παρρησία;" i. e. in direct words: for that St. John uſes it in that ſenſe we may ſee, chap. xi. 11—14. "Jeſus ſaith to "them, Lazarus ſleepeth. His diſciples ſaid, If he "ſleeps, he ſhall do well. Howbeit, Jeſus ſpake of "his death; but they thought he had ſpoken of taking "reſt in ſleep. Then ſaid Jeſus to them plainly, παρ- "ρησία, Lazarus is dead." Here we ſee what is meant by παρρησία, PLAIN, direct words, ſuch as expreſs the ſame thing without a figure; and ſo they would have had Jeſus pronounce himſelf to be the Meſſiah. And the ſame thing they preſs again, Matt. xxvi. 63, the high prieſt adjuring him by the living God, to tell them whether he were the Meſſiah, the Son of God; as we ſhall have occaſion to take notice by-and-by.

This we may obſerve in the whole management of their deſign againſt his life. It turned upon this, that they wanted and wiſhed for a declaration from him in direct words, that he was the Meſſiah; ſomething from his own mouth that might offend the roman power, and render him criminal to Pilate. In the 21ſt verſe of this xxth of Luke, "They aſked him, ſaying, Maſter, we "know that thou ſayeſt and teacheſt rightly; neither "accepteſt thou the perſon of any, but teacheſt the "way of God truly. Is it lawful for us to give tribute "to Cæſar, or no?" By this captious queſtion they hoped to catch him, which way ſoever he anſwered.

For

For if he had said, they ought to pay tribute to Cæsar, it would be plain he allowed their subjection to the romans; and so in effect disowned himself to be their King and Deliverer; whereby he would have contradicted what his carriage and doctrine seemed to aim at, the opinion that was spread amongst the people, that he was the Messiah. This would have quashed the hopes, and destroyed the faith of those that believed on him; and have turned the ears and hearts of the people from him. If on the other side he answered, No, it is not lawful to pay tribute to Cæsar; they had had out of his own mouth, wherewithal to condemn him before Pontius Pilate. But St. Luke tells us, ver. 23, " He " perceived their craftiness, and said unto them, Why " tempt ye me?" i. e. Why do ye lay snares for me? " Ye hypocrites, show me the tribute-money;" so it is, Matt. xxii. 19, " Whose image and inscription has " it? They said, Cæsar's." He said unto them, " Ren-" der therefore to Cæsar the things that are Cæsar's, " and to God the things that are God's." By the wisdom and caution of which unexpected answer, he defeated their whole design: " And they could not take " hold of his words before the people; and they mar-" velled at his answer, and held their peace." Luke xx. 26. " And leaving him, they departed." Matt. xxii. 22.

He having, by this reply, (and what he answered to the sadducees, concerning the resurrection, and to the lawyer, about the first commandment, Mark xii.) answered so little to their satisfaction or advantage, they durst ask him no more questions, any of them. And now, their mouths being stopped, he himself begins to question them about the Messiah; asking the pharisees, Matt. xxii. 41, " What think ye of the Messiah? whose " son is he? They say unto him, The Son of David." Wherein though they answered right, yet he shows them in the following words, that, however they pretended to be studiers and teachers of the law, yet they understood not clearly the scriptures concerning the Messiah; and thereupon he sharply rebukes their hypocrisy, vanity, pride, malice, covetousness, and ignorance; and particularly tells them, ver. 13. " Ye shut up the kingdom " of heaven against men: for ye neither go in your-
" selves,

" felves, nor fuffer ye them that are entering, to go
" in." Whereby he plainly declares to them, that the
Meffiah was come, and his kingdom begun; but that
they refufed to believe in him themfelves, and did all
they could to hinder others from believing in him; as
is manifeft throughout the New Teftament: the hiftory
whereof fufficiently explains what is meant here by
" the kingdom of heaven," which the fcribes and pharifees would neither go into themfelves, nor fuffer others
to enter into. And they could not choofe but underftand
him, though he named not himfelf in the cafe.

Provoked anew by his rebukes, they get prefently to
council, Matt. xxvi. 3, 4. " Then affembled together
" the chief priefts, and the fcribes, and the elders of
" the people, unto the palace of the high prieft, who
" was called Caiaphas, and confulted that they might
" take Jefus by fubtlety, and kill him. But they faid,
" Not on the feaft-day, left there fhould be an uproar
" among the people. For they feared the people,"
fays Luke, chap. xxii. 2.

Having in the night got Jefus into their hands, by
the treachery of Judas, they prefently led him away
bound to Annas, the father-in-law of Caiaphas. Annas,
probably, having examined him, and getting nothing
out of him for his purpofe, fends him away to Caiaphas,
John xviii. 24, where the chief priefts, the fcribes, and
the elders were affembled, Matt. xxvi. 57. John xviii.
13, 19. " The high prieft then afked Jefus of his difci-
" ples, and of his doctrine. Jefus anfwered him, I
" fpake openly to the world: I ever taught in the fyna-
" gogue, and in the temple, whither the jews always
" refort, and in fecret have I faid nothing." A proof
that he had not in private, to his difciples, declared
himfelf in exprefs words to be the Meffiah, the Prince.
But he goes on: " Why afkeft thou me?" Afk Judas,
who has been always with me. " Afk them who heard
" me, what I have faid unto them; behold, they know
" what I faid." Our Saviour, we fee here, warily de-
clines, for the reafons above-mentioned, all difcourfe
of his doctrine. The fanhedrim, Matt. xxvi. 59,
" fought falfe witnefs againft him:" but when " they
" found none that were fufficient," or came up to the

point they defired, which was to have fomething againft him to take away his life, (for fo, I think, the words ἴσαι and ἴση mean, Mark xiv. 56, 59.) they try again what they can get out of him himfelf, concerning his being the Meffiah; which if he owned in exprefs words, they thought they fhould have enough againft him at the tribunal of the roman governor, to make him " læ-" fæ majeftatis reum," and fo take away his life. They therefore fay to him, Luke xxii. 67, " If thou be the " Meffiah, tell us." Nay, as St. Matthew hath it, the high prieft adjures him by the living God, to tell him whether he were the Meffiah. To which our Saviour replies, " If I tell you, ye will not believe; and if I " alfo afk you, ye will not anfwer me, nor let me go." If I tell you, and prove to you, by the teftimony given me from heaven, and by the works that I have done among you, you will not believe in me, that I am the Meffiah. Or if I fhould afk where the Meffiah is to be born, and what ftate he fhould come in; how he fhould appear, and other things that you think in me are not reconcileable with the Meffiah; you will not anfwer me, nor let me go, as one that has no pretence to be the Meffiah, and you are not afraid fhould be received for fuch. But yet I tell you, " Hereafter fhall the Son " of man fit on the right hand of the power of God," ver. 70. " Then fay they All, Art thou then the Son of " God? And he faid unto them, Ye fay that I am." By which difcourfe with them, related at large here by St. Luke, it is plain, that the anfwer of our Saviour, fet down by St. Matthew, chap. xxvi. 64, in thefe words, " Thou haft faid;" and by St. Mark, chap. xiv. 62, in thefe, " I am;" is an anfwer only to this queftion, " Art thou then the Son of God?" And not to that other, " Art thou the Meffiah?" which preceded, and he had anfwered to before; though Matthew and Mark, contracting the ftory, fet them down together, as if making but one queftion, omitting all the intervening difcourfe; whereas it is plain out of St. Luke, that they were two diftinct queftions, to which Jefus gave two diftinct anfwers. In the firft whereof he, according to his ufual caution, declined faying in plain
exprefs

exprefs words, that he was the Meffiah ; though in the latter he owned himfelf to be " the Son of God." Which, though they, being jews, underftood to fignify the Meffiah, yet he knew could be no legal or weighty accufation againft him, before a heathen ; and fo it proved. For upon his anfwering to their queftion, " Art thou then the Son of God ? Ye fay that I am ;" they cry out, Luke xxii. 71, " What need we any fur- " ther witnefs ? For we ourfelves have heard out of his " own mouth." And fo thinking they had enough againft him, they hurry him away to Pilate. Pilate afking them, John xviii. 29—32, " What accufation " bring you againft this man ? They anfwered and faid, " If he were not a malefactor, we would not have de- " livered him up unto thee." Then faid Pilate unto them, " Take ye him, and judge him according to " your law." But this would not ferve their turn, who aimed at his life, and would be fatisfied with no- thing elfe. " The jews therefore faid unto him, It is " not lawful for us to put any man to death." And this was alfo, " That the faying of Jefus might be ful- " filled, which he fpake, fignifying what death he " fhould die." Purfuing therefore their defign of making him appear, to Pontius Pilate, guilty of treafon againft Cæfar, Luke xxiii. 2, " They began to accufe " him, faying, We found this fellow perverting the na- " tion, and forbidding to give tribute to Cæfar ; fay- " ing, that he himfelf is the Meffiah, the King ;" all which were inferences of theirs, from his faying, he was " the Son of God :" which Pontius Pilate finding, (for it is confonant that he examined them to the precife words he had faid) their accufation had no weight with him. However, the name of king being fuggefted againft Jefus, he thought himfelf concerned to fearch it to the bottom, John xviii. 33—37. " Then " Pilate entered again into the judgment-hall, and " called Jefus, and faid unto him, Art thou the king " of the jews ? Jefus anfwered him, Sayeft thou this of " thyfelf, or did others tell it thee of me ? Pilate an- " fwered, Am I a jew ? Thine own nation and the " chief priefts have delivered thee unto me : What haft

" thou

" thou done? Jesus answered, My kingdom is not of this
" world : if my kingdom were of this world, then
" would my servants fight, that I should not be deli-
" vered to the jews; but now my kingdom is not from
" hence.   Pilate therefore said unto him, Art thou a
" king then? Jesus answered, Thou sayest that I am a
" king.   For this end was I born, and for this cause
" came I into the world, that I should bear witness to
" the truth : every one that is of the truth heareth my
" voice."   In this dialogue between our Saviour and
Pilate, we may observe, 1. That being asked, Whether
he were " The King of the Jews?" he answered so,
that though he deny it not, yet he avoids giving the
least umbrage, that he had any design upon the government.   For, though he allows himself to be a king, yet,
to obviate any suspicion, he tells Pilate, " his kingdom
" is not of this world;" and evidences it by this, that
if he had pretended to any title to that country, his followers, which were not a few, and were forward enough
to believe him their king, would have fought for him ;
if he had had a mind to set himself up by force, or his
kingdom were so to be erected.   " But my kingdom,"
says he, " is not from hence," is not of this fashion, or
of this place.

2. Pilate being, by his words and circumstances, satisfied that he laid no claim to his province, or meant
any disturbance of the government ; was yet a little
surprized to hear a man in that poor garb, without re-
tinue, or so much as a servant, or a friend, own himself
to be a king ; and therefore asks him, with some kind of
wonder, " Art thou a king then?"

3. That our Saviour declares, that his great business
into the world was, to testify and make good this great
truth, that he was a king ; i. e. in other words, that he
was the Messiah.

4. That whoever were followers of truth, and got
into the way of truth and happiness, received this doctrine concerning him, viz. That he was the Messiah,
their King.

Pilate being thus satisfied, that he neither meant, nor
could there arise, any harm from his pretence, what-

ever

6

ever it was, to be a king; tells the jews, ver. 31, " I
" find no fault in this man." But the jews were the
more fierce, Luke xxiii. 5, saying, " He ſtirreth up the
" people to ſedition, by his preaching through all
" Jewry, beginning from Galilee to this place." And
then Pilate, learning that he was of Galilee, Herod's
juriſdiction, ſent him to Herod; to whom alſo " the
" chief prieſts and ſcribes," ver. 10, " vehemently ac-
" cuſed him." Herod, finding all their accuſations
either falſe or frivolous, thought our Saviour a bare object of contempt; and ſo turning him only into ridicule, ſent him back to Pilate: who, calling unto him
the chief prieſts, and the rulers, and the people, ver.
14, " Said unto them, Ye have brought this man unto
" me, as one that perverteth the people; and behold, I
" having examined him before you, have found no
" fault in this man, touching theſe things whereof ye
" accuſe him; no, nor yet Herod; for I ſent you to
" him: and lo, nothing worthy of death is done by
" him." And therefore he would have releaſed him:
" For he knew the chief prieſts had delivered him
" through envy," Mark xv. 10. And when they demanded Barabbas to be releaſed, but as for Jeſus, cried,
" Crucify him;" Luke xxiii. 22, " Pilate ſaid unto
" them the third time, Why? What evil hath he done?
" I have found no cauſe of death in him; I will, there-
" fore, chaſtiſe him, and let him go."
We may obſerve, in all this whole proſecution of the
jews, that they would fain have got it out of Jeſus's own
mouth, in expreſs words, that he was the Meſſiah:
which not being able to do, with all their art and endeavour; all the reſt that they could allege againſt him
not amounting to a proof before Pilate, that he claimed
to be king of the jews; or that he had cauſed, or
done any thing towards a mutiny or inſurrection among
the people (for upon theſe two, as we ſee, their whole
charge turned); Pilate again and again pronounced him
innocent: for ſo he did a fourth, and a fifth time;
bringing him out to them, after he had whipped him,
John xix. 4, 6. And after all, " When Pilate ſaw that
" he could prevail nothing, but that rather a tumult
" was

" was made, he took water, and wafhed his hands be-
" fore the multitude, faying, I am innocent of the
" blood of this juft man: fee you to it:" Matt. xxvii.
24. Which gives us a clear reafon of the cautious and
wary conduct of our Saviour, in not declaring himfelf,
in the whole courfe of his miniftry, fo much as to his
difciples; much lefs to the multitude, or to the rulers
of the jews, in exprefs words, to be the Meffiah the
King; and why he kept himfelf always in prophetical,
or parabolical terms, (he and his difciples preaching
only the kingdom of God, i. e. of the Meffiah, to be
come); and left to his miracles to declare who he was;
though this was the truth, which he came into the
world, as he fays himfelf, John xviii. 37, to teftify, and
which his difciples were to believe.

When Pilate, fatisfied of his innocence, would have
releafed him; and the jews perfifted to cry out, " Cru-
" cify him, crucify him," John xix. 6. " Pilate fays
" to them, Take ye him yourfelves, and crucify him:
" for I do not find any fault in him." The jews then,
fince they could not make him a ftate criminal, by
alleging his faying, that he was " the Son of God,"
fay, by their law it was a capital crime, ver. 7. " The
" jews anfwered to Pilate, We have a law, and by our
" law he ought to die; becaufe he made himfelf the
" Son of God," i. e. becaufe, by faying " he is the Son
" of God," he has made himfelf the Meffiah, the prophet, which was to come. For we find no other law
but that againft falfe prophets, Deut. xviii. 20, whereby
" making himfelf the Son of God" deferved death.
After this, Pilate was the more defirous to releafe him,
ver. 12, 13. " But the jews cried out, faying, If thou
" let this man go, thou art not Cæfar's friend; whofo-
" ever maketh himfelf a king, fpeaketh againft Cæfar."
Here we fee the ftrefs of their charge againft Jefus;
whereby they hoped to take away his life, viz. that he
" made himfelf king." We fee alfo upon what they
grounded this accufation, viz. becaufe he had owned
himfelf to be " the Son of God." For he had, in their
hearing, never made or profeffed himfelf to be a king.
We fee here, likewife, the reafon why they were fo defirous

firous to draw from his own mouth a confeffion in exprefs words, that he was the Meffiah; viz. That they might have what might be a clear proof that he did fo. And, laft of all, we fee reafon why, though in expreffions which they underftood, he owned himfelf to them to be the Meffiah; yet he avoided declaring it to them, in fuch words as might look criminal at Pilate's tribunal. He owned himfelf to be the Meffiah plainly, to the un-derftanding of the jews; but in ways that could not, to the underftanding of Pilate, make it appear that he had laid claim to the kingdom of Judea; or went about to make himfelf king of that country. But whether his faying, that he was "the Son of God," was criminal by their law, that Pilate troubled not himfelf about.

He that confiders what Tacitus, Suetonius, Seneca de benef. l. 3. c. 26. fay of Tiberius and his reign, will find how neceffary it was for our Saviour, if he would not die as a criminal and a traitor, to take great heed to his words and actions; that he did or faid not any thing that might be offenfive, or give the leaft umbrage to the roman government. It behoved an innocent man, who was taken notice of, for fomething extraordinary in him; to be very wary under a jealous and cruel prince, who encouraged informations, and filled his reign with executions for treafon; under whom, words fpoken in-nocently, or in jeft, if they could be mifconftrued, were made treafon, and profecuted with a rigour, that made it always the fame thing to be accufed and con-demned. And therefore we fee, that when the jews told Pilate, John xix. 12, that he fhould not be a friend to Cæfar, if he let Jefus go (for that whoever made himfelf king, was a rebel againft Cæfar): he afks them no more, whether they would take Barabbas, and fpare Jefus; but (though againft his confcience) gives him up to death, to fecure his own head.

One thing more there is, that gives us light into this wife and neceffarily cautious management of himfelf, which manifeftly agrees with it, and makes a part of it: and that is, the choice of his apoftles; exactly fuited to the defign and forefight of the neceffity of keeping the declaration of the kingdom of the Meffiah, which was now expeċted, within certain general terms, during his miniſtry.   It was not fit to open himſelf too plainly or forwardly to the heady jews, that he himſelf was the Meſſiah: that was to be left to the obſervation of thoſe, who would attend to the purity of his life, the teſtimony of his miracles, and the conformity of all with the prediċtions concerning him: by theſe marks, thoſe he lived amongſt were to find it out, without an expreſs promulgation that he was the Meſſiah, until after his death.   His kingdom was to be opened to them by degrees, as well to prepare them to receive it, as to enable him to be long enough amongſt them, to perform what was the work of the Meſſiah to be done; and fulfil all thoſe ſeveral parts of what was foretold of him in the Old Teſtament, and we ſee applied to him in the New.

The jews had no other thoughts of their Meſſiah, but of a mighty temporal prince, that ſhould raiſe their nation into an higher degree of power, dominion and proſperity, than ever it had enjoyed.   They were filled with the expeċtation of a glorious earthly kingdom.   It was not, therefore, for a poor man, the ſon of a carpenter, and (as they thought) born in Galilee, to pretend to it. None of the jews, no, not his diſciples, could have born this, if he had expreſsly avowed this at firſt, and began his preaching and the opening of his kingdom this way, eſpecially if he had added to it, that in a year or two, he ſhould die an ignominious death upon the croſs.   They are therefore prepared for the truth by degrees.   Firſt, John the Baptiſt tells them, " The king " dom of God" (a name by which the jews called the kingdom of the Meſſiah) " is at hand."   Then our Saviour comes, and he tells them " of the kingdom of " God;" ſometimes that it is at hand, and upon ſome occaſions, that it is come; but ſays, in his public preaching, little or nothing of himſelf.   Then come the apoſtles and evangeliſts after his death, and they, in expreſs words, teach what his birth, life, and doċtrine had done before, and had prepared the well-diſpoſed to receive, viz. That " Jeſus is the Meſſiah."

To this deſign and method of publiſhing the goſpel,
was

was the choice of the apoftles exactly adjufted; a company of poor, ignorant, illiterate men; who, as Chrift
himfelf tells us, Matt. xi. 25. and Luke x. 21, were not
of the " wife and prudent" men of the world : they
were, in that refpect, but mere children.   Thefe, convinced by the miracles they faw him daily do, and the
unblameable life he led, might be difpofed to believe
him to be the Meffiah : and though they, with others,
expected a temporal kingdom on earth, might yet reft
fatisfied in the truth of their mafter, (who had honoured
them with being near his perfon) that it would come,
without being too inquifitive after the time, manner, or
feat of his kingdom, as men of letters, more ftudied in
their rabbins, or men of bufinefs, more verfed in the
world, would have been forward to have been.   Men,
great or wife in knowledge, or ways of the world,
would hardly have been kept from prying more nar-
rowly into his defign and conduct ; or from queftioning
him about the ways and meafures he would take, for
afcending the throne ; and what means were to be ufed
towards it, and when they fhould in earneft fet about
it.   Abler men, of higher births or thoughts, would
hardly have been hindered from whifpering, at leaft to
their friends and relations, that their mafter was the
Meffiah ; and that, though he concealed himfelf to a
fit opportunity, and until things were ripe for it, yet
they fhould, ere long, fee him break out of his obfcurity, caft off the cloud, and declare himfelf, as he was,
King of Ifrael.   But the ignorance and lownefs of thefe
good, poor men, made them of another temper.   They
went along, in an implicit truft on him, punctually
keeping to his commands, and not exceeding his commiffion.   When he fent them to preach the gofpel, he
bid them preach " the kingdom of God" to be at hand;
and that they did, without being more particular than
he had ordered, or mixing their own prudence with his
commands, to promote the kingdom of the Meffiah.
They preached it, without giving, or fo much as intimating that their mafter was he : which men of another
condition, and an higher education, would fcarce have
forborn to have done.   When he afked them, who they

thought

thought him to be; and Peter answered, "The Messiah,
"the Son of God," Matt. xvi. 16, he plainly shows by
the following words, that he himself had not told them
so; and at the same time, ver. 20, forbids them to tell
this their opinion of him to any body. How obedient
they were to him in this, we may not only conclude
from the silence of the evangelists concerning any such
thing, published by them any where before his death;
but from the exact obedience three of them paid to a
like command of his. He takes Peter, James, and
John, into a mountain; and there Moses and Elias
coming to him, he is transfigured before them, Matt.
xvii. 9. He charges them, saying, "See that ye tell
"no man what ye have seen, until the Son of man shall
"be risen from the dead." And St. Luke tells us, what
punctual observers they were of his orders in this case,
chap. ix. 36. "They kept it close, and told no man,
"in those days, any of those things which they had
"seen."

Whether twelve other men, of quicker parts, and of
a station or breeding, which might have given them any
opinion of themselves, or their own abilities, would have
been so easily kept from meddling, beyond just what was
prescribed them, in a matter they had so much interest
in; and have said nothing of what they might, in human prudence, have thought would have contributed to
their master's reputation, and made way for his advance-
ment to his kingdom; I leave to be considered. And
it may suggest matter of meditation, whether St. Paul
was not for this reason, by his learning, parts, and
warmer temper, better fitted for an apostle after, than
during our Saviour's ministry: and therefore, though a
chosen vessel, was not by the divine wisdom called, until
after Christ's resurrection.

I offer this only as a subject of magnifying the admirable contrivance of the divine wisdom, in the whole
work of our redemption, as far as we are able to trace
it, by the footsteps which God hath made visible to human reason. For though it be as easy to omnipotent
power to do all things by an immediate over-ruling
will, and so to make any instruments work, even contrary

trary to their nature, in fubferviency to his ends; yet
his wifdom is not ufually at the expence of miracles,
(if I may fo fay) but only in cafes that require them,
for the evidencing of fome revelation or miffion to be
from-him. He does conftantly (unlefs where the confirmation of fome truth requires it otherwife) bring
about his purpofes by means operating according to
their natures. If it were not fo, the courfe and evidence
of things would be confounded, miracles would lofe
their name and force; and there could be no diftinction
between natural and fupernatural.

There had been no room left to fee and admire the
wifdom, as well as innocence of our Saviour, if he had
rafhly every-where expofed himfelf to the fury of the
jews, and had always been preferved by a miraculous
fufpenfion of their malice, or a miraculous refcuing
him out of their hands. It was enough for him once
to efcape from the men of Nazareth, who were going to throw him down a precipice, for him never to
preach to them again. Our Saviour had multitudes
that followed him for the loaves; who barely feeing the
miracles that he did, would have made him king. If
to the miracles he did, he had openly added, in exprefs
words, that he was the Meffiah, and the king they expected to deliver them, he would have had more followers, and warmer in the caufe, and readier to fet him
up at the head of a tumult. Thefe indeed God, by a
miraculous influence, might have hindered from any
fuch attempt: but then pofterity could not have believed, that the nation of the jews did, at that time, expect the Meffiah, their king and deliverer; or that Jefus, who declared himfelf to be that king and deliverer,
fhowed any miracles amongft them, to convince them
of it; or did any thing worthy to make him be credited or received: If he had gone about preaching to
the multitude, which he drew after him, that he was
the " Meffiah, the king of Ifrael," and this had been
evidenced to Pilate; God could indeed, by a fupernatural influence upon his mind, have made Pilate pronounce him innocent, and not condemn him as a malefactor, who had openly, for three years together, preached

fedition

sedition to the people, and endeavoured to persuade them, that he was " the Messiah, their king," of the royal blood of David, come to deliver them.   But then I ask, Whether posterity would not either have suspected the story, or that some art had been used to gain that testimony from Pilate?   Because he could not (for nothing) have been so favourable to Jesus, as to be willing to release so turbulent and seditious a man; to declare him innocent, and to cast the blame and guilt of his death, as unjust, upon the envy of the jews.

But now, the malice of the chief priests, scribes and pharisees; the headiness of the mob, animated with hopes, and raised with miracles; Judas's treachery, and Pilate's care of his government, and of the peace of his province, all working naturally as they should; Jesus, by the admirable wariness of his carriage, and an extraordinary wisdom, visible in his whole conduct; weathers all these difficulties, does the work he comes for, uninterruptedly goes about preaching his full appointed time, sufficiently manifests himself to be the Messiah, in all the particulars the scriptures had foretold of him; and when his hour is come, suffers death: but is acknowledged, both by Judas that betrayed, and Pilate that condemned him, to die innocent.   For, to use his own words, Luke xxiv. 46, " Thus it is written, and " thus it behoved the Messiah to suffer."   And of his whole conduct we have a reason and clear resolution in those words to St. Peter, Matt. xxvi. 53, " Thinkest " thou that I cannot now pray to my Father, and he " shall presently give me more than twelve legions of " angels? But how then shall the scripture be fulfilled, " that thus it must be?"

Having this clew to guide us, let us now observe, how our Saviour's preaching and conduct comported with it in the last scene of his life.   How cautious he had been in the former part of his ministry, we have already observed.   We never find him to use the name of the Messiah but once, until he now came to Jerusalem, this last passover.   Before this, his preaching and miracles were less at Jerusalem, (where he used to make but very short stays) than any where else.   But now he comes six days

before

before the feaft, and is every day in the temple teaching; and there publicly heals the blind and the lame,
in the prefence of the fcribes, pharifees, and chief
priefts. The time of his miniftry drawing to an end,
and his hour coming, he cared not how much the chief
priefts, elders, rulers, and the fanhedrim, were provoked
againft him by his doctrine and miracles: he was as
open and bold in his preaching, and doing the works
of the Meffiah now at Jerufalem, and in the fight of the
rulers, and of all the people; as he had been before
cautious and referved there, and careful to be little taken
notice of in that place, and not to come in their way
more than needs. All that he now took care of was,
not what they fhould think of him, or defign againft
him, (for he knew they would feize him) but to fay or
do nothing that might be a juft matter of accufation
againft him, or render him criminal to the governor.
But, as for the grandees of the jewifh nation, he fpares
them not, but fharply now reprehends their mifcarriages publicly in the temple; where he calls them,
more than once, " hypocrites;" as is to be feen, Matt.
xxiii. And concludes all with no fofter a compellation
than " ferpents," and " a generation of vipers."

After this fevere reproof of the fcribes and pharifees,
being retired with his difciples into the " Mount of
Olives" over-againft the temple, and there foretelling
the deftruction of it; his difciples afk him, Matt. xxiv.
3, &c. " When it fhould be, and what fhould be the
" fign of his coming?" He fays, to them, " Take heed
" that no man deceive you: for many fhall come in my
" name," (i. e. taking on them the name and dignity of
the Meffiah, which is only mine) faying, " I am the
" Meffiah, and fhall deceive many." But be not you by
them mifled, nor by perfecution driven away from this
fundamental truth, that I am the Meffiah; " for many
" fhall be fcandalized," and apoftatize; " but he that
" endures to the end, the fame fhall be faved: and this
" gofpel of the kingdom fhall be preached in all the
" world;" i. e. the good news of me, the Meffiah, and
my kingdom, fhall be fpread through the world. This
was the great and only point of belief they were warned
to ftick to; and this is inculcated again, ver. 23,—26,

and

and Mark xiii. 21,—23, with this emphatical application to them, in both these evangelists, " Behold, I have
" told you beforehand ; remember, you are fore-
" warned."

This was in answer to the apostles inquiry, concerning his " coming, and the end of the world," ver. 3.
For so we translate τῆς συν]ελείας τῶ αἰῶνος. We must understand the disciples here to put their question, according to the notion and way of speaking of the Jews. For
they had two worlds, as we translate it, ὁ νῦν αἰὼν, ῃ ὁ
μέλλων αἰὼν; " the present world," and the " world to
" come." The kingdom of God, as they called it, or
the time of the Messiah, they called ὁ μέλλων αἰὼν, " the
world to come," which they believed was to put an end
to " this world ;" and that then the just should be raised
from the dead, to enjoy in that " new world" a happy
eternity, with those of the jewish nation, who should
be then living.

These two things, viz. the visible and powerful appearance of his kingdom, and the end of the world,
being confounded in the apostles question, our Saviour
does not separate them, nor distinctly reply to them
apart ; but, leaving the inquirers in the common opinion, answers at once concerning his coming to take
vengeance on the jewish nation, and put an end to their
church worship and commonwealth ; which was their
ὁ νῦν αἰὼν, " present world," which they counted should
last till the Messiah came ; and so it did, and then had
an end put to it. And to this he joins his last coming
to judgment, in the glory of his Father, to put a final
end to this world, and all the dispensation belonging
to the posterity of Adam upon earth. This joining
them together, made his answer obscure, and hard to be
understood by them then ; nor was it safe for him to
speak plainer of his kingdom, and the destruction of
Jerusalem ; unless he had a mind to be accused for having designs against the government. For Judas was
amongst them : and whether no other but his apostles
were comprehended under the name of " his disciples,"
who were with him at this time, one cannot determine.
Our Saviour, therefore, speaks of his kingdom in no
other style, but that which he had all along hitherto
used,

ufed, viz. " the kingdom of God," Luke xxi. 31.
" When you fee thefe things come to pafs, know ye
" that the kingdom of God is nigh at hand." And
continuing on his difcourfe with them, he has the fame
expreffion, Matt. xxv. 1. " Then the kingdom of
" heaven fhall be like unto ten virgins." At the end
of the following parable of the talents, he adds, ver. 31,
" When the Son of man fhall come in his glory, and
" all the holy angels with him, then fhall he fit upon
" the throne of his glory. And before him fhall be
" gathered all the nations. And he fhall fet the fheep
" on his right hand, and the goats on his left. Then
" fhall the King fay, &c." Here he defcribes to his
difciples the appearance of his kingdom, wherein he
will fhow himfelf a king in glory upon his throne; but
this in fuch a way, and fo remote, and fo unintelligible
to an heathen magiftrate; that, if it had been alleged
againft him, it would have feemed rather the dream of
a crazy brain, than the contrivance of an ambitious or
dangerous man, defigning againft the government: the
way of expreffing what he meant, being in the prophetic ftyle, which is feldom fo plain as to be underftood, till accomplifhed. It is plain, that his difciples
themfelves comprehended not what kingdom he here
fpoke of, from their queftion to him after his refurrection, " Wilt thou at this time reftore again the king-
" dom unto Ifrael?"

Having finifhed thefe difcourfes, he takes order for
the paffover, and eats it with his difciples; and at fup-
per tells them, that one of them fhould betray him;
and adds, John xiii. 19, " I tell it you now, before it
" come, that when it is come to pafs, you may know
" that I am." He does not fay out, " the Meffiah;"
Judas fhould not have that to fay againft him, if he
would; though that be the fenfe in which he ufes this
expreffion, ἐγώ εἰμι, " I am," more than once. And
that this is the meaning of it, is clear from Mark xii. 6.
Luke xxi. 8. In both which evangelifts the words are,
" For many fhall come in my name, faying, ἐγώ εἰμι, I
" am:" the meaning whereof we fhall find explained
in the parallel place of St. Matthew, chap. xxiv. 5,
" For

" For many shall come in my name, saying, ἐγὼ εἰμι ὁ
Χριϛὸς, " I am the Messiah." Here, in this place of
John xiii. Jesus foretels what should happen to him,
viz. that he should be betrayed by Judas; adding this
prediction to the many other particulars of his death
and suffering, which he had at other times foretold to
them. And here he tells them the reason of these his
predictions, viz. that afterwards they might be a confirmation to their faith. And what was it that he would
have them believe, and be confirmed in the belief of?
Nothing but this, ὅτι ἐγὼ εἰμι ὁ Χριϛὸς, " that he was the
" Messiah." The same reason he gives, John xiv. 28,
" You have heard how I said unto you, I go away, and
" come again unto you : and now I have told you, be-
" fore it comes to pass, that when it comes to pass, ye
" might believe."

When Judas had left them, and was gone out, he
talks a little freer to them of his glory and his kingdom, than ever he had done before. For now he speaks
plainly of himself, and of his kingdom, John xiii. 31,
" Therefore when he [Judas] was gone out, Jesus said,
Now is the Son of man glorified, and God is also glorified in him. And, if God be glorified in him, God
" shall also glorify him in himself, and shall straitway
" glorify him." And Luke xxii. 29, " And I will
" appoint unto you a kingdom, as my Father hath
" appointed unto me ; that ye may eat and drink with
" me at my table, in my kingdom." Though he has
every where, all along through his ministry, preached
the " gospel of the kingdom," and nothing else but
that and repentance, and the duties of a good life :
yet it has been always " the kingdom of God,"
and " the kingdom of heaven :" and I do not remember, that any where, till now, he uses any such expression, as " my kingdom." But here now he speaks in
the first person, " I will appoint you a kingdom," and,
" in my kingdom :" and this we see is only to the eleven, now Judas was gone from them.

With these eleven, whom he was just now leaving, he
has a long discourse, to comfort them for the loss of
him ; and to prepare them for the persecution of the
world,

world, and to exhort them to keep his commandments, and to love one another. And here one may expect all the articles of faith should be laid down plainly, if any thing elfe were required of them to believe, but what he had taught them, and they believed already, viz. " That he was the Meffiah." John xiv. 1, " Ye be-" lieve in God, believe alfo in me." Ver. 29. " I have " told you before it come to pafs, that when it is come " come to pafs, ye may believe." It is believing on him without any thing elfe. John xvi. 31, " Jefus an-" fwered them, Do ye now believe?" This was in an-fwer to their profeffion, ver. 30, " Now are we fure " that thou knoweft all things, and needeft not that " any man fhould afk thee: by this we believe that thou " cameft forth from God."

John xvii. 20, " Neither pray I for thefe alone, but " for them alfo which fhall believe on me through their " word." All that is fpoke of believing, in this his laft fermon to them, is only " believing on him," or believing that " he came from God;" which was no other than believing him to be the Meffiah.

Indeed, John xiv. 9, our Saviour tells Philip, " He " that hath feen me, hath feen the Father." And adds, ver. 10, " Believeft thou not that I am in the Father, " and the Father in me? The words that I fpeak unto " you, I fpeak not of myfelf: but the Father that dwel-" leth in me, he doth the works." Which being in anfwer to Philip's words, ver. 9, " Show us the Father," feem to import thus much: " No man hath feen God " at any time," he is known only by his works. And that he is my Father, and I the Son of God, i. e. the Meffiah, you may know by the works I have done; which it is impoffible I could do of myfelf, but by the union I have with God my Father. For that by being " in God," and " God in him," he fignifies fuch an union with God, that God operates in and by him, appears not only by the words above cited out of ver. 10. (which can fcarce otherwife be made coherent fenfe) but alfo from the fame phrafe, ufed again by our Saviour prefently after, ver. 20, " At that day," viz. after his refurrection, when they fhould fee him again, " you fhall
" know

" know that I am in the Father, and you in me, and I
" in you ;" i. e. by the works that I shall enable you to
do, through a power I have received from the Father:
which whosoever sees me do, must acknowledge the Father to be in me; and whosoever sees you do, must acknowledge me to be in you.   And therefore he says,
ver. 12, " Verily, verily, I say unto you, he that believ-
" eth on me, the works that I do shall he do also, be-
" cause I go unto my Father."   Though I go away,
yet I shall be in you, who believe in me; and ye shall
be enabled to do miracles also, for the carrying on of my
kingdom, as I have done; that it may be manifested to
others, that you are sent by me, as I have evidenced to
you, that I am sent by the Father.   And hence it is
that he says, in the immediately preceding ver. 11,
" Believe me, that I am in the Father, and the Father
" in me; if not, believe me for the sake of the works
" themselves."   Let the works that I have done convince
you, that I am sent by the Father; that he is with me,
and that I do nothing but by his will; and by virtue of
the union I have with him; and that consequently I am
the Messiah, who am anointed, sanctified, and separated
by the Father, to the work for which he sent me.

To confirm them in this faith, and to enable them to
do such works as he had done, he promises them the
Holy Ghost, John xiv. 25, 26. " These things I have
" said unto you, being yet present with you."   But
when I am gone, " The Holy Ghost, the Paraclet,"
(which may signify Monitor, as well as Comforter, or
Advocate) " which the Father shall send you in my
" name, he shall show you all things, and bring to your
" remembrance all things which I have said."   So that,
considering all that I have said, and laying it together,
and comparing it with what you shall see come to pass;
you may be more abundantly assured, that I am the
Messiah; and fully comprehend, that I have done and
suffered all things foretold of the Messiah, and that
were to be accomplished and fulfilled by him, according
to the scriptures.   But be not filled with grief, that I leave
you, John xvi. 7, " It is expedient for you, that I go
" away; for if I go not away, the Paraclet will not
come

"come unto you." One reafon why, if he went not away, the Holy Ghoft could not come, we may gather from what has been obferved, concerning the prudent and wary carriage of our Saviour all through his miniftry, that he might not incur death with the leaft fufpicion of a malefactor. And therefore, though his difciples believed him to be the Meffiah, yet they neither under-ftood it fo well, nor were fo well confirmed in the belief of it, as after that, he being crucified and rifen again, they had received the Holy Ghoft; and with the gifts of the Holy Spirit, a fuller and clearer evidence and knowledge that he was the Meffiah. They then were enlightened to fee how his kingdom was fuch as the fcriptures foretold; though not fuch as they, till then, had expected. And now this knowledge and affurance, received from the Holy Ghoft, was of ufe to them after his refurrection; when they could now boldly go about, and openly preach, as they did, that Jefus was the Mef-fiah; confirming that doctrine by the miracles which the Holy Ghoft empowered them to do. But till he was dead and gone, they could not do this. Their go-ing about openly preaching, as they did after his refur-rection, that Jefus was the Meffiah, and doing miracles every where, to make it good, would not have confifted with that character of humility, peace and innocence, which the Meffiah was to fuftain, if they had done it before his crucifixion. For this would have drawn upon him the condemnation of a malefactor, either as a ftirrer of fedition againft the public peace, or as a pretender to the kingdom of Ifrael. Hence we fee, that they, who before his death preached only the "gofpel of "the kingdom;" that "the kingdom of God was at "hand;" as foon as they had received the Holy Ghoft, after his refurrection, changed their ftyle, and every where in exprefs words declare, that Jefus is the Mef-fiah, that King which was to come. This, the following words here in St. John xvi. 8—14. confirm; where he goes on to tell them, "And when he is come, he will "convince the world of fin; becaufe they believed not "on me." Your preaching then, accompanied with miracles, by the affiftance of the Holy Ghoft, fhall be a

conviction

conviction to the world, that the jews finned in not believing me to be the Messiah. " Of righteousnefs," or
justice ; " becaufe I go to my Father, and ye fee me no
more." By the fame preaching and miracles you fhall
confirm the doctrine of my afcenfion ; and thereby convince the world, that I was that juft one, who am, therefore, afcended to the Father into heaven, where no unjuft perfon fhall enter. " Of judgment ; becaufe the
prince of this world is judged." And by the fame affiftance of the Holy Ghoft ye fhall convince the world,
that the devil is judged or condemned by your cafting
of him out, and deftroying his kingdom, and his worfhip, where-ever you preach. Our Saviour adds, " I
" have yet many things to fay unto you, but you
" cannot bear them now." They were yet fo full of
a temporal kingdom, that they could not bear the difcovery of what kind of kingdom his was, nor what a
king he was to be : and therefore he leaves them to the
coming of the Holy Ghoft, for a farther and fuller difcovery of himfelf, and the kingdom of the Messiah ; for
fear they fhould be fcandalized in him, and give up the
hopes they now had in him, and forfake him. This
he tells them, ver. 1, of this xvith chapter : " Thefe
" things I have faid unto you, that you may not be
" fcandalized." The laft thing he had told them, before his faying this to them, we find in the laft verfes
of the preceding chapter: " When the Paraclet is come,
" the Spirit of truth, he fhall witnefs concerning me."
He fhall fhow you who I am, and witnefs it to the
world ; and then, " Ye alfo fhall bear witnefs, becaufe
" ye have been with me from the beginning." He
fhall call to your mind what I have faid and done, that
ye may underftand it, and know, and bear witnefs concerning me. And again here, John xvi, after he had
told them they could not bear what he had more to fay,
he adds, ver. 13, " Howbeit, when the Spirit of truth
" is come, he will guide you into all truth ; and he will
" fhow you things to come : he fhall glorify me." By
the Spirit, when he comes, ye fhall be fully inftructed
concerning me ; and though you cannot yet, from what
I have faid to you, clearly comprehend my kingdom
and

5

and glory, yet he shall make it known to you wherein it consists : and though I am now in a mean state, and ready to be given up to contempt, torment, and death, so that ye know not what to think of it ; yet the Spirit, when he comes, " shall glorify me," and fully satisfy you of my power and kingdom ; and that I sit on the right hand of God, to order all things for the good and increase of it, till I come again at the last day, in the fulness of glory.

Accordingly, the apostles had a full and clear sight and persuasion of this, after they had received the Holy Ghost; and they preached it every where boldly and openly, without the least remainder of doubt or uncertainty. But that, even so late as this, they understood not his death and resurrection, is evident from ver. 17, 18, " Then said some of his disciples among themselves, " What is it that he saith unto us ; A little while, and " ye shall not see me ; and again, a little while, and ye " shall see me ; and because I go to the Father ? They " said therefore, What is this that he saith, A little " while ? We know not what he saith." Upon which he goes on to discourse to them of his death and resurrection, and of the power they should have of doing miracles. But all this he declares to them in a mystical and involved way of speaking : as he tells them himself, ver. 25, " These things have I spoken to you in pro- " verbs ;" i. e. in general, obscure, ænigmatical, or figurative terms (all which, as well as allusive apologues, the jews called proverbs or parables.) Hitherto my declaring of myself to you hath been obscure, and with reserve ; and I have not spoken of myself to you in plain and direct words, because ye " could not bear it." A Messiah, and not a King, you could not understand : and a King living in poverty and persecution, and dying the death of a slave and malefactor upon a cross ; you could not put together. And had I told you in plain words, that I was the Messiah, and given you a direct commission to preach to others, that I professedly owned myself to be the Messiah ; you and they would have been ready to have made a commotion, to have set me upon the throne of my father David, and to fight for

me ;

me; and that your Messiah, your King, in whom are
your hopes of a kingdom, should not be delivered up
into the hands of his enemies, to be put to death; and
of this Peter will instantly give you a proof. But "the
"time cometh, when I shall no more speak unto you
"in parables; but I shall show unto you plainly of the
"Father." My death and resurrection, and the coming
of the Holy Ghost, will speedily enlighten you, and then
I shall make you know the will and design of my Father; what a kingdom I am to have, and by what means,
and to what end, ver. 27. And this the Father himself
will show unto you; "For he loveth you, because ye
"have loved me, and have believed that I came out
"from the Father." Because ye have believed that I
am "the Son of God, the Messiah;" that he hath
anointed and sent me; though it hath not yet been fully
discovered to you, what kind of kingdom it shall be, nor
by what means brought about. And then our Saviour,
without being asked, explaining to them what he had
said, and making them understand better what before
they stuck at, and complained secretly among themselves that they understood not; they thereupon declare,
ver. 30, "Now are we sure that thou knowest all things,
"and needest not that any man should ask thee." It is
plain, thou knowest men's thoughts and doubts before
they ask. "By this we believe that thou camest forth
"from God. Jesus answered, Do ye now believe?"
Notwithstanding that you now believe, that I came from
God, and am the Messiah, sent by him; "Behold, the
"hour cometh, yea, is now come, that ye shall be scat-
"tered;" and as it is Matth. xxvi. 31, and "shall all
"be scandalized in me." What it is to be scandalized
in him, we may see by what followed hereupon, if that
which he says to St. Peter, Mark xiv, did not sufficiently
explain it.

This I have been the more particular in; that it may
be seen, that in this last discourse to his disciples (where
he opened himself more than he had hitherto done; and
where, if any thing more was required to make them
believers than what they already believed, we might
have expected they should have heard of it) there were
no

no new articles propofed to them, but what they believed before, viz. that he was the Meffiah, the Son of
God, fent from the Father; though of his manner of
proceeding, and his fudden leaving of the world, and
fome few particulars, he made them underftand fomething more than they did before. But as to the main
defign of the gofpel, viz. that he had a kingdom, that
he fhould be put to death, and rife again, and afcend
into heaven to his Father, and come again in glory to
judge the world; this he had told them: and fo had
acquainted them with the great counfel of God, in fending him the Meffiah, and omitted nothing that was neceffary to be known or believed in it. And fo he tells
them himfelf, John xv. 15, " Henceforth I call you
" not fervants; for the fervant knoweth not what his
" Lord does: but I have called you friends; for ALL
" THINGS that I have heard of my Father, I have made
" known unto you;" though perhaps ye do not fo
fully comprehend them, as you will fhortly, when I
am rifen and afcended.

To conclude all, in his prayer, which fhuts up this
difcourfe, he tells the Father, what he had made known
to his apoftles; the refult whereof we have, John xvii. 8.
" I have given unto them the words which thou gaveft
" me, and they have received them, and THEY HAVE
" BELIEVED THAT THOU DIDST SEND ME." Which is,
in effect, that he was the Meffiah promifed and fent by
God. And then he prays for them, and adds, ver.
20, 21, " Neither pray I for thefe alone, but for them
" alfo who fhall believe on me through their word."
What that word was, through which others fhould believe in him, we have feen in the preaching of the apoftles, all through the hiftory of the Acts, viz. this one
great point, that Jefus was the Meffiah. The apoftles,
he fays, ver. 25, " know that thou haft fent me;" i. e.
are affured that I am the Meffiah. And in ver. 21 and
23, he prays, " That the world may believe" (which,
ver. 23, is called knowing) " that thou haft fent me."
So that what Chrift would have believed by his difciples, we may fee by this his laft prayer for them, when

he was leaving the world, as by what he preached whilst he was in it.

And, as a testimony of this, one of his last actions, even when he was upon the cross, was to confirm his doctrine, by giving salvation to one of the thieves that was crucified with him, upon his declaration, that he believed him to be the Messiah: for so much the words of his request imported, when he said, " Remember " me, Lord, when thou comest into thy kingdom," Luke xxiii. 42. To which Jesus replied, ver. 43, " Verily, I say unto thee, To-day shalt thou be with " me in paradise." An expression very remarkable: for as Adam, by sin, lost paradise, i. e. a state of happy immortality; here the believing thief, through his faith in Jesus the Messiah, is promised to be put in paradise, and so re-instated in an happy immortality.

Thus our Saviour ended his life. And what he did after his resurrection, St. Luke tells us, Acts i. 3, That he showed himself to the apostles, " forty days, speak- " ing things concerning the kingdom of God." This was what our Saviour preached in the whole course of his ministry, before his passion: and no other mysteries of faith does he now discover to them after his resurrec- tion. All he says, is concerning the kingdom of God; and what it was he said concerning that, we shall see presently out of the other evangelists; having first only taken notice, that when now they asked him, ver. 6, " Lord, wilt thou at this time restore again the king- " dom of Israel? He said unto them, ver. 7, It is not " for you to know the times and the seasons, which the " Father hath put in his own power: but ye shall " receive power, after that the Holy Ghost is come " upon you; and ye shall be witnesses unto me, un- " to the utmost parts of the earth." Their great business was to be witnesses to Jesus, of his life, death, resurrection, and ascension; which, put together, were undeniable proofs of his being the Messiah. This was what they were to preach, and what he said to them, concerning the kingdom of God; as will appear by what is recorded of it in the other evangelists.

When

When on the day of his refurrection he appeared to
the two going to Emmaus, Luke xxiv, they declare,
ver. 21, what his difciples faith in him was : " But we
" trufted that it had been he that fhould have redeemed
" Ifrael ;" i. e. we believed that he was the Meffiah,
come to deliver the nation of the jews. Upon this,
Jefus tells them, they ought to believe him to be the
Meffiah, notwithftanding what had happened; nay, they
ought, by his fufferings and death, to be confirmed in
that faith, that he was the Meffiah. And ver. 26, 27,
" Beginning at Mofes and all the prophets, he ex-
" pounded unto them, in all the fcriptures, the things
" concerning himfelf," how, " that the Meffiah ought
" to have fuffered thefe things, and to have entered into
" his glory." Now he applies the prophecies of the
Meffiah to himfelf, which we read not, that he did ever
do before his paffion. And afterwards appearing to the
eleven, Luke xxiv. 36, he faid unto them, ver. 44—47,
" Thefe are the words, which I fpake unto you, while
" I was yet with you, that all things muft be fulfilled
" which are written in the law of Mofes, and in the
" prophets, and in the pfalms concerning me. Then
" opened he their underftanding, that they might un-
" derftand the fcripture, and faid unto them : Thus it
" is written, and thus it behoved the Meffiah to fuffer,
" and to rife from the dead the third day; and that re-
" pentance and remiffion of fins fhould be preached in
" his name among all nations, beginning at Jerufalem."
Here we fee what it was he had preached to them, though
not in fo plain open words, before his crucifixion ; and
what it is he now makes them underftand ; and what it
was that was to be preached to all nations, viz. That he
was the Meffiah that had fuffered, and rofe from the
dead the third day, and fulfilled all things that were
written in the Old Teftament concerning the Meffiah ;
and that thofe who believed this, and repented, fhould
receive remiffion of their fins, through this faith in him.
Or, as St. Mark has it, chap. xvi. 15, " Go into all the
" world, and preach the gofpel to every creature ; he
" that believeth, and is baptized, fhall be faved ; but
" he that believeth not, fhall be damned," ver. 16.

What

What the " gofpel," or " good news," was, we have
fhowed already, viz. The happy tidings of the Meffiah
being come. Ver. 20, And " they went forth and
" preached every where, the Lord working with them,
" and confirming the word with figns following."
What the " word" was which they preached, and the
Lord confirmed with miracles, we have feen already,
out of the hiftory of their Acts. I have already given
an account of their preaching every-where, as it is recorded in the Acts, except fome few places, where the
kingdom of " the Meffiah" is mentioned under the
name of " the kingdom of God ;" which I forbore to
fet down, till I had made it plain out of the evangelifts,
that that was no other but the kingdom of the Meffiah.

It may be feafonable therefore, now, to add to thofe
fermons we have formerly feen of St. Paul, (wherein
he preached no other article of faith, but that " Jefus
" was the Meffiah," the King, who being rifen from the
dead, now reigneth, and fhall more publicly manifeft
his kingdom, in judging the world at the laft day) what
farther is left upon record of his preaching.   Acts xix.
8, at Ephefus, " Paul went into the fynagogues, and
" fpake boldly for the fpace of three months ; difputing
" and perfuading concerning the kingdom of God."
And, Acts xx. 25, at Miletus he thus takes leave of the
elders of Ephefus : " And now, behold, I know that ye
" all, among whom I have gone preaching the king-
" dom of God, fhall fee my face no more."   What
this preaching the kingdom of God was, he tells you,
ver. 20, 21, " I have kept nothing back from you,
" which was profitable unto you ; but have fhowed you,
" and have taught you publicly, and from houfe to
" houfe ; teftifying both to the jews, and to the greeks,
" repentance towards God, and faith towards our Lord
" Jefus Chrift."   And fo again, Acts xxviii. 23, 24,
" When they [the jews at Rome] had appointed him
" [Paul] a day, there came many to him into his lodg-
" ing ; to whom he expounded and teftified the king-
" dom of God ; perfuading them concerning Jefus,
" both out of the law of Mofes, and out of the pro-
" phets, from morning to evening. And fome believed
                                                " the

" the things which were fpoken, and fome believed not."
And the hiftory of the Acts is concluded with this account of St. Paul's preaching : " And Paul dwelt two
" whole years in his own hired houfe, and received all
" that came in unto him, preaching the kingdom of
" God, and teaching thofe things which concern the
" Lord Jefus the Meffiah." We may therefore here
apply the fame conclufion to the hiftory of our Saviour,
writ by the evangelifts, and to the hiftory of the apoftles, writ in the acts, which St. John does to his own
gofpel, chap. xx. 30, 31, " Many other figns did Jefus
" before his difciples ;" and in many other places the
apoftles preached the fame doctrine, " which are not
" written" in thefe books ; " but thefe are written that
" you may believe that Jefus is the Meffiah, the Son of
" God ; and that believing you may have life in his
" name."

What St. John thought neceffary and fufficient to be
believed, for the attaining eternal life, he here tells us.
And this not in the firft dawning of the gofpel ; when,
perhaps, fome will be apt to think lefs was required to
be believed, than after the doctrine of faith, and myftery of falvation, was more fully explained, in the
epiftles writ by the apoftles, for it is to be remembered,
that St. John fays this, not as foon as Chrift was a-
fcended ; for thefe words, with the reft of St. John's
gofpel, were not written till many years after not only
the other gofpels, and St. Luke's hiftory of the Acts,
but in all appearance, after all the epiftles writ by the
other apoftles. So that above threefcore years after our
Saviour's paffion (for fo long after, both Epiphanius and
St. Jerom affure us this gofpel was written) St. John
knew nothing elfe required to be believed, for the attaining of life, but that " Jefus is the Meffiah, the Son
" of God."

To this, it is likely, it will be objected by fome, that
to believe only that Jefus of Nazareth is the Meffiah, is
but an hiftorical, and not a juftifying, or faving faith.

To which I anfwer, That I allow to the makers of
fyftems and their followers to invent and ufe what dif-
tinctions they pleafe, and to call things by what names

H 3   they

they think fit.   But I cannot allow to them, or to any man, an authority to make a religion for me, or to alter that which God hath revealed.   And if they please to call the believing that which our Saviour and his apostles preached, and proposed alone to be believed, an historical faith ; they have their liberty.   But they must have a care, how they deny it to be a justifying or saving faith, when our Saviour and his apostles have declared it so to be ; and taught no other which men should receive, and whereby they should be made believers unto eternal life : unless they can so far make bold with our Saviour, for the sake of their beloved systems, as to say, that he forgot what he came into the world for ; and that he and his apostles did not instruct people right in the way and mysteries of salvation.   For that this is the sole doctrine pressed and required to be believed in the whole tenour of our Saviour's and his apostles preaching, we have showed through the whole history of the evangelists and the Acts.   And I challenge them to show that there was any other doctrine, upon their assent to which, or disbelief of it, men were pronounced believers or unbelievers ; and accordingly received into the church of Christ, as members of his body ; as far as mere believing could make them so ; or else kept out of it.   This was the only gospel-article of faith which was preached to them.   And if nothing else was preached every where, the apostle's argument will hold against any other articles of faith to be believed under the gospel, Rom. x. 14, " How shall they believe that where- " of they have not heard ?" For, to preach any other doctrines necessary to be believed, we do not find that any body was sent.

Perhaps it will farther be urged, that this is not a " saving faith ;" because such a faith as this the devils may have, and it was plain they had ; for they believed and declared " Jesus to be the Messiah." And St. James, ch. ii. 19, tells us, " The devils believe and tremble ;" and yet they shall not be saved.   To which I answer, 1. That they could not be saved by any faith, to whom it was not proposed as a means of salvation, nor ever promised to be counted for righteousness.   This was an act
of

of grace fhown only to mankind. God dealt fo favour-ably with the pofterity of Adam, that if they would be-lieve Jefus to be the Meffiah, the promifed King and Saviour, and perform what other conditions were re-quired of them by the covenant of grace; God would juftify them, becaufe of this belief. He would account this faith to them for righteoufnefs, and look on it as making up the defects of their obedience; which being thus fupplied, by what was taken inftead of it, they were looked on as juft or righteous; and fo inherited eternal life. But this favour fhown to mankind, was never offered to the fallen angels. They had no fuch propofals made to them: and therefore, whatever of this kind was propofed to men, it availed not devils, what-ever they performed of it. This covenant of grace was never offered to them.

2. I anfwer; that though the devils believed, yet they could not be faved by the covenant of grace; be-caufe they performed not the other condition required in it, altogether as neceffary to be performed as this of believing: and that is repentance. Repentance is as abfolute a condition of the covenant of grace as faith; and as neceffary to be performed as that. John the Baptift, who was to prepare the way for the Meffiah, " Preached the baptifm of repentance for the remiffion " of fins," Mark i. 4.

As John began his preaching with " Repent; for " the kingdom of heaven is at hand," Matt. iii. 2. So did our Saviour begin his, Matt. iv. 17, " From that " time began Jefus to preach, and to fay, Repent; for " the kingdom of heaven is at hand." Or, as St. Mark has it in that parallel place, Mark i. 14, 15, " Now, " after that John was put in prifon, Jefus came into " Galilee, preaching the gofpel of the kingdom of God, " and faying, The time is fulfilled, and the kingdom of " God is at hand: repent ye, and believe the gofpel." This was not only the beginning of his preaching, but the fum of all that he did preach; viz. That men fhould repent, and believe the good tidings which he brought them; that " the time was fulfilled" for the coming of the Meffiah. And this was what his apoftles

H 4   preached,

preached, when he sent them out, Mark vi. 12. "And
" they, going out, preached that men should repent."
Believing Jesus to be the Messiah, and repenting, were
so necessary and fundamental parts of the covenant of
grace, that one of them alone is often put for both. For
here St. Mark mentions nothing but their preaching
repentance: as St. Luke, in the parallel place, chap. ix.
6, mentions nothing but their evangelizing, or preaching the good news of the kingdom of the Messiah: and
St. Paul often, in his epistles, puts faith for the whole
duty of a christian.   But yet the tenour of the gospel is
what Christ declares, Luke xii. 3, 5, "Unless ye re-
" pent, ye shall all likewise perish."   And in the parable of the rich man in hell, delivered by our Saviour,
Luke xvi. repentance alone is the means proposed, of
avoiding that place of torment, ver. 30, 31.   And what
the tenour of the doctrine which should be preached to
the world should be, he tells his apostles, after his resurrection, Luke xxiv. 27. viz. That repentance and
remission of sins should be preached " in his name,"
who was the Messiah.   And accordingly, believing Jesus
to be the Messiah, and repenting, was what the apostles
preached.   So Peter began, Acts ii. 38, "Repent, and
" be baptized." These two things were required for
the remission of sins, viz. entering themselves in the
kingdom of God; and owning and professing themselves the subjects of Jesus, whom they believed to be
the Messiah, and received for their Lord and King; for
that was to be " baptized in his name:" baptism being
an initiating ceremony, known to the jews, whereby
those, who leaving heathenism, and professing a submission to the law of Moses, were received into the
commonwealth of Israel.   And so it was made use of
by our Saviour, to be that solemn visible act, whereby
those who believed him to be the Messiah, received him
as their King, and professed obedience to him, were admitted as subjects into his kingdom: which in the gospel, is called "the kingdom of God;" and in the
Acts and epistles, often by another name, viz. the
" Church."

The same St. Peter preaches again to the jews, Acts
iii. 19,

iii. 19, " Repent, and be converted, that your fins may " be blotted out."

What this repentance was which the new covenant required, as one of the conditions to be performed by all thofe who fhould receive the benefits of that covenant; is plain in the fcripture, to be not only a forrow for fins paft, but (what is a natural confequence of fuch forrow, if it be real) a turning from them into a new and contrary life. And fo they are joined together, Acts iii. 19, " Repent and turn about;" or, as we render it, " be converted." And Acts xxvi. 20, " Repent and " turn to God."

And fometimes " turning about" is put alone to fignify repentance, Matt. xiii. 15. Luke xxii. 32, which in other words is well expreffed by " newnefs of life." For it being certain that he, who is really forry for his fins, and abhors them, will turn from them, and forfake them; either of thefe acts, which have fo natural a connexion one with the other, may be, and is often put for both together. Repentance is an hearty forrow for our paft mifdeeds, and a fincere refolution and endeavour, to the utmoft of our power, to conform all our actions to the law of God. So that repentance does not confift in one fingle act of forrow, (though that being the firft and leading act, gives denomination to the whole) but in " doing works meet for repentance;" in a fincere obedience to the law of Chrift, the remainder of our lives. This was called for by John the Baptift, the preacher of repentance, Matt. iii. 8, " Bring forth " fruits meet for repentance." And by St. Paul here, Acts xxvi. 20. " Repent and turn to God, and do works " meet for repentance." There are works to follow belonging to repentance, as well as forrow for what is paft.

Thefe two, faith and repentance, i. e. believing Jefus to be the Meffiah, and a good life, are the indifpenfable conditions of the new covenant, to be performed by all thofe who would obtain eternal life. The reafonablenefs, or rather neceffity of which, that we may the better comprehend, we muft a little look back to what vas faid in the beginning.

Adam

Adam being the Son of God, and so St. Luke calls him, chap. iii. 38, had this part also of the likeness and image of his Father, viz. that he was immortal. But Adam, transgressing the command given him by his heavenly Father, incurred the penalty; forfeited that state of immortality, and became mortal. After this, Adam begot children: but they were " in his own " likeness, after his own image;" mortal, like their father.

God nevertheless, out of his infinite mercy, willing to bestow eternal life on mortal men, sends Jesus Christ into the world; who being conceived in the womb of a virgin (that had not known man) by the immediate power of God, was properly the Son of God; according to what the angel declared unto his mother, Luke i. 30—35, " The Holy Ghost shall come upon thee, and " the power of the Highest shall over-shadow thee: " therefore also that holy thing, which shall be born of " thee, shall be called the SON OF GOD." So that being the Son of God, he was, like the Father, immortal; as he tells us, John v. 26, " As the Father hath life in " himself, so hath he given to the Son to have life in " himself."

And that immortality is a part of that image, wherein those (who were the immediate sons of God, so as to have no other father) were made like their father, appears probable, not only from the places in Genesis concerning Adam, above taken notice of, but seems to me also to be intimated in some expressions, concerning Jesus the Son of God, in the New Testament. Col. i. 15, he is called " the image of the invisible God." Invisible seems put in, to obviate any gross imagination, that he (as images used to do) represented God in any corporeal or visible resemblance. And there is farther subjoined, to lead us into the meaning of it, " The " first-born of every creature;" which is farther explained, ver. 18, where he is termed " The first-born " from the dead:" thereby making out, and showing himself to be the image of the invisible; that death hath no power over him; but being the Son of God, and not having forfeited that sonship by any transgression;

9

was

was the heir of eternal life, as Adam fhould have been, had he continued in his filial duty. In the fame fenfe the apoftle feems to ufe the word image in other places, viz. Rom. viii. 29, "Whom he did foreknow, he alfo "did predeftinate to be conformed to the image of his "Son, that he might be the firft-born among many "brethren." This image, to which they were conformed, feems to be immortality and eternal life: for it is remarkable, that in both thefe places, St. Paul fpeaks of the refurrection; and that Chrift was "The firft-born "among many brethren;" he being by birth the Son of God, and the others only by adoption, as we fee in this fame chapter, ver. 15—17, "Ye have received the "Spirit of adoption, whereby we cry, Abba, Father; "the Spirit itfelf bearing witnefs with our fpirit, that "we are the children of God. And if children, then "heirs, and joint-heirs with Chrift; if fo be that we "fuffer with him, that we may alfo be glorified toge- "ther." And hence we fee, that our Saviour vouch- fafes to call thofe, who at the day of judgment are, through him, entering into eternal life, his brethren; Matt. xxv. 40, "Inafmuch as ye have done it unto one "of the leaft of thefe my brethren." May we not in this find a reafon, why God fo frequently in the New Teftament, and fo feldom, if at all, in the Old, is men- tioned under the fingle title of THE FATHER? And there- fore our Saviour fays, Matt. xi. "No man knoweth the "Father, fave the Son, and he to whomfoever the Son "will reveal him." God has now a Son again in the world, the firft-born of many brethren, who all now, by the Spirit of adoption, can fay, Abba, Father. And we, by adoption, being for his fake made his brethren, and the fons of God, come to fhare in that inheritance, which was his natural right; he being by birth the Son of God: which inheritance is eternal life. And again, ver. 23, "We groan within ourfelves, waiting for the "adoption, to wit, the redemption of our body;" whereby is plainly meant, the change of thefe frail mortal bodies, into the fpiritual immortal bodies at the refurrection; "When this mortal fhall have put on "immortality," 1 Cor. xv. 54. which in that chapter,

ver.

ver. 42—44, he farther expresses thus ; " So also is the
" resurrection of the dead.   It is sown in corruption,
" it is raised in incorruption ; it is sown in dishonour,
" it is raised in glory; it is sown in weakness, it is
" raised in power ; it is sown a natural body, it is raised
" a spiritual body, &c."   To which he subjoins, ver.
49, " As we have born the image of the earthy," (i. e.
as we have been mortal, like earthy Adam, our father,
from whom we are descended, when he was turned out
of paradise) " we shall also bear the image of the hea-
" venly ;" into whose sonship and inheritance being
adopted, we shall, at the resurrection, receive that
adoption we expect, " even the redemption of our bo-
" dies ;" and after his image, which is the image of
the Father, become immortal.   Hear what he says
himself, Luke xx. 35, 36, " They who shall be ac-
" counted worthy to obtain that world, and the resur-
" rection from the dead, neither marry, nor are given
" in marriage.   Neither can they die any more ; for
" they are equal to the angels, and are the SONS OF
" GOD, being the sons of the resurrection."   And he
that shall read St. Paul's arguing, Acts xiii. 32, 33,
will find that the great evidence that Jesus was the
" Son of God," was his resurrection.   Then the image
of his Father appeared in him, when he visibly entered
into the state of immortality.   For thus the apostle reasons, " We preach to you, how that the promise which
" was made to our fathers, God hath fulfilled the same
" unto us, in that he hath raised up Jesus again ; as it
" is also written in the second psalm, Thou art my
" Son, this day have I begotten thee."

This may serve a little to explain the immortality of
the sons of God, who are in this like their Father,
made after his image and likeness. But that our Saviour
was so, he himself farther declares, John x. 18, where
speaking of his life, he says, " No one taketh it from
" me, but I lay it down of myself : I have power to lay
" it down, and I have power to take it up again."
Which he could not have had, if he had been a mortal
man, the son of a man, of the seed of Adam ; or else had
by any transgression forfeited his life.   For " the wages
						" of

" of fin is death:" and he that hath incurred death for his own tranfgreffion, cannot lay down his life for another, as our Saviour profeffes he did. For he was the juft one, Acts vii. 52. and xxii. 14. " Who knew no " fin," 2 Cor. v. 21. " Who did no fin, neither was " guile found in his mouth." And thus, " As by man " came death, fo by man came the refurrection of the " dead. For as in Adam all die, fo in Chrift fhall all " be made alive."

For this laying down his life for others, our Saviour tells us, John x. 17, " Therefore does my Father love " me, becaufe I lay down my life, that I might take it " again." And this his obedience and fuffering was rewarded with a kingdom : which he tells us, Luke xxii, " His Father had appointed unto him ;" and which, it is evident out of the epiftle to the Hebrews, chap. xii. 2, he had a regard to in his fufferings : " Who for the " joy that was fet before him, endured the crofs, de- " fpifing the fhame, and is fet down at the right hand " of the throne of God." Which kingdom, given him upon this account of his obedience, fuffering and death, he himfelf takes notice of in thefe words, John xvii. 1—4, " Jefus lifted up his eyes to heaven, and faid, " Father, the hour is come : glorify thy Son, that thy " Son alfo may glorify thee : as thou haft given him " power over all flefh, that he fhould give eternal life " to as many as thou haft given him. And this is life " eternal, that they may know thee the only true God, " and Jefus, the Meffiah, whom thou haft fent. I have " glorified thee on earth : I have finifhed the work " which thou gaveft me to do." And St. Paul, in his epiftle to the philippians, chap. ii. 8—11, " He hum- " bled himfelf, and became obedient unto death, even " the death of the crofs. Wherefore God alfo hath " highly exalted him, and given him a name that is " above every name ; that at the name of Jefus every " knee fhould bow, of things in heaven, and things in " earth, and things under the earth ; and that every " tongue fhould confefs, that Jefus Chrift is Lord."

Thus God, we fee, defigned his Son Jefus Chrift a kingdom, an everlafting kingdom in heaven. But

though

though, " as in Adam all die, fo in Chrift fhall all be
" made alive ;" and all men fhall return to life again
at the laft day ; yet all men having finned, and thereby
" come fhort of the glory of God," as St. Paul aflures
us, Rom. iii. 23, i. e. not attaining to the heavenly
kingdom of the Mefliah, which is often called the glory
of God ; (as may be feen, Rom. v. 2. and xv. 7. and ii.
7. Matt. xvi. 27. Mark viii. 38.   For no one who is
unrighteous, i. e. comes fhort of perfect righteoufnefs,
fhall be admitted into the eternal life of that kingdom ;
as is declared, 1 Cor. vi. 9. " The unrighteous fhall not
" inherit the kingdom of God ;") and death, the wages
of fin, being the portion of all thofe who had tranfgreffed the righteous law of God ; the fon of God would
in vain have come into the world, to lay the foundations of a kingdom, and gather together a felect people
out of the world, if, (they being found guilty at their
appearance before the judgment-feat of the righteous
Judge of all men at the laft day) inftead of entrance
into eternal life in the kingdom he had prepared for
them, they fhould receive death, the juft reward of fin
which every one of them was guilty of : this fecond
death would have left him no fubjects ; and inftead of
thofe ten thoufand times ten thoufand, and thoufands
of thoufands, there would not have been one left him to
fing praifes unto his name, faying, " Blefling, and ho-
" nour, and glory, and power, be unto him that fitteth
" on the throne, and unto the lamb for ever and ever."
God therefore, out of his mercy to mankind, and for
the erecting of the kingdom of his Son, and furnifhing
it with fubjects out of every kindred, and tongue, and
people, and nation ; propofed to the children of men,
that as many of them as would believe Jefus his Son
(whom he fent into the world) to be the Mefliah, the
promifed Deliverer ; and would receive him for their
King and Ruler ; fhould have all their paft fins, difobedience, and rebellion forgiven them : and if for the future they lived in a fincere obedience to his law, to
the utmoft of their power ; the fins of human frailty for
the time to come, as well as all thofe of their paft
lives ; fhould, for his Son's fake, becaufe they gave
themfelves

themfelves up to him, to be his fubjects, be forgiven them: and fo their faith, which made them be baptized into his name, (i. e. enrol themfelves in the kingdom of Jefus the Meffiah, and profefs themfelves his fubjects, and confequently live by the laws of his kingdom) fhould be accounted to them for righteoufnefs; i. e. fhould fupply the defects of a fcanty obedience in the fight of God; who, counting faith to them for righteoufnefs, or complete obedience, did thus juftify, or make them juft, and thereby capable of eternal life.

Now, that this is the faith for which God of his free grace juftifies finful man, (for "it is God alone that juftifieth," Rom. viii. 33. Rom. iii. 26.) we have already fhowed, by obferving through all the hiftory of our Saviour and the apoftles, recorded in the evangelifts, and in the Acts, what he and his apoftles preached, and propofed to be believed. We fhall fhow now, that befides believing him to be the Meffiah, their King, it was farther required, that thofe who would have the privilege, advantage, and deliverance of his kingdom, fhould enter themfelves into it; and by baptifm being made denizens, and folemnly incorporated into that kingdom, live as became fubjects obedient to the laws of it. For if they believed him to be the Meffiah, their King, but would not obey his laws, and would not have him to reign over them; they were but the greater rebels; and God would not juftify them for a faith that did but increafe their guilt, and oppofe diametrically the kingdom and defign of the Meffiah; "Who gave himfelf " for us, that he might redeem us from all iniquity, " and purify unto himfelf a peculiar people zealous of " good works," Titus ii. 14. And therefore St. Paul tells the galatians, That that which availeth is faith; but "faith working by love." And that faith without works, i. e. the works of fincere obedience to the law and will of Chrift, is not fufficient for our juftification, St. James fhows at large, chap. ii.

Neither, indeed, could it be otherwife; for life, eternal life, being the reward of juftice or righteoufnefs only, appointed by the righteous God (who is of purer eyes than to behold iniquity) to thofe who only had no

taint

taint or infection of sin upon them, it is impossible that he should justify those who had no regard to justice at all, whatever they believed.   This would have been to encourage iniquity, contrary to the purity of his nature; and to have condemned that eternal law of right, which is holy, just, and good; of which no one precept or rule is abrogated or repealed; nor indeed can be, whilst God is an holy, just, and righteous God, and man a rational creature.   The duties of that law, arising from the constitution of his very nature, are of eternal obligation; nor can it be taken away or dispensed with, without changing the nature of things, overturning the measures of right and wrong, and thereby introducing and authorizing irregularity, confusion, and disorder in the world.   Christ's coming into the world was not for such an end as that; but, on the contrary, to reform the corrupt state of degenerate man; and out of those who would mend their lives, and bring forth fruit meet for repentance, erect a new kingdom.

This is the law of that kingdom, as well as of all mankind; and that law, by which all men shall be judged at the last day.   Only those who have believed Jesus to be the Messiah, and have taken him to be their King, with a sincere endeavour after righteousness, in obeying his law; shall have their past sins not imputed to them; and shall have that faith taken instead of obedience, where frailty and weakness made them transgress, and sin prevailed after conversion; in those who hunger and thirst after righteousness, (or perfect obedience) and do not allow themselves in acts of disobedience and rebellion, against the laws of that kingdom they are entered into.

He did not expect, it is true, a perfect obedience, void of slips and falls: he knew our make, and the weakness of our constitution too well, and was sent with a supply for that defect. Besides, perfect obedience was the righteousness of the law of works; and then the reward would be of debt, and not of grace; and to such there was no need of faith to be imputed to them for righteousness.   They stood upon their own legs, were just already, and needed no allowance to be made them for
believing

believing Jesus to be the Messiah, taking him for their king, and becoming his subjects. But that Christ does require obedience, sincere obedience, is evident from the law he himself delivers, (unless he can be supposed to give and inculcate laws, only to have them disobeyed) and from the sentence he will pass when he comes to judge.

The faith required was, to believe Jesus to be the Messiah, the Anointed; who had been promised by God to the world. Among the jews (to whom the promises and prophecies of the Messiah were more immediately delivered) anointing was used to three sorts of persons, at their inauguration; whereby they were set apart to three great offices, viz. of priests, prophets, and kings. Though these three offices be in holy writ attributed to our Saviour, yet I do not remember that he any where assumes to himself the title of a priest, or mentions any thing relating to his priesthood; nor does he speak of his being a prophet but very sparingly, and only once or twice, as it were by the bye: but the gospel, or the good news of the kingdom of the Messiah, is what he preaches every where, and makes it his great business to publish to the world. This he did, not only as most agreeable to the expectation of the jews, who looked for their Messiah, chiefly as coming in power to be their king and deliverer; but as it best answered the chief end of his coming, which was to be a king, and, as such, to be received by those who would be his subjects in the kingdom which he came to erect. And though he took not directly on himself the title of King, until he was in custody, and in the hands of Pilate; yet it is plain, "King" and "King of Israel" were the familiar and received titles of the Messiah. See John i. 50. Luke xix. 38. compared with Matt. xxi. 9. and Mark xi. 9. John xii. 13. Matth. xxi. 5. Luke xxiii. 2. compared with Matt. xxvii. 11. and John xviii. 33—37. Mark xv. 12. compared with Matth. xxvii. 22, 42.

What those were to do, who believed him to be the Messiah, and received him for their king, that they might be admitted to be partakers with him of his kingdom in glory, we shall best know by the laws he

gives

gives them, and requires them to obey; and by the sentence which he himself will give, when, sitting on his throne, they shall all appear at his tribunal, to receive every one his doom from the mouth of this righteous judge of all men.

What he proposed to his followers to be believed, we have already seen, by examining his and his apostles preaching, step by step, all through the history of the four evangelists, and the Acts of the Apostles. The same method will best and plainest show us, whether he required of those who believed him to be the Messiah, any thing besides that faith, and what it was. For, he being a king, we shall see by his commands what he expects from his subjects: for, if he did not expect obedience to them, his commands would be but mere mockery; and if there were no punishment for the transgressors of them, his laws would not be the laws of a king, and that authority to command, and power to chastise the disobedient, but empty talk, without force, and without influence.

We shall therefore from his injunctions (if any such there be) see what he has made necessary to be performed, by all those who shall be received into eternal life, in his kingdom prepared in the heavens. And in this we cannot be deceived. What we have from his own mouth, especially if repeated over and over again, in different places and expressions, will be past doubt and controversy. I shall pass by all that is said by St. John Baptist, or any other before our Saviour's entry upon his ministry, and public promulgation of the laws of his kingdom.

He began his preaching with a command to repent, as St. Matthew tells us, iv. 17, " From that time Jesus " began to preach, saying, Repent; for the kingdom " of heaven is at hand." And Luke v. 32, he tells the scribes and pharisees, "I come not to call the righteous;" (those who were truly so, needed no help, they had a right to the tree of life,) " but sinners to repentance."

In his sermon, as it is called, in the mount, Luke vi. and Matth. v, &c. he commands they should be exemplary

plary in good works : " Let your light fo fhine amongft
" men, that they may fee your good works, and glorify
" your Father which is in heaven," Matth. v. 15. And
that they might know what he came for, and what he
expected of them, he tells them, ver. 17—20, " Think
" not that I am come to diffolve," or loofen, " the law,
" or the prophets : I am not come to diffolve," or loofen,
" but to make it full," or complete ; by giving it you in
its true and ftrict fenfe. Here we fee he confirms, and at
once re-enforces all the moral precepts in the Old Teftament. " For verily I fay to you, Till heaven and earth
" pafs, one jot, or one tittle, fhall in no wife pafs from
" the law, till all be done. Whofoever therefore fhall
" break one of thefe leaft commandments, and fhall
" teach men fo, he fhall be called the leaft (i. e. as it
" is interpreted, fhall not be at all) in the kingdom of
" heaven." Ver. 21, " I fay unto you, That except
" your righteoufnefs," i. e. your performance of the
eternal law of right, " fhall exceed the righteoufnefs
" of the fcribes and pharifees, ye fhall in no cafe enter
" into the kingdom of heaven." And then he goes on
to make good what he faid, ver. 17, viz. " That he was
" come to complete the law," viz. by giving its full
and clear fenfe, free from the corrupt and loofening
gloffes of the fcribes and pharifees, ver. 22—26. He
tells them, That not only murder, but caufelefs anger,
and fo much as words of contempt, were forbidden. He
commands them to be reconciled and kind towards
their adverfaries ; and that upon pain of condemnation.
In the following part of his fermon, which is to be read
Luke vi. and more at large, Matth. v, vi, vii. he not
only forbids actual uncleannefs, but all irregular defires,
upon pain of hell-fire ; caufelefs divorces ; fwearing in
converfation, as well as forfwearing in judgment ; re-
venge ; retaliation ; oftentation of charity, of devotion,
and of fafting ; repetitions in prayer, covetoufnefs,
worldly care, cenforioufnefs : and on the other fide
commands loving our enemies, doing good to thofe
that hate us, bleffing thofe that curfe us, praying for
thofe that defpitefully ufe us ; patience and meeknefs
under injuries, forgivenefs, liberality, compaffion : and
clofes all his particular injunctions, with this general

golden rule, Matth. vii. 12, " All things whatfoever ye
" would that men fhould do to you, do you even fo to
" them, for this is the law and the prophets." And to
fhow how much he is in earneft, and expects obedience
to thefe laws; he tells them, Luke vi. 35, That if they
obey, " great fhall be their REWARD;" they " fhall be
" called, the fons of the Higheft." And to all this, in
the conclufion, he adds the folemn fanction; " Why
" call ye me, Lord, Lord, and do not the things that
" I fay?" It is in vain for you to take me for the Meffiah your King, unlefs you obey me. " Not every one
" who calls me Lord, Lord, fhall enter into the king-
" dom of heaven," or be the fons of God; " but he
" that doth the will of my Father which is in heaven."
To fuch difobedient fubjects, though they have prophefied and done miracles in my name, I fhall fay at the day
of judgment, " Depart from me, ye workers of iniquity;
" I know you not."

When, Matt. xii, he was told, that his mother and
brethren fought to fpeak with him, ver. 49, " Stretch-
" ing out his hands to his difciples, he faid, "Behold my
" mother and my brethren; for whofoever fhall do the
" will of my Father, who is in heaven, he is my bro-
" ther, and fifter, and mother." They could not be
children of the adoption, and fellow-heirs with him of
eternal life, who did not do the will of his heavenly
Father.

Matth. xv. and Mark vi, the pharifees finding fault,
that his difciples eat with unclean hands, he makes this
declaration to his apoftles: " Do not ye perceive, that
" whatfoever from without entereth into a man, cannot
" defile him, becaufe it entereth not into his heart, but
" his belly? That which cometh out of the man, that
" defileth the man; for from within, out of the heart of
" men, proceed evil thoughts, adulteries, fornications,
" murders, thefts, falfe witneffes, covetoufnefs, wick-
" ednefs, deceit, lafcivioufnefs, an evil eye, blafphemy,
" pride, foolifhnefs. All thefe ill things come from
" within, and defile a man."

He commands felf-denial, and the expofing ourfelves
to fuffering and danger, rather than to deny or difown
him:

him: and this upon pain of losing our souls; which are
of more worth than all the world. This we may read,
Matt. xvi. 24—27, and the parallel places, Mark viii.
and Luke ix.

The apostles disputing among them, who should be
greatest in the kingdom of the Messiah, Matt. xviii. 1,
he thus determines the controversy, Mark ix. 35, " If
" any one will be first, let him be last of all, and servant
" of all:" and setting a child before them, adds, Matt.
xviii. 3, " Verily, I say unto you, Unless ye turn, and
" become as children, ye shall not enter into the king-
" dom of heaven."

Matth. xviii. 15, " If thy brother shall trespass
" against thee, go and tell him his fault between thee
" and him alone: if he shall hear thee, thou hast gained
" thy brother. But if he will not hear thee, then take
" with thee one or two more, that in the mouth of two
" or three witnesses every word may be established.
" And if he shall neglect to hear them, tell it to the
" church: but if he neglect to hear the church, let him
" be unto thee as an heathen and publican." Ver. 21,
" Peter said, Lord, how often shall my brother sin against
" me, and I forgive him? Till seven times? Jesus said
" unto him, I say not unto thee, till seven times; but
" until seventy times seven." And then ends the parable of the servant, who being himself forgiven, was
rigorous to his fellow-servant, with these words, ver. 34,
" and his Lord was wroth, and delivered him to the
" tormentors, till he should pay all that was due to him.
" So likewise shall my heavenly Father do also unto you,
" if you from your hearts forgive not every one his bro-
" ther their trespasses."

Luke x. 25, to the lawyer, asking him, " What shall
" I do to inherit eternal life? He said, What is written
" in the law? How readest thou?" He answered,
" Thou shalt love the Lord thy God with all thy heart,
" and with all thy soul, and with all thy strength, and
" with all thy mind; and thy neighbour as thyself."
Jesus said, " This do, and thou shalt live." And when
the lawyer, upon our Saviour's parable of the good Sa-
maritan, was forced to confess, that he that showed

I 3   mercy

mercy was his neighbour; Jesus dismissed him with this charge, ver. 37, " Go, and do thou likewise."

Luke xi. 41, " Give alms of such things as ye have : " behold, all things are clean unto you."

Luke xii. 15, " Take heed, and beware of covetous-" ness." Ver. 22, " Be not solicitous what ye shall " eat, or what ye shall drink, nor what ye shall put " on ;" be not fearful, or apprehensive of want ; " for " it is your Father's pleasure to give you a kingdom. " Sell that you have, and give alms : and provide your-" selves bags that wax not old, a treasure in the heavens, " that faileth not : for where your treasure is, there will " your heart be also. Let your loins be girded, and " your lights burning ; and ye yourselves like unto men " that wait for the Lord, when he will return. Blessed " are those servants, whom the Lord, when he cometh, " shall find watching. Blessed is that servant, whom " the Lord having made ruler of his houshold, to give " them their portion of meat in due season, the Lord, " when he cometh, shall find so doing. Of a truth I " say unto you, that he will make him ruler over all " that he hath. But if that servant say in his heart, " my Lord delayeth his coming ; and shall begin to " beat the men-servants, and maidens, and to eat and " drink, and to be drunken ; the Lord of that servant " will come in a day when he looketh not for him, and " at an hour when he is not aware ; and will cut him " in sunder, and will appoint him his portion with un-" believers. And that servant who knew his lord's " will, and prepared not himself, neither did according " to his will, shall be beaten with many stripes. But " he that knew not, and did commit things worthy of " stripes, shall be beaten with few stripes. For unto " whomsoever much is given, of him shall much be " required : and to whom men have committed much, " of him they will ask the more."

Luke xiv. 11, " Whosoever exalteth himself, shall be " abased : and he that humbleth himself, shall be ex-" alted."

Ver. 12, When thou makest a dinner, or supper, call " not thy friends, or thy brethren, neither thy kinsmen,

nor

" nor thy neighbours ; left they alfo bid thee again, and
" a recompence be made thee. But when thou makeft
" a feaft, call the poor and maimed, the lame and the
" blind ; and thou fhalt be bleffed, for they cannot re-
" compence thee ; for thou fhalt be recompenfed at the
" refurrection of the juft."

Ver. 33, " So likewife, whofoever he be of you, that
" is not ready to forego all that he hath, he cannot be
" my difciple."

Luke xvi. 9, "I fay unto you, make to yourfelves
" friends of the mammon of unrighteoufnefs; that
" when ye fail, they may receive you into everlafting
" habitations. If ye have not been faithful in the un-
" righteous mammon, who will commit to your truft the
" true riches? And if ye have not been faithful in that
" which is another man's, who fhall give you that
" which is your own?"

Luke xvii. 3, " If thy brother trefpafs againft thee,
" rebuke him ; and if he repent, forgive him. And
" if he trefpafs againft thee feven times in a day, and
" feven times in a day turn again unto thee, faying, I
" repent ; thou fhalt forgive him."

Luke xviii. 1, " he fpoke a parable to them, to this
" end, that men ought always to pray, and not to
" faint."

Ver. 18, " One comes to him, and afks him, faying,
" Mafter, what fhall I do to inherit eternal life? Jefus
" faid unto him, if thou wilt enter into life, keep the
" commandments. He fays, Which? Jefus faid, Thou
" knoweft the commandments. Thou fhalt not kill;
" thou fhalt not commit adultery ; thou fhalt not fteal ;
" thou fhalt not bear falfe witnefs ; defraud not ; ho-
" nour thy father and thy mother ; and thou fhalt love
" thy neighbour as thyfelf. He faid, all thefe have I
" obferved from my youth. Jefus hearing this, loved
" him ; and faid unto him, Yet lackeft thou one thing:
" fell all that thou haft, and give it to the poor, and
" thou fhalt have treafure in heaven ; and come, follow
" me." To underftand this right, we muft take notice, that this young man afks our Saviour, what he
muft do, to be admitted effectually into the kingdom

of the Messiah? The jews believed, that when the Messiah came, those of their nation that received him, should not die; but that they, with those who, being dead, should then be raised again by him, should enjoy eternal life with him. Our Saviour, in answer to this demand, tells the young man, that to obtain the eternal life of the kingdom of the Messiah, he must keep the commandments. And then enumerating several of the precepts of the law, the young man says, he had observed these from his childhood. For which, the text tells us, Jesus loved him. But our Saviour, to try whether in earnest he believed him to be the Messiah, and resolved to take him to be his king, and to obey him as such; bids him give all that he has to the poor, and come, and follow him; and he should have treasure in heaven. This I look on to be the meaning of the place; this, of selling all he had, and giving it to the poor, not being a standing law of his kingdom; but a probationary command to this young man; to try whether he truly believed him to be the Messiah, and was ready to obey his commands, and relinquish all to follow him, when he, his prince, required it.

And therefore we see, Luke xix. 14, where our Saviour takes notice of the jews not receiving him as the Messiah, he expresses it thus: " We will not have this " man to reign over us." It is not enough to believe him to be the Messiah, unless we also obey his laws, and take him to be our king, to reign over us.

Matt. xxii. 11—13, he that had not on the wedding garment, though he accepted of the invitation, and came to the wedding, was cast into utter darkness. By the wedding-garment, it is evident good works are meant here; that wedding-garment of fine linen, clean and white, which we are told, Rev. xix. 8, is the δικαιώματα, " righteous acts of the saints;" or, as St. Paul calls it, Ephes. iv. 1, " The walking worthy of the vocation " wherewith we are called." This appears from the parable itself: " The kingdom of heaven," says our Saviour, ver. 2, " is like unto a king, who made a mar- " riage for his son." And here he distinguishes those who were invited, into three sorts: 1. Those who were
invited,

invited, and came not; i. e. thofe who had the gofpel, the good news of the kingdom of God propofed to them, but believed not. 2. Thofe who came, but had not on a wedding-garment; i. e. believed Jefus to be the Meffiah, but were not new clad (as I may fo fay) with a true repentance, and amendment of life: nor adorned with thofe virtues, which the apoftle, Col. iii, requires to be put on. 3. Thofe who were invited did come, and had on the wedding-garment; i. e. heard the gofpel, believed Jefus to be the Meffiah, and fincerely obeyed his laws. Thefe three forts are plainly defigned here; whereof the laft only were the bleffed, who were to enjoy the kingdom prepared for them.

Matt. xxiii, " Be not ye called Rabbi; for one is
" your mafter, even the Meffiah, and ye are all brethren.
" And call no man your father upon the earth: For
" one is your Father which is in heaven. Neither
" be ye called mafters: for one is your mafter, even the
" Meffiah. But he that is greateft amongft you, fhall
" be your fervant. And whofoever fhall exalt himfelf,
" fhall be abafed; and he that fhall humble himfelf,
" fhall be exalted."

Luke xxi. 34. " Take heed to yourfelves, left your
" hearts be at any time overcharged with furfeiting and
" drunkennefs, and cares of this life."

Luke xxii. 25, " He faid unto them, the kings of
" the gentiles exercife lordfhip over them; and they
" that exercife authority upon them, are called bene-
" factors. But ye fhall not be fo. But he that is greateft
" among you, let him be as the younger; and he that
" is chief, as he that doth ferve."

John xiii. 34, " A new commandment I give unto
" you, That ye love one another: as I have loved you,
" that ye alfo love one another. By this fhall all men
" know that ye are my difciples, if ye love one ano-
" ther." This command, of loving one another, is
repeated again, chap. xv. 12, and 17.

John xiv. 15, " If ye love me, keep my command-
" ments. Ver. 21, " He that hath my command-
" ments, and keepeth them, he it is that loveth me:
" and he that loveth me, fhall be loved of my Father,
" and

" and I will love him, and manifest myself to him."
Ver. 23, "If a man loveth me, he will keep my words."
Ver. 24, "He that loveth me not, keepeth not my
" sayings."

John xv. 8. "In this is my Father glorified, that ye
" bear much fruit; so shall ye be my disciples." Ver.
14, "Ye are my friends, if ye do whatsoever I com-
" mand you."

Thus we see our Saviour not only confirmed the
moral law; and clearing it from the corrupt glosses of
the scribes and pharisees, showed the strictness as well
as obligation of its injunctions; but moreover, upon
occasion, requires the obedience of his disciples to several of the commands he afresh lays upon them; with the
inforcement of unspeakable rewards and punishments in
another world, according to their obedience or disobedience. There is not, I think, any of the duties of morality, which he has not, somewhere or other, by himself and his apostles, inculcated over and over again to
his followers in express terms. And is it for nothing
that he is so instant with them to bring forth fruit?
Does he, their King, command, and is it an indifferent
thing? Or will their happiness or misery not at all depend upon it, whether they obey or no? They were required to believe him to be the Messiah; which faith is
of grace promised to be reckoned to them, for the com-
pleting of their righteousness, wherein it was defective:
but righteousness, or obedience to the law of God, was
their great business, which if they could have attained
by their own performances, there would have been no
need of this gracious allowance, in reward of their
faith: but eternal life, after the resurrection, had been
their due by a former covenant, even that of works; the
rule whereof was never abolished, though the rigour
was abated. The duties enjoined in it were duties still.
Their obligations had never ceased; nor a wilful neglect of them was ever dispensed with. But their past
transgressions were pardoned, to those who received Jesus, the promised Messiah, for their king; and their future slips covered, if renouncing their former iniquities,
they entered into his kingdom, and continued his subjects

jects with a steady resolution and endeavour to obey his laws. This righteousness therefore, a complete obedience and freedom from sin, are still sincerely to be endeavoured after. And it is no where promised, that those who persist in a wilful disobedience to his laws, shall be received into the eternal bliss of his kingdom, how much soever they believe in him.

A sincere obedience, how can any one doubt to be, or scruple to call, a condition of the new covenant, as well as faith; whoever reads our Saviour's sermon in the mount, to omit all the rest? Can any thing be more express than these words of our Lord? Matt. vi. 14, " If you forgive men their trespasses, your heavenly Fa-" ther will also forgive you : but if you forgive not men " their trespasses, neither will your Father forgive your " trespasses." And John xiii. 17, " If ye know these " things, happy are ye if you do them." This is so indispensable a condition of the new covenant, that believing without it, will not do, nor be accepted ; if our Saviour knew the terms on which he would admit men into life. " Why call ye me, Lord, Lord," says he, Luke vi. 46, " and do not the things which I say?" It is not enough to believe him to be the Messiah, the Lord, without obeying him. For that these he speaks to here, were believers, is evident from the parallel place, Matt. vii. 21—23, where it is thus recorded: " Not every one who says Lord, Lord, shall enter into " the kingdom of heaven; but he that doth the will of " my Father, which is in heaven." No rebels, or refractory disobedient, shall be admitted there, though they have so far believed in Jesus, as to be able to do miracles in his name : as is plain out of the following words : " Many will say to me in that day, Have we not " prophesied in thy name, and in thy name have cast " out devils, and in thy name have done many wonderful " works ? And then will I profess unto them, I never " knew you : depart from me, ye workers of iniquity."

This part of the new covenant, the apostles also, in their preaching the gospel of the Messiah, ordinarily joined with the doctrine of faith.

St. Peter, in his first sermon. Acts ii, when they were
pricked

pricked in heart, and asked, "What shall we do?" says, ver. 38, "Repent, and be baptized, every one of "you, in the name of Jesus Christ, for the remission of "sins." The same he says to them again in his next speech, Acts iv. 26, "Unto you first, God having raised "up his Son Jesus, sent him to bless you." How was this done? "IN TURNING AWAY EVERY ONE FROM YOUR "INIQUITIES."

The same doctrine they preach to the high priest and rulers, Acts v. 30, "The God of our fathers raised up "Jesus, whom ye slew, and hanged on a tree Him "hath God exalted with his right hand, to be a Prince "and a Saviour, for to give REPENTANCE to Israel, and "forgiveness of sins; and we are witnesses of these "things, and so is also the Holy Ghost, whom God "hath given to them that obey him."

Acts xvii. 30, St. Paul tells the Athenians, That now under the gospel, "God commandeth all men every "where to REPENT."

Acts xx. 21, St. Paul, in his last conference with the elders of Ephesus, professes to have taught them the whole doctrine necessary to salvation: "I have," says he, "kept back nothing that was profitable unto you; "but have showed you, and have taught you publicly, "and from house to house; testifying both to the jews "and to the greeks:" and then gives an account what his preaching had been, viz. "REPENTANCE towards "God, and faith towards our Lord Jesus the Messiah." This was the sum and substance of the gospel which St. Paul preached, and was all that he knew necessary to salvation; viz. "Repentance, and believing Jesus to "be the Messiah:" and so takes his last farewell of them, whom he should never see again, ver. 32, in these words, "And now, brethren, I commend you to "God, and to the word of his grace, which is able to "build you up, and to give you an inheritance among "all them that are sanctified." There is an inheritance conveyed by the word and covenant of grace; but it is only to those who are sanctified.

Acts xxiv. 24, "When Felix sent for Paul," that he and his wife Drusilla might hear him, "concerning the
"faith

" faith in Chrift;" Paul reafoned of righteoufnefs, or juftice; and temperance; the duties we owe to others, and to ourfelves; and of the judgment to come; until he made Felix to tremble. Whereby it appears, that " temperance and juftice" were fundamental parts of the religion that Paul profeffed, and were contained in the faith which he preached. And if we find the duties of the moral law not preffed by him every where, we muft remember, that moft of his fermons left upon record, were preached in their fynagogues to the jews, who acknowledged their obedience due to all the precepts of the law; and would have taken it amifs to have been fufpected not to have been more zealous for the law than he. And therefore it was with reafon that his difcourfes were directed chiefly to what they yet wanted, and were averfe to, the knowledge and embracing of Jefus, their promifed Meffiah. But what his preaching generally was, if we will believe him himfelf, we may fee Acts xxvi, where giving an account to king Agrippa, of his life and doctrine, he tells him, ver. 20, " I " fhowed unto them of Damafcus, and at Jerufalem, " and throughout all the coafts of Judea, and then to " the gentiles, that they fhould repent, and turn to " God, and do works meet for repentance."

Thus we fee, by the preaching of our Saviour and his apoftles, that he required of thofe who believed him to be the Meffiah, and received him for their Lord and Deliverer, that they fhould live by his laws: and that (though in confideration of their becoming his fubjects, by faith in him, whereby they believed and took him to be the Meffiah, their former fins fhould be forgiven, yet) he would own none to be his, nor receive them as true denizens of the new Jerufalem, into the inheritance of eternal life; but leave them to the condemnation of the unrighteous; who renounced not their former mifcarriages, and lived in a fincere obedience to his commands. What he expects from his followers, he has fufficiently declared as a legiflator: and that they may not be deceived, by miftaking the doctrine of faith, grace, free-grace, and the pardon and forgivenefs of fins, and falvation by him, (which was the great end of his coming) he more than once declares to them, for what omissions and miscarriages he shall judge and condemn to death, even those who have owned him, and done miracles in his name: when he comes at last to render to every one according to what he had DONE in the flesh, sitting upon his great and glorious tribunal, at the end of the world.

The first place where we find our Saviour to have mentioned the day of judgment, is John v. 28, 29, in these words: " The hour is coming, in which all that " are in their graves shall hear his [i. e. the Son of " God's] voice, and shall come forth; they that have " DONE GOOD, unto the resurrection of life; and they " that have DONE EVIL, unto the resurrection of damna- " tion." That which puts the distinction, if we will believe our Saviour, is the having done good or evil. And he gives a reason of the necessity of his judging or condemning those " who have done evil," in the following words, ver. 30, " I can of myself do nothing. " As I hear I judge; and my judgment is just; be- " cause I seek not my own will, but the will of my Fa- " ther who hath sent me." He could not judge of himself; he had but a delegated power of judging from the Father, whose will he obeyed in it; and who was of purer eyes than to admit any unjust person into the kingdom of heaven.

Matt. vii. 22, 23, speaking again of that day, he tells what his sentence will be, " Depart from me, ye WORK- " ERS of iniquity." Faith in the penitent and sincerely obedient, supplies the defect of their performances; and so by grace they are made just. But we may observe, none are sentenced or punished for unbelief, but only for their misdeeds. " They are workers of iniquity" on whom the sentence is pronounced.

Matt. xiii. 41, " At the end of the world, the Son of " man shall send forth his angels; and they shall ga- " ther out of his kingdom all scandals, and them which " DO INIQUITY; and cast them into a furnace of fire; " there shall be wailing and gnashing of teeth." And again, ver. 49, " The angels shall sever the WICKED " from

" from among the JUST; and fhall caft them into the
" furnace of fire."

Matt. xvi. 24. " For the Son of man fhall come in
" the glory of his Father, with his angels: and then he
" fhall reward every man according to his WORKS."

Luke xiii. 26, " Then fhall ye begin to fay, We have
" eaten and drank in thy prefence, and thou haft taught
" in our ftreets. But he fhall fay, I tell you, I know
" you not; depart from me, ye workers of iniquity."

Matt. xxv. 31—46, " When the Son of man fhall
" come in his glory; and before him fhall be gathered
" all nations; he fhall fet the fheep on his right hand,
" and the goats on his left. Then fhall the King fay
" to them on his right hand, Come, ye bleffed of my
" Father, inherit the kingdom prepared for you from
" the foundation of the world; for I was an hungred,
" and ye gave me meat; I was thirfty, and ye gave me
" drink; I was a ftranger, and ye took me in; naked,
" and ye clothed me; I was fick and ye vifited me; I
" was in prifon, and ye came unto me. Then fhall the
" righteous anfwer him, faying, Lord, when faw we
" thee an hungred, and fed thee? &c. And the King
" fhall anfwer and fay unto them, Verily, I fay unto
" you, Inafmuch as ye have done it unto one of the
" leaft of thefe my brethren, ye have done it unto me.
" Then fhall he fay unto them on the left hand, Depart
" from me, ye curfed, into everlafting fire, prepared for
" the devil and his angels: for I was an hungred, and
" ye gave me no meat; I was thirfty, and ye gave me
" no drink; I was a ftranger, and ye took me not in;
" naked, and ye clothed me not; fick, and in prifon,
" and ye vifited me not.. Infomuch that ye did it not
" to one of thefe, ye did it not to me. And thefe fhall
" go into everlafting punifhment; but the righteous
" into life eternal."

Thefe, I think, are all the places where our Saviour
mentions the laft judgment, or defcribes his way of proceeding in that great day; wherein, as we have obferved, it is remarkable, that every-where the fentence
follows doing or not doing, without any mention of believing or not believing. Not that any, to whom the

gofpel

gospel hath been preached, shall be saved, without believing Jesus to be the Messiah: for all being sinners, and transgressors of the law, and so unjust; are all liable to condemnation; unless they believe, and so through grace are justified by God, for this faith, which shall be accounted to them for righteousness. But the rest wanting this cover, this allowance for their transgressions, must answer for all their actions; and being found transgressors of the law, shall, by the letter and sanction of that law, be condemned, for not having paid a full obedience to that law; and not for want of faith. That is not the guilt on which the punishment is laid; though it be the want of faith, which lays open their guilt uncovered; and exposes them to the sentence of the law, against all that are unrighteous.

The common objection here, is, If all sinners shall be condemned, but such as have a gracious allowance made them; and so are justified by God, for believing Jesus to be the Messiah, and so taking him for their King, whom they are resolved to obey to the utmost of their power; "What shall become of all mankind, who " lived before our Saviour's time, who never heard of " his name, and consequently could not believe in " him?" To this the answer is so obvious and natural, that one would wonder how any reasonable man should think it worth the urging. No body was, or can be required to believe, what was never proposed to him to believe. Before the fulness of time, which God from the counsel of his own wisdom had appointed to send his Son in, he had, at several times, and in different manners, promised to the people of Israel, an extraordinary person to come; who, raised from amongst themselves, should be their Ruler and Deliverer. The time, and other circumstances of his birth, life, and person, he had in sundry prophecies so particularly described, and so plainly foretold, that he was well known, and expected by the jews, under the name of the Messiah, or Anointed, given him in some of these prophesies. All then that was required, before his appearing in the world, was to believe what God had revealed, and to rely with a full assurance on God, for the performance

of

of his promife; and to believe, that in due time he
would fend them the Meffiah, this anointed King, this
promifed Saviour and Deliverer, according to his word.
This faith in the promifes of God, this relying and ac-
quiefcing in his word and faithfulnefs, the Almighty
takes well at our hands, as a great mark of homage, paid
by us poor frail creatures, to his goodnefs and truth,
as well as to his power and wifdom: and accepts it as
an acknowledgment of his peculiar providence, and be-
nignity to us. And therefore our Saviour tells us, John
xii. 44, " He that believes on me, believes not on me,
" but on him that fent me." The works of nature fhow
his wifdom and power: but it is his peculiar care of
mankind moft eminently difcovered in his promifes to
them, that fhows his bounty and goodnefs; and confequently engages their hearts in love and affection to
him. This oblation of an heart, fixed with dependence
on, and affection to him, is the moft acceptable tribute
we can pay him, the foundation of true devotion, and
life of all religion. What a value he puts on this depending on his word, and refting fatisfied in his promifes, we have an example in Abraham; whofe faith
" was counted to him for righteoufnefs," as we have
before remarked out of Rom. iv. And his relying firmly
on the promife of God, without any doubt of its performance, gave him the name of the father of the faithful; and gained him fo much favour with the Almighty,
that he was called the " friend of God;" the higheft
and moft glorious title that can be beftowed on a creature. The thing promifed was no more but a fon by
his wife Sarah; and a numerous pofterity by him, which
fhould poffefs the land of Canaan. Thefe were but
temporal bleffings, and (except the birth of a fon) very
remote, fuch as he fhould never live to fee, nor in his
own perfon have the benefit of. But becaufe he queftioned not the performance of it; but refted fully fatisfied in the goodnefs, truth, and faithfulnefs of God,
who had promifed, it was counted to him for righteoufnefs. Let us fee how St. Paul expreffes it, Rom. iv.
18—22, " Who, againft hope, believed in hope, that
" he might become the father of many nations; ac-

" cording to that which was spoken, So shall thy seed
" be. And being not weak in faith, he considered not
" his own body now dead, when he was above an hun-
" dred years old, neither yet the deadness of Sarah's
" womb. He staggered not at the promise of God
" through unbelief, but was strong in faith: giving
" glory to God, and being fully persuaded, that what
" he had promised he was able to perform. And
" THEREFORE it was imputed to him for righteousness."
St. Paul having here emphatically described the strength
and firmness of Abraham's faith, informs us, that he
thereby " gave glory to God;" and therefore it was
" accounted to him for righteousness." This is the
way that God deals with poor frail mortals. He is
graciously pleased to take it well of them, and give it
the place of righteousness, and a kind of merit in his
sight; if they believe his promises, and have a stedfast
relying on his veracity and goodness. St. Paul, Heb.
xi. 6, tells us, " Without faith it is impossible to please
" God:" but at the same time tells us what faith that
is. " For," says he, " he that cometh to God, must
" believe that he is ; and that he is a rewarder of them
" that diligently seek him." He must be persuaded of
God's mercy and goodwill to those who seek to obey
him ; and rest assured of his rewarding those who rely
on him, for whatever, either by the light of nature, or
particular promises, he has revealed to them of his tender mercies, and taught them to expect from his bounty.
This description of faith, (that we might not mistake
what he means by that faith, without which we cannot
please God, and which recommended the saints of old)
St. Paul places in the middle of the list of those who
were eminent for their faith ; and whom he sets as pat-
terns to the converted Hebrews, under persecution, to
encourage them to persist in their confidence of deliverance by the coming of Jesus Christ, and in their belief of the promises they now had under the gospel. By
those examples he exhorts them not to " draw back"
from the hope that was set before them, nor apostatize
from the profession of the christian religion. This is
plain from ver. 35—38, of the precedent chapter:
" Cast

" Caſt not away therefore your confidence, which hath
" great recompence of reward. For ye have great need
" of perſiſting or perſeverance ;" (for ſo the greek word
ſignifies here, which our tranſlation renders " patience."
Vide Luke viii. 15.) " that after ye have done the will
" of God, ye might receive the promiſe. For yet a
" little while, and he that ſhall come will come, and
" will not tarry. Now the juſt ſhall live by faith. But
" if any man draw back, my ſoul ſhall have no plea-
" ſure in him."

The examples of faith, which St. Paul enumerates and
propoſes in the following words, chap. xi, plainly ſhow,
that the faith whereby thoſe believers of old pleaſed God,
was nothing but a ſtedfaſt reliance on the goodneſs and
faithfulneſs of God, for thoſe good things, which either
the light of nature, or particular promiſes, had given
them grounds to hope for. Of what avail this faith was
with God, we may ſee, ver. 4, " By faith Abel offered
" unto God a more excellent ſacrifice than Cain ; by
" which he obtained witneſs that he was righteous."
Ver. 5, " By faith Enoch was tranſlated, that he ſhould
" not ſee death : for before his tranſlation he had this
" teſtimony, that he pleaſed God." Ver. 7, " Noah
" being warned of God of things not ſeen as yet ;" being
wary, " by faith prepared an ark, to the ſaving of his
" houſe ; by the which he condemned the world, and
" became heir of the righteouſneſs which is by faith."
And what it was that God ſo graciouſly accepted and
rewarded, we are told, ver. 11, " Through faith alſo
" Sarah herſelf received ſtrength to conceive ſeed, and
" was delivered of a child, when ſhe was paſt age."
How ſhe came to obtain this grace from God, the
apoſtle tells us, " Becauſe ſhe judged him faithful who
" had promiſed." Thoſe therefore, who pleaſed God,
and were accepted by him before the coming of Chriſt,
did it only by believing the promiſes, and relying on
the goodneſs of God, as far as he had revealed it to
them. For the apoſtle, in the following words, tells us,
ver. 13, " Theſe all died in faith, not having received
" (the accompliſhment of) the promiſes ; but having
" ſeen them afar off : and were perſuaded of them, and

K 2   " embraced

" embraced them." This was all that was required of
them; to be persuaded of, and embrace the promises
which they had. They could be " persuaded of " no
more than was proposed to them; " embrace" no more
than was revealed; according to the promises they had
received, and the dispensations they were under. And if
the faith of things " seen afar off;" if their trusting in
God for the promises he then gave them; if a belief of
the Messiah to come; were sufficient to render those who
lived in the ages before Christ acceptable to God, and
righteous before him : I desire those who tell us, that
God will not (nay, some go so far as to say, cannot) accept any, who do not believe every article of their particular creeds and systems, to consider, why God, out of
his infinite mercy, cannot as well justify men now, for
believing Jesus of Nazareth to be the promised Messiah,
the King and Deliverer; as those heretofore, who believed only that God would, according to his promise,
in due time, send the Messiah, to be a King and Deliverer.

There is another difficulty often to be met with,
which seems to have something of more weight in it :
and that is, that " though the faith of those before
" Christ, (believing that God would send the Messiah,
" to be a Prince and a Saviour to his people, as he had
" promised) and the faith of those since his time, (be-
" lieving Jesus to be that Messiah, promised and sent
" by God) shall be accounted to them for righteous-
" ness; yet what shall become of all the rest of man-
" kind, who, having never heard of the promise or
" news of a Saviour; not a word of a Messiah to be
" sent, or that was come; have had no thought or be-
" lief concerning him ?"

To this I answer; that God will require of every man,
" according to what a man hath, and not according to
" what he hath not." He will not expect the im-
provement of ten talents, where he gave but one; nor
require any one should believe a promise of which he
has never heard. The apostle's reasoning, Rom. x. 14,
is very just : " How shall they believe in him, of whom
" they have not heard ?" But though there be many,
who

who being ftrangers to the commonwealth of Ifrael, were alfo ftrangers to the oracles of God, committed to that people; Many, to whom the promife of the Meffiah never came, and fo were never in a capacity to believe or reject that revelation; yet God had, by the light of reafon, revealed to all mankind, who would make ufe of that light, that he was good and merciful. The fame fpark of the divine nature and knowledge in man, which making him a man, fhowed him the law he was under, as a man; fhowed him alfo the way of atoning the merciful, kind, compaffionate Author and Father of him and his being, when he had tranfgreffed that law. He that made ufe of this candle of the Lord, fo far as to find what was his duty, could not mifs to find alfo the way to reconciliation and forgivenefs, when he had failed of his duty: though, if he ufed not his reafon this way, if he put out or neglected this light, he might, perhaps, fee neither.

The law is the eternal, immutable ftandard of right. And a part of that law is, that a man fhould forgive, not only his children, but his enemies, upon their repentance, afking pardon, and amendment. And therefore he could not doubt that the author of this law, and God of patience and confolation, who is rich in mercy, would forgive his frail offspring, if they acknowledged their faults, difapproved the iniquity of their tranfgreffions, begged his pardon, and refolved in earneft, for the future, to conform their actions to this rule, which they owned to be juft and right. This way of reconciliation, this hope of atonement, the light of nature revealed to them: and the revelation of the gofpel, having faid nothing to the contrary, leaves them to ftand and fall to their own Father and Mafter, whofe goodnefs and mercy is over all his works.

I know fome are forward to urge that place of the Acts, chap. iv, as contrary to this. The words, ver. 10 and 12, ftand thus: " Be it known unto you all, and " to all the people of Ifrael, that by the name of Jefus " Chrift of Nazareth, whom ye crucified, whom God " raifed from the dead, even by him, doth this man" [i. e. the lame man reftored by Peter] " ftand here be-

K 3 " fore

" fore you whole. This is the stone which is set at
" nought by you builders, which is become the head of
" the corner. Neither is there salvation in any other:
" for there is none other name under heaven given
" among men, in which we must be saved." Which,
in short, is, that Jesus is the only true Messiah, neither
is there any other person, but he, given to be a mediator
between God and man; in whose name we may ask, and
hope for salvation.

It will here possibly be asked, " Quorsum perditio
" hæc?" What need was there of a Saviour? What advantage have we by Jesus Christ?

It is enough to justify the fitness of any thing to be
done, by resolving it into the " wisdom of God," who
has done it; though our short views, and narrow understandings, may utterly incapacitate us to see that wisdom, and to judge rightly of it. We know little of this
visible, and nothing at all of the state of that intellectual
world, wherein are infinite numbers and degrees of spirits out of the reach of our ken, or guess; and therefore
know not what transactions there were between God
and our Saviour, in reference to his kingdom. We
know not what need there was to set up an head and a
chieftain, in opposition to " the prince of this world,
" the prince of the power of the air," &c. whereof
there are more than obscure intimations in scripture.
And we shall take too much upon us, if we shall call God's
wisdom or providence to account, and pertly condemn
for needless, all that our weak, and perhaps biassed, understanding cannot account for.

Though this general answer be reply enough to the
forementioned demand, and such as a rational man, or
fair searcher after truth, will acquiesce in; yet in this
particular case, the wisdom and goodness of God has
shown itself so visibly to common apprehensions, that it
hath furnished us abundantly wherewithal to satisfy the
curious and inquisitive; who will not take a blessing,
unless they be instructed what need they had of it, and
why it was bestowed upon them. The great and many
advantages we receive by the coming of Jesus the Messiah,

fiah, will fhow, that it was not without need, that he was fent into the world.

The evidence of our Saviour's miffion from heaven is fo great, in the multitude of miracles he did before all all forts of people, that what he delivered cannot but be received as the oracles of God, and unqueftionable verity. For the miracles he did were fo ordered by the divine providence and wifdom, that they never were, nor could be denied by any of the enemies, or oppofers of chriftianity.

Though the works of nature, in every part of them, fufficiently evidence a Deity; yet the world made fo little ufe of their reafon, that they faw him not, where, even by the impreffions of himfelf, he was eafy to be found. Senfe and luft blinded their minds in fome, and a carelefs inadvertency in others, and fearful apprehenfions in moft (who either believed there were, or could not but fufpect there might be, fuperiour unknown beings) gave them up into the hands of their priefts, to fill their heads with falfe notions of the Deity, and their worfhip with foolifh rites, as they pleafed: and what dread or craft once began, devotion foon made facred, and religion immutable. In this ftate of darknefs and ignorance of the true God, vice and fuperftition held the world. Nor could any help be had, or hoped for from reafon; which could not be heard, and was judged to have nothing to do in the cafe; the priefts, every where, to fecure their empire, having excluded reafon from having any thing to do in religion. And in the crowd of wrong notions, and invented rites, the world had almoft loft the fight of the one only true God. The rational and thinking part of mankind, it is true, when they fought after him, they found the one fupreme, invifible God; but if they acknowledged and worfhipped him, it was only in their own minds. They kept this truth locked up in their own breafts as a fecret, nor ever durft venture it amongft the people; much lefs amongft the priefts, thofe wary guardians of their own creeds and profitable inventions. Hence we fee, that reafon, fpeaking ever fo clearly to the wife and virtuous, had never authority enough to prevail on the multitude; and to

K 4 perfuade

persuade the societies of men, that there was but one God, that alone was to be owned and worshipped. The belief and worship of one God, was the national religion of the Israelites alone: and if we will consider it, it was introduced and supported amongst the people by revelation. They were in Goshen, and had light, whilst the rest of the world were in almost Egyptian darkness, " without God in the world." There was no part of mankind, who had quicker parts, or improved them more; that had a greater light of reason, or followed it farther in all sorts of speculations, than the Athenians: and yet we find but one Socrates amongst them, that opposed and laughed at their polytheism, and wrong opinions of the Deity; and we see how they rewarded him for it: Whatsoever Plato, and the soberest of the philosophers, thought of the nature and being of the one God, they were fain, in their outward professions and worship, to go with the herd, and keep to the religion established by law: which what it was, and how it had disposed the minds of these knowing and quick-sighted Grecians, St. Paul tells us, Acts xvii. 22—29, " Ye " men of Athens," says he, " I perceive, that in all " things ye are too superstitious. For as I passed by, " and beheld your devotions, I found an altar with this " inscription, TO THE UNKNOWN GOD. Whom there-" fore ye ignorantly worship, him declare I unto you. " God that made the world, and all things therein, see-" ing that he is Lord of heaven and earth, dwelleth " not in temples made with hands: neither is wor-" shipped with men's hands, as though he needed any " thing, seeing that he giveth unto all life, and breath, " and all things; and hath made of one blood all the " nations of men, for to dwell on the face of the earth; " and hath determined the times before appointed, and " the bounds of their habitations; that they should seek " the Lord, if haply they might feel him out and find " him, though he be not far from every one of us." Here he tells the Athenians, that they, and the rest of the world (given up to superstition) whatever light there was in the works of creation and providence, to lead them to the true God; yet few of them found him,

He

He was every where near them; yet they were but like people groping and feeling for fomething in the dark, and did not fee him with a full and clear day-light; " But thought the Godhead like to gold and filver, and " ftone, graven by art and man's device."

In this ftate of darknefs and errour, in reference to the " true God," our Saviour found the world. But the clear revelation he brought with him, diffipated this darknefs; made the " one invifible true God" known to the world: and that with fuch evidence and energy, that polytheifm and idolatry have no where been able to withftand it: but wherever the preaching of the truth he delivered, and the light of the gofpel hath come, thofe mifts have been difpelled. And, in effect, we fee, that fince our Saviour's time, the " belief of one " God" has prevailed and fpread itfelf over the face of the earth. For even to the light that the Meffiah brought into the world with him, we muft afcribe the owning and profeffion of one God, which the Mahometan religion hath derived and borrowed from it. So that in this fenfe it is certainly and manifeftly true of our Saviour, what St. John fays of him, 1 John iii. 8, " For " this purpofe the Son of God was manifefted, that he " might deftroy the works of the devil." This light the world needed, and this light is received from him: that there is but " one God," and he " eternal, invifi- " ble;" not like to any vifible objects, nor to be reprefented by them.

If it be afked, whether the revelation to the patriarchs by Mofes did not teach this, and why that was not enough? The anfwer is obvious; that however clearly the knowledge of one invifible God, maker of heaven and earth, was revealed to them; yet that revelation was fhut up in a little corner of the world; amongft a people, by that very law, which they received with it, excluded from a commerce and communication with the reft of mankind. The Gentile world, in our Saviour's time, and feveral ages before, could have no atteftation of the miracles on which the Hebrews built their faith, but from the Jews themfelves, a people not known to the greateft part of mankind; contemned

and

and thought vilely of, by those nations that did know them; and therefore very unfit and unable to propagate the doctrine of one God in the world, and diffuse it through the nations of the earth, by the strength and force of that ancient revelation, upon which they had received it. But our Saviour, when he came, threw down this wall of partition; and did not confine his miracles or message to the land of Canaan, or the worshippers at Jerusalem. But he himself preached at Samaria, and did miracles in the borders of Tyre and Sidon, and before multitudes of people gathered from all quarters. And after his resurrection, sent his apostles amongst the nations, accompanied with miracles; which were done in all parts so frequently, and before so many witnesses of all sorts, in broad day-light, that, as I have before observed, the enemies of christianity have never dared to deny them; no, not Julian himself: who neither wanted skill nor power to inquire into the truth: nor would have failed to have proclaimed and exposed it, if he could have detected any falshood in the history of the gospel; or found the least ground to question the matter of fact published of Christ and his apostles. The number and evidence of the miracles done by our Saviour and his followers, by the power and force of truth, bore down this mighty and accomplished emperor, and all his parts, in his own dominions. He durst not deny so plain a matter of fact, which being granted, the truth of our Saviour's doctrine and mission unavoidably follows; notwithstanding whatsoever artful suggestions his wit could invent, or malice should offer to the contrary.

Next to the knowledge of one God; maker of all things; " a clear knowledge of their duty was wanting " to mankind." This part of knowledge, though cultivated with some care by some of the heathen philosophers, yet got little footing among the people. All men, indeed, under pain of displeasing the gods, were to frequent the temples: every one went to their sacrifices and services: but the priests made it not their business to teach them virtue. If they were diligent in their observations and ceremonies; punctual

in

in their feafts and folemnities, and the tricks of religion ; the holy tribe affured them the gods were pleafed, and they looked no farther. Few went to the fchools of the philofophers to be inftructed in their duties, and to know what was good and evil in their actions. The priefts fold the better pennyworths, and therefore had all the cuftom. Luftrations and proceffions were much eafier than a clean confcience, and a fteady courfe of virtue ; and an expiatory facrifice that atoned for the want of it, was much more convenient than a ftrict and holy life. No wonder then, that religion was every where diftinguifhed from, and preferred to virtue ; and that it was dangerous herefy and profanenefs to think the contrary. So much virtue as was neceffary to hold focieties together, and to contribute to the quiet of governments, the civil laws of commonwealths taught, and forced upon men that lived under magiftrates. But thefe laws being for the moft part made by fuch, who had no other aims but their own power, reached no farther than thofe things that would ferve to tie men together in fubjection ; or at moft were directly to conduce to the profperity and temporal happinefs of any people. But natural religion, in its full extent, was no where, that I know, taken care of, by the force of natural reafon. It fhould feem, by the little that has hitherto been done in it, that it is too hard a tafk for unaffifted reafon to eftablifh morality in all its parts, upon its true foundation, with a clear and convincing light. And it is at leaft a furer and fhorter way, to the apprehenfions of the vulgar, and mafs of mankind, that one manifeftly fent from God, and coming with vifible authority from him, fhould, as a king and law-maker, tell them their duties ; and require their obedience ; than leave it to the long and fometimes intricate deductions of reafon, to be made out to them. Such trains of reafoning the greateft part of mankind have neither leifure to weigh ; nor, for want of education and ufe, fkill to judge of. We fee how unfuccefsful in this the attempts of philofophers were before our Saviour's time. How fhort their feveral fyftems came of the perfection of a true and complete morality, is

9   very

very visible. And if, since that, the christian philosophers have much out-done them ; yet we may observe,
that the first knowledge of the truths they have added,
is owing to revelation : though as soon they are heard
and considered, they are found to be agreeable to reason; and such as can by no means be contradicted.
Every one may observe a great many truths, which he
receives at first from others, and readily assents to, as
consonant to reason, which he would have found it
hard, and perhaps beyond his strength, to have discovered himself. Native and original truth is not so
easily wrought out of the mine, as we, who have it delivered already dug and fashioned into our hands, are
apt to imagine. And how often at fifty or threescore
years old are thinking men told what they wonder how
they could miss thinking of ? Which yet their own
contemplations did not, and possibly never would have
helped them to. Experience shows, that the knowledge
of morality, by mere natural light, (how agreeable soever it be to it) makes but a slow progress, and little
advance in the world. And the reason of it is not hard
to be found in men's necessities, passions, vices, and
mistaken interests ; which turn their thoughts another
way : and the designing leaders, as well as following
herd, find it not to their purpose to employ much of
their meditations this way. Or whatever else was the
cause, it is plain, in fact, that human reason unassisted
failed men in its great and proper business of morality.
It never from unquestionable principles, by clear deductions, made out an entire body of the " law of na-
" ture." And he that shall collect all the moral rules
of the philosophers, and compare them with those contained in the New Testament, will find them to come
short of the morality delivered by our Saviour, and
taught by his apostles; a college made up, for the most
part, of ignorant, but inspired fishermen.

Though yet, if any one should think, that out of the
sayings of the wise heathens before our Saviour's time,
there might be a collection made of all those rules of
morality, which are to be found in the christian religion; yet this would not at all hinder, but that the
world,

world, neverthelefs, ftood as much in need of our Saviour, and the morality delivered by him. Let it be
granted (though not true) that all the moral precepts
of the gofpel were known by fomebody or other, amongft
mankind before. But where, or how, or of what ufe, is
not confidered. Suppofe they may be picked up here
and there; fome from Solon and Bias in Greece, others
from Tully in Italy: and to complete the work, let
Confucius, as far as China, be confulted; and Anachar-
fis, the Scythian, contribute his fhare. What will all
this do, to give the world a complete morality, that may
be to mankind the unqueftionable rule of life and manners? I will not here urge the impoffibility of collecting
from men, fo far diftant from one another, in time and
place, and languages. I will fuppofe there was a Sto-
beus in thofe times, who had gathered the moral fayings
from all the fages of the world. What would this
amount to, towards being a fteady rule; a certain tranf-
cript of a law that we are under? Did the faying of
Ariftippus, or Confucius, give it an authority? Was
Zeno a law-giver to mankind? If not, what he or any
other philofopher delivered, was but a faying of his.
Mankind might hearken to it, or reject it, as they pleafed; or as it fuited their intereft, paffions, principles or
humours. They were under no obligation; the opinion
of this or that philofopher was of no authority. And
if it were, you muft take all he faid under the fame character. All his dictates muft go for law, certain and
true; or none of them. And then, if you will take any
of the moral fayings of Epicurus (many whereof Seneca
quotes with efteem and approbation) for precepts of the
law of nature, you muft take all the reft of his doctrine
for fuch too; or elfe his authority ceafes: and fo no
more is to be received from him, or any of the fages of
old, for parts of the law of nature, as carrying with it an
obligation to be obeyed, but what they prove to be fo.
But fuch a body of ethics, proved to be the law of nature, from principles of reafon, and teaching all the
duties of life; I think nobody will fay the world had
before our Saviour's time. It is not enough, that there
were up and down fcattered fayings of wife men, con-
                                                    formable

formable to right reason. The law of nature, is the law
of convenience too : and it is no wonder, that those men
of parts, and studious of virtue (who had occasion to
think on any particular part of it) should, by meditation,
light on the right even from the observable convenience
and beauty of it ; without making out its obligation
from the true principles of the law of nature, and foundations of morality. But these incoherent apophthegms
of philosophers, and wise men, however excellent in
themselves, and well intended by them ; could never
make a morality, whereof the world could be convinced ; could never rise to the force of a law, that
mankind could with certainty depend on. Whatsoever
should thus be universally useful, as a standard to which
men should conform their manners, must have its authority, either from reason or revelation. It is not every
writer of morality, or compiler of it from others, that
can thereby be erected into a law-giver to mankind ;
and a dictator of rules, which are therefore valid, because they are to be found in his books ; under the authority of this or that philosopher. He, that any one
will pretend to set up in this kind, and have his rules
pass for authentic directions, must show, that either he
builds his doctrine upon principles of reason, self-evi-
dent in themselves ; and that he deduces all the parts
of it from thence, by clear and evident demonstration :
or must show his commission from heaven, that he
comes with authority from God, to deliver his will and
commands to the world. In the former way, no-body
that I know, before our Saviour's time, ever did, or
went about to give us a morality. It is true, there is a
law of nature : but who is there that ever did, or undertook to give it us all entire, as a law ; no more, nor no
less, than what was contained in, and had the obligation
of that law ? Who ever made out all the parts of it, put
them together, and showed the world their obligation ?
Where was there any such code, that mankind might
have recourse to, as their unerring rule, before our Saviour's time ? If there was not, it is plain there was
need of one to give us such a morality ; such a law,
which might be the sure guide of those who had a desire

to

to go right; and, if they had a mind, need not miftake their duty, but might be certain when they had performed, when failed in it. Such a law of morality Jefus Chrift hath given us in the New Teftament; but by the latter of thefe ways, by revelation. We have from him a full and fufficient rule for our direction, and conformable to that of reafon. But the truth and obligation of its precepts have their force, and are put paft doubt to us, by the evidence of his miffion. He was fent by God: his miracles fhow it; and the authority of God in his precepts cannot be queftioned. Here morality has a fure ftandard, that revelation vouches, and reafon cannot gainfay, nor queftion; but both together witnefs to come from God the great law-maker. And fuch an one as this, out of the New Teftament, I think the world never had, nor can any one fay, is any where elfe to be found. Let me afk any one, who is forward to think that the doctrine of morality was full and clear in the world, at our Saviour's birth; whither would he have directed Brutus and Caffius, (both men of parts and virtue, the one whereof believed, and the other difbelieved a future being) to be fatisfied in the rules and obligations of all the parts of their duties; if they fhould have afked him, Where they might find the law they were to live by, and by which they fhould be charged, or acquitted, as guilty, or innocent? If to the fayings of the wife, and the declarations of philofophers, he fends them into a wild wood of uncertainty, to an endlefs maze, from which they fhould never get out: if to the religions of the world, yet worfe: and if to their own reafon, he refers them to that which had fome light and certainty; but yet had hitherto failed all mankind in a perfect rule; and, we fee, refolved not the doubts that had rifen amongft the ftudious and thinking philofophers; nor had yet been able to convince the civilized parts of the world, that they had not given, nor could, without a crime, take away the lives of their children, by expofing them.

If any one fhall think to excufe human nature, by laying blame on men's negligence, that they did not carry morality to an higher pitch; and make it out entire

tire in every part, with that clearnefs of demonftration which fome think it capable of; he helps not the matter. Be the caufe what it will, our Saviour found mankind under a corruption of manners and principles, which ages after ages had prevailed, and muft be confeffed, was not in a way or tendency to be mended. The rules of morality were in different countries and fects different. And natural reafon no where had cured, nor was like to cure the defects and errours in them. Thofe juft meafures of right and wrong, which neceffity had any where introduced, the civil laws prefcribed, or philofophy recommended, ftood on their true foundations. They were looked on as bonds of fociety, and conveniencies of common life, and laudable practices. But where was it that their obligation was thoroughly known and allowed, and they received as precepts of a law; of the higheft law, the law of nature? That could not be, without a clear knowledge and acknowledgement of the law-maker, and the great rewards and punifhments, for thofe that would, or would not obey him. But the religion of the heathens, as was before obferved, little concerned itfelf in their morals. The priefts, that delivered the oracles of heaven, and pretended to fpeak from the gods, fpoke little of virtue and a good life. And, on the other fide, the philofophers, who fpoke from reafon, made not much mention of the Deity in their ethics. They depended on reafon and her oracles, which contain nothing but truth: but yet fome parts of that truth lie too deep for our natural powers eafily to reach, and make plain and vifible to mankind; without fome light from above to direct them. When truths are once known to us, though by tradition, we are apt to be favourable to our own parts; and afcribe to our own underftandings the difcovery of what, in reality, we borrowed from others: or, at leaft, finding we can prove, what at firft we learn from others, we are forward to conclude it an obvious truth, which, if we had fought, we could not have miffed. Nothing feems hard to our underftandings that is once known: and becaufe what we fee, we fee with our own eyes; we are apt to overlook, or forget the help we had from others

who

who fhowed it us, and firft made us fee it; as if we
were not at all beholden to them, for thofe truths they
opened the way to, and led us into. For knowledge
being only of truths that are perceived to be fo, we are
favourable enough to our own faculties, to conclude,
that they of their own ftrength would have attained
thofe difcoveries, without any foreign affiftance; and
that we know thofe truths, by the ftrength and native
light of our own minds, as they did from whom we received them by theirs, only they had the luck to be before us. Thus the whole ftock of human knowledge is
claimed by every one, as his private poffeffion, as foon
as he (profiting by others difcoveries) has got it into
his own mind: and fo it is; but not properly by his
own fingle induftry, nor of his own acquifition. He
ftudies, it is true, and takes pains to make a progrefs in
what others have delivered: but their pains were of
another fort, who firft brought thofe truths to light,
which he afterwards derives from them. He that tra-
vels the roads now, applauds his own ftrength and legs
that have carried him fo far in fuch a fcantling of time;
and afcribes all to his own vigour; little confidering
how much he owes to their pains, who cleared the
woods, drained the bogs, built the bridges, and made
the ways paffable; without which he might have toiled
much with little progrefs. A great many things which
we have been bred up in the belief of, from our cradles,
(and are notions grown familiar, and, as it were, natural
to us, under the gofpel) we take for unqueftionable obvious truths, and eafily demonftrable; without confidering how long we might have been in doubt or ignorance of them, had revelation been filent. And many
are beholden to revelation, who do not acknowledge it.
It is no diminifhing to revelation, that reafon gives its
fuffrage too, to the truths revelation has difcovered.
But it is our miftake to think, that becaufe reafon confirms them to us, we had the firft certain knowledge of
them from thence; and in that clear evidence we now
poffefs them. The contrary is manifeft, in the defective morality of the gentiles, before our Saviour's time;
and the want of reformation in the principles and meafures of it, as well as practice. Philofophy feemed to

have fpent its ftrength, and done its utmoft : or if it
fhould have gone farther, as we fee it did not, and
from undeniable principles given us ethics in a fcience
like mathematics, in every part demonftrable ; this
yet would not have been fo effectual to man in this
imperfect ftate, nor proper for the cure.   The greateft
part of mankind want leifure or capacity for demonftration ; nor can carry a train of proofs, which in that way
they muft always depend upon for conviction, and cannot be required to affent to, until they fee the demonftration.   Wherever they ftick, the teachers are always
put upon proof, and muft clear the doubt by a thread
of coherent deductions from the firft principle, how
long, or how intricate foever they be.   And you may as
foon hope to have all the day-labourers and tradefmen,
the fpinfters and dairy-maids, perfect mathematicians,
as to have them perfect in ethics this way.   Hearing
plain commands, is the fure and only courfe to bring
them to obedience and practice. The greateft part cannot know, and therefore they muft believe.   And I afk,
whether one coming from heaven in the power of God,
in full and clear evidence and demonftration of miracles, giving plain and direct rules of morality and obedience ; be not likelier to enlighten the bulk of mankind, and fet them right in their duties, and bring them
to do them, than by reafoning with them from general
notions and principles of human reafon ? And were all
the duties of human life clearly demonftrated, yet I
conclude, when well confidered, that method of teaching men their duties would be thought proper only for
a few, who had much leifure, improved underftandings,
and were ufed to abftract reafonings.   But the inftruction of the people were beft ftill to be left to the precepts and principles of the gofpel.   The healing of the
fick, the reftoring fight to the blind by a word, the raif-
ing and being raifed from the dead, are matters of fact,
which they can without difficulty conceive, and that he
who does fuch things, muft do them by the affiftance of
a divine power.   Thefe things lie level to the ordina-
rieft apprehenfion : he that can diftinguifh between fick
and well, lame and found, dead and alive, is capable of
this doctrine.   To one who is once perfuaded that Jefus
                                                        Chrift

Chrift was fent by God to be a King, and a Saviour of thofe who do believe in him; all his commands become principles; there needs no other proof for the truth of what he fays, but that he faid it. And then there needs no more, but to read the infpired books, to be inftruct-ed: all the duties of morality lie there clear, and plain, and eafy to be underftood. And here I appeal, whether this be not the fureft, the fafeft, and moft effectual way of teaching: efpecially if we add this farther confidera-tion, that as it fuits the loweft capacities of reafonable creatures, fo it reaches and fatisfies, nay, enlightens the higheft. The moft elevated underftandings cannot but fubmit to the authority of this doctrine as divine; which coming from the mouths of a company of illiterate men, hath not only the atteftation of miracles, but reafon to confirm it: fince they delivered no precepts but fuch, as though reafon of itfelf had not clearly made out, yet it could not but affent to, when thus difcovered, and think itfelf indebted for the difcovery. The credit and authority our Saviour and his'apoftles had over the minds of men, by the miracles they did, tempted them not to mix (as we find in that of all the fects and philofophers, and other religions) any conceits, any wrong rules, any thing tending to their own by-intereft, or that of a party, in their morality. No tang of prepoffeffion, or fancy; no footfteps of pride, or vanity; no touch of oftentation or ambition; appears to have a hand in it. It is all pure, all fincere; nothing too much, nothing wanting; but fuch a complete rule of life, as the wifeft men muft acknowledge, tends entirely to the good of mankind, and that all would be happy, if all would practife it.

3. The outward forms of worfhipping the Deity, wanted a reformation. Stately buildings, coftly orna-ments, peculiar and uncouth habits, and a numerous huddle of pompous, fantaftical, cumberfome ceremo-nies, every where attended divine worfhip. This, as it had the peculiar name, fo it was thought the principal part, if not the whole of religion. Nor could this, pof-fibly, be amended, whilft the jewifh ritual ftood; and there was fo much of it mixed with the worfhip of the true God. To this alfo our Saviour, with the know-ledge of the infinite, invifible, fupreme Spirit, brought

L 2 a remedy,

a remedy, in a plain, spiritual, and suitable worship. Jesus says to the woman of Samaria, " The hour cometh, " when ye shall neither in this mountain, nor yet at " Jerusalem, worship the Father. But the true wor- " shippers shall worship the Father, both in spirit and " in truth; for the Father seeketh such to worship him." To be worshipped in spirit and truth, with application of mind, and sincerity of heart, was what God hence- forth only required. Magnificent temples, and con- finement to certain places, were now no longer necessary for his worship, which by a pure heart might be per- formed any where. The splendour and distinction of ha- bits, and pomp of ceremonies, and all outside perfor- mances, might now be spared. God, who was a spirit, and made known to be so, required none of those, but the spirit only; and that in public assemblies, (where some actions must lie open to the view of the world) all that could appear and be seen, should be done decently, and in order, and to edification. Decency, order, and edification, were to regulate all their public acts of wor- ship, and beyond what these required, the outward ap- pearance (which was of little value in the eyes of God) was not to go. Having shut indecency and confusion out of their assemblies, they need not be solicitous about use- less ceremonies. Praises and prayer, humbly offered up to the Deity, were the worship he now demanded; and in these every one was to look after his own heart, and to know that it was that alone which God had re- gard to, and accepted.

4. Another great advantage received by our Saviour, is the great encouragement he brought to a virtuous and pious life; great enough to surmount the difficul- ties and obstacles that lie in the way to it, and reward the pains and hardships of those who stuck firm to their duties, and suffered for the testimony of a good con- science. The portion of the righteous has been in all ages taken notice of, to be pretty scanty in this world. Virtue and prosperity do not often accompany one ano- ther; and therefore virtue seldom had many followers. And it is no wonder she prevailed not much in a state, where the inconveniencies that attended her were visi- ble,

ble, and at hand; and the rewards doubtful, and at a distance. Mankind, who are and muft be allowed to purfue their happinefs, nay, cannot be hindered; could not but think themfelves excufed from a ftrict obferva-tion of rules, which appeared fo little to confift of their chief end, happinefs; whilft they kept them from the en-joyments of this life; and they had little evidence and fecurity of another. It is true they might have argued the other way, and concluded, That, becaufe the good were moft of them ill-treated here, there was another place where they fhould meet with better ufage; but it is plain they did not: their thoughts of another life were at beft obfcure, and their expectations uncertain. Of manes, and ghofts, and the fhades of departed men, there was fome talk; but little certain, and lefs minded. They had the names of Styx and Acheron, of Elyfian fields, and feats of the bleffed: but they had them gene-rally from their poets, mixed with their fables. And fo they looked more like the inventions of wit, and or-naments of poetry; than the ferious perfuafions of the grave and the fober. They came to them bundled up among their tales, and for tales they took them. And that which rendered them more fufpected, and lefs ufe-ful to virtue, was, that the philofophers feldom fet their rules on men's minds and practices, by confideration of another life. The chief of their arguments were from the excellency of virtue; and the higheft they generally went, was the exalting of human nature, whofe per-fection lay in virtue. And if the prieft at any time talked of the ghofts below, and a life after this; it was only to keep men to their fuperftitious and idolatrous rites; whereby the ufe of this doctrine was loft to the credulous multitude, and its belief to the quicker-fighted; who fufpected it prefently of prieftcraft. Be-fore our Saviour's time, the doctrine of a future ftate, though it were not wholly hid, yet it was not clearly known in the world. It was an imperfect view of rea-fon, or, perhaps, the decayed remains of an ancient tradition, which feemed rather to float on men's fan-cies, than fink deep into their hearts. It was fome-thing, they knew not what, between being and not being. Something in man they imagined might escape the grave; but a perfect complete life, of an eternal duration, after this, was what entered little into their thoughts, and less into their persuasions. And they were so far from being clear herein, that we see no nation of the world publicly professed it, and built upon it: no religion taught it; and it was no where made an article of faith, and principle of religion until Jesus Christ came; of whom it is truly said, that he, at his appearing, " brought life and immortality to light." And that not only in the clear revelation of it, and in instances shown of men raised from the dead; but he has given us an unquestionable assurance and pledge of it in his own resurrection and ascension into heaven. How has this one truth changed the nature of things in the world, and given the advantage to piety over all that could tempt or deter men from it? The philosophers, indeed, showed the beauty of virtue; they set her off so, as drew men's eyes and approbation to her; but leaving her unendowed, very few were willing to espouse her. The generality could not refuse her their esteem and commendation; but still turned their backs on her, and forsook her, as a match not for their turn. But now there being put into the scales on her side, " an exceeding and immortal weight of glory;" interest is come about to her, and virtue now is visibly the most enriching purchase, and by much the best bargain. That she is the perfection and excellency of our nature; that she is herself a reward, and will recommend our names to future ages, is not all that can now be said of her. It is not strange that the learned heathens satisfied not many with such airy commendations. It has another relish and efficacy to persuade men, that if they live well here, they shall be happy hereafter. Open their eyes upon the endless, unspeakable joys of another life, and their hearts will find something solid and powerful to move them. The view of heaven and hell will cast a slight upon the short pleasures and pains of this present state, and give attractions and encouragements to virtue, which reason and interest, and the care of ourselves, cannot but allow and prefer. Upon this foundation,

dation, and upon this only, morality ſtands firm, and may defy all competition. This makes it more than a name; a ſubſtantial good, worth all our aims and endeavours; and thus the goſpel of Jeſus Chriſt has delivered it to us.

5. To theſe I muſt add one advantage more by Jeſus Chriſt, and that is the promiſe of aſſiſtance. If we do what we can, he will give us his Spirit to help us to do what, and how we ſhould. It will be idle for us, who know not how our own ſpirits move and act us, to aſk in what manner the Spirit of God ſhall work upon us. The wiſdom that accompanies that Spirit knows better than we, how we are made, and how to work upon us. If a wiſe man knows how to prevail on his child, to bring him to what he deſires; can we ſuſpect that the ſpirit and wiſdom of God ſhould fail in it; though we perceive or comprehend not the ways of his operation? Chriſt has promiſed it, who is faithful and juſt; and we cannot doubt of the performance. It is not requiſite on this occaſion, for the inhancing of this benefit, to enlarge on the frailty of our minds, and weakneſs of our conſtitutions; how liable to miſtakes, how apt to go aſtray, and how eaſily to be turned out of the paths of virtue. If any one needs go beyond himſelf, and the teſtimony of his own conſcience in this point; if he feels not his own errours and paſſions always tempting, and often prevailing, againſt the ſtrict rules of his duty; he need but look abroad into any ſtage of the world, to be convinced. To a man under the difficulties of his nature, beſet with temptations, and hedged in with prevailing cuſtom; it is no ſmall encouragement to ſet himſelf ſeriouſly on the courſes of virtue, and practice of true religion; that he is from a ſure hand, and an Almighty arm, promiſed aſſiſtance to ſupport and carry him through.

There remains yet ſomething to be ſaid to thoſe, who will be ready to object, " If the belief of Jeſus of Na-
" zareth to be the Meſſiah, together with thoſe con-
" comitant articles of his reſurrection, rule, and com-
" ing again to judge the world, be all the faith required,
" as neceſſary to juſtification; to what purpoſe were
" the epiſtles written; I ſay, if the belief of thoſe many

" doctrines

" doctrines contained in them be not also necessary to
" salvation; and what is there delivered a christian
" may believe or disbelieve, and yet, nevertheless, be a
" member of Christ's Church, and one of the faithful?"

To this I answer, that the epistles are written upon
several occasions: and he that will read them as he
ought, must observe what it is in them, which is principally aimed at; find what is the argument in hand, and
and how managed; if he will understand them right,
and profit by them. The observing of this will best
help us to the true meaning and mind of the writer:
for that is the truth which is to be received and believed; and not scattered sentences in scripture-lan-
guage, accommodated to our notions and prejudices.
We must look into the drift of the discourse, observe
the coherence and connexion of the parts, and see how
it is consistent with itself and other parts of scripture;
if we will conceive it right.   We must not cull out, as
best suits our system, here and there a period or verse;
as if they were all distinct and independent aphorisms;
and make these the fundamental articles of the christian
faith, and necessary to salvation; unless God has made
them so.   There be many truths in the bible, which a
good christian may be wholly ignorant of, and so not
believe; which, perhaps, some lay great stress on and
call fundamental articles, because they are the distin-
guishing points of their communion.   The epistles,
most of them, carry on a thread of argument, which, in
the style they are writ, cannot every where be observed
without great attention, and to consider the texts as
they stand, and bear a part in that, is to view them in
their due light, and the way to get the true sense of
them.   They were writ to those who were in the faith,
and true christians already: and so could not be designed to teach them the fundamental articles and points
necessary to salvation.   The epistle to the romans was
writ to all " that were at Rome, beloved of God, called
" to be saints, whose faith was spoken of through the
" world," chap. i. 7, 8.   To whom St. Paul's first
epistle to the corinthians was, he shows, chap. i. 2, 4,
&c. " Unto the church of God which is at Corinth,
" to them that are sanctified in Christ Jesus, called to
                                                    " be

" be faints; with all them that in every place call upon
" the name of Jefus Chrift our Lord, both theirs and
" ours. I thank my God always on your behalf, for the
" grace of God which is given you by Jefus Chrift; that
" in every thing ye are enriched by him, in all utterance,
" and in all knowledge : even as the teftimony of Chrift
" was confirmed in you. So that ye come behind in no
" gift; waiting for the coming of our Lord Jefus
" Chrift." And fo likewife the fecond was, " To the
" church of God at Corinth, with all the faints in
" Achaia," chap. i. 1. His next is to the churches of
Galatia. That to the ephefians, was, " To the faints
" that were at Ephefus, and to the faithful in Chrift
" Jefus." So likewife, " To the faints and faithful bre-
" thren in Chrift at Coloffe, who had faith in Chrift
" Jefus, and love to the faints. To the church of the
" Theffalonians. To Timothy his fon in the faith.
" To Titus his own fon after the common faith. To
" Philemon his dearly beloved, and fellow-labourer."
And the author to the hebrews calls thofe he writes to
" Holy brethren, partakers of the heavenly calling,"
chap. iii. 1. From whence it is evident, that all thofe
whom St. Paul writ to, were brethren, faints, faithful
in the church, and fo chriftians already ; and, therefore,
wanted not the fundamental articles of the chriftian religion ; without a belief of which they could not be
faved ; nor can it be fuppofed, that the fending of fuch
fundamentals was the reafon of the apoftle's writing to
any of them. To fuch alfo St. Peter writes, as is plain
from the firft chapter of each of his epiftles. Nor is it
hard to obferve the like in St. James's and St. John's
epiftles. And St. Jude directs his thus : " To them
" that are fanctified by God the Father, and preferved
" in Jefus Chrift, and called." The epiftles, therefore, being all written to thofe who were already believers and chriftians, the occafion and end of writing
them could not be to inftruct them in that which was
neceffary to make them chriftians. This, it is plain,
they knew and believed already ; or elfe they could not
have been chriftians and believers. And they were writ
upon particular occafions ; and without thofe occafions,

had

had not been writ; and so cannot be thought necessary to salvation: though they resolving doubts, and reforming mistakes, are of great advantage to our knowledge and practice. I do not deny, but the great doctrines of the christian faith are dropt here and there, and scattered up and down in most of them. But it is not in the epistles we are to learn what are the fundamental articles of faith, where they are promiscuously and without distinction mixed with other truths, in discourses that were (though for edification, indeed, yet) only occasional. We shall find and discern those great and necessary points best, in the preaching of our Saviour and the apostles, to those who were yet strangers, and ignorant of the faith; to bring them in, and convert them to it. And what that was, we have seen already, out of the history of the evangelists, and the acts; where they are plainly laid down, so that nobody can mistake them. The epistles to particular churches, besides the main argument of each of them, (which was some present concernment of that particular church, to which they severally were addressed) do in many places explain the fundamentals of the christian religion, and that wisely; by proper accommodations to the apprehensions of those they were writ to; the better to make them imbibe the christian doctrine, and the more easily to comprehend the method, reasons, and grounds of the great work of salvation. Thus we see, in the epistle to the romans, adoption (a custom well known amongst those of Rome) is much made use of, to explain to them the grace and favour of God, in giving them eternal life; to help them to conceive how they became the children of God, and to assure them of a share in the kingdom of heaven, as heirs to an inheritance. Whereas the setting out, and confirming the christian faith to the hebrews, in the epistle to them, is by allusions and arguments, from the ceremonies, sacrifices, and oeconomy of the jews, and references to the records of the Old Testament. And as for the general epistles, they, we may see, regard the state and exigencies, and some peculiarities of those times. These holy writers, inspired from above, writ nothing but truth; and in most

placees,

places, very weighty truths to us now ; for the expound‑
ing, clearing, and confirming of the chriftian doctrine,
and eftablifhing thofe in it who had embraced it.   But
yet every fentence of theirs muft not be taken up, and
looked on as a fundamental article, neceffary to falva‑
tion ; without an explicit belief whereof, no‑body could
be a member of Chrift's church here, nor be admitted
into his eternal kingdom hereafter.   If all, or moft of
the truths declared in the epiftles, were to be received
and believed as fundamental articles, what then became
of thofe chriftians who were fallen afleep (as St. Paul
witneffes in his firft to the corinthians, many were) be‑
fore thefe things in the epiftles were revealed to them?
Moft of the epiftles not being written till above twenty
years after our Saviour's afcenfion, and fome after
thirty.

But farther, therefore, to thofe who will be ready to
fay, " May thofe truths delivered in the epiftles, which
" are not contained in the preaching of our Saviour and
" his apoftles, and are therefore, by this account, not
" neceffary to falvation ; be believed, or difbelieved
" without any danger ? May a chriftian fafely queftion
" or doubt of them ?"

To this I anfwer, That the law of faith, being a co‑
venant of free grace, God alone can appoint what fhall
be neceffarily believed by every one whom he will
juftify.   What is the faith which he will accept and ac‑
count for righteoufnefs, depends wholly on his good
pleafure.   For it is of grace, and not of right, that this
faith is accepted.   And therefore he alone can fet the
meafures of it : and what he has fo appointed and de‑
clared, is alone neceffary.   No body can add to thefe
fundamental articles of faith ; nor make any other ne‑
ceffary, but what God himfelf hath made, and declared
to be fo.   And what thefe are which God requires of
thofe who will enter into, and receive the benefits of
the new covenant, has already been fhown.   An explicit
belief of thefe is abfolutely required of all thofe to
whom the gofpel of Jefus Chrift is preached, and falva‑
tion through his Name propofed.

The

The other parts of divine revelation are objects of faith, and are so to be received. They are truths, whereof no one can be rejected; none that is once known to be such, may, or ought to be disbelieved. For to acknowledge any proposition to be of divine revelation and authority; and yet to deny, or disbelieve it; is to offend against this fundamental article and ground of faith, that God is true. But yet a great many of the truths revealed in the gospel, every one does, and must confess, a man may be ignorant of; nay, disbelieve, without danger to his salvation: as is evident in those, who, allowing the authority, differ in the interpretation and meaning of several texts of scripture, not thought fundamental: in all which, it is plain, the contending parties on one side or the other, are ignorant of, nay, disbelieve the truths delivered in holy writ; unless contrarieties and contradictions can be contained in the same words; and divine revelation can mean contrary to itself.

Though all divine revelation requires the obedience of faith, yet every truth of inspired scriptures is not one of those, that by the law of faith is required to be explicitly believed to justification. What those are, we have seen by what our Saviour and his apostles proposed to, and required in those whom they converted to the faith. Those are fundamentals, which it is not enough not to disbelieve: every one is required actually to assent to them. But any other proposition contained in the scripture, which God has not thus made a necessary part of the law of faith, (without an actual assent to which, he will not allow any one to be a believer) a man may be ignorant of, without hazarding his salvation by a defect in his faith. He believes all that God has made necessary for him to believe, and assent to; and as for the rest of divine truths, there is nothing more required of him, but that he receive all the parts of divine revelation, with a docility and disposition prepared to embrace and assent to all truths coming from God; and submit his mind to whatsoever shall appear to him to bear that character. Where he, upon fair endeavours, understands it not, how can he avoid being ignorant? And where

he

he cannot put several texts, and make them confist together, what remedy? He must either interpret one by the other, or suspend his opinion. He that thinks that more is, or can be required of poor frail man in matters of faith will do well to consider what absurdities he will run into. God, out of the infiniteness of his mercy, has dealt with man, as a compassionate and tender Father. He gave him reason, and with it a law: that could not be otherwise than what reason should dictate; unless we should think, that a reasonable creature should have an unreasonable law. But, considering the frailty of man, apt to run into corruption and misery, he promised a Deliverer, whom in his good time he sent; and then declared to all mankind, that whoever would believe him to be the Saviour promised, and take him now raised from the dead, and constituted the Lord and Judge of all men, to be their King and Ruler, should be saved. This is a plain intelligible proposition; and the all-merciful God seems herein to have consulted the poor of this world, and the bulk of mankind. These are articles that the labouring and illiterate man may comprehend. This is a religion suited to vulgar capacities; and the state of mankind in this world, destined to labour and travel. The writers and wranglers in religion fill it with niceties, and dress it up with notions, which they make necessary and fundamental parts of it; as if there were no way into the church, but through the academy or lyceum. The greatest part of mankind have not leisure for learning and logic, and superfine distinctions of the schools. Where the hand is used to the plough and the spade, the head is seldom elevated to sublime notions, or exercised in mysterious reasoning. It is well if men of that rank (to say nothing of the other sex) can comprehend plain propositions, and a short reasoning about things familiar to their minds, and nearly allied to their daily experience. Go beyond this, and you amaze the greatest part of mankind; and may as well talk Arabic to a poor day-labourer, as the notions and language that the books and disputes of religion are filled with; and as soon you will be understood. The dissenting congregation are supposed by

their

their teachers to be more accurately inftructed in matters of faith, and better to underftand the chriftian religion, than the vulgar conformifts, who are charged with great ignorance; how truly, I will not here determine. But I afk them to tell me ferioufly, " Whether " half their people have leifure to ftudy? Nay, Whe " ther one in ten, of thofe who come to their meetings " in the country, if they had time to ftudy them, do or " can underftand the controverfies at this time fo " warmly managed amongft them, about "juftifica " tion," the fubject of this prefent treatife?" I have talked with fome of their teachers, who confefs themfelves not to underftand the difference in debate between them. And yet the points they ftand on, are reckoned of fo great weight, fo material, fo fundamental in religion, that they divide communion, and feparate upon them. Had God intended that none but the learned fcribe, the difputer, or wife of this world, fhould be chriftians, or be faved, thus religion fhould have been prepared for them, filled with fpeculations and niceties, obfcure terms, and abftract notions. But men of that expectation, men furnifhed with fuch acquifitions, the apoftle tells us, 1 Cor. i. are rather fhut out from the fimplicity of the gofpel; to make way for thofe poor, ignorant, illiterate, who heard and believed promifes of a Deliverer, and believed Jefus to be him; who could conceive a man dead and made alive again; and believe that he fhould, at the end of the world, come again and pafs fentence on all men, according to their deeds. That the poor had the gofpel preached to them; Chrift makes a mark, as well as bufinefs of his miffion, Matt. xi. 5: And if the poor had the gofpel preached to them, it was, without doubt, fuch a gofpel as the poor could underftand; plain and intelligible: and fo it was, as we have feen, in the preachings of Chrift and his apoftles.

A

VINDICATION

OF THE

REASONABLENESS

OF

CHRISTIANITY, &c.

FROM MR. EDWARDS's

REFLECTIONS.

A

V I N D I C A T I O N

OF THE

R E A S O N A B L E N E S S

OF

C H R I S T I A N I T Y, &c.

MY Book had not been long out, before it fell under the correction of the author of a Treatife, en-
titled, "Some Thoughts concerning the feveral Caufes
" and Occafions of Atheifm, efpecially in the prefent
" Age." No contemptible adverfary, I'll affure you;
fince, as it feems, he has got the faculty to heighten
every thing that difpleafes him, into the capital crime
of atheifm; and breathes againft thofe, who come in
his way, a peftilential air, whereby every the leaft dif-
temper is turned into the plague, and becomes mortal.
For whoever does not juft fay after Mr. Edwards, cannot, it is evident, efcape being an atheift, or a promoter
of atheifm. I cannot but approve of any one's zeal, to
guard and fecure that great and fundamental article of
all religion and morality, " That there is a God :" but

atheifm being a crime, which, for its madnefs as well as
guilt, ought to fhut a man out of all fober and civil
fociety, fhould be very warily charged on any one, by
deductions and confequences, which he himfelf does not
own, or, at leaft, do not manifeftly and unavoidably flow
from what he afferts. This caution, charity, I think,
obliges us to: and our author would poffibly think himfelf hardly dealt with, if, for neglecting fome of thofe
rules he himfelf gives, p. 31 and 34, againft atheifm,
he fhould be pronounced a promoter of it: as rational
a charge, I imagine, as fome of thofe he makes; and as
fitly put together, as "the treatife of the Reafonablenefs
"of Chriftianity, &c." brought in among the caufes
of atheifm. However I fhall not much complain of
him, fince he joins me, p. 104, with no worfe company, than two eminently pious and learned * prelates
of our church, whom he makes favourers of the fame
conceit, as he calls it. But what has that conceit to do
with atheifm? Very much. That conceit is of kin to
focinianifm, and focinianifm to atheifm. Let us hear
Mr. Edwards himfelf. He fays, p. 113, I am "all over
"focinianized:" and therefore, my book, fit to be
placed among the caufes of atheifm. For in the 64th,
and following pages, he endeavours to fhow, That "a
"focinian is an atheift;" or, left that fhould feem harfh,
"one that favours the caufe of atheifm," p. 75. For
fo he has been pleafed to mollify, now it is publifhed as
a treatife, what was much more harfh, and much more
confident in it, when it was preached as a fermon. In
this abatement, he feems a little to comply with his own
advice, againft his fourth caufe of atheifm; which we
have in thefe words, p. 34, "Wherefore, that we may
"effectually prevent this folly in ourfelves, let us banifh
"prefumption, confidence, and felf-conceit; let us ex-
"tirpate all pride and arrogance; let us not lift ourfelves
"in the number of capricious opiniators."

I fhall leave the focinians themfelves to anfwer his
charge againft them, and fhall examine his proof of my
being a focinian. It ftands thus, page 112, "When he"

---

* Bp. Taylor, and the author of "the Naked Truth."

(the

(the author of the Reasonableness of Christianity, &c.)
" proceeds to mention the advantages and benefits of
" Christ's coming into the world, and appearing in the
" flesh, he hath not one syllable of his satisfying for us;
" or, by his death, purchasing life or salvation, or any
" thing that sounds like it. This, and several other
" things, show, that he is all over socinianized." Which
in effect is, that because I have not set down all that
this author perhaps would have done, therefore I am a
socinian. But what if I should say, I set down as much
as my argument required, and yet am no socinian?
Would he, from my silence and omission, give me the
lie, and say, I am one? Surmises that may be overturned
by a single denial, are poor arguments, and such as some
men would be ashamed of: at least, if they are to be
permitted to men of this gentleman's skill and zeal,
who knows how to make a good use of conjectures,
suspicions, and uncharitable censures in the cause of
God; yet even there too (if the cause of God can need
such arts) they require a good memory to keep them
from recoiling upon the author. He might have taken
notice of these words in my book, (page 9. of this Vol.)
" From this estate of death, JESUS CHRIST RESTORES
" all mankind to life." And a little lower. " The life
" which Jesus Christ restores to all men." And p. 109,
" He that hath incurred death for his own transgression,
" cannot LAY DOWN HIS LIFE FOR ANOTHER, as our Sa-
" viour professes he did." This, methinks, SOUNDS
SOMETHING LIKE " Christ's purchasing life for us by
" his death." But this reverend gentleman has an answer ready; it was not in the place he would have had
it in, it was not where I mention the advantages and
benefits of Christ's coming. And therefore, I not having
there one syllable of Christ's purchasing life and salvation
for us by his death, or any thing that sounds like it: this,
and several other things, that might be offered, show that
I am " all over socinianized." A very clear and ingenuous proof, and let him enjoy it.

But what will become of me, that I have not mentioned satisfaction!

Possibly, this reverend gentleman would have had

charity

charity enough for a known writer of the brotherhood,
to have found it by an " innuendo," in thofe words
above quoted, of laying down his life for another.   But
every thing is to be ftrained here the other way.   For
the author of " the Reafonablenefs of Chriftianity, &c."
is of neceffity to be reprefented as a focinian; or elfe his
book may be read, and the truths in it, which Mr. Edwards likes not, be received, and people put upon examining.   Thus one, as full of happy conjectures and
fufpicions as this gentleman, might be apt to argue.
But what if the author defigned his treatife, as the title
fhows, chiefly for thofe who were not yet thoroughly,
or firmly, chriftians, propofing to work on thofe, who
either wholly difbelieved, or doubted of the truth of the
chriftian religion?   Would any one blame his prudence,
if he mentioned only thofe advantages, which all chriftians are agreed in?   Might he not remember and obferve that command of the apoftle, Rom. xiv. 1, " Him
" that is weak in the faith, receive ye, but not to doubt-
" ful difputations;" without being a focinian?   Did he
amifs, that he offered to the belief of thofe who ftood
off, that, and only that, which our Saviour and his apoftles preached, for the reducing the unconverted world:
and would any one think he in earneft went about to
perfuade men to be chriftians, who fhould ufe that as an
argument to recommend the gofpel, which he has obferved men to lay hold on, as an objection againft it?
To urge fuch points of controverfy, as neceffary articles
of faith, when we fee our Saviour and the apoftles, in
their preaching, urged them not as neceffary to be believed, to make men chriftians, is (by our own authority) to add prejudices to prejudices, and to block up
our own way to thofe men, whom we would have accefs
to, and prevail upon.   But fome men had rather you
fhould write booty, and crofs your own defign of removing men's prejudices to chriftianity, than leave out
one tittle of what they put into their fyftems.   To fuch,
I fay, convince but men of the miffion of Jefus Chrift,
make them but fee the truth, fimplicity and reafonablenefs, of what he himfelf taught, and required to be believed by his followers; and you need not doubt, but,

4   being

being once fully perfuaded of his doctrine, and the advantages which all chriftians agree are received by him,
fuch converts will not lay by the fcriptures, but by a
conftant reading and ftudy of them get all the light they
can from this divine revelation, and nourifh themfelves
up in the words of faith, and of good doctrine, as St.
Paul fpeaks to Timothy.   But fome men will not bear
it, that any one fhould fpeak of religion, but according
to the model that they themfelves have made of it.
Nay, though he propofes it upon the very terms, and
in the very words which our Saviour and his apoftles
preached it in, yet he fhall not efcape cenfures and the
fevereft infinuations.   To deviate in the leaft, or to
omit any thing contained in their articles, is herefy,
under the moft invidious names in fafhion, and 'tis well
if he efcapes being a downright atheift.   Whether this
be the way for teachers to make themfelves hearkened
to, as men in earneft in religion, and really concerned
for the falvation of men's fouls, I leave them to confider.
What fuccefs it has had, towards perfuading men of the
truth of chriftianity, their own complaints of the prevalency of atheifm, on the one hand, and the number of
deifts on the other, fufficiently fhow.

Another thing laid to my charge, p. 105 and 107, is
my " forgetting, or rather wilful omitting, fome plain
" and obvious paffages," and fome " famous teftimo-
" nies in the evangelifts; namely Matth. xxviii. 19,
" Go, teach all nations, baptizing them in the name of
" the Father, and of the Son, and of the Holy Ghoft."
And John i, 1, " In the beginning was the Word, and
" the word was with God, and the word was God."
And verfe 14, " And the word was made flefh."   Mine,
it feems, in this book, are all fins of omiffion.   And yet,
when it came out, the buz, the flutter, and noife which
was made, and the reports which were raifed, would
have perfuaded the world, that it fubverted all morality,
and was defigned againft the chriftian religion.   I muft
confefs, difcourfes of this kind, which I met with,
fpread up and down, at firft amazed me; knowing
the fincerity of thofe thoughts, which perfuaded me
to publifh it (not without fome hope of doing fome

fervice

fervice to decaying piety, and miftaken and flandered chriftianity. I fatisfied myfelf againft thofe heats, with this affurance, that, if there was any thing in my book againft what any one called religion, it was not againft the religion contained in the gofpel. And for that, I appeal to all mankind.

But to return to Mr. Edwards, in particular, I muft take leave to tell him, that if " omitting plain and ob-" vious paffages, the famous teftimonies in the evange-" lifts," be a fault in me, I wonder why he, among fo many of this kind that I am guilty of, mentions fo few. For I muft acknowledge I have omitted more, nay, many more, that are " plain and obvious paffages, and " famous teftimonies in the evangelifts," than thofe he takes notice of. But if I have left out none of thofe " paffages or teftimonies," which contain what our Sa-viour and his apoftles preached, and required affent to, to make men believers, I fhall think my omiffions (let them be what they will) no faults in the prefent cafe. Whatever doctrines Mr. Edwards would have to be be-lieved, if they are fuch as our Saviour and his apoftles required to be believed, to make a man a chriftian, he will be fure to find them in thofe preachings and " fa-" mous teftimonies," of our Saviour and his apoftles, that I have quoted. And if they are not there, he may reft fatisfied, that they were not propofed by our Saviour and his apoftles, as neceffary to be believed, to make men Chrift's difciples.

If the omiffion of other texts in the evangelifts (which are all true alfo, and no one of them to be difbelieved) be a fault, it might have been expected that Mr. Ed-wards fhould have accufed me for leaving out Matth. i. 18—23, and Matth. xxvii. 24, 35, 50, 60, for thefe are " plain and obvious paffages and famous teftimonies in " the evangelifts ;" and fuch, whereon thefe articles of the apoftles creed, viz. " born of the virgin Mary, fuf-" fered under Pontius Pilate, was crucified, dead and " buried," are founded. Thefe, being articles of the apoftles creed, are looked upon as " fundamental doc-" trines :" and one would wonder, why Mr. Edwards fo quietly paffes by their omiffion; did it not appear, that

that he was so intent on fixing his imputation of so-cinianism upon me, that, rather than miss that, he was content to drop the other articles of his creed. For I must observe to him, that if he had blamed me for the omission of the places last quoted out of St. Matthew (as he had as much reason as for any other) it would plainly have appeared, how idle and ill-grounded his charging socinianism on me was. But, at any rate, he was to give the book an ill name; not because it was socinian; for he has no more reason to charge it with socinianism for the omissions he mentions, than the apostles creed. It is therefore well for the compilers of that creed, that they lived not in Mr. Edwards's days: for he would, no doubt, have found them " all over " socinianized," for omitting the texts he quotes, and the doctrines he collects out of John i, and John xiv, p. 107, 108. Socinianism then is not the fault of the book, whatever else it be. For I repeat it again, there is not one word of socinianism in it. I, that am not so good at conjectures as Mr. Edwards, shall leave it to him to say, or to those who can bear the plainness and simplicity of the gospel, to guess, what its fault is.

Some men are shrewd guessers, and others would be thought to be so : but he must be carried far by his forward inclination, who does not take notice, that the world is apt to think him a diviner, for any thing rather than for the sake of truth, who sets up his own suspicions against the direct evidence of things; and pretends to know other men's thoughts and reasons, better than they themselves. I had said, that the epistles, being writ to those who were already believers, could not be supposed to be writ to them to teach them fundamentals, without which they could not be believers.

And the reason I gave, why I had not gone through the writings in the epistles, to collect the fundamental articles of faith, as I had through the preachings of our Saviour and the apostles, was, because those fundamental articles were in those epistles promiscuously, and without distinction, mixed with other truths. And, therefore, we shall find and discern those great and ne-

M 4

ceffary points beft in the preachings of our Saviour and
the apoftles, to thofe who were yet ignorant of the faith,
and unconverted. This, as far as I know my own
thoughts, was the reafon why I did (as Mr. Edwards
complains, p. 109.) " not proceed to the epiftles, and
" not give an account of them, as I had done of the
" gofpels and acts." This, I imagined, I had in the
clofe of my book fo fully and clearly expreffed, particularly p. 152. of this Vol. that I fuppofed no-body,
how willing foever, could have miftaken me. But this
gentleman is fo much better acquainted with me, than
I am with myfelf; fees fo deeply into my heart, and
knows fo perfectly every thing that paffes there; that
he, with affurance, tells the world, p. 109, " That I
" purpofely omitted the epiftolary writings of the apo-
" ftles, becaufe they are fraught with other funda-
" mental doctrines, befides that one which I mention."
And then he goes to enumerate thofe fundamental articles, p. 110, 111, viz. " The corruption and degeneracy
" of human nature, with the true original of it (the
" defection of our firft parents) the propagation of fin
" and mortality, (our reftoration and reconciliation by
" Chrift's blood, the eminency and excellency of his
" priefthood, the efficacy of his death, the full fatisfac-
" tion made, thereby, to divine juftice, and his being
" made an all-fufficient facrifice for fin. Chrift's
" righteoufnefs, our juftification by it, election, adop-
" tion, fanctification, faving faith, the nature of the
" gofpel, the new covenant, the riches of God's mercy
" in the way of falvation by Jefus Chrift, the certainty
" of the refurrection of human bodies, and of the future
" glory."
Give me leave now to afk you ferioufly, whether thefe,
which you have here fet down under the title of " fun-
" damental doctrines," are fuch (when reduced to propofitions) that every one of them is required to be believed to make a man a chriftian, and fuch as, without
the actual belief thereof, he cannot be faved. If they
are not fo, every one of them, you may call them " fun-
" damental doctrines," as much as you pleafe, they are
not of thofe doctrines of faith I was fpeaking of, which
are

are only such as are required to be actually believed to make a man a christian. If you say, some of them are such necessary points of faith, and others not, you, by this specious list of well-sounding, but unexplained terms, arbitrarily collected, only make good what I have said, viz. that the necessary articles of faith, are, in the epistles, promiscuously delivered with other truths, and, therefore, they cannot be distinguished but by some other mark, than being barely found in the epistles. If you say, that they are all of them necessary articles of faith, I shall then desire you to reduce them to so many plain doctrines, and then prove them to be every one of them required to be believed by every christian man, to make him a member of the christian church. For, to begin with the first, it is not enough to tell us, as you do, that " the corruption and degeneracy of human na-
" ture, with the true original of it, (the defection of
" our first parents) the propagation of sin and morta-
" lity, is one of the great heads of christian divinity."
But you are to tell us, what are the propositions we are required to believe concerning this matter : for nothing can be an article of faith, but some proposition ; and then it will remain to be proved, that these articles are necessary to be believed to salvation. The apostles creed was taken, in the first ages of the church, to contain all things necessary to salvation ; I mean, necessary to be believed : but you have now better thought on it, and are pleased to enlarge it, and we, no doubt, are bound to submit to your orthodoxy.

The list of materials for his creed (for the articles are not yet formed) Mr. Edwards closes, p. 111, with these words, " These are the matters of faith contained in the
" epistles, and they are essential and integral parts of
" the gospel itself." What, just these? Neither more nor less? If you are sure of it, pray let us have them speedily, for the reconciling of differences in the christian church, which has been so cruelly torn, about the articles of the christian faith, to the great reproach of christian charity, and scandal of our true religion.

Mr. Edwards, having thus, with two learned terms of
" essential and integral parts," sufficiently proved the

matter

matter in queſtion, viz. That all thoſe he has ſet down
are articles of faith neceſſary to be believed to make a
man a chriſtian, he grows warm at my omiſſion of them.
This I cannot complain of as unnatural: the ſpirit of
creed-making always riſing from an heat of zeal for our
own opinions, and warm endeavours, by all ways poſſi-
ble, to decry and bear down thoſe who differ in a tittle
from us.   What then could I expect more gentle and
candid, than what Mr. Edwards has ſubjoined in theſe
words? " And therefore it is no wonder that our au-
" thor, being ſenſible of this" (viz. That the points he
has named were eſſential and integral parts of the goſpel)
" would not vouchſafe to give us an abſtract of thoſe
" inſpired writings [the epiſtles]; but paſſes them by
" with ſome contempt."   Sir, when your angry fit is
over, and the abatement of your paſſion has given way
to the return of your ſincerity, I ſhall beg you to read
this paſſage in page 154. of this vol. " Theſe holy wri-
" ters (viz. the pen-men of the ſcriptures) INSPIRED
" from above, writ nothing but truth, and, in moſt
" places, very weighty truths to us now, for the ex-
" pounding, clearing, and confirming of the chriſtian
" doctrine; and eſtabliſhing thoſe in it who had
" embraced it."   And again, p. 156, " The other
" parts of DIVINE REVELATION are objects of faith, and
" are ſo to be received. They are truths, of which none
" that is once known to be ſuch, i. e. revealed, may or
" ought to be diſbelieved." And if this does not ſatisfy
you, that I have as high a veneration for the epiſtles, as
you or any one can have, I require you to publiſh to the
world thoſe paſſages, which ſhow my contempt of them.
In the mean time, I ſhall deſire my reader to examine
what I have writ concerning the epiſtles, which is all
contained between p. 151, and 158. of this vol. and then
to judge, whether I have made bold with the epiſtles in
what I have ſaid of them, or this gentleman made bold
with truth in what he has writ of me.   Human frailty
will not, I ſee, eaſily quit its hold; what it loſes in one
part, it will be ready to regain in another; and not be
hindered from taking repriſals, even on the moſt privi-
leged ſort of men.   Mr. Edwards, who is intrenched
                                                    in

in orthodoxy, and so is as safe in matters of faith almost as infallibility itself, is yet as apt to err as others in matters of fact.

But he has not yet done with me about the epistles: all his fine draught of my slighting that part of the scripture will be lost, unless the strokes complete it into socinianism. In his following words you have the conclusion of the whole matter. His words are these: "And more especially, if I may conjecture," (by all means, sir, conjecturing is your proper talent: you have hitherto done nothing else; and I will say that for you, you have a lucky hand at it.) "He doth this, (i. e. pass "by the epistles with contempt) because he knew that "there are so many and frequent, and those so illustri- "ous and eminent attestations to the doctrine of the "ever to be adored Trinity, in these epistles." Truly, sir, if you will permit me to know what I know, as well as you do allow yourself to conjecture what you please, you are out for this once; the reason why I went not through the epistles, as I did the gospels and the acts, was that very reason I printed, and that will be found so sufficient a one to all considerate readers, that I believe, they will think you need not strain your conjectures for another. And, if you think it to be so easy to distinguish fundamentals from non-fundamentals in the epistles, I desire you to try your skill again, in giving the world a perfect collection of propositions out of the epistles, that contain all that is required, and no more than what is absolutely required to be believed by all christians, without which faith they cannot be of Christ's church. For I tell you, notwithstanding the show you have made, you have not yet done it, nor will you affirm that you have.

His next page, p. 112, is made up of the same, which he calls, not uncharitable conjectures. I expound, he says, "John xiv. 9, &c. after the antitrinitarian mode:" and I make "Christ and Adam to be Sons of God, in "the same sense, and by their birth, as the racovians "generally do." I know not but it may be true, that the antitrinitarians and racovians understand those places as I do: but it is more than I know, that they

do

do fo.   I took not my fenfe of thofe texts from thofe
writers, but from the fcripture itfelf, giving light to
its own meaning, by one place compared with another:
what in this way appears to me its true meaning, I fhall
not decline, becaufe I am told that it is fo underftood
by the racovians, whom I never yet read ; nor embrace
the contrary, though the "generality of divines" I
more converfe with, fhould declare for it.   If the fenfe,
wherein I underftand thofe texts, be a miftake, I fhall
be beholden to you, if you will fet me right.   But they
are not popular authorities, or frightful names, whereby
I judge of truth or falfhood.   You will now, no doubt,
applaud your conjectures ; the point is gained, and I
am openly a focinian, fince I will not difown, that I
think the Son of God was a phrafe, that among the
jews, in our Saviour's time, was ufed for the Meffiah,
though the focinians underftand it in the fame fenfe ;
and therefore I muft certainly be of their perfuafion in
every thing elfe.   I admire the acutenefs, force, and
fairnefs of your reafoning, and fo I leave you to triumph
in your conjectures.   Only I muft defire you to take
notice, that that ornament of our church, and every
way eminent prelate, the late archbifhop of Canterbury,
underftood that phrafe in the fame fenfe that I do, without being a focinian.   You may read what he fays concerning Nathanael, in his firft "fermon of fincerity,"
publifhed this year : his words are thefe, p. 4, "And
" being fatisfied that he [our Saviour] was the Meffiah,
" he prefently owned him for fuch, calling him the
" Son of God, and the king of Ifrael."
   Though this gentleman knows my thoughts as perfectly as if he had for feveral years paft lain in my bo-
fom, yet he is mightily at a lofs about my perfon : as if
it at all concerned the truth contained in my book,
what hand it came from.   However, the gentleman is
mightily perplexed about the author.   Why, fir, what
if it were writ by a fcribbler of Bartholomew-fair drolls,
with all that flourifh of declamatory rhetoric, and all
that fmartnefs of wit and jeft about captain Tom, unitarians, units, and cyphers, &c. which are to be found
between pages 115, and 123 of a book, that came out
                                          during

during the merry time of rope-dancing, and puppet-
plays? What is truth, would, I hope, neverthele∫s be
truth in it, however oddly ∫pruced up by ∫uch an author:
though, perhaps, it is likely ∫ome would be apt to ∫ay,
∫uch merriment became not the gravity of my ∫ubject,
and that I writ not in the ∫tyle of a graduate in divinity.
I confe∫s, (as Mr. Edwards rightly ∫ays) my fault lies
on the other ∫ide, in a want of " vivacity and elevation:"
and I cannot wonder, that one of his character and
palate, ∫hould find out and complain of my flatne∫s,
which has ∫o over-charged my book with plain and direct texts of ∫cripture, in a matter capable of no other
proofs. But yet I mu∫t acknowledge his exce∫s of civility to me; he ∫hows me more kindne∫s than I could expect or wi∫h, ∫ince he prefers what I ∫ay to him my∫elf
to what is offered to him from the word of God; and
makes me this compliment, that I begin to mend,
about the clo∫e, i. e. when I leave off quoting of ∫crip-
ture: and the dull work was done, of " going through
" the hi∫tory of the Evangeli∫ts and Acts," which he
computes, p. 105, to take up three quarters of my book.
Does not all this de∫erve, at lea∫t, that I ∫hould, in return, take ∫ome care of his credit? Which I know not
how better to do, than by entreating him, that when he
takes next in hand ∫uch a ∫ubject as this, wherein the
∫alvation of ∫ouls is concerned, he would treat it a little
more ∫eriou∫ly, and with a little more candour; left
men ∫hould find in his writings, another cau∫e of
athei∫m, which, in this treati∫e, he has not thought fit to
mention. " O∫tentation of wit" in general he has made
a " cau∫e of athei∫m," p. 28. But the world will tell
him, that frothy light di∫cour∫es concerning the ∫erious
matters of religion; and o∫tentation of trifling and mi∫-
becoming wit in tho∫e who come as amba∫∫adors from
God, under the title of ∫ucce∫∫ors of the apo∫tles, in the
great commi∫∫ion of the go∫pel; are none of the lea∫t
cau∫es of athei∫m.

Some men have ∫o peculiar a way of arguing, that
one may ∫ee it influences them in the repeating another
man's rea∫oning, and ∫eldom fails to make it their own.
In the next paragraph I find the∫e words: " what makes
" him

" him contend for one single article, with the exclusion
" of all the rest? He pretends it is this, that all men
" ought to understand their religion." This, I confess, is a reasoning I did not think of; nor could it
hardly, I fear, have been used but by one who had first
took up his opinion from the recommendation of
fashion or interest, and then sought topics to make it
good. Perhaps the deference due to your character,
excused you from the trouble of quoting the page, where
I pretend, as you say; and it is so little like my way of
reasoning, that I shall not look for it in a book where I
remember nothing of it, and where, without your direction, I fear the reader will scarce find it. Though I
have not " that vivacity of thought, that elevation of
mind," which Mr. Edwards demands, yet common
sense would have kept me from contending that there
is but one article, because all men ought to understand
their religion. Numbers of propositions may be harder
to be remembered, but it is the abstruseness of the notions, or obscurity, inconsistency, or doubtfulness of the
terms or expressions that makes them hard to be understood: and one single proposition may more perplex the
understanding than twenty others. But where did you
find " I contended for one single article, so as to ex-
" clude all the rest?" You might have remembered,
that I say, p. 16, 17, That the article of the one only
true God, was also necessary to be believed. This might
have satisfied you, that I did not so contend for one article of faith, as to be at defiance with more than one.
However, you insist on the word one with great vigour,
from p. 108 to 121. And you did well, you had else
lost all the force of that killing stroke reserved for the
close, in that sharp jest of unitarians, and a clench or
two more of great moment.

Having found, by a careful perusal of the preachings
of our Saviour and his apostles, that the religion they
proposed, consisted in that short, plain, easy and intelligible summary which I set down, p. 157, in these words:
" Believing Jesus to be the Saviour promised, and tak-
" ing him, now raised from the dead, and constituted
" the Lord and Judge of men, to be their King and
　　　　　　　　　　　　　　　　　　　Ruler ;"

" Ruler ;" I could not forbear magnifying the wisdom
and goodness of God (which infinitely exceeds the
thoughts of ignorant, vain, and narrow-minded man) in
these following words : " The All-merciful God seems
" herein to have consulted the poor of this world, and
" the bulk of mankind : THESE ARE ARTICLES that the
" labouring and illiterate man may comprehend."
Having thus plainly mentioned more than one article,
I might have taken it amiss, that Mr. Edwards should
be at so much pains as he is, to blame me for " con-
" tending for one" article ; because I thought more
than one could not be understood ; had he not had many
fine things to say in his declamation upon one article,
which affords him so much matter, that less than seven
pages could not hold it. Only here and there, as men
of oratory often do, he mistakes the business, as p. 115,
where he says, " I urge, that there must be nothing in
" christianity that is not plain, and exactly levelled to
" all men's mother-wit." I desire to know where I
said so, or that " the very manner of every thing in
" christianity must be clear and intelligible, every thing
" must be presently comprehended by the weakest nod-
" dle, or else it is no part of religion, especially of
" christianity ;" as he has it p. 119. I am sure it is not
in p. 133—136, 149—151, of my book : these, therefore,
to convince him that I am of another opinion, I shall
desire somebody to read to Mr. Edwards, for he himself
reads my book with such spectacles, as make him find
meanings and words in it, neither of which I put there.
He should have remembered, that I speak not of all the
doctrines of christianity, nor all that is published to the
world in it ; but of those truths only, which are absolutely required to be believed to make any one a christian. And these, I find, are so plain and easy, that I
see no reason why every body, with me, should not magnify the goodness and condescension of the Almighty,
who having, out of his free grace, proposed a new law
of faith to sinful and lost man ; hath, by that law, required no harder terms, nothing as absolutely necessary
to be believed, but what is suited to vulgar capacities,
and the comprehension of illiterate men.

You

You are a little out again, p. 118, where you ironi-
cally fay, as if it were my fenfe, "Let us have but one
" article, though it be with defiance to all the reft."
Jefting apart, fir, this is a ferious turn, that what our
Saviour and his apoftles preached, and admitted men
into the church for believing, is all that is abfolutely
required to make a man a chriftian.   But this is, without any "defiance to all the reft," taught in the word
of God.   This excludes not the belief of any of thofe
many other truths contained in the fcriptures of the Old
and New Teftaments, which it is the duty of every
chriftian to ftudy, and thereby build himfelf up in our
moft holy faith ; receiving with ftedfaft belief, and ready
obedience, all thofe things which the fpirit of truth
hath therein revealed.   But that all the reft of the infpired writings, or, if you pleafe, "articles, are of equal
" neceffity" to be believed to make a man a chriftian,
with what was preached by our Saviour and his apoftles,
that I deny.   A man, as I have fhown, may be a chriftian and believer, without actually believing them,
becaufe thofe whom our Saviour and his apoftles, by
their preaching and difcourfes, converted to the faith,
were made chriftians and believers, barely upon the receiving what they preached to them.

I hope it is no derogation to the chriftian religion,
to fay, that the fundamentals of it, i. e. all that is neceffary to be believed in it, by all men, is eafy to be
underftood by all men.   This I thought myfelf authorized to fay, by the very eafy and very intelligible articles, infifted on by our Saviour and his apoftles ; which
contain nothing but what could be underftood by the
bulk of mankind ; a term which, I know not why, Mr.
Edwards, p. 117, is offended at ; and thereupon is, after
his fafhion, fharp upon me about captain Tom and his
myrmidons, for whom, he tells me, I am "going to
make a religion."   The making of religions and creeds
I leave to others.   I only fet down the chriftian religion
as I find our Saviour and his apoftles preached it, and
preached it to, and left it for, the "ignorant and un-
" learned multitude."   For I hope you do not think,
how contemptibly foever you fpeak of the "venerable
                                        " mob,"

" mob," as you are pleased to dignify them, p. 117, that the bulk of mankind, or, in your phrase, the " rabble," are not concerned in religion, or ought to understand it, in order to their salvation. Nor are you, I hope, acquainted with any who are of that muscovite divine's mind, who, to one that was talking to him about religion, and the other world, replied, That for the czar, indeed, and bojars, they might be permitted to raise their hopes to heaven; but that, for such poor wretches as he, they were not to think of salvation.

I remember the pharisees treated the common people with contempt, and said, " Have any of the rulers, or " of the pharisees, believed in him? But this people, " who knoweth not the law, are cursed." But yet these, who, in the censure of the pharisees, were cursed, were some of the poor; or, if you please to have it so, the mob, to whom the " gospel was preached" by our Saviour, as he tells John's disciples, Matt. xi. 5.

Pardon me, sir, that I have here laid these examples and considerations before you; a little to prevail with you, not to let loose such a torrent of wit and eloquence against the " bulk of mankind," another time, and that for a mere fancy of your own: for I do not see how they here came in your way; but that you were resolved to set up something to have a fling at, and show your parts, in what you call your " different strain," though besides the purpose. I know nobody was going to " ask " the mob, What you must believe?" And as for me, I suppose you will take my word for it, that I think no mob, no, not your " venerable mob," is to be asked, what I am to believe; nor that " Articles of faith" are to be " received by the vote of club-men," or any other sort of men, you will name instead of them.

In the following words, p. 115, you ask, " Whether " a man may not understand those articles of faith, " which you mentioned out of the gospels and epistles, " if they be explained to him, as well as that one, I " speak of?" It is as the articles are, and as they are explained. There are articles that have been some hundreds of years explaining; which there are many, and those not of the most illiterate, who profess they do not yet underſtand. And to inſtance in no other, but "He deſcended into hell," the learned are not yet agreed in the ſenſe of it, though great pains have been taken to explain it.

Next, I aſk, Who are to explain your articles? The papiſts will explain ſome of them one way, and the reformed another. The remonſtrants, and anti-remonſtrants, give them different ſenſes. And probably, the trinitarians and unitarians will profeſs, that they underſtand not each others explications. And at laſt, I think it may be doubted, whether any articles, which need men's explications, can be ſo clearly and certainly underſtood, as one which is made ſo very plain by the ſcripture itſelf, as not to need any explication at all. Such is this, that Jeſus is the Meſſiah. For though you learnedly tell us, that Meſſiah is a hebrew word, and no better underſtood by the vulgar, than arabic; yet I gueſs it is ſo fully explained in the New Teſtament, and in thoſe places I have quoted out of it, that nobody, who can underſtand any ordinary ſentence in the ſcripture, can be at a loſs about it. And it is plain, it needs no other explication, than what our Saviour and the apoſtles gave it in their preaching; for, as they preached it, men received it, and that ſuffced to make them believers.

To conclude, when I heard that this learned gentleman, who had a name for his ſtudy of the ſcriptures, and writings on them, had done me the honour to conſider my treatiſe, I promiſed myſelf, that his degree, calling, and fame in the world, would have ſecured to me ſomething of weight in his remarks, which might have convinced me of my miſtakes; and, if he had found any in it, juſtified my quitting of them. But having examined what, in his, concerns my book, I to my wonder find, that he has only taken pains to give it an ill name, without ſo much as attempting to refute any one poſition in it, how much ſoever he is pleaſed to make a noiſe againſt ſeveral propoſitions, which he might be free with, becauſe they are his own: and I have no reaſon to take it amiſs if he has ſhown his zeal and ſkill againſt them. He has been ſo favourable to what is

mine,

mine, as not to ufe any one argument againft any paffage in my book. This, which I take for a public teftimony of his approbation, I fhall return him my thanks
for, when I know whether I owe it to his miftake, conviction, or kindnefs. But if he writ only for his bookfeller's fake, he alone ought to thank him.

AFTER the foregoing papers were fent to the prefs,
the "Witneffes to Chriftianity," of the reverend and
leared Dr. Patrick, now lord bifhop of Ely, fell into
my hands. I regretted the not having feen it, before I
writ my treatife of the "Reafonablefs of Chriftianity,
" &c." I fhould then, poffibly, by the light given me
by fo good a guide, and fo great a man, with more confidence directly have fallen into the knowledge of
chriftianity; which, in the way I fought it, in its fource,
required the comparing of texts with texts, and the more
than once reading over the Evangelifts and Acts, befides
other parts of fcripture. But I had the ill-luck not to
fee that treatife, until fo few hours fince, that I have
had time only to read as far as the end of the introduction, or firft chapter: and there Mr. Edwards may
find, that this pious bifhop (whofe writings fhow he
ftudies, as well as his life that he believes, the fcriptures) owns what Mr. Edwards is pleafed to call, "a
" plaufible conceit," which, he fays, "I give over and
" over again in thefe formal words, viz. That nothing
" is required to be believed by any chriftian man, but
" this, That Jefus is the Meffiah."
The liberty Mr. Edwards takes, in other places, deferves not it fhould be taken upon his word, "That
" thefe formal words" are to be found "over and over
" again" in my book, unlefs he had quoted the pages.
But I will fet him down the "formal words," which
are to be found in this reverend prelate's book, p. 14.
" To be the Son of God, and to be Chrift, being but
different "expreffions of the fame thing." And, p. 10,
" It is the very fame thing to believe, that Jefus is the
" Chrift, and to believe, that Jefus is the Son of God;
" exprefs it how you pleafe. This ALONE is the faith
" which can regenerate a man, and put a divine fpirit

N 2   " into

" into him ; that is, make him a conqueror over
" the world, as Jefus was." I have quoted only thefe
few words ; but Mr. Edwards, if he pleafes, or any
body elfe, may, in this firft chapter, fatisfy himfelf
more fully, that the defign of it is to fhow, that in our
Saviour's time, " Son of God," was a known and received name and appellation of the Meffiah, and fo ufed
in the holy writers. And that the faith that was to
make men chriftians, was only the believing, " that
" Jefus is the Meffiah." It is to the truth of this propofition that he " examines his witneffes," as he fpeaks
p. 21. And this, if I miftake not, in his epiftle dedi-
catory, he calls " chriftianity;" fol. A 3, where he
calls them " witneffes to chriftianity." But thefe two
propofitions, viz. That " Son of God," in the gofpel,
ftands for Meffiah ; and that the faith, which alone
makes men chriftians, is the believing " Jefus to be the
" Meffiah," difpleafes Mr. Edwards fo much in my
book, that he thinks himfelf authorized from them, to
charge me with focinianifm, and want of fincerity. How
he will be pleafed to treat this reverend prelate, whilft
he is alive (for the dead may, with good manners, be
made bold with) muft be left to his decifive authority.
This, I am fure, which way foever he determine, he
muft, for the future, either afford me more good company, or fairer quarter.

A SECOND

VINDICATION

OF THE

REASONABLENESS

OF

CHRISTIANITY, &c.

PREFACE

TO THE

READER.

IT hath pleafed Mr. Edwards, in anfwer to the " Rea-
" fonablenefs of Chriftianity, &c." and its " Vindi-
" cation," to turn one of the moft weighty and important points that can come into queftion, (even no lefs,
than the very fundamentals of the chriftian religion)
into a mere quarrel againft the author; as every one,
with Mr. Bold, may obferve. In my reply to him, I
have endeavoured, as much as his objections would allow me, to bring him to the fubject-matter of my book,
and the merits of the caufe; though his peculiar way of
writing controverfy has made it neceffary for me, in following him ftep by ftep, to wipe off the dirt he has
thrown on me, and clear myfelf from thofe falfhoods he
has filled his book with. This I could not but do, in
dealing with fuch an antagonift; that, by the untruths
I have proved upon him, the reader may judge of thofe
other allegations of his, whereof the proof lying on his
fide, the bare denial is enough on mine, and, indeed,
are wholly nothing to the truth or falfhood of what is
contained in my " Reafonablenefs of Chriftianity, &c."
To which I fhall defire the reader to add this farther
confideration from his way of writing, not againft my

N 4   book,

book, but againſt me, for writing it, that if he had had
a real concern for truth and religion in this diſpute, he
would have treated it after another manner; and we
ſhould have had from him more argument, reaſoning,
and clearneſs, and leſs boaſting, declamation, and rail_
ing.   It has been unavoidable for me to take notice of
a great deal of this ſort of ſtuff, in anſwering a writer,
who has very little elſe to ſay in the controverſy, and
places his ſtrength in things beſide the queſtion: but
yet I have been ſo careful, to take all occaſions to explain the doctrine of my book, that I hope the reader
will not think his pains wholly loſt labour, in peruſing
this reply; wherein he will find ſome farther, and, I
hope, ſatisfying account, concerning the writings of the
New Teſtament, and the Chriſtian Religion contained
in it.

Mr. Edwards's ill language, which I thought perſonally to me, (though I know not how I had provoked a
man whom I had never had to do with) I am now ſatisfied,
by his rude and ſcurrilous treating of Mr. Bold, is his
way and ſtrength in management of controverſy; and
therefore requires a little more conſideration in this diſ-
putant, than otherwiſe it would deſerve. Mr. Bold, with
the calmneſs of a chriſtian, the gravity of a divine, the
clearneſs of a man of parts, and the civility of a well-
bred man, made ſome " animadverſions" on his " So-
" cinianiſm unmaſked;" which, with a ſermon preached
on the ſame ſubject with my " Reaſonableneſs of Chri-
" ſtianity," he publiſhed: and how he has been uſed by
Mr. Edwards, let the world judge.

I was extremely ſurpriſed with Mr. Bold's book, at a
time when there was ſo great an outcry againſt mine,
on all hands.   But, it ſeems, he is a man that does not
take up things upon hearſay; nor is afraid to own truth,
whatever clamour or calumny it may lie under.   Mr.
Edwards confidently tells the world, that Mr. Bold has
been drawn in to eſpouſe this cauſe, upon baſe and mean
conſiderations.   Whoſe picture of the two, ſuch a de-
ſcription is moſt likely to give us, I ſhall leave to the
reader to judge, from what he will find in their writings
on this ſubject.   For as to the perſons themſelves, I am

equally

equally a ftranger to them both: I know not the face of either of them: and having hitherto never had any communication with Mr. Bold, I fhall begin with him, as I did with Mr. Edwards in print; and here publicly return him this following acknowledgment, for what he has printed in this controverfy.

To Mr. Bold.

Sir,

Though I do not think I ought to return thanks to any one, for being of my opinion, any more than to fall out with him, for differing from me; yet I cannot but own to all the world, the efteem, that I think is due to you, for that proof you have given, of a mind and temper becoming a true minifter of the gofpel; in appearing, as you have done, in the defence of a point, a great point of chriftianity, which it is evident you could have no other temptation to declare for, but the love of truth. It has fared with you herein, no better than with me. For Mr. Edwards not being able to anfwer your arguments, he has found out already, that you are a mercenary, defending a caufe againft your perfuafion, for hire; and that you " are failing to Racovia by " a fide-wind:" fuch inconfiftencies can one (whofe bufinefs it is to rail for a caufe he cannot defend) put together to make a noife with: and he tells you plainly, what you muft expect, if you write any more on this argument, viz. to be pronounced a downright apoftate and renegado.

As foon as I faw your fermon and animadverfions, I wondered what fcarecrow Mr. Edwards would fet up, wherewith he might hope to deter men of more caution than fenfe, from reading of them; fince focinianifm, from which you were known to be as remote as he, I concluded would not do. The unknown author of the " Reafonablenefs of Chriftianity," he might make a focinian, mahometan, atheift, or what fort of raw-head and bloody-bones he pleafed. But I imagined he had had more fenfe than to venture any fuch afperfions, on

a man

a man whom, though I have not yet the happiness perfonally to know; yet, I know, hath justly a great and settled reputation amongst worthy men: and I thought that that coat, which you had worn with so much reputation, might have preserved you from the besspatterings of Mr. Edwards's dunghill. But what is to be expected from a warrior that hath no other ammunition, and yet ascribes to himself victory from hence, and, with this artillery, imagines he carries all before him? And so Skimmington rides in triumph, driving all before him, by the ordures that he bestows on those that come in his way. And, were not christianity concerned in the case, a man would scarce excuse to himself the ridiculousness of entering into the lift with such a combatant. I do not, therefore, wonder that this mighty boaster, having no other way to answer the books of his opponents, but by popular calumnies, is fain to have recourse to his only refuge, and lay out his natural talent in vilifying and slandering the authors. But I see, by what you have already writ, how much you are above that; and, as you take not up your opinions from fashion or interest, so you quit them not, to avoid the malicious reports of those that do: out of which number, they can hardly be left, who (unprovoked) mix, with the management of their cause, injuries and ill-language, to those they differ from. This, at least, I am sure, zeal or love for truth can never permit falshood to be used in the defence of it.

Your mind, I see, prepared for truth, by resignation of itself, not to the traditions of men, but the doctrine of the gospel, has made you more readily entertain, and more easily enter into the meaning of my book, than most I have heard speak of it. And since you seem to me to comprehend what I have laid together, with the same disposition of mind, and in the same sense that I received it from the holy scriptures, I shall, as a mark of my respect to you, give you a particular account of it.

The beginning of the year in which it was published, the controversy that made so much noise and heat amongst some of the dissenters, coming one day accidentally
dentally

dentally into my mind, drew me, by degrees, into a ftricter and more thorough inquiry into the queftion about juftification. The fcripture was direct and plain, that it was faith that juftified: The next queftion then, was, What faith that was that juftified; what it was which, if a man believed, it fhould be imputed to him for righteoufnefs. To find out this, I thought the right way was, to fearch the fcriptures; and thereupon betook myfelf ferioufly to the reading of the New Teftament, only to that purpofe. What that produced, you and the world have feen.

The firft view I had of it feemed mightily to fatisfy my mind, in the reafonablenefs and plainnefs of this doctrine; but yet the general filence I had in my little reading met with, concerning any fuch thing, awed me with the apprehenfion of fingularity; until going on in the gofpel-hiftory, the whole tenour of it made it fo clear and vifible, that I more wondered that every body did not fee and embrace it; than that I fhould affent to what was fo plainly laid down, and fo frequently inculcated in holy writ, though fyftems of divinity faid nothing of it. That which added to my fatisfaction was, that it led me into a difcovery of the marvellous and divine wifdom of our Saviour's conduct, in all the circumftances of his promulgating this doctrine; as well as of the neceffity that fuch a law-giver fhould be fent from God, for the reforming the morality of the world; two points, that, I muft confefs, I had not found fo fully and advantageoufly explained in the books of divinity I had met with, as the hiftory of the gofpel feemed to me, upon an attentive perufal, to give occafion and matter for. But the neceffity and wifdom of our Saviour's opening the doctrine (which he came to publifh) as he did in parables and figurative ways of fpeaking, carries fuch a thread of evidence through the whole hiftory of the evangelifts, as, I think, is impoffible to be refifted; and makes it a demonftration, that the facred hiftorians did not write by concert, as advocates for a bad caufe, or to give colour and credit to an impofture they would ufher into the world: fince they, every one of them, in fome place or other, omit fome paffages of our Saviour's

life,

life, or circumftancee of his actions; which fhow the wifdom and warinefs of his conduct; and which, even thofe of the evangelifts who have recorded, do barely and tranfiently mention, without laying any ftrefs on them, or making the leaft remark of what confequence they are, to give us our Saviour's true character, and to prove the truth of their hiftory. Thefe are evidences of truth and fincerity, which refult alone from the nature of things, and cannot be produced by any art or contrivance.

How much I was pleafed with the growing difcovery, every day, whilft I was employed in this fearch, I need not fay. The wonderful harmony, that the farther I went difclofed itfelf, tending to the fame points, in all the parts of the facred hiftory of the gofpel, was of no fmall weight with me and another perfon, who every day, from the beginning to the end of my fearch, faw the progrefs of it, and knew, at my firft fetting out, that I was ignorant whither it would lead me; and therefore, every day afked me, What more the fcripture had taught me? So far was I from the thoughts of focinianifm, or an intention to write for that, or any other party, or to publifh any thing at all. But, when I had gone through the whole, and faw what a plain, fimple, reafonable thing chriftianity was, fuited to all conditions and capacities; and in the morality of it now, with divine authority, eftablifhed into a legible law, fo far furpaffing all that philofophy and human reafon had attained to, or could poffibly make effectual to all degrees of mankind; I was flattered to think it might be of fome ufe in the world; efpecially to thofe, who thought either that there was no need of revelation at all, or that the revelation of our Saviour required the belief of fuch articles for falvation, which the fettled notions, and their way of reafoning in fome, and want of underftanding in others, made impoffible to them. Upon thefe two topics, the objections feemed to turn, which were with moft affurance made by deifts, againft chriftianity; but againft chriftianity mifunderftood. It feemed to me, that there needed no more to fhow them the weaknefs of their exceptions, but to lay plainly before them the

doctrine

doctrine of our Saviour and his apostles, as delivered in the scriptures, and not as taught by the several sects of christians.

This tempted me to publish it, not thinking it deserved an opposition from any minister of the gospel; and least of all, from any one in the communion of the church of England. But so it is, that Mr. Edwards's zeal for he knows not what (for he does not yet know his own creed, nor what is required to make him a christian) could not brook so plain, simple, and intelligible a religion: but yet, not knowing what to say against it, and the evidence it has from the word of God, he thought fit to let the book alone, and fall upon the author. What great matter he has done in it, I need not tell you, who have seen and showed the weakness of his wranglings. You have here, Sir, the true history of the birth of my " Reasonableness of Christianity, as delivered in the Scriptures," and my design in publishing it, &c. What it contains, and how much it tends to peace and union among christians, if they would receive christianity as it is, you have discovered. I am,

SIR,

Your most humble servant,

A. B.

My readers will pardon me, that, in my preface to them, I make this particular address to Mr. Bold. He hath thought it worth his while to defend my book. How well he has done it, I am too much a party to say. I think it so sufficient to Mr. Edwards, that I needed not to have troubled myself any farther about him, on the account of any argument that remained in his book to be answered. But a great part of the world judging of the contests about truth, as they do of popular elections, that the side carries it where the greatest noise is; it was necessary they should be undeceived, and be let see, that sometimes such writers may be let alone, not because they cannot, but because they deserve not to be answered.

This

This farther I ought to acknowledge to **Mr. Bold,** and own to the world, that he hath entered into the true fenfe of my treatife, and his notions do fo perfectly agree with mine, that I fhall not be afraid, by thoughts and expreffions very like his, in this my fecond vindication, to give Mr. Edwards (who is exceedingly quick-fighted, and pofitive in fuch matters) a handle to tell the world, that either I borrowed this my "vindication" from Mr. Bold, or writ his "animadverfions" for him. The former of thefe I fhall count no difcredit, if Mr. Edwards think fit to charge me with it; and the latter, Mr. Bold's character is anfwer enough to. Though the impartial reader, I doubt not, will find, that the fame uniform truth, confidered by us, fuggefted the fame thoughts to us both, without any other communication.

There is another author, who in a civiler ftyle, hath made it neceffary for me to vindicate my book from a reflection or two of his, wherein he feems to come fhort of that candour he profeffes. All that I fhall fay on this occafion here, is, that it is a wonder to me, that having publifhed what I thought the fcripture told me was the faith that made a chriftian, and defired, that if I was miftaken, any one that thought fo, would have the goodnefs to inform me better; fo many with their tongues, and fome in print, fhould intemperately find fault with a poor man out of his way, who defires to be fet right; and no one, who blames his faith, as coming fhort, will tell him what that faith is, which is required to make him a chriftian. But I hope, that amongft fo many cenfurers, I fhall at laft find one, who knowing himfelf to be a chriftian upon other grounds than I am, will have fo much chriftian charity, as to fhow me what more is abfolutely neceffary to be believed, by me, and every man, to make him a chriftian.

A SECOND

VINDICATION

OF THE

REASONABLENESS

OF

CHRISTIANITY, &c.

A CAUSE that ſtands in need of falſhoods to ſupport it, and an adverſary that will make uſe of them, deſerve nothing but contempt; which I doubt not but every conſiderate reader thought anſwer enough to " Mr. " Edwards's Socinianiſm unmaſked." But, ſince in his late " Socinian Creed," he ſays, " I would have an- " ſwered him if I could," that the intereſt of chriſtianity may not ſuffer by my ſilence, nor the contemptibleneſs of his treatiſe afford him matter of triumph among thoſe who lay any weight on ſuch boaſting, it is fit it ſhould be ſhown what an arguer he is, and how well he deſerves, for his performance, to be dubbed, by himſelf, " irre- " fragable."

Thoſe who, like Mr. Edwards, dare to publiſh in- ventions of their own, for matters of fact, deſerve a

name

name fo abhorred, that it finds not room in civil converfation. This fecures him from the proper anfwer,
due to his imputations to me, in print, of matters of
fact utterly falfe, which, without any reply of mine, fix
upon him that name (which, without a profligate mind,
a man cannot expofe himfelf to) till he hath proved
them. Till then, he muft wear what he has put upon
himfelf. This being a rule, which common juftice hath
prefcribed to the private judgments of mankind, as well
as to the public judicatures of courts, that all allegations of facts, brought by contending parties, fhould be
prefumed to be falfe, till they are proved.

There are two ways of making a book unanfwerable.
The one is by the clearnefs, ftrength, and fairnefs of the
argumentation. Men who know how to write thus, are
above bragging what they have done, or boafting to the
world that their adverfaries are baffled. Another way to
make a book unanfwerable, is to lay a ftrefs on matters
of fact foreign to the queftion, as well as to truth ; and
to ftuff it with fcurrility and fiction. This hath been
always fo evident to common fenfe, that no man, who
had any regard to truth, or ingenuity, ever thought
matters of fact befides the argument, and ftories made
at pleafure, the way of managing controverfies. Which
fhowing only the want of fenfe and argument, could, if
ufed on both fides, end in nothing but downright railing : and he muft always have the better of the caufe,
who has lying and impudence on his fide.

The unmafker, in the entrance of his book, fets a
great diftance between his and my way of writing. I
am not forry that mine differs fo much as it does from
his. If it were like his, I fhould think, like his, it
wanted the author's commendations. For, in his firft
paragraph, which is all laid out in his own teftimony of
his own book, he fo earneftly befpeaks an opinion of
maftery in politenefs, order, coherence, pertinence,
ftrength, ferioufnefs, temper, and all the good qualities
requifite in controverfy, that I think, fince he pleafes
himfelf fo much with his own good opinion, one in
pity ought not to go about to rob him of fo confiderable
an admirer. I fhall not, therefore, conteft any of thofe
excel-

excellencies he ascribes to himself, or faults he blames
in me, in the management of the dispute between us,
any farther than as particular passages of his book, as I
come to examine them, shall suggest unavoidable remarks
to me. I think the world does not so much concern
itself about him, or me, that it need be told in that in-
ventory, he has given of his own good parts, in his first
paragraph, which of us two has the better hand at
" flourishes, jesting, and common-places ;" if I am,
as he says, p. 2, troubled with " angry fits, and passio-
" nate ferments, which, though I strive to palliate, are
" easily discernible, &c." and he be more laudably ingenuous in the openness of that temper, which he shows
in every leaf ; I shall leave to him the entire glory of
boasting of it. Whatever we brag of our performances,
they will be just as they are, however he may think to
add to his, by his own encomium on them. The difference in style, order, coherence, good breeding (for all
those, amongst others, the unmasker mentions) the reader will observe, whatever I say of them ; and at best
they are nothing to the question in hand. For though
I am a " tool, pert, childish, starch'd, impertinent, in-
" coherent, trifling, weak, passionate, &c." commendations I meet with, before I get to the 4th page, besides
what follows, as, " upstart Racovian," p. 24. " Flou-
" rishing scribbler," p. 41. " Dissembler," 106. " Pe-
" dantic," 107. I say, although I am all this, and what
else he liberally bestows on me in the rest of his book,
I may have truth on my side, and that in the present
case serves my turn.

Having thus placed the laurels on his own head, and
sung applause to his own performance, he, p. 4, enters,
as he thinks, upon his businefs, which ought to be, as he
confesses, p. 3, " to make good his former charges."
The first whereof he sets down in these words : That
" I unwarrantably crowded all the necessary articles of
" faith into one, with a design of favouring soci-
" nianism."

If it may be permitted to the subdued, to be so bold
with one, who is already conqueror, I desire to know,
where that proposition is laid down in these terms, as

O laid

laid to my charge. Whether it be true, or falfe, fhall, if he pleafes, be hereafter examined: but it is not, at prefent, the matter in queftion. There are certain pro-pofitions, which he having affirmed, and I denied, are under debate between us: and that the difpute may not run into an endlefs ramble, by multiplying of new, before the points in conteft are decided, thofe ought firft to be brought to an iffue.

To go on, therefore, in the order of his " Socinian-" ifm unmafked," (for, p. 3, he has, out of the Mifhna, taught me good breeding, " to anfwer the firft, and fo " in order.") The next thing he has againft me is p. 5, which, that the reader may underftand the force of, I muft inform him, that in p. 105, of his " Thoughts " concerning the caufes of atheifm" he faid, that I " give this plaufible conceit," as he calls it, " over " and over again, in thefe formal words," viz. " That " nothing is required to be believed by any chriftian " man, but this, that Jefus is the Meffiah." This I denied. To make it good, " Socinianifm unmafked," p. 5, he thus argues. Firft, " It is obfervable, that this " guilty mah would be fhifting off the indictment, by " excepting againft the formality of words, as if fuch " were not to be found in his book: but when doth he " do this? In the clofe of it, when this matter was ex-" haufted, and he had nothing elfe to fay," Vind. p. 113, " then he bethinks himfelf of his falvo, &c." Anfw. As if a falfhood were ever the lefs a falfhood, be-caufe it was not oppofed, or would grow into a truth, if it were not taken notice of, before the 38th page of the anfwer. I defire him to fhow me thefe " formal words " over and over again," in my " reafonablenefs of chrif-" tianity:" nor let him hope to evade, by faying I would be " fhifting, by excepting againft the formality " of the words."

To fay, that " I have, over and over again, thofe for-" mal words," in my book, is an affertion of a matter of fact; let him produce the words, and juftify his allegation, or confefs, that this is an untruth pub-lifhed to the world: and fince he makes fo bold with truth, in a matter vifible to every body, let the
world

world be judge, what credit is to be given to his allegations of matters of fact, in things foreign to what I
have printed; and that are not capable of a negative
proof. A sample whereof the reader has at the entrance, in his introduction, p. A. 4, and the three or
four following pages. Where he affirms to the world,
not only what I know to be false; but that every one
must see, he could not know to be true. For he pretends to know and deliver my thoughts. And what the
character is of one that confidently affirms what he does
not know, no body need be told.

But he adds, "I had before pleaded to the indict-
" ment, and thereby owned it to be true." This is to
make good his promise, p. 3, to keep at a distance from
my " feeble strugglings." Here this strong arguer must
prove, that what is not answered or denied, in the very
beginning of a reply, or before the 11th page, "is
" owned to be true." In the mean time, 'till he does
that, I shall desire such of my readers, as think the unmasker's veracity worth examining, to see in my Vindication, from p. 174, &c. wherein is contained, what I
have said about one article, whether I have owned what
he charged me with, on that subject.

This proposition then remains upon him still to be
proved, viz.

I. " That I have, over and over again, these formal
" words in my reasonableness of christianity, viz.
" That nothing is required to be believed by
" any christian man, but this, That Jesus is the
" Messiah."

He goes on, p. 5. "And indeed he could do no
" other; for it was the main work he set himself about,
" to find but one article of faith in all the chapters of
" the four evangelists, and the acts of the apostles;"
this is to make good his promise, p. 3, " To clear his
" book from those sorry objections and cavils I had
" raised against it." Several of my " sorry objections
" and cavils" were to represent to the reader, that a
great part of what is said was nothing but suspicions and

conjectures;

conjectures; and such he could not but then own them to be. But now he has rid himself of all his conjectures; and has raised them up into direct, positive affirmations, which, being said with confidence without proof, who can deny but he has cleared, thoroughly cleared, that part from my " sorry objections and ca-
" vils ?" He says, " it was the main work I set myself
" about, to find but one article of faith." This I must take the liberty to deny; and I desire him to prove it. A man may " set himself to find two," or as many as there be, and yet find but one : or a man may " set
" himself to find but one," and yet find two more. It is no argument, from what a man has found, to prove what was his main work to find, unless where his aim was only to find what there was, whether more or less. For a writer may find the reputation of a poor contemptible railer; nay of a downright impudent lyar; and yet no body will think it was his main work to find that. Therefore, sir, if you will not find what it is like you did not seek, you must prove those many confident assertions you have published, which I shall give you in tale, whereof this is the second, viz.

II. That " the main business I set myself about, was
" to find but one article of faith."

In the following part of this sentence, he quotes my own words with the pages where they are to be found; the first time, that, in either of his two books against me, he has vouchsafed to do so, concerning one article, wherewith he has made so much noise. My words in (p. 102. of) my " reasonableness of christianity" stand thus : " for that this is the sole doctrine pressed and re-
" quired to be believed, in the whole tenour of our Sa-
" viour's and his apostles preaching, we have showed,
" through the whole history of the Evangelists and Acts,
" and I challenge them to show, that there was any
" other doctrine upon their assent to which, or disbelief
" of it, men were pronounced believers, or unbelievers,
" and accordingly received into the church of Christ,
" as members of his body, as far as mere believing
" could

" could make them fo; or elfe kept out. This was
" the only gofpel article of faith, which was preached
" to them." Out of this paffage, the unmafker fets
down thefe words, " This is the SOLE doctrine preffed
" and required to be believed, in the whole tenour of
" our Saviour's and his apoftles preaching," p. 129.
" this was the ONLY gofpel article of faith, which was
" preached to them."

I fhall pafs by all other obfervations, that this way of
citing thefe words would fuggeft, and only remark, that,
if he brought thefe words, to prove the immediately
preceding affertion of his, viz. That " to find out but
" one article of faith was the main work I fet myfelf
" about." This argument, reduced into form, will
ftand thus :

He who fays, that this is the fole doctrine preffed and
required to be believed in the whole tenour of our Saviour's and his apoftles preaching, upon their affent to
which, or difbelief of it, men were pronounced believers,
or unbelievers; and accordingly received into the church
of Chrift, as members of his body, as far as mere believing could make them fo, or elfe kept out ; fets himfelf to find out but one article of faith, as his main
work. But the vindicator did fo : ergo.

If this were the ufe he would make of thofe words of
mine cited, I muft defire him to prove the major. But
he talks fo freely, and without book every where, that I
fuppofe he thought himfelf, by the privilege of a declaimer, exempt from being called ftrictly to an account,
for what he loofely fays, and from proving what he
fhould be called to an account for. Rail luftily, is a
good rule; fomething of it will ftick, true or falfe,
proved or not proved.

If he alleges thefe words of mine, to anfwer my demand, Vind. p. 175, where he found that " I contended
" for one fingle article of faith, with the exclufion and
" defiance of all the reft," which he had charged me
with. I fay, it proves this as little as the former. For
to fay, " That I had fhowed through the whole hiftory
" of the Evangelifts, and the Acts, that this is the fole
" doctrine, or only gofpel-article preffed and required

" to

" to be believed in the whole tenour of our Saviour and
" his apostles preaching; upon their assent to which,
" or disbelieving of it, men were pronounced believers
" or unbelievers, and accordingly received into the
" church of Christ, or kept out;" is the simple assertion of a positive matter of fact, and so carries in it no
defiance, no, nor exclusion of any other doctrinal, or
historical truth, contained in the scripture: and therefore it remains still on the unmasker to show, where it
is I express any defiance of any other truth contained in
the word of God; or where I exclude any one doctrine
of the scriptures. So that if it be true, that "I contend
" for one article," my contention may be without any
defiance, or so much as exclusion of any of the rest,
notwithstanding any thing contained in these words.
Nay, if it should happen that I am in a mistake, and that
this was not the sole doctrine, which our Saviour and
his apostles preached, and, upon their assent to which,
men were admitted into the church: yet the unmasker's
accusation would be never the truer for that, unless it
be necessary, that he that mistakes in one matter of fact,
should be at defiance with all other truths; or, that he
who erroneously says, that our Saviour and his apostles
admitted men into the church, upon the believing him
to be the Messiah, does thereby exclude all other truths
published to the jews before, or to christian believers
afterwards.

If these words be brought to prove that I contended
" for one article," barely "one article," without any
defiance, or exclusion annexed to that contention; I say
neither do they prove that, as is manifest from the words
themselves, as well as from what I said elsewhere, concerning the article of one God. For here, I say, this is
the only gospel article, &c. upon which men were pronounced believers; which plainly intimates some other
article, known and believed in the world before, and
without the preaching of the gospel.

To this the unmasker thinks he has provided a salvo,
in these words, " Socinianism unmasked," p. 6, " And
" when I told him of this one article, he knew well
" enough, that I did not exclude the article of the
                                        " Deity,

" Deity for that is a principle of natural religion."
If it be fit for an unmasker to perceive what is in debate, he would know, that the question is not, what he
excluded, or excluded not, but what articles he charged
me to have excluded.

Taking it therefore to be his meaning (which it must
be, if he meant any thing to the purpose), viz. That
when he charged me so often and positively, for contest-
ing for " one article," viz. that " Jesus was the Mes-
" siah," he did not intend to accuse me for excluding
" the article of the Deity." To prove that he did not so
intend it, he tells me, that " I knew that he did not."

Ans. How should I know it? He never told me so,
either in his book, or otherwise. This I know, that he
said, p. 115, that, " I contended for one article, with
" the exclusion of all the rest." If then the belief of
the Deity be an article of faith, and be not the article
of Jesus being the Messiah, it is one " of the rest;" and
if " all the rest" were excluded, certainly that being
one of " all the rest," must be excluded. How then he
could say, " I knew that he excluded it not." i. e.
meant not that I excluded it, when he positively says,
I did " exclude it," I cannot tell, unless he thought
that I knew him so well, that when he said one thing,
I knew that he meant another, and that the quite contrary.

He now, it seems, acknowledges that I affirmed,
that the belief of the Deity, as well as of Jesus being
the Messiah, was required to make a man a believer.
The believing in " one God, the Father Almighty,
" maker of heaven and earth," is one article; and in
" Jesus Christ, his only Son our Lord," is another article. These, therefore, being " two articles," and
both asserted by me, to be required to make a man a
christian, let us see with what truth or ingenuity the unmasker could apply, besides that above-mentioned, these
following expressions to me, as he does without any exception: " Why then must there be one article and no
" more?" p. 115. " Going to make a religion for his
" myrmidons, he contracts all into one article, and will
" trouble them with no more," p. 117. " Away with

O 4 " systems,

" fyftems, away with creeds, let us have but one arti-
" cle, though it be with defiance to all the reft," p.
118.   " Thus we fee, why he reduces all belief to that
" one article before rehearfed," p. 120.   And all this,
without any the leaft exception of the article of a
Deity, as he now pretends.   Nor could he, indeed, as
is evident from his own words, p. 121, 122.   " To con-
" clude, this gentleman and his fellows are refolved to
" be unitarians ; they are for One article of faith, as
" well as One perfon in the Godhead : —— But, if thefe
" learned men were not prejudiced, ——— they would
" perceive, that, when the catholic faith is thus brought
" down to one fingle article, it will foon be reduced to
" none; the unit will dwindle into a cypher."   By
which the reader may fee that his intention was, to perfuade the world, that I reduced ALL BELIEF, the CATHO-
LIC FAITH, (they are in his own words) " to one fingle
" article, and no more."   For if he had given but the
leaft hint, that I allowed of Two, all the wit and ftrength
of argument, contained in unitarians, unit and cypher,
with which he winds up all, had been utterly loft, and
dwindled into palpable nonfenfe.

To demonftrate that this was the fenfe he would
be underftood in, we are but to obferve what he fays
again, p. 50. of his " Socinianifm unmafked," where
he tells his readers, that " I and my friends have new
" modelled the apoftle's creed ; yea, indeed, have pre-
" fented them with ONE article, inftead of TWELVE."
And hence we may fee, what fincerity there is, in the
reafon he brings, to prove that he did not exclude the
" article of the Deity."   " For, fays he, p. 6, that is a
" principle of natural religion."

Anf. Ergo, he did not in pofitive words, without
any exception, fay, I reduced " all belief, the catholic
" faith, to one fingle article, and no more."   But to
make good his promife, " not to refemble me in the
" little artifices of evading," he wipes his mouth, and
fays at the bottom of this page, " But the reader fees
" his [the vindicator's] fhuffling."   Whilft the article
of " One God" is a part of " ALL belief, a part of the
" catholic faith," ALL which he affirmed I excluded,
but

but the one article concerning the Messiah ; every one will see where the shuffling is: and, if it be not clear enough from those words themselves, let those above quoted, out of p. 50, of his " Socinianism unmasked," where he says, that " I have new modelled the apostles " creed, and presented the world with ONE article in- " stead of TWELVE," by an interpretation of them. For, if the article of " one eternal God, maker of heaven and " earth," be one of the articles of the apostles creed, and the one article I presented them with, be not that, it is plain, he did, and would be understood to mean, that by my one article, I excluded that of the one eter- nal God, which branch soever of religion, either natural, or revealed, it belongs to.

· I do not endeavour to " persuade the reader," as he says, p. 6, "that he misunderstood me," but yet every body will see that he misrepresented me. And I chal- lenge him to say, that those expressions above quoted out of him, concerning " one article," in the obvious sense of the words, as they stand in his accusation of me, were true.

This flies so directly in his face, that he labours mightily to get it off, and therefore adds these words, " My discourse did not treat, (neither doth his book run " that way) of principles of natural religion, but of the " revealed, and particularly the christian : accordingly, " this was it that I taxed him with, That, of all the " principles and articles of christianity, he chose out " but one, as necessary to be believed to make a man a " christian."

Answ. His book was of ———— atheism, which one may think should make his " discourse treat of natural " religion." But I pass by that, and bid him tell me where he taxed me, " That, of all the principles and ar- " ticles of christianity, I chose out but one :" let him show, in all his discourse, but such a word, or any thing said, like " one article of christianity," and I will grant that he meant particularly, but spoke generally ; misled his reader, and left himself a subterfuge. But if there be no expression to be found in him, tending that way, all this is but the covering of one falshood with another,

which

which thereby only becomes the groffer. Though if he
had in exprefs words taxed me, " That, of all the principles and articles of the chriftian religion, I chofe
out but one, that would not at all help him, till he farther declares, that the belief of one God is not an " ar-
" ticle of the chriftian religion." For, of " ALL the ar-
" ticles of the chriftian religion," he fays, " I chofe but
" one ;" which not being that of a Deity, his words
plainly import, that that was left out amongſt the reſt,
unleſs it be poffible for a man to choofe but one article
of the chriftian religion, viz. That " Jefus is the Mef-
" fiah ;" and at the fame time, to choofe two articles of
the chriftian religion, viz. That there is one eternal
God, and that Jefus is the Meſſiah. If he had fpoken
clearly, and like a fair man, he fhould have faid, That
he taxed me with choofing but one article of revealed religion. This had been plain and direct to his purpofe :
but then he knew the falfhood of it would be too obvious : for, in the feven pages, wherein he taxes me fo
much with One article, chriftianity is feveral times
named, though not once to the purpofe he here pretends.
But revelation is not fo much as once mentioned in
them, nor, as I remember, in any of the pages he be-
ſtows upon me.

To conclude, the feveral paffages above quoted out
of him, concerning one fole article, are all in general
terms, without any the leaſt limitation or reſtriction ;
and, as they ſtand in him, fit to perfuade the reader,
that I excluded all other articles whatfoever, but that
one, of " Jefus the Meſſiah :" and if, in that fenfe, they
are not true, they are fo many falfhoods of his, repeated
there, to miflead others into a wrong opinion of me.
For, if he had a mind his readers fhould have been rightly
informed, why was it not as eafy once to explain himfelf, as fo often to affirm it in general and unreſtrained
terms ? This, all the boafted ſtrength of the unmafker
will not be able to get him out of. This very well becomes one, who fo loudly charges me with fhuffling.
Having repeated the fame thing over and over again,
in as general terms as was poffible, without any the
leaſt limitation, in the whole difcourfe, to have nothing
elfe to plead when required to prove it, but that it was
                                                    meant

meant in a limited sense, in an unmasker, is not shuffling. For, by this way, he may have the convenience to say, and unsay, what he pleases; to vent what stuff he thinks for his turn; and, when he is called to account for it, reply, He meant no such thing. Should any one publish, that the unmasker had but " one article of " faith, and no more," viz. That the doctrines in fashion, and likely to procure preferment, are alone to be received; that all his belief was comprised in this " one " single article:" and, when such a talker was demanded to prove his assertion, should he say, he meant to except his belief of the apostles creed: would he not, notwithstanding such a plea, be thought a shuffling lyar? And, if the unmasker can no otherwise prove those universal propositions above cited, but by saying, he meant them with a tacit restriction, (for none is expressed) they will still, and for ever remain to be accounted for, by his veracity.

What he says in the next paragraph, p. 7, of my " splitting one article into two," is just of the same force, and with the same ingenuity. I had said, That the belief of one God was necessary; which is not denied: I had also said, " That the belief of Jesus of Na-" zareth to be the Messiah, together with those con-" comitant articles of his resurrection, rule, and com-" ing again to judge the world, was necessary, p. 151. " And again, p. 157, That God had declared, whoever " would believe Jesus to be the Saviour promised, and " take him now raised from the dead, and constituted " the Lord and Judge of all men, to be their King and " Ruler, should be saved." This made me say, " These, " and those articles" (in words of the plural number) more than once; evidence enough to any but a caviller, that I " contend not for one single article, and no " more." And to mind him of it, I, in my Vindication, reprinted one of those places, where I had done so; and, that he might not, according to his manner, overlook what does not please him, the words, THESE ARE ARTICLES, were printed in great characters. Whereupon he makes this remark, p. 7, " And though since " he has tried to split this one into two, p. 28, " yet
" he

" he labours in vain: for to believe Jefus to be the
" Meffiah, amounts to the fame with believing him to
" be King and Ruler; his being anointed, (i. e. being
" the Meffiah) including that in it: yet he has the va-
" nity to add in great characters, THESE ARE ARTICLES;
" as if the putting them into thefe great letters, would
" make one article two."

Anf. Though no letters will make one article two;
yet that there is one God, and Jefus Chrift his only Son
our Lord, who rofe again from the dead, afcended into
heaven, and fitteth at the right hand of God, fhall come
to judge the quick and the dead, are, in the apoftles
creed, fet down as more than one article, and therefore
may, very properly, be called THESE ARTICLES, without
fplitting one into two.

What, in my " Reafonablenefs of Chriftianity," I
have faid of one article, I fhall always own; and in what
fenfe I have faid it, is eafy to be underftood; and with
a man of the leaft candour, whofe aim was truth, and
not wrangling, it would not have occafioned one word
of difpute. But as for this unmafker, who makes it
his bufinefs, not to convince me of any miftakes in my
opinion, but barely to mifreprefent me; my bufinefs at
prefent with him is, to fhow the world, that what he
has captioufly and fcurriloufly faid of me, relating to
one article, is falfe; and that he neither has, nor can
prove one of thofe affertions concerning it, above cited
out of him, in his own words. Nor let him pretend a
meaning againft his direct words: fuch a caviller as he,
who would fhelter himfelf under the pretence of a meaning, whereof there are no footfteps; whofe difputes are
only calumnies directed againft the author, without examining the truth or falfhood of what I had publifhed;
is not to expect the allowances one would make to a fair
and ingenuous adverfary, who fhowed fo much concern
for truth, that he treated of it with a ferioufnefs due to the
weightinefs of the matter, and ufed other arguments,
befides obloquy, clamour and falfhoods, againft what he
thought errour. And therefore I again pofitively demand of him to prove thefe words of his to be true, or
confefs that he cannot; viz,

III. " That

III. " That I contend for one article of faith, with
" the exclusion and defiance of all the rest."

Two other instances of this sort of arguments, I gave
in the 175th page of my Vindication, out of the 115th
and 119th pages of his " thoughts concerning the causes
of " atheism ;" and I here demand of him again to show,
since he has not thought fit hitherto to give any answer
to it,

IV. " Where I urge, that there must be nothing in
" christianity, that is not plain, and exactly le-
" velled to all men's mother-wit, and every com-
" mon apprehension."

Or, where he finds, in my " Reasonableness of Chris-
" tianity," this other proposition :

V. " That the very manner of every thing in chris-
" tianity, must be clear and intelligible ; every
" thing must immediately be comprehended by
" the weakest noddle ; or else it is no part of re-
" ligion, especially of christianity."

These things he must prove that I have said : I put it
again upon him to show where I said them, or else to
confess the forgery : for till he does one or the other, he
shall be sure to have these, with a large catalogue of other
falshoods, laid before him.

Page 26, of his " Socinianism unmasked," he endeavours to make good his saying, that " I set up one arti-
" cle, with defiance to all the rest," in these words: " for
" what is excluding them wholly, but defying them ?
" Wherefore, seeing he utterly excludes all the rest, by
" representing them as USELESS to the making a man a
" christian, which is the design of his whole under-
" taking, it is manifest that he defies them."

Answ. This at least is manifest from hence, that
the unmasker knows not, or cares not what he says.
For whoever, but he, thought, that a bare exclusion, or
passing by, was defiance ? If he understands so, I would
advise him not to seek preferment. For exclusions will

happen :

happen; and if every exclufion be defiance, a man had need be well affured of his own good temper, who fhall not think his peace and charity in danger, amongft fo many enemies that are at defiance with him? Defiance, if, with any propriety, it can be fpoken of an article of faith, muft fignify a profeffed enmity to it. For, in its proper ufe, which is to perfons, it fignifies an open and declared enmity, raifed to that height, that he, in whom it is, challenges the party defied to battle, that he may there wreak his hatred on his enemy, in his deftruction. So that "my defiance of all the reft" remains ftill to be proved.

But, fecondly, There is another thing manifeft from thefe words of his, viz. that, notwithftanding his great brags in his firft paragraph, his main fkill lies in fancying what would be for his turn, and then confidently fathering it upon me. It never entered into my thoughts, nor, I think, into any body's elfe, (I muft always except the acute unmafker, who makes no difference between ufeful and neceffary) that all but the fundamental articles of the chriftian faith, were ufelefs to make a man a chriftian; though, if it be true, that the belief of the fundamentals alone (be they few, or many) is all that is neceffary to his being made a chriftian, all that may any way perfuade him to believe them, may certainly be ufeful towards the making him a chriftian: and therefore here again, I muft propofe to him, and leave it with him to be fhowed where it is,

> VI. "I have reprefented all the reft as ufelefs to the "making a man a chriftian?" And how it appears, that "this is the defign of my whole undertaking."

In his "thoughts concerning the caufes of atheifm," he fays, page 115, "What makes him contend for one "fingle article, with the exclufion of all the reft? He "pretends it is this, that all men ought to underftand "their religion." This reafoning I difowned, p. 174. of my Vindication, and intimated, that he fhould have quoted the page where I fo pretended.

To this, p. 26, he tells me with great confidence, and

and in abundance of words, as we shall see by and by, that I had done so; as if repetition were a proof. He had done better to have quoted one place, where I so pretend. Indeed, p. 27, for want of something better, he quotes these words of mine out of p. 157, of the Reasonableness of Christianity: " The all-merciful God " seems herein to have consulted the poor of this " world, and the bulk of mankind. THESE ARE ARTI- " CLES that the labouring and illiterate man may com- " prehend." I ask, whether it be possible for one to bring any thing more direct against himself? The thing he was to prove, was, that " I contended for one single " article, with the exclusion of all the rest, because I " pretended, that all men ought to understand their " religion;" i. e. the reason I gave, why there was to be " but one single article in religion, with the exclu- " sion of all the rest," was, because men ought to un- derstand their religion. And the place he brings, to prove my contending upon that ground, " for one single " article, with the exclusion of all the rest," is a pas- sage wherein I speak of more than one article, and say, " these articles." Whether I said, " these articles," properly or improperly, it matters not, in the present case (and that we have examined in another place) it is plain, I meant more than one article, when I said, " these articles;" and did not think, that the labour- ing and illiterate man could not understand them, if they were more than one: and therefore, I pretended not, that there must be but one, because by illiterate men, more than one could not be understood. The rest of this paragraph is nothing but a repetition of the same asser- tion, without proof, which, with the unmasker, often passes for a way of proving, but with no body else.

But, that I may keep that distance, which he boasts, there is betwixt his and my way of writing, I shall not say this without proof. One instance of his repetition, of which there is such plenty in his book, pray take here. His business, p. 26, is to prove, that " I pre- " tended that I contended for one single article, with " the exclusion of all the rest, because all men ought to " understand their religion;" p. 174. of my Vindication,

I denied

I denied that I had fo pretended.   To convince me that I had, thus he proceeds:

Unmafker.   " He founds his conceit" of one article, "partly upon this, that a multitude of doctrines is " obfcure, and hard to be underftood."

Anfwer.   You fay it, and had faid it before : but I afk you, as I did before, Where I did fo?

Unm.   " And therefore he truffes all up in one article, " that the poor people and bulk of mankind may " bear it."

Anfw.   I defire again to know where I made that inference, and argued fo, for "one article?"

Unm.   " This is the fcope of a great part of his " book."

Anfw.   This is faying again, fhow it once.

Unm.   " But his memory does not keep pace with his " invention, and thence he fays, he remembers nothing " of this in his book," Vind. p. 174.

Anfw.   This is to fay that it is in my book.   You have faid it more than once already; I demand of you to fhow me where.

Unm.   " This worthy writer does not know his own " reafoning, that he ufes."

Anfw.   I afk, Where does he ufe that reafoning?

Unm.   " As particularly thus, that he troubles chrif" tian men with no more, but one article : BECAUSE that " is intelligible, and all people, high and low, may " comprehend it."

Anfw.   We have heard it affirmed by you, over and over again, but the queftion ftill is, " Where is that way " of arguing to be found in my book?"

Unm.   " For he has chofen out, as he thinks, a plain " and eafy article.   Whereas the others, which are com" monly propounded, are not generally agreed on (he " faith) and are dubious and uncertain.   But the be" lieving that Jefus is the Meffiah, has nothing of doubt" fulnefs or obfcurity in it."

Anfw.   The word " For," in the beginning of this fentence, makes it ftand for one of your reafons ; though it be but a repetion of the fame thing in other words.

Unm,

Unm. " This the reader will find to be the drift and
" deſign of ſeveral of his pages."

Anſw. This muſt ſignify " that I trouble men with no
" more but one article, becauſe only one is intelligi-
" ble," and then it is but a repetition. If any thing
elſe be meant by the word This, it is nothing to the
purpoſe. For that I ſaid, that all things neceſſary to
be believed are plain in ſcripture, and eaſy to be under
ſtood, I never denied ; and ſhould be very ſorry, and recant it, if I had.

Unm. " And the reaſon why I did not quote any ſin-
" gle one of them, was, becauſe he inſiſts on it, ſo long
" together : and ſpins it out after his way, in p. 156. of
" his " Reaſonableneſs of Chriſtianity," where he ſets
" down the ſhort, plain, eaſy, and intelligible ſummary
" (as he calls it) of religion," couched in a ſingle article : he immediately adds : " the all-merciful God
" ſeems herein to have conſulted the poor of this world,
" and the bulk of mankind : theſe are articles" (whereas
" he had ſet down but one) " that the labouring and
" illiterate man may comprehend."

Anſw. If " my inſiſting on it ſo long together" was
" the cauſe why, in your thoughts of the cauſes of
" atheiſm," you did not quote any ſingle paſſage ; methinks here, in your " Socinianiſm unmaſked," where
you knew it was expected of you, my " inſiſting on it,"
as you ſay, " ſo long together," might have afforded, at
leaſt, one quotation to your purpoſe.

Unm. " He aſſigns this, as a ground, why it was
" God's pleaſure, that there ſhould be but ONE POINT
" of faith, BECAUSE thereby religion may be underſtood
" the better ; the generality of people may compre-
" hend it."

Anſw. I hear you ſay it again, but want a proof ſtill,
and aſk, " where I aſſign that ground ?"

Unm. " This he repreſents as a great kindneſs done
" by God to man ; whereas the variety of articles would
" be hard to be underſtood."

Anſw. Again the ſame cabbage ; an affirmation, but
no proof.

Unm. " This he enlarges upon, and flouriſhes it

P " over,

" over, after his fashion : and yet defires to know,
" When he faid fo?" p. 175. Vindic.

Anfw. And if I did, let the world here take a fample of the unmafker's ability, or truth, who fpends above
two whole pages, 26, 27, in repetitions of the fame affertion, without the producing any but one place for
proof; and that too againft him, as I have fhown. But
he has not yet done with confounding me by dint of repetition; he goes on,

Unm.   " Good fir, let me be permitted to acquaint
" you, that your memory is as defective as your judg-
" ment."

Anfw.   I thank you for the regard you have had to
it; for often repetition is a good help to a bad memory.
In requital, I advife you to have fome eye to your own
memory and judgment too.   For one, or both of them,
feem a little to blame, in the reafon you fubjoin to the
foregoing words, viz.

Unm.   " For in the very vindication, you attribute
" it to the goodnefs and condefcenfion of the Almighty,
" that he requires nothing, as abfolutely neceffary to be
" believed, but what is fuited to vulgar capacities, and
" the comprehenfion of illiterate men."

Anfw.   I will, for the unmafker's fake, put this argument of his into a fyllogifm. If the vindicator, in his
vindication, attributes it to the goodnefs and condefcenfion of the Almighty, that he requires nothing to be
believed, but what is fuited to vulgar capacities, and the
comprehenfion of illiterate men; then he did, in his
" Reafonablenefs of Chriftianity," pretend, that the
reafon, why he contended for One article, with the exclufion of all the reft, was becaufe all men ought to underftand their religion.

But the vindicator, in his vindication, attributes it
to the goodnefs and condefcenfion of Almighty God,
that he requires nothing to be believed, but what is
fuited to vulgar capacities, and the comprehenfion of
illiterate men,

   " Ergo," in his " Reafonablenefs of Chriftianity,"
he pretended, that the reafon why he contended for one
                                                        article,

article, with the exclusion of all the rest, was, because all men ought to understand their religion.

This was the proposition to be proved, and which, as he confesses here, p. 26, I denied to remember to be in my "Reasonableness of Christianity." Who can but admire his logic!

But, besides the strength of judgment, which you have showed in this clear and cogent reasoning, Does not your memory too deserve its due applause? You tell me, in your "Socinianism unmasked," that in p. 175. of my Vindication, I desired to know when I said so. To which desire of mine, you reply in these words before cited: "Good sir, let me be permitted to acquaint
" you, that your memory is as defective as your judg-
" ment; for, in the very Vindication, you attribute it
" to the goodness and condescension of the Almighty,
" that he requires nothing, as absolutely necessary to be
" believed, but what is suited to vulgar capacities, and
" the comprehension of illiterate men," p. 30.

Sure the unmasker thinks himself at cross questions. I ask him, in the 29th page of my Vindication, WHEN I said so? And he answers, that I had said so in the 30th page of my Vindication; i. e. when I writ the 29th page, I asked the question, When I had said, what he charged me with saying? And I am answered, I had said in the 30th page; which was not yet written: i. e. I asked the question to-day, WHEN I had said so? And I am answered, I had said it to-morrow. As opposite and convincing an answer, to make good his charge, as if he had said, To-morrow I found a horse-shoe. But perhaps this judicious disputant will ease himself of this difficulty, by looking again into the 175th page of my Vindication, out of which he cites these words for mine: "I desire to know, When I said so?" But my words in that place are, "I desire to know, WHERE I said so?" A mark of his exactness in quoting, when he vouchsafes to do it. For unmaskers, when they turn disputants, think it the best way to talk at large, and charge home in generals: but do not often find it convenient to quote pages, set down words, and come to particulars. But, if he had quoted my words right, his anfwer had been juft as pertinent. For I afk him, WHERE, in my " Reafonablenefs of Chriftianity," I had faid fo? And he anfwers, I had faid fo in my Vindication. For where, in my queftion, refers to my " Reafonablenefs of Chri-" ftianity," which the unmafker had feen, and charged with this faying; and could not refer to my Vindication, which he had not yet feen, nor to a paffage in it, which was not then written. But this is nothing with an un-mafker; therefore, what is yet worfe, thefe words of mine, Vindication, p. 175, relate not to the paffage he is here proving, I had faid, but to another different from it; as different as it is to fay, " That, becaufe all men " are to underftand their religion, therefore there is to " be but one article in it;" and to fay, " that there " muft be nothing in chriftianity, that is not plain, and " exactly levelled to all men's mother-wit:" both which he falfly charges on me; but it is only to the latter of them, that my words, " I defire to know, where I faid " fo?" are applied.

Perhaps the well-meaning man fees no difference be-tween thefe propofitions, yet I fhall take the liberty to afk him again, Where I faid either of them, as if they were two? Although he fhould accufe me again, of " excepting againft the formality of words," and doing fo foolifh a thing, as to expect, that a difputing un-mafker fhould account for his words, or any propofition he advances. It is his privilege to plead, he did not mean as his words import, and without any more ado he is affoiled; and he is the fame unmafker he was be-fore. But let us hear him out on the argument he was upon, for his repetitions on it are not yet done. His next words are,

Unm. " It is clear then, that you found your ONE " article on this, that it is fuited to the vulgar capaci-" ties: whereas the other articles mentioned by me, " are obfcure and ambiguous, and therefore furpafs the " comprehenfion of the illiterate."

Anfw. The latter part, indeed, is now the firft time imputed to me; but all the reft is nothing but an un-

proved

proved repetition, though ushered in with " it is clear
" then;" words that should have a proof going before
them.

Unm. " But yet you pretend, that you have forgot
" that any such thing was said by you."

Answ. I have indeed forgot, and notwithstanding all
your pains by so many repetitions, to beat it into my
head, I fear I shall never remember it.

Unm. " Which shows that you are careless of your
" words, and that you forget what you write."

Answ. So you told me before, and this repeating of
it does no more convince me, than that did.

Unm. " What shall we say to such an oblivious au-
" thor?"

Answ. Show it him in his book, or else he will never
be able to remember that it is there, nor any body else
be able to find it.

Unm. " He takes no notice of what falls from his
" own pen."

Answ. So you have told him more than once. Try
him once with showing it him, amongst other things
which fell from his own pen, and see what then he will
say: that perhaps may refresh his memory.

Unm. " And therefore, within a page or two, he
" confutes himself, and gives himself the lye."

Answ. It is a fault he deserves to be told of, over
and over again. But he says, he shall not be able to
find the two pages wherein he " gives himself the lye,"
unless you set down their numbers, and the words in
them, which confute, and which are confuted.

I beg my reader's pardon, for laying before him so
large a pattern of our unmasker's new-fashioned stuff;
his fine tissue of argumentation not easily to be match-
ed, but by the same hand. But it lay all together in
p. 26, 27, 28; and it was fit the reader should have
this one instance of the excellencies he promises in his
first paragraph, in opposition to my " impertinencies,
" incoherences, weak and feeble strugglings." Other
excellencies he there promised, upon the same ground,
which I shall give my reader a taste of in fit places:
not but that the whole is of a piece, and one cannot miss

some

some of them in every page; but to transcribe them all, would be more than they are worth. If any one desires more plenty, I send him to his book itself. But saying a thousand times, not being proving once, it remains upon him still to show,

VII. Where, in my "Reasonableness of Christianity,
    "I pretend that I contend for one single article,
    "with the exclusion of all the rest, because all
    "men ought to understand their religion."

And in the next place, where it is that I say,

VIII. "That there must be nothing in christianity,
    "that is not plain and exactly level to all men's
    "mother-wit."

Let us now return to his 8th page: for the bundling together, as was fit, all that he has said, in distant places, upon the subject of One article, has made me trespass a little, against the Jewish character of a well-bred man, recommended by him to me, out of the Mishna. Though I propose to myself to follow him, as near as I can, step by step, as he proceeds.

In the 110th and 111th pages of his "Thoughts con-
"cerning the Causes of Atheism," he gave us a list of his "fundamental articles:" upon which, I thus applied myself to him, Vind. p. 168, &c. "Give me leave
"now to ask you seriously, Whether these you have
"here set down under the title of "fundamental
"doctrines," are such (when reduced to proposi-
"tions) that every one of them is required, to make
"a man a christian, and such as, without the ac-
"tual belief thereof, he cannot be saved? If they are
"not so, every one of them, you may call them "fun-
"damental doctrines," as much as you please, they are
"not of those doctrines of faith I was speaking of;
"which are only such as are required to be actually
"believed, to make a man a christian." And again,
Vindic. p. 169, I asked him, "Whether just these, nei-
"ther more nor less," were those necessary articles?

To

To which we have his anſwer, " Socinianiſm un-
" maſked," p. 8, &c. From p. 8. to 20, he has quoted
near forty texts of ſcripture, of which he ſaith, p. 21,
" Thus I have briefly ſet before the reader, thoſe evan-
" gelical truths, thoſe chriſtian principles, which belong
" to the very eſſence of chriſtianity : I have proved
" them to be ſuch, and I have reduced moſt of them
" to certain propoſitions, which is a thing the vindi-
" cator called for."

Anſw. Yes : but that was not all the vindicator called for, and had reaſon to expect. For I aſked, " Whe-
" ther thoſe the unmaſker gave us, in his Thoughts
" concerning the Cauſes of Atheiſm," were the fundamental articles, " without an actual belief whereof, a
" man could not be a chriſtian ; juſt all, neither more
" nor leſs ?" This I had reaſon to demand from him,
or from any one, who queſtions that part of my book ;
and I ſhall inſiſt upon it, until he does it, or confeſſes
he cannot. For having ſet down the articles, which the
ſcripture, upon a diligent ſearch, ſeemed to me to require as neceſſary, and only neceſſary ; I ſhall not loſe
my time in examining what another ſays againſt thoſe
fundamentals, which I have gathered out of the preachings of our Saviour and his apoſtles, until he gives me
a liſt of his fundamentals, which he will abide by ; that
ſo, by comparing them together, I may ſee which is the
true catalogue of neceſſaries. For after ſo ſerious and
diligent a ſearch, which has given me light and ſatisfac-
tion in this great point, I ſhall not quit it, and ſet myſelf on float again, at the demand of any one, who would
have me be of his faith, without telling me what it is.
Thoſe fundamentals the ſcripture has ſo plainly given,
and ſo evidently determined, that it would be the
greateſt folly imaginable, to part with this rule for aſk-
ing ; and give up myſelf blindly to the conduct of one,
who either knows not, or will not tell me, what are the
points neceſſary to be believed to make me a chriſtian. He
that ſhall find fault with my collection of fundamentals,
only to unſettle me, and not give me a better of his own,
I ſhall not think worth minding, until, like a fair man,
he puts himſelf upon equal terms, and makes up the de-

fects

fects of mine, by a complete one of his own. For a deficiency, or errour, in one neceſſary, is as fatal, and as certainly excludes a man from being a chriſtian, as in an hundred. When any one offers me a complete catalogue of his fundamentals, he does not unreaſonably demand me to quit mine for nothing: I have then one, that being ſet by mine, I may compare them; and ſo be able to chooſe the true and perfect one, and relinquiſh the other.

He that does not do this, plainly declares, that, (without ſhowing me the certain way to ſalvation) he expects, that I ſhould depend on him with an implicit faith, whilſt he reſerves to himſelf the liberty to require of me to believe, what he ſhall think fit, as he ſees occaſion; and in effect ſays thus, " Diſtruſt thoſe funda-
" mentals, which the preachings of our Saviour and his
" apoſtles have ſhowed to be all that is neceſſary to be
" believed, to make a man a chriſtian; and, though I
" cannot tell you, what are thoſe other articles which
" are neceſſary and ſufficient to make a man a chriſtian,
" yet take me for your guide, and that is as good as if
" I made up, in a complete liſt, the defects of your fun-
" damentals." To which this is a ſufficient anſwer,
" Si quid noviſti rectiùs, imperti; ſi non, his utere
" mecum."

The unmaſker, of his own accord, p. 110, of his
" Thoughts concerning the Cauſes of Atheiſm," ſets down ſeveral, which he calls " fundamental doctrines." I aſk him, whether thoſe be all? For anſwer, he adds more to them in his " Socinianiſm unmaſked:" but in a great pet refuſes to tell me, whether this ſecond liſt of fundamentals be complete: and, inſtead of anſwering ſo reaſonable a demand, pays me with ill language, in theſe words, p. 22, ſubjoined to thoſe laſt quoted, " If
" what I have ſaid will not content him, I am ſure I
" can do nothing that will; and, therefore, if he ſhould
" capriciouſly require any thing more, it would be as
" great folly in me to comply with it, as it is in him to
" move it." If I did aſk a queſtion, which troubles you, be not ſo angry; you yourſelf were the occaſion of it. I propoſed my collection of fundamentals, which I had, with

with great care, fought; and thought I had found clear in the fcripture; you tell me no, it is imperfect, and offer me one of your own. I afk, whether that be per-fect? Thereupon you grow into choler, and tell me it is a foolifh queftion. Why! then I think it was not very wife in you fo forwardly to offer one, unlefs you had one ready, not liable to the fame exception. Would you have me fo foolifh, to take a lift of fundamentals from you, who have not yet one for yourfelf; nor are yet refolved with yourfelf, what doctrines are to be put in, or left out of it? Farther, pray tell me, if you had a fettled collection of fundamentals, that you would ftand to, why fhould I take them from you, upon your word, rather than from an anabaptift, or a quaker, or an arminian, or a focinian, or a lutheran, or a papift; who, I think, are not perfectly agreed with you, or one another in fundamentals? And yet, there is none amongft them, that I have not as much reafon to believe, upon his bare word, as an unmafker, who, to my certain knowledge, will make bold with truth. If you fet up for infallibility, you may have fome claim to have your bare word taken, before any other but the pope. But yet, if you demand to be an unqueftionable propofer, of what is abfolutely neceffary to be believed to make a man a chriftian, you muft perform it a little better, than hitherto you have done. For it is not enough, fome-times to give us texts of fcripture; fometimes propofi-tions of your own framing, and fometimes texts of fcrip-ture, out of which they are to be framed; as page 14, you fay, " Thefe and the like places afford us fuch fun-" damental and neceffary doctrines as thefe:" and again, p. 16, after the naming feveral other texts of fcripture, you add, " which places yield us fuch propofitions as " thefe;" and then in both places fet down what you think fit to draw out of them. And page 15, you have thefe words: " and here, likewife, it were eafy to fhow, " that adoption, juftification, pardon of fins, &c. which " are privileges and benefits beftowed upon us by the " Meffiah, are neceffary matters of our belief." By all which, as well as the whole frame, wherein you make fhow of giving us your fundamental articles, it is plain,

that

that what you have given us there, is nothing lefs than
a complete collection of fundamentals, even in your own
opinion of it.

But, good fir, Why is it a foolifh queftion in me?
You have found fault with my fummary for being fhort :
the defect in my collection of neceffary articles, has
raifed your zeal into fo fevere cenfures, and drawn upon
me, from you, fo heavy a condemnation, that, if half you
have faid of me be true, I am in a very ill cafe, for having fo curtailed the fundamental doctrines of chriftianity.
Is it folly, then, for me to afk from you a complete
creed? If it be fo dangerous (as certainly it is) to fail
in any neceffary article of faith, Why is it folly in me, to
be inftant with you, to give me them all? Or why is it
folly in you, to grant fo reafonable a demand? A fhort
faith, defective in neceffaries, is no more tolerable in
you, than in me; nay, much more inexcufable, if it
were for no other reafon but this, that you reft in it
yourfelf, and would impofe it on others; and yet do not
yourfelf know, or believe it to be complete. For if you
do, why dare you not fay fo, and give it us all entire, in
plain propofitions: and not, as you have in a great meafure done here, give only the texts of fcripture, from
whence, you fay, neceffary articles are to be drawn?
Which is too great an uncertainty for doctrines, abfolutely neceffary. For, poffibly all men do not underftand thofe texts alike, and fome may draw articles
out of them quite different from your fyftem; and fo,
though they agree in the fame texts, may not agree in the
fame fundamentals: and, till you have fet down plainly
and diftinctly your articles, that you think contained in
them, cannot tell whether you will allow them to be
chriftians, or no. For you know, fir, feveral inferences
are often drawn from the fame text; and the different
fyftems of diffenting (I was going to fay chriftians, but
that none muft be fo, but thofe who receive your collection of fundamentals, when you pleafe to give it
them) profeffors are all founded on the fcripture.

Why, I befeech you, is mine a foolifh queftion to afk,
" What are the neceffary articles of faith?" It is of no
lefs confequence than, nor much different from the jai-

1...'s

ler's queftion in the fixteenth of the Acts, " What fhall " I do to be faved?" And that was not, that ever I heard, counted by any one a foolifh queftion. You grant, there are articles neceffary to be believed for falvation: Would it not then be wifdom to know them? Nay, is it not our duty to know and believe them? If not, why do you, with fo much outcry, reprehend me, for not knowing them? Why do you fill your books with fuch variety of invectives, as if you could never fay enough, nor bad enough, againft me, for having left out fome of them? And, if it be fo dangerous, fo criminal to mifs any of them, Why is it a folly in me, to move you to give me a complete lift?

If fundamentals are to be known, eafy to be known, (as, without doubt, they are) then a catalogue may be given of them. But, if they are not, if it cannot certainly be determined, which are they; but the doubtful knowledge of them depends upon gueffes; Why may not I be permitted to follow my gueffes, as well as you yours? Or why, of all others, muft you prefcribe your gueffes to me, when there are fo many that are as ready to prefcribe as you, and of as good authority? The pretence, indeed, and clamour is religion, and the faving of fouls: but your bufinefs, it is plain, is nothing but to over-rule and prefcribe, and be hearkened to as a dictator; and not to inform, teach, and inftruct in the fure way to falvation. Why elfe do you fo ftart and fling, when I defire to know of you, what is neceffary to be believed to make a man a chriftian, when this is the only material thing in controverfy between us; and my miftake in it has made you begin a quarrel with me, and let loofe your pen againft me in no ordinary way of reprehenfion?

Befides, in this way which you take, you will be in no better a cafe than I. For, another having as good a claim to have his gueffes give the rule, as you yours; or to have his fyftem received, as well as you yours; he will complain of you as well, and upon as good grounds, as you do of me; and (if he have but as much zeal for his orthodoxy, as you fhow for yours) in as civil, well-bred, and chriftian-like language.

In

In the next place, pray tell me, Why would it be folly in you, to comply with what I require of you? Would it not be useful to me, to be set right in this matter? If so, Why is it folly in you to set me right? Consider me, if you please, as one of your parishioners, who (after you have resolved which catalogue of fundamentals to give him, either that in your " Thoughts of the Causes of " Atheism," or this other here, in your " Socinianism " unmasked ;" for they are not both the same, nor either of them perfect) asked you, " Are these all fundamental " articles necessary to be believed to make a man a " christian; and are there no more but these?" Would you answer him, that it was folly in you to comply with him, in what he desired? Is it of no moment to know, what is required of men to be believed; without a belief of which, they are not christians, nor can be saved? And is it folly in a minister of the gospel, to inform one committed to his instruction, in so material a point as this, which distinguishes believers from unbelievers? Is it folly in one, whose business it is to bring men to be christians, and to salvation, to resolve a question, by which they may know, whether they are christians or no; and, without a resolution of which, they cannot certainly know their condition, and the state they are in? Is it besides your commission and business, and therefore a folly, to extend your care of souls so far as this, to those who are committed to your charge?

Sir, I have a title to demand this of you, as if I were your parishioner: you have forced yourself upon me for a teacher, in this very point, as if you wanted a parishioner to instruct: and therefore I demand it of you, and shall insist upon it, till you either do it, or confess you cannot. Nor shall it excuse you, to say it is capriciously required. For this is no otherwise capricious, than all questions are capricious to a man, that cannot answer them; and such an one, I think, this is to you. For, if you could answer it, no body can doubt, but that you would, and that with confidence: for no body will suspect it is the want of that makes you so reserved. This is, indeed, a frequent way of answering questions, by men, that cannot otherwise

cover

cover the abfurdities of their opinions, and their info-
lence of expecting to be believed upon their bare words,
by faying they are capriciously afked, and deferve no
other anfwer.

But how far foever capriciousfnefs (when proved, for
faying is not enough) may excufe from anfwering a material queftion, yet your own words here will clear this
from being a capricious queftion in me. For that thofe
texts of fcripture which you have fet down, do not, upon
your own grounds, contain all the fundamental doctrines
of religion, all that is neceffary to be believed to make a
man a chriftian; what you fay a little lower, in this very
page, as well as in other places, does demonftrate. Your
words are, " I think I have fufficiently proved, that
" there are other doctrines befides that [Jefus is the
" Meffiah] which are required to be believed to make
" a man a chriftian; Why did the apoftles write thefe
" doctrines? Was it not, that thofe they writ to, might
" give their affent to them?" This argument, for the
neceffity of believing the texts you cite from their being
fet down in the " New Teftament," you urged thus,
p. 9, " Is this fet down to no purpofe in thefe infpired
" epiftles? Is it not requifite that we fhould know it
" and believe?" And again, p. 29, " they are in our
" bibles to that very purpofe, to be believed." If then
it be neceffary to know and believe thofe texts of fcripture you have collected, becaufe the apoftles writ them,
and they were not " fet down to no purpofe: and they
" are fet down in our bibles on purpofe to be believed:"
I have reafon to demand of you other texts, befides thofe
you have enumerated, as containing points neceffary to
be believed; becaufe there are other texts which the
apoftles writ, and were not " fet down to no purpofe,
" and are in our bibles, on purpofe to be believed," as
well as thofe which you have cited.

Another reafon of doubting, and confequently of demanding, whether thofe propofitions you have fet down
for fundamental doctrines, be every one of them neceffary
to be believed, and all that are neceffary to be believed
to make a man a chriftian, I have from your next argument; which, joined to the former, ftands thus, p. 22 ;
" Why

" Why did the apoftles write thefe doctrines? Was it
" not that thofe they writ to, might give their affent to
" them? Nay, did they not require affent to them?
" Yes verily; for this is to be proved from the nature
" of the things contained in thefe doctrines, which are
" fuch as had immediate refpect to the occafion, au-
" thor, way, means and iffue, of their redemption and
" falvation." If therefore all "things which have an
" immediate refpect to the occafion, author, way,
" means and iffue of men's redemption and falvation,"
are thofe and thofe only, which are neceffary to be believed to make a man a chriftian; may a man not juftly
doubt, whether thofe propofitions, which the unmafker
has fet down, contain all thofe things, and whether there
be not other things contained in other texts of fcripture,
or in fome of thofe cited by him, but otherwife underftood, that have as immediate a " refpect to the occa-
" fion, author, way, means and iffue, of men's redemp-
" tion and falvation," as thofe he has fet down? and
therefore I have reafon to demand a completer lift.
For at beft, to tell us of " all things that have an im-
" mediate refpect to the occafion, author, way, means
" and iffue, of men's redemption and falvation," is but
a general defcription of fundamentals, with which fome
may think fome articles agree, and others, others: and
the terms, " immediate refpect," may give ground
enough for difference about them, to thofe who agree
that the reft of your defcription is right. My demand
therefore is not a general defcription of fundamentals,
but, for the reafons above mentioned, the particular articles themfelves, which are neceffary to be believed to
make a man a chriftian.

　　It is not my bufinefs at prefent, to examine the va-
lidity of thefe arguments of his, to prove all the propofitions to be neceffary to be believed, which he has here,
in his " Socinianifm unmafked," fet down as fuch.
The ufe I make of them now, is to fhow the reafon they
afford me to doubt, that thofe propofitions, which he
has given us, for doctrines neceffary to be believed, are
either not all fuch, or more than all, by his own rule:
and therefore, I muft defire him to give us a completer
creed,

creed, that we may know, what in his fenfe, is neceffary, and enough to make a man a chriftian.

Nor will it be fufficient, in this cafe, to do what he
tells us he has done, in thefe words, p. 21, " I have
" briefly fet before the reader thofe evangelical truths,
" thofe chriftian principles, which belong to the very
" effence of chriftianity ;"————and " I have reduced
" moft of them to certain propofitions, which is a thing
" the vindicator called for," p. 16. With fubmiffion,
I think he miftakes the vindicator. What I called for,
was, not that, " moft of them fhould be reduced to cer-
" tain propofitions," but that all of them fhould : and
the reafon of my demanding that was plain, viz. that
then, having the unmafker's creed in clear and diftinct
propofitions, I might be able to examine whether it was
what God in the fcriptures indifpenfably required of
every man to make him a chriftian, that fo I might
thereby correct the errours or defects of what I at prefent apprehend the fcripture taught me in the cafe.

The unmafker endeavours to excufe himfelf from
anfwering my queftion by another exception againft it,
p. 24, in thefe words : " Surely none, but this upftart
" racovian, will have the confidence to deny, that thefe
" articles of faith are fuch as are neceffary to conftitute
" a chriftian, as to the intellectual and doctrinal part of
" chriftianity ; fuch as muft, IN SOME MEASURE, be
" known and affented to by him. Not that a man is
" fuppofed, every moment, actually to exert his affent
" and belief ; for none of the moral virtues, none of the
" evangelical graces, are exerted thus always. Where-
" fore that queftion," in p. 168, " though he fays he
" afks it" (ferioufly) "might have been fpared," "Whe-
" ther every one of thefe fundamentals is required to
" be believed to make a man a chriftian, and fuch as,
" without the actual belief thereof, he cannot be faved ?"
" Here is ferioufnefs pretended where there is none ;
" for the defign is only to cavil, and (if he can) to ex-
" pofe my affertion. But he is not able to do it ; for
" all his critical demands are anfwered in thefe few
" words, viz. That the intellectual (as well as moral
" endowments) are never fuppofed to be always in act :
" they

" they are exerted upon occasion, not all of them at a
" time.   And therefore he mistakes, if he thinks, or
" rather as he objects without thinking, that these doc-
" trines, if they be fundamental and necessary, must be
" always actually believed.   No man, besides himself,
" ever started such a thing."

This terrible long combat has the unmasker managed
with his own shadow, to confound the seriousness of my
question ; and, as he says himself, is come off, not only
safe and sound, but triumphant.   But for all that, sir,
may not a man's question be serious, though he should
chance to express it ill ? I think you and I were not best
to set up for critics in language, and nicety of expression, for fear we should set the world a laughing.   Yet,
for this once, I shall take the liberty to defend mine
here.   For I demand, in what expression of mine, I said
or supposed, that a man should, every moment, actually
exert his assent to any proposition required to be believed ? Cannot a man say, that the unmasker cannot
be admitted to any preferment in the church of England, without an actual assent to, or subscribing of the
thirty-nine articles ; unless it be supposed, that he must
every moment, from the time he first read, assented to,
and subscribed those articles, until he received institution and induction, " actually exert his assent" to every
one of them, and repeat his subscription ? In the same
sense it is literally true, that a man cannot be admitted
into the church of Christ, or into heaven, without actually believing all the articles necessary to make a man
a christian, without supposing that he must " actually
" exert that assent every moment," from the time that
he first gave it, until the moment that he is admitted
into heaven.   He may eat, drink, make bargains, study
Euclid, and think of other things between ; nay, sometimes sleep, and neither think of those articles, nor any
thing else ; and yet it be true, that he shall not be admitted into the church, or heaven, without an actual
assent to them : that condition of an actual assent, he
has performed, and until he recal that assent, by actual
unbelief, it stands good : and though a lunacy, or lethargy, should seize on him presently after, and he
                                                        should

should never think of it again as long as he lived, yet it is literally true, he is not saved without an actual assent. You might therefore have spared your pains, in saying, "that none of the moral virtues, none of the evangeli-"cal graces, are exerted THUS always," until you had met with some body who said THUS. That I did so, I think, would have entered into no body's thoughts but yours, it being evident from p. 156, of my book, that by actual, I meant explicit. You should rather have given a direct answer to my question, which I here again seri-ously ask you, viz. Whether

IX. Those you called "fundamental doctrines," in your "Thoughts concerning the causes of atheism," or those "christian principles, which "belong to the very essence of christianity," so many as you have given us of them in your "So-"cinianism unmasked," (for you may take which of your two creeds you please) are just those, nei-ther more or less, that are every one of them re-quired to be believed to make a man a christian, and such as, without the actual, or (since that word displeases you) the explicit belief whereof, he can-not be saved?

When you have answered this question, we shall then see, which of us two is nearest the right: but if you shall forbear railing, which, I fear, you take for arguing, against that summary of faith, which our Saviour and his apostles taught, and which only they proposed to their hearers to be believed, to make them christians, until you have found another perfect creed, of only ne-cessary articles, that you dare own for such; you are like to have a large time of silence. Before I leave the pas-sage above-cited, I must desire the reader to take no-tice of what he says, concerning his list of fundamentals, viz. That "these his articles of faith," necessary to con-stitute a christian, are such as must, IN SOME MEASURE, be known and assented to by him: a very wary expression concerning fundamentals! The question is about articles necessary to be explicitly believed to make a man a

chriftian.   Thefe, in his lift, the unmafker tells us, are
" neceffary to conftitute a chriftian, and muft, IN SOME
" MEASURE, be known and affented to."   I would now
fain know of the reader, Whether he underftands thereby, that the unmafker means, that thefe his neceffary
articles muft be explicitly believed or not ? If he means
an explicit knowledge and belief, why does he puzzle his
reader, by fo improper a way of fpeaking ? For what is
as complete and perfect as it ought to be, cannot properly be faid to be " in fome meafure."   If his, " in
" fome meafure," falls fhort of explicitly knowing and
believing his fundamentals, his neceffary articles are
fuch, as a man may be a chriftian, without explicitly
knowing and believing, i. e. are no fundamentals, no neceffary articles at all.   Thus men, uncertain what to fay,
betray themfelves by their great caution.

Having pronounced it folly in himfelf, to make up
the defects of my fhort, and therefore fo much blamed
collection of fundamentals, by a full one of his own,
though his attempt fhows he would if he could ; he goes
on thus, p. 22, " From what I [the unmafker] have
" faid, it is evident, that the vindicator is grofsly mif-
" taken, when he faith," " Whatever doctrines the
" apoftles required to be believed to make a man a
" chriftian, are to be found in thofe places of fcripture
" which he has quoted in his book."   And a little
lower, " I think I have fufficiently proved, that there
" are other doctrines befides that, which are required
" to be believed to make a man a chriftian."

Anfw.   Whatever you have proved, or (as you never
fail to do) boaft you have proved, will fignify nothing,
until you have proved one of thefe propofitions ; and
have fhown either,

X. That what our Saviour and his apoftles preached,
   and admitted men into the church for believing, is
   not all that is abfolutely required to make a man a
   chriftian.   Or,
That the believing him to be the Meffiah, was not the
   only article they infifted on, to thofe who acknowledged one God, and, upon the belief whereof,
                                                they

they admitted converts into the church, in any one of those many places quoted by me out of the history of the New Testament."

I say, any one: for though it be evident, throughout the whole gospel, and the Acts, that this was the one doctrine of faith, which, in all their preachings every where, they principally drive at: yet, if it were not so, but that in other places they taught other things, that would not prove that those other things were articles of faith, absolutely necessarily required to be believed to make a man a christian, unless it had been so said. Because, if it appears, that ever any one was admitted into the church, by our Saviour or his apostles, without having that article explicitly laid before him, and without his explicit assent to it, you must grant, that an explicit assent to that article is not necessary to make a man a christian: unless you will say, that our Saviour and his apostles admitted men into the church that were not qualified with such a faith as was absolutely necessary to make a man a christian; which is as much as to say, that they allowed and pronounced men to be christians, who were not christians. For he that wants what is necessary to make a man a christian, can no more be a christian, than he that wants what is necessary to make him a man, can be a man. For what is necessary to the being of any thing, is essential to its being; and any thing may be as well without its essence, as without any thing that is necessary to its being: and so a man be a man, without being a man; and a christian a christian, without being a christian; and an unmasker may prove this, without proving it. You may, therefore, set up, by your unquestionable authority, what articles you please, as necessary to be believed to make a man a christian: if our Saviour and his apostles admitted converts into the church, without preaching those your articles to them, or requiring an explicit assent to what they did not preach and explicitly lay down, I shall prefer their authority to yours, and think it was rather by them, than by you, that God promulgated the

law

law of faith, and manifefted what that faith was, upon
which he would receive penitent converts.

And, though, by his apoftles, our Saviour taught a
great many other truths, for the explaining this fundamental article of the law of faith, that Jefus is the Meffiah; fome whereof have a nearer, and fome a more
remote connexion with it, and fo cannot be denied by any chriftian, who fees that connexion, or
knows they are fo taught: yet an explicit belief of any
one of them, is no more neceffarily required to make a
man a chriftian, than an explicit belief of all thofe
truths, which have a connexion with the being of a
God, or are revealed by him, is neceffarily required to
make a man not to be an atheift: though none of them
can be denied by any one who fees that connexion, or
acknowledges that revelation, without his being an
atheift. All thefe truths, taught us from God, either by
reafon or revelation, are of great ufe, to enlighten our
minds, confirm our faith, ftir up our affections, &c.
And the more we fee of them, the more we fhall fee,
admire, and magnify the wifdom, goodnefs, mercy, and
love of God, in the work of our redemption. This will
oblige us to fearch and ftudy the fcripture, wherein it is
contained and laid open to us.

All that we find, in the revelation of the " New Tef-
" tament," being the declared will and mind of our
Lord and Mafter, the Meffiah, whom we have taken to
be our king, we are bound to receive as right and truth,
or elfe we are not his fubjects, we do not believe him to
be the Meffiah, our King, but caft him off, and with the
jews fay, " We will not have this man reign over us."
But it is ftill what we find in the fcripture, not in this
or that fyftem; what we, fincerely feeking to know the
will of our Lord, difcover to be his mind. Where it is
fpoken plainly, we cannot mifs it; and it is evident he
requires our affent: where there is obfcurity, either in
the expreffions themfelves, or by reafon of the feeming
contrariety of other paffages, there a fair endeavour, as
much as our circumftances will permit, fecures us from
a guilty difobedience of his will, or a finful errour in
faith, which way foever our inquiry refolves the doubt,

or perhaps leaves it unresolved. If he had required more of us in those points, he would have declared his will plainer to us, and discovered the truth contained in in those obscure, or seemingly contradictory places, as clearly, and as uniformly as he did that fundamental article, that we were to believe him to be the Messiah, our King.

As men, we have God for our King, and are under the law of reason: as christians, we have Jesus the Messiah for our King, and are under the law revealed by him in the gospel. And though every christian, both as a deist and a christian, be obliged to study both the law of nature and the revealed law, that in them he may know the will of God, and of Jesus Christ, whom he hath sent; yet, in neither of these laws, is there to be found a select set of fundamentals, distinct from the rest, which are to make him a deist, or a christian. But he that believes one eternal, invisible God, his Lord and King, ceases thereby to be an atheist; and he that believes Jesus to be the Messiah, his King, ordained by God, thereby becomes a christian, is delivered from the power of darkness, and is translated into the kingdom of the Son of God; is actually within the covenant of grace, and has that faith, which shall be imputed to him for righteousness; and, if he continues in his allegiance to this his King, shall receive the reward, eternal life.

He that considers this, will not be so hot as the unmasker, to contend for a number of fundamental articles, all necessary, every one of them, to be explicitly believed by every one for salvation, without knowing them himself, or being able to enumerate them to another. Can there be any thing more absurd than to say, there are several fundamental articles, each of which every man must explicitly believe, upon pain of damnation, and yet not be able to say, which they be? The unmasker has set down no small number; but yet dares not say, these are all. On the contrary, he has plainly confessed there are more; but will not, i. e. cannot tell what they are, that remain behind: Nay, has given a general description of his fundamental articles, by which it is not evident, but there may be ten times as many as

those

thofe he had named; and amongft them (if he durft, or could name them) probably feveral, that many a good chriftian, who died in the faith, and is now in heaven, never once thought of; and others, which many, of as good authority as he, would, from their different fyf-tems, certainly deny and contradict.

This, as great an abfurdity as it is, cannot be other-wife, whilft men will take upon them to alter the terms of the gofpel; and when it is evident, that our Saviour and his apoftles received men into the church, and pro-nounced them believers, for taking him to be the Mef-fiah, their King and deliverer, fent by God, have a bold-nefs to fay, "this is not enough." But, when you would know of them, what then is enough, they cannot tell you: the reafon whereof is vifible, viz. becaufe they be-ing able to produce no other reafon for their collection of fundamental articles, to prove them neceffary to be believed, but becaufe they are of divine authority, and contained in the holy fcriptures; and are, as the un-mafker fays, "writ there on purpofe to be believed;" they know not where to ftop, when they have once be-gun: thofe texts that they leave out, or from which they deduce none of their fundamentals, being of the fame divine authority, and fo upon that account equally fundamental with what they culled out, though not fo well fuited to their particular fyftems.

Hence come thofe endlefs and unreafonable conten-tions about fundamentals, whilft each cenfures the de-fect, redundancy, or falfhood of what others require, as neceffary to be believed: and yet he himfelf gives not a catalogue of his own fundamentals, which he will fay is fufficient and complete. Nor is it to be wondered; fince, in this way, it is impoffible to ftop fhort of put-ting every propofition, divinely revealed, into the lift of fundamentals; all of them being of divine, and fo of equal authority; and, upon that account, equally ne-ceffary to be believed by every one that is a chriftian, though they are not all neceffary to be believed, to make any one a chriftian. For the New Teftament contain-ing the laws of the Meffiah's kingdom, in regard of all the actions, both of mind and body, of all his fubjects;

every

every chriftian is bound, by his allegiance to him, to believe all that he fays in it to be true ; as well as to affent,
that all he commands in it is juft and good : and what
negligence, perverfenefs, or guilt there is, in his miftaking in the one, or failing in his obedience to the
other, that this righteous judge of all men, who cannot
be deceived, will at the laft day lay open, and reward accordingly,

It is no wonder, therefore, there have been fuch fierce
contefts, and fuch cruel havock made amongft chriftians
about fundamentals ; whilft every one would fet up his
fyftem, upon pain of fire and faggot in this, and hell-fire
in the other world.   Though, at the fame time, whilft
he is exercifing the utmoft barbarities againft others, to
prove himfelf a true chriftian, he profeffes himfelf fo
ignorant, that he cannot tell, or fo uncharitable, that he
will not tell, what articles are abfolutely neceffary and
fufficient to make a man a chriftian.   If there be any
fuch fundamentals, as it is certain there are, it is as certain they muft be very plain.   Why then does every
one urge and make a ftir about fundamentals, and no
body give a lift of them ?   But becaufe (as I have faid)
upon the ufual grounds, they cannot : for I will be bold
to fay, that every one who confiders the matter, will fee,
that either only the article of his being the Meffiah their
King, which alone our Saviour and his apoftles preached to the unconverted world, and received thofe that
believed it into the church, is the only neceffary article
to be believed by a theift, to make him a chriftian ; or
elfe, that all the truths contained in the New Teftament,
are neceffary articles to be believed to make a man a
chriftian : and that between thefe two, it is impoffible
any where to ftand ; the reafon whereof is plain.   Becaufe, either the believing Jefus to be the Meffiah, i. e.
the taking him to be our King, makes us fubjects and
denizens of his kingdom, that is, chriftians : or elfe an
explicit knowledge of, and actual obedience to the laws
of his kingdom, is what is required to make us fubjects ; which, I think, it was never faid of any other
kingdom.   For a man muft be a fubject, before he is
bound to obey.

Q 4   Let

Let us fuppofe it will be faid here, that an obedience to the laws of Chrift's kingdom, is what is neceffary to make us fubjects of it, without which we cannot be admitted into it, i. e. be chriftians: and, if fo, this obedience muft be univerfal; I mean, it muft be the fame fort of obedience to all the laws of this kingdom: which, fince no body fays is in any one fuch as is wholly free from errour, or frailty, this obedience can only lie in a fincere difpofition and purpofe of mind, to obey every one of the laws of the Meffiah, delivered in the New Teftament, to the utmoft of our power. Now, believing right being one part of that obedience, as well as acting right is the other part, the obedience of affent muft be implicitly to all that is delivered there, that it is true. But for as much as the particular acts of an explicit affent, cannot go any farther than his underftanding, who is to affent; what he underftands to be truth, delivered by our Saviour, or the apoftles commiffioned by him, and affifted by his Spirit, that he muft neceffarily believe: it becomes a fundamental article to him, and he cannot refufe his affent to it, without renouncing his allegiance. For he that denies any of the doctrines that Chrift has delivered, to be true, denies him to be fent from God, and confequently to be the Meffiah; and fo ceafes to be a chriftian. From whence it is evident, that if any more be neceffary to be believed to make a man a chriftian, than the believing Jefus to be the Meffiah, and thereby taking him for our King, it cannot be any fet bundle of fundamentals, culled out of the fcripture, with an omiffion of the reft, according as beft fuits any one's fancy, fyftem, or intereft: but it muft be an explicit belief of all thofe propofitions, which he, according to the beft of his underftanding, really apprehends to be contained and meant in the fcripture; and an implicit belief of all the reft, which he is ready to believe, as foon as it fhall pleafe God, upon his ufe of the means, to enlighten him, and make them clear to his underftanding. So that, in effect, almoft every particular man in this fenfe has, or may have, a diftinct catalogue of fundamentals, each whereof it is neceffary for him explicitly to believe, now that he

is

is a christian; whereof, if he should disbelieve, or deny
any one, he would cast off his allegiance, disfranchise
himself, and be no longer a subject of Christ's kingdom.
But, in this sense, no body can tell what is fundamental
to another, what is necessary for another man to believe.
This catalogue of fundamentals, every one alone can
make for himself: no body can fix it for him; no body
can 'collect or prescribe it to another: but this is, according as God has dealt to every one the measure of
light and faith; and has opened each man's understanding, that he may understand the scriptures. Whoever
has used what means he is capable of, for the informing
of himself, with a readiness to believe and obey what
shall be taught and prescribed by Jesus, his Lord and
King, is a true and faithful subject of Christ's kingdom;
and cannot be thought to fail in any thing necessary to
salvation.

Supposing a man and his wife, barely by seeing the
wonderful things that Moses did, should have been persuaded to put themselves under his government; or by
reading his law, and liking it; or by any other motive,
had been prevailed on sincerely to take him for their
ruler and law-giver; and accordingly (renouncing their
former idolatry and heathenish pollutions) in token
thereof had, by baptism and circumcision, the initiating
ceremonies, solemnly entered themselves into that communion, under the law of Moses; had they not, thereby
been made denizens of the common-wealth of Israel,
and invested with all the privileges and prerogatives of
true children of Abraham, leaving to their posterity a
right to their share in the promised land, though they had
died before they had performed any other act of obedience to that law; nay, though they had not known
whose son Moses was, nor how he had delivered the
children of Israel out of Egypt, nor whither he was leading them? I do not say, it is likely they should be so
far ignorant. But, whether they were or no, it was
enough that they took him for their prince and ruler,
with a purpose to obey him, to submit themselves entirely to his commands and conduct; and did nothing
afterwards, whereby they disowned or rejected his authority

thority over them. In that refpect, none of his laws were greater or more neceffary to be fubmitted to, one than another, though the matter of one might be of much greater confequence than of another. But a difobedience to any law of the leaft confequence, if it carry with it a difowning of the authority that made it, forfeits all, and cuts off fuch an offender from that commonwealth, and all the privileges of it.

This is the cafe, in refpect of other matters of faith, to thofe who believe Jefus to be the Meffiah, and take him to be their King, fent from God, and fo are already chriftians. It is not the opinion, that any one may have of the weightinefs of the matter, (if they are, without their own fault, ignorant that our Saviour hath revealed it) that fhall disfranchife them, and make them forfeit their intereft in his kingdom: they may ftill be good fubjects, though they do not believe a great many things, which creed-makers may think neceffary to be believed. That which is required of them, is a fincere endeavour to know his mind, declared in the gofpel, and an explicit belief of all that they underftand to be fo. Not to believe what he has revealed, whether in a lighter, or more weighty matter, calls his veracity into queftion, deftroys his miffion, denies his authority, and is a flat difowning him to be the Meffiah, and fo overturns that fundamental and neceffary article whereby a man is a chriftian. But this cannot be done by a man's ignorance, or unwilful miftake of any of the truths publifhed by our Saviour himfelf, or his authorized and infpired minifters, in the New Teftament. Whilft a man knows not that it was his will or meaning, his allegiance is fafe, though he believe the contrary.

If this were not fo, it is impoffible that any one fhould be a chriftian. For in fome things we are ignorant, and err all, not knowing the fcriptures. For the holy infpired writings, being all of the fame divine authority, muft all equally in every article be fundamental, and neceffary to be believed; if that be a reafon, that makes any one propofition in it neceffary to be believed. But the law of faith, the covenant of the gofpel, being a covenant of grace, and not of natural right, or debt; nothing

nothing can be abfolutely neceffary to be believed, but what, by this new law of faith, God of his good plea-fure hath made to be fo. And this, it is plain, by the preaching of our Saviour and his apoftles, to all that be-lieved not already in him, was only the believing the only true God, and Jefus to be the Meffiah, whom he hath fent. The performance of this puts a man within the covenant, and is that, which God will impute to him for righteoufnefs. All the other acts of affent to other truths, taught by our Saviour, and his apoftles, are not what make a man a chriftian; but are neceffary acts of obedience to be performed by one, who is a chriftian; and therefore, being a chriftian, ought to live by the laws of Chrift's kingdom.

Nor are we without fome glimpfe of light, why it hath pleafed God of his grace, that the believing Jefus to be the Meffiah fhould be that faith which he would impute to men for righteoufnefs. It is evident from fcripture, that our Saviour defpifed the fhame and en-dured the crofs for the joy fet before him; which joy, it is alfo plain, was a kingdom. But, in this kingdom, which his Father had appointed to him, he could have none but voluntary fubjects; fuch as leaving the king-dom of darknefs, and of the prince of this world, with all the pleafures, pomps, and vanities thereof, would put themfelves under his dominion, and tranflate them-felves into his kingdom; which they did, by believing and owning him to be the Meffiah their King, and thereby taking him to rule over them. For the faith for which God juftifieth, is not an empty fpeculation, but a faith joined with repentance, and working by love. And for this, which was, in effect, to return to God himfelf, and to their natural allegiance due to him, and to advance, as much as lay in them, the glory of the kingdom, which he had promifed his Son; God was pleafed to declare, he would accept them, receive them to grace, and blot out all their former tranfgreffions.

This is evidently the covenant of grace, as delivered in the fcriptures: and if this be not, I defire any one to tell me what it is, and what are the terms of it. It is a law of faith, whereby God has promifed to forgive all

our

our fins, upon our repentance and believing fomething; and to impute that faith to us for righteoufnefs. Now I afk, what it is by the law of faith, we are required to believe? For until that be known, the law of faith is not diftinctly known; nor the terms of the covenant, upon which the all-merciful God gracioufly offers us falvation. And, if any one will fay, this is not known, nay, is not eafily and certainly to be known under the gofpel, I defire him to tell me, what the greateft enemies of chriftianity can fay worfe againft it? For a way propofed to falvation, that does not certainly lead thither, or is propofed, fo as not to be known, are very little different as to their confequence; and mankind would be left to wander in darknefs and uncertainty, with the one as well as the other.

I do not write this for controverfy's fake; for had I minded victory, I would not have given the unmafker this new matter of exception. I know whatever is faid, he muft be bawling for his fafhionable and profitable orthodoxy, and cry out againft this too, which I have here added, as focinianifm; and caft that name upon all that differs from what is held by thofe he would recommend his zeal to in writing. I call it bawling, for whether what he has faid be reafoning, I fhall refer to thofe of his own brotherhood, if he be of any brotherhood, and there be any that will join with him in his fet of fundamentals, when his creed is made.

Had I minded nothing but how to deal with him, I had tied him up fhort to his lift of fundamentals, without affording him topics of declaiming, againft what I have here faid. But I have enlarged on this point, for the fake of fuch readers, who, with the love of truth, read books of this kind, and endeavour to inform themfelves in the things of their everlafting concernment: it being of greater confideration with me to give any light and fatisfaction to one fingle perfon, who is really concerned to underftand, and be convinced of the religion he profeffes, than what a thoufand fafhionable, or titular profeffors of any fort of orthodoxy fhall fay, or think of me, for not doing as they do; i. e. for not fay-

ing

ing after others, without understanding what is said, or upon what grounds, or caring to understand it.

Let us now consider his argument, to prove the articles he has given us to be fundamentals. In his "Thoughts concerning the causes of atheism," p. 119, he argues from 1 Tim. iii. 16, where he says, "Christi- " anity is called a mystery; that all things in christi- " anity are not plain, and exactly level to every com- " mon apprehension; and that every thing in christi- " anity is not clear, and intelligible and comprehensible " by the weakest noddle." Let us take this for proved, as. much as he pleases; and then let us see the force of this subtile disputant's argument, for the necessity there is, that every christian man should believe those, which he has given us for fundamental articles, out of the epistles. The reason of that obligation, and the necessity of every man's and woman's believing in them, he has laid in this, that they are to be found in the epistles, or in the bible. This argument for them we have, over and over again, in his "Socinianism unmasked," as here, p. 9, thus: "Are " they set down to no purpose, in these inspired epistles? " Why did the apostles write these doctrines, was it not, " that those they writ to, might give their assent to " them?" p. 22. "They are in our bibles, for that " very purpose, to be believed," p. 25. Now I ask, Can any one more directly invalidate all he says here, for the necessity of believing his articles? Can any one more apparently write booty, than by saying, that "these his " doctrines, these his fundamental articles" (which are, after his fashion, set down between the 8th and 20th pages of this his first chapter) are of necessity to be be- lieved by every one, before he can be a christian, be- cause they are in the epistles and in the bible; and yet affirm, that in christianity, i. e. in the epistles and in the bible, there are mysteries, there are things "not " plain, not clear, not intelligible to common appre- " hensions?" If his articles, some of which contain mysteries, are necessary to be believed to make a man a christian, because they are in the bible; then, according to this rule, it is necessary for many men to believe what is not intelligible to them; what their noddles cannot apprehend,

apprehend, (as the unmafker is pleafed to turn the fuppofition of vulgar people's underftanding the fundamentals of their religion into ridicule) i. e. it is neceffary for many men to do, what is impoffible for them
to do, before they can be chriftians.   But if there be
feveral things in the bible, and in the epiftles, that are
not neceffary for men to believe, to make them chriftians; then all the unmafker's arguments, upon their
being in the epiftles, are no proofs, that all his articles
are neceffary to be believed to make a man a chriftian,
becaufe they are fet down in the epiftles : much lefs,
becaufe he thinks they may be drawn, according to his
fyftem, out of what is fet down in the epiftles.   Let
him therefore, either confefs thefe and the like queftions,
" Why did the apoftles write thefe? Was it not, that
" thofe they writ to, might give their affent to them?
" Why fhould not every one of thefe evangelical truths
" be believed and embraced? They are in our bibles,
" for that very purpofe;" and the like; to be impertinent and ridiculous.   Let him ceafe to propofe them
with fo much oftentation, for they can ferve only to miflead unwary readers : or let him unfay what he has faid,
of things " not plain to common apprehenfions, not
" clear and intelligible."   Let him recant what he has
faid of myfteries in chriftianity.   For I afk with him,
p. 8, " where can we be informed, but in the facred and
" infpired writings?"   It is ridiculous to urge, that any
thing is neceffary to be explicitly believed, to make a
man a chriftian, becaufe it is writ in the epiftles, and
in the bible; unlefs he confefs that there is no myftery,
nothing not plain, or unintelligible to vulgar underftandings, in the epiftles, or in the bible.

   This is fo evident, that the unmafker himfelf, who,
p. 119, of his " Thoughts concerning the Caufes of
" Atheifm," thought it ridiculous to fuppofe, that the
vulgar fhould underftand chriftianity, is here of another
mind : and, p. 30, fays of his evangelical doctrines and
articles, neceffary to be affented to, that they are intelligible and plain; there is no " ambiguity and doubtful-
" nefs in them; they fhine with their own light, and
                                        " to

" to an unprejudiced eye are plain, evident, and illuf-
" trious."

To draw the unmafker out of the clouds, and prevent
his hiding himfelf in the doubtfulnefs of his expreffions,
I fhall defire him to fay directly, whether the articles,
which are neceffary to be believed, to make a man a
chriftian, and particularly thofe he has fet down for
fuch, are all plain and intelligible, and fuch as may be
underftood and comprehended (I will not fay in the
unmafker's ridiculous way, by the weakeft noddles, but)
by every illiterate country man and woman, capable of
church-communion?

If he fays, Yes; then all myfteries are excluded out
of his articles neceffary to be believed to make a man a
chriftian. For that which can be comprehended by every
day-labourer, every poor fpinfter, that is a member of
the church, cannot be a myftery. And, if what fuch illiterate people cannot underftand be required to be believed to make them chriftians, the greateft part of
mankind are fhut out from being chriftians.

But the unmafker has provided an anfwer, in thefe
words, p. 31, " There is," fays he, " a difficulty in the
" doctrine of the trinity, and feveral truths of the gof-
" pel, as to the exact manner of the things themfelves,
" which we fhall never be able to comprehend, at leaft
" on this fide of heaven: but there is no difficulty as
" to the reality and certainty of them, becaufe we know
" they are revealed to us by God in the holy fcrip-
" tures."

Which anfwer of " difficulty in the manner," and
" no difficulty in the reality," having the appearance of
a diftinction, looks like learning; but when it comes
to be applied to the cafe in hand, will fcarce afford us
fenfe.

The queftion is about a propofition to be believed,
which muft firft neceffarily be underftood. For a man
cannot poffibly give his affent to any affirmation or ne-
gation, unlefs he underftand the terms as they are joined
in that propofition, and has a conception of the thing
affirmed or denied, and alfo a conception of the thing,
concerning which it is affirmed or denied, as they are
there

there put together.   But let the propofition be what it will, there is no more to be underftood, than is expreffed in the terms of that propofition.   If it be a propofition concerning a matter of fact, it is enough to conceive, and believe the matter of fact.   If it be a propofition concerning the manner of the fact, the manner of the fact muft alfo be believed, as it is intelligibly expreffed in that propofition ; v. g. fhould this propofition νεκροὶ ἐγείρονται be offered as an article of faith, to an illiterate countryman of England, he could not believe it : becaufe, though a true propofition, yet it being propofed in words, whofe meaning he underftood not, he could not give any affent to it.   Put it into Englifh, he underftands what is meant by the " dead fhall rife."   For he can conceive, that the fame man, who was dead and fenfelefs, fhould be alive again ; as well as he can, that the fame man, who is now in a lethargy, fhould awake again ; or the fame man that is now out of his fight, and he knows not whether he be alive or dead, fhould return and be with him again : and fo he is capable of believing it, though he conceives nothing of the manner, how a man revives, wakes or moves.   But none of thefe manners of thofe actions being included in thofe propofitions, the propofition concerning the matter of fact (if it imply no contradiction in it) may be believed ; and fo all that is required may be done, whatever difficulty may be, as to the exact manner, how it is brought about.

But where the propofition is about the manner, the belief too muft be of the manner, v. g. the article is, " The dead fhall be raifed with fpiritual bodies :" and then the belief muft be as well of this manner of the fact, as of the fact itfelf.   So that what is faid here, by the unmafker, about the manner, fignifies nothing at all in the cafe.   What is underftood to be expreffed in each propofition, whether it be of the manner, or not of the manner, is (by its being a revelation from God) to be believed, as far as it is underftood : but no more is required to be believed concerning any article, than is contained in that article.

What the unmafker, for the removing of difficulties,

adds

adds farther, in these words, " But there is no difficulty
" as to the reality and certainty of the truths of the
" gospel ; because we know, they are revealed to us by
" God in the holy scripture ;" is yet farther from signi-
fying any thing to the purpose, than the former. The
question is about understanding, and in what sense they are
understood ; not believing several propositions, or articles
of faith, which are to be found in the scripture. To
this, the unmasker says, there can be " no difficulty at
" all as to their reality and certainty ; because they are
" revealed by God." Which amounts to no more but
this, that there is no difficulty at all in the understanding and believing this proposition, " that whatever is
" revealed by God, is really and certainly true." But
is the understanding and believing this single proposition, the understanding and believing all the articles of
faith necessary to believed ? Is this all the explicit faith
a christian need have ? If so, then a christian need explicitly believe no more, but this one proposition, viz.
That all the propositions between the two covers of his
bible, are certainly true. But I imagine the unmasker
will not think the believing this one proposition, is a
sufficient belief of all those fundamental articles, which
he has given us, as necessary to be believed to make a
man a christian. For, if that will serve the turn, I conclude he may make his set of fundamentals as large and
express to his system as he pleases : calvinists, arminians,
anabaptists, socinians, will all thus own the belief of
them, viz. that all that God has revealed in the scripture, is really and certainly true.

But if believing this proposition, that all that is revealed by God in the scripture is true, be not all the
faith which the unmasker requires, what he says about
the reality and certainty of all truths revealed by God,
removes nothing of the difficulty. A proposition of divine authority is found in the scripture : it is agreed
presently between him and me, that it contains a real,
certain truth : but the difficulty is, what is the truth it
contains, to which he and I must assent ; v. g. the profession of faith made by the eunuch, in these words,
" Jesus Christ is the Son of God," upon which he was

admitted into the church, as a chriftian, I believe, contains a " real and certain truth." Is that enough? No, fays the unmafker, p. 87, it " includes in it, that Chrift was God;" and therefore it is not enough for me to believe, that thefe words contain a real certain truth: but I muft believe, they contain this truth, that Jefus Chrift is God; that the eunuch fpoke them in that fenfe, and in that fenfe I muft affent to them: whereas they appear to me to be fpoken, and meant here, as well as in feveral other places of the " New Teftament," in this fenfe, viz. " That Jefus Chrift is the Meffiah," and in that fenfe, in this place, I affent to them. The meaning then of thefe words, as fpoken by the eunuch, is the difficulty: and I defire the unmafker, by the application of what he has faid here, to remove that difficulty. For granting all revelation from God to be really and certainly true, (as certainly it is) how does the believing that general truth remove any difficulty about the fenfe and interpretation of any particular propofition, found in any paffage of the holy fcriptures? Or is it poffible for any man to underftand it in one fenfe, and believe it in another; becaufe it is a divine revelation, that has reality and certainty in it? Thus much, as to what the unmafker fays of the fundamentals, he has given us, p. 30, viz. That " no true lover of God and " truth, need doubt of any of them: for there is no " ambiguity and doubtfulnefs in them." If the diftinction he has ufed, " of difficulty as to the exact manner, " and no difficulty, as to the reality and certainty of " gofpel-truths," will remove all ambiguity and doubt- fulnefs from all thofe texts of fcripture, from whence he and others deduce fundamental articles, fo that they will be " plain and intelligible" to every man, in the fenfe he underftands them; he has done great fervice to chriftianity.

But he feems to diftruft that himfelf, in the following words: " They fhine," fays he, " with their own light, " and, to an unprejudiced eye, are plain, evident, and " illuftrious; and they would always continue fo, if " fome ill-minded men did not perplex and entangle " them." I fee the matter would go very fmooth, if the

the unmaſker might be the ſole, authentic interpreter of
ſcripture. He is wiſely of that judge's mind, who was
againſt hearing the counſel on the other ſide, becauſe
they always perplexed the cauſe.

But if thoſe who differ from the unmaſker, ſhall in
their turns call him the " prejudiced and ill-minded
" man," who perplexes theſe matters (as they may, with
as much authority as he) we are but where we were;
each muſt underſtand for himſelf, the beſt he can, until
the unmaſker be received, as the only unprejudiced man,
to whoſe dictates every one, without examination, is
with an implicit faith to ſubmit.

Here again, p. 32, the unmaſker puts upon me, what
I never ſaid : and therefore I muſt deſire him to ſhow,
where it is, that I pretend,

XI. That this " propoſition," that Jeſus is the Meſſiah, " is more intelligible, than any of thoſe he
" has named."

In his " Thoughts concerning the Cauſes of Atheiſm,"
p. 120, he argues, that this propoſition [Jeſus is the
Meſſiah] has more difficulty in it, than the article of the
holy Trinity. And his proofs are worthy of an unmaſker. " For," ſays he, " here is an Hebrew word
" firſt to be explained;" or (as he has this ſtrong argument again, " Socinaniſm unmaſked," p. 32,) " Here
" firſt the name Jeſus, which is of hebrew extraction,
" though ſince grecized, muſt be expounded."

Anſw. Jeſus being a proper name, only denoting a
certain perſon, needs not to be expounded, of what extraction ſoever it be. Is this propoſition, Jonathan was
the ſon of Saul, king of Iſrael, any thing the harder, becauſe the three proper names in it, Jonathan, Saul, and
Iſrael, are of Hebrew extraction? And is it not as eaſy,
and as " level to the underſtanding of the vulgar," as
this, Arthur was the ſon of Henry, king of England;
though neither of theſe names be of Hebrew extraction?
Or cannot any vulgar capacity underſtand this propoſition, " John Edwards writ a book, intitled," Socinianiſm unmaſked; until the name of John, which is of hebrew extraction, be explained to him? If this be ſo, parents were beſt beware, how hereafter they give their chil-

dren

dren fcripture-names, if they cannot underftand what they fay to one another about them, until thefe names of Hebrew extraction are expounded to them; and every propofition, that is in writings and contracts, made concerning perfons, that have names of hebrew extraction, become thereby as hard to be underftood, as the doctrine of the holy trinity.

His next argument is juft of the fame fize. The word Meffias muft, he fays, be explained too. Of what extraction foever it be, there needs no more explication of it, than what our Englifh bible gives of it, where it is plain to any vulgar capacity, that it was ufed to denote that King and Deliverer, whom God had promifed. So that this propofition, " Jefus is the Meffiah," has no more difficulty in it than this, Jefus is the promifed King and Deliverer; or than this, Cyrus was king and deliverer of Perfia; which, I think, requires not much depth of Hebrew to be underftood. He that underftood this propofition, and took Cyrus for his king, was a fubject, and a member of his kingdom; and he that underftands the other, and takes Jefus to be his King, is his fubject, and a member of his kingdom. But if this be as hard as it is to fome men, to underftand the doctrine of the trinity, I fear many of the kings in the world have but few true fubjects. To believe Jefus to be the Meffiah, is (as he has been told, over and over again) to take him for our King and Ruler, promifed, and fent by God. This is that which will make any one from a jew, or heathen, to be a chriftian. In this fenfe it is very intelligible to vulgar capacities. Thofe who fo underftand and believe it, are fo far from " pronouncing thefe words " as a fpell," (as the unmafker ridiculoufly fuggefts, p. 33.) that they thereby become chriftians.

But what if I tell the unmafker, that there is one Mr. Edwards, who (when he fpeaks his mind without confidering how it will make for, or againft him) in another place, thinks this propofition, " Jefus is the Mef- " fias," very eafy and intelligible? To convince him of it, I fhall defire him to turn to the 74th page of his " Socinianifm unmafked," where he will find, that Mr. Edwards, without any great fearch into Hebrew extractions, interprets " Jefus the Meffiah," to fignify this,

" That

" That Jesus of Nazareth was that eminent and ex-
" traordinary person prophesied of long before, and
" that he was sent and commissioned by God :" which,
I think, is no very hard proposition to be understood.
But it is no strange thing, that that which was very easy
to an unmasker in one place, should be terribly hard in
another, where want of something better requires to
have it so.

Another argument that he uses to prove the articles
he has given us to be necessary to salvation, p. 22, is,
because they are doctrines which contain things, that in
their nature have an " immediate respect to the occa-
" sion, author, way, end, means, and issue of men's re-
" demption and salvation." And here I desire him to
prove,

XII. That every one of his articles contains things
so immediately relating to the " occasion, author,
" way, means, and issue of our redemption and
" salvation, that no body can be saved, without
" understanding the texts from whence he draws
" them, in the very same sense that he does ; and
" explicitly believing all these propositions that he
" has deduced, and all that he will deduce from
" scripture, when he shall please to complete his
" creed."

Page 23, he says of his fundamentals, " Not without
" good reason, THEREFORE, I called them essential and
" integral parts of our christian and evangelical faith :
" and why the Vindicator sneers at these terms, I know
" no reason, but that he cannot confute the application
" of them."

Answ. One would think by the word, Therefore,
which he uses here, that in the preceding paragraph, he
had produced some reason to justify his ridiculous use
of those terms, in his " Thoughts concerning Atheism,"
p. 111. But nothing therein will be found tending to it.
Indeed, the foregoing paragraph begins with these words,
" Thus I have briefly set before the reader those evan-
" gelical truths, those christian principles, which belong

R 3   to

" to the very effence of chriftianity." Amongft thefe,
there is the word Effence: but that from thence, or any
thing elfe in that paragraph, the unmafker could, with
good fenfe, or any fenfe at all, infer, as he does, " not
" without good reafon, THEREFORE I called them the
" ESSENTIAL and INTEGRAL parts of our chriftian and
" evangelical faith ;" requires an extraordinary fort of
logic to make out. What, I befeech you, is your good
reafon too, here, upon which you infer, "Therefore," &c.?
For it is impoffible for any one, but an unmafker, to find
one word, juftifying his ufe of the terms effential and
integral. But it would be a great reftraint to the running of the unmafker's pen, if you fhould not allow him
the free ufe of illative particles, where there are no pre-
mifes to fupport them : and if you fhould not take affirmations without proof, for reafoning, you at once ftrike
off above three quarters of his book ; and he will often,
for feveral pages together, have nothing to fay. As for
example, from p. 28. to p. 35.

But to fhow, that I did not, without reafon fay, his
ufe of the terms effential and integral, in the place before quoted, was ridiculous ; I muft mind my reader,
that, p. 109. of his " Thoughts concerning the Caufes
" of Atheifm," he having faid, that " the epiftolary
" writings are fraught with other fundamentals, befides
" that one which I mention ;" and then having fet
them down, he clofes his catalogue of them thus :
" Thefe are matters of faith contained in the epiftles,
" and they are effential and integral parts of the gofpel
" itfelf," p. 111. Now what could be more ridiculous, than, where the queftion is about fundamental
doctrines, which are effentials of the chriftian religion,
without an affent to which a man cannot be a chriftian ;
and fo he himfelf calls them, p. 21, of his " Socinianifm
" unmafked ;" that he fhould clofe the lift he had made
of fundamental doctrines, i. e. effential points of the
chriftian religion, with telling his reader, " Thefe are
" effential and integral parts of the gofpel itfelf? i. e.
Thefe, which I have given you for fundamental, for effential doctrines of the gofpel, are the fundamental and
not fundamental, effential and not effential parts of the
gofpel

gospel mixed together. For integral parts, in all the writers I have met with, besides the unmasker, are contradistinguished to essential; and signify such parts as the thing can be without, but without them will not be so complete and entire as with them. Just such an acuteness, as our unmasker, would any one show, who taking upon him to set down the parts essential to a man, without the having of which, he could not be a man, should name the soul, the head, the heart, lungs, stomach, liver, spleen, eyes, ears, tongue, arms, legs, hair, and nails; and, to make all sure, should conclude with these words; " These are parts contained" in a man, " and are essential and integral parts of a man " himself;" i. e. They are parts, without some of which he cannot be a man; and others, which though they make the man intire, yet he may be a man without them; as a man ceases not to be a man, though he wants a nail, a finger, or an arm, which are integral parts of a man, " Risum teneatis?" If the unmasker can make any better sense of his " essential and integral parts of " the gospel itself," I will ask his pardon for my laughing: until then he must not be angry, if the reader and I laugh too. Besides, I must tell him, that those, which he has set down, are not the " integral parts of the chris- " tian faith," any more than the head, the trunk, and the arms, hands, and thighs are the integral parts of a man: for a man is not entire without the legs and feet too. They are some of the integral parts indeed; but cannot be called the integral parts, where any, that go to make up the whole man, are left out; nor those the integral, but some of the integral parts of the christian faith, out of which any of the doctrines, proposed in the " New Testament," are omitted: for whatever is there proposed, is proposed to be believed, and so is a part of the christian faith.

Before I leave his catalogue of the " essential and in- " tegral parts" of the gospel, which he has given us, instead of one, containing the articles necessary to be believed to make a man a christian, I must take notice of what he says, whilst he is making it, p. 9. " Why " then is there a treatise published, to tell the world,

" that the bare belief of a Meſſiah, is all that is required
" of a chriſtian?" As if there were no difference between believing a Meſſiah, and believing Jeſus to be the
Meſſiah; no difference between "required of a chriſ-
" tian," and required to make a man a chriſtian.   As
if you ſhould ſay, renouncing his former idolatry, and
being circumciſed and baptized into Moſes, was all that
was required to make a man an iſraelite; therefore it
was all that was required of an iſraelite.   For theſe two
falſhoods has he, in this one ſhort ſentence, thought fit
ſlily to father upon me, the " humble imitator of the
" jeſuits," as he is pleaſed to call me.   And, therefore, I muſt deſire him to ſhow,

XIII. Where the " world is told, in the treatiſe that
    " I publiſhed, That the bare belief of a Meſſiah,
    " is all that is required of a chriſtian?"

The ſix next pages, i. e. from the twenty-eighth to
the end of his ſecond chapter, being taken up with nothing but pulpit oratory, out of its place; and without
any reply, applied, or applicable to any thing I have
ſaid, in my Vindication; I ſhall paſs by, until he ſhows
any thing in them that is ſo.

In page 36, this giant in argument falls on me, and
mauls me unmercifully, about the epiſtles.   He begins
thus: " The gentleman is not without his evaſions, and
" he ſees it is high time to make uſe of them.   This puts
" him in ſome diſorder.   For, when he comes to ſpeak
" of my mentioning his ill treatment of the epiſtles,——
" you may obſerve, that he begins to grow warmer than
" before.   Now this meek man is nettled, and one may
" perceive he is ſenſible of the ſcandal that he hath
" given to good people, by his ſlighting the epiſtolary
" writings of the holy apoſtles; yet he is ſo cunning as
" to diſguiſe his paſſion as well as he can."   Let all
this impertinent and inconſiſtent ſtuff be ſo.   I am angry
and cannot diſguiſe it, I am cunning and would diſguiſe
it, but yet, the quick-ſighted unmaſker has found me
out, that I am nettled.   What does all this notable pro-
logue of " hiciius dociius," of a cunning man, and in
                                                        effect

effect " no cunning man, in diforder, warmed, nettled,
" in a paffion," tend to? but to fhow, that thefe following words of mine, p. 170, of my Vindication, viz.
" I require you to publifh to the world thofe paffages
" which fhow my contempt of the epiftles," are fo full
of heat and diforder, that they need no other anfwer:
" But what need I, good fir, do this, when you have
" done it yourfelf?" A reply, I own, very foft; and
whether I may not fay, very filly, let the reader judge.
The unmafker having accufed me of contemning the
epiftles, my reply, in my Vindication, ibid. was thus:
" Sir, when your angry fit is over, and the abatement
" of your paffion has given way to the return of your
" fincerity, I fhall beg you to read this paffage in the
" 154th page of my book: Thefe holy writers (viz. the
" penmen of the epiftles) infpired from above, writ no-
" thing but truth; and in moft places very weighty
" truths to us now, for the expounding, clearing and
" confirming of the chriftian doctrine, and eftablifhing
" thofe in it, who had embraced it." And again, p.
156, "The other parts [i. e. befides the gofpels and the
" Acts] of DIVINE REVELATION are objects of faith, and
" are fo to be received; they are truths, of which none
" that is once known to be fuch, i. e. revealed, may, or
" ought to be difbelieved. And if this does not fatisfy
" you, that I have as high a veneration for the epiftles
" as you, or any one can have, I require you to publifh
" to the world thofe PASSAGES which fhow my con-
" tempt of them." After fuch direct words of mine,
expreffing my veneration for that part of divine revelation, which is contained in the epiftles, any one, but an
unmafker, would blufh to charge me with contempt of
them; without alleging, when fummoned to it, any
word in my book to juftify that charge.

If hardnefs of forehead were ftrength of brains, it
were two to one of his fide againft any man I ever yet
heard of. I require him to publifh to the world, thofe
paffages, that fhow my contempt of the epiftles;
and he anfwers me, " He need not do it, for I have
" done it myfelf." Whoever had common fenfe,
would underftand, that what I demanded was, that he

fhould fhow the world where, amongft all I had publifhed, there were any paffages that expreffed contempt
of the epiftles: for it was not expected he fhould quote
paffages of mine, that I had never publifhed. And this
acute unmafker (to this) fays, I had publifhed them myfelf. So that the reafon why he cannot find them, is,
becaufe I had publifhed them myfelf. But, fays he,
" I appeal to the reader, whether (after your tedious
" collection out of the four evangelifts) your paffing by
" the epiftles, and neglecting wholly what the apoftles
" fay in them," be not publifhing to the " world your
" contempt of them?" I demand of him to publifh to
the world 'thofe paffages, which fhow my contempt of
the epiftles: and he anfwers, " He need not, I have
" done it myfelf." How does that appear? I have
paffed by the epiftles, fays he. My paffing them by
then, are paffages publifhed againft the epiftles? For
" publifhing of paffages" is what you faid, you " need
" not do," and what " I had done." So that the paffages I have publifhed containing a contempt of the
epiftles, are extant in my faying nothing of them?
Surely this fame paffing by has done fome very fhrewd
difpleafure to our poor unmafker, that he fo ftarts whenever it is but named, and cannot think it contains lefs
than exclufion, defiance, and contempt. Here therefore the propofition remaining to be proved by you,
is,

XIV. " That one cannot pafs by any thing, without
contempt of it."

And when you have proved it, I fhall then afk you,
what will become of all thofe parts of fcripture, all
thofe chapters and verfes, that you have paffed by, in
your collection of fundamental articles? Thofe that
you have vouchfafed to fet down, you tell us, " are in
" the bible, on purpofe to be believed." What muft
become of all the reft, which you have omitted? Are
they there not to be believed? And muft the reader underftand your paffing them by, to be a publifhing to the
world your contempt of them? If fo, you have unmafked
yourfelf:

yourself: If not, but you may pass by some parts of
scripture, nay, whole epistles, as you have those of St.
James and St. Jude, without contempt; why may not
I, without contempt, pass by others; but because you
have a liberty to do what you will, and I must do but
what you, in your good pleasure, will allow me? But if
I ask you, whence you have this privilege above others;
you will have nothing to say, except it be, according to
your usual skill in divining, that you know my heart,
and the thoughts that are in it, which you find not like
yours, right orthodox, and good; but always evil and
perverse, such as I dare not own, but hypocritically
either say nothing of or declare against: but yet, with all
my cunning, I cannot hide them from you; your all-
knowing penetration always finds them out: you know
them, or you guess at them, as is best for your turn, and
that is as good: and then presently I am confounded.
I doubt, whether the world has ever had any two-eyed
man your equal, for penetration and a quick sight.
The telling by the spectator's looks, what card he guesses,
is nothing to what you can do.   You take the height of
an author's parts, by numbering the pages of his book;
you can spy an heresy in him, by his saying not a syllable of it; distinguish him from the orthodox, by his
understanding places of scripture, just as several of the
orthodox do; you can repeat by heart whole leaves of
what is in his mind to say, before he speaks a word of
it; you can discover designs before they are hatched, and
all the intrigues of carrying them on, by those who never
thought of them. All this and more you can do, by the
spirit of orthodoxy; or, which is as certain, by your own
good spirit of invention informing you. Is not this to
be an errant conjurer?

But to your reply. You say, " After my TEDIOUS
" collection out of the four evangelists, my passing by
" the epistles, and neglecting wholly what the apostles
" say," &c. I wondered at first why you mentioned not
the Acts here, as well as the four evangelists: for I have
not, as you have in other places observed, been sparing
of collections out of the Acts too. But there was, it
seems, a necessity here for your omitting it: for that
                                                    would

would have stood too near what followed, in these words; and " neglecting wholly what the apostles say." For if it appeared to the reader, out of your own confession, that I allowed and built upon the divine authority of what the apostles say in the Acts, he could not so easily be misled into an opinion, that I contemned what they say in their epistles. But this is but a slight touch of your leger-de-main.

And now I ask the reader, what he will think of a minister of the gospel, who cannot bear the texts of scripture I have produced, nor my quotations out of the four evangelists? This, which in his " Thoughts of the " Causes of Atheism," p. 114, was want of " vivacity " and elevation of mind," want of " a vein of sense " and reason, yea, and of elocution too;" is here, in his " Socinianism unmasked," a " tedious collection " out of the four evangelists." Those places I have quoted lie heavy, it seems, upon his stomach, and are too many to be got off. But it was my business not to omit one of them, that the reader might have a full view of the whole tenour of the preaching of our Saviour and his apostles, to the unconverted Jews and Gentiles; and might therein see, what faith they were converted to, and upon their assent to which, they were pronounced believers, and admitted into the christian church. But the unmasker complains, there are too many of them : he thinks the gospel, the good news of salvation, tedious from the mouth of our Saviour and his apostles : he is of opinion, that before the epistles were writ, and with-out believing precisely what he thinks fit to cull out of them, there could be no christians ; and if we had no-thing but the four evangelists, we could not be saved. And yet it is plain, that every single one of the four con-tains the gospel of Jesus Christ ; and, at least, they alto-gether contain all that is necessary to salvation. If any one doubt of this, I refer him to Mr. Chillingworth for satisfaction, who hath abundantly proved it.

His following words (were he not the same unmasker all through) would be beyond parallel : " But let us hear " why the Vindicator did not attempt to collect any ar-" ticles out of these writings ; he assigns this as one
" reason :

" reason: " The epistles being writ to those who were
" already believers, it could not be supposed that they
" were writ to them, to teach them fundamentals,"
p. 167. Vindic. " Certainly no man would have con-
" jectured, that he would have used such an evasion as
" this. I will say that for him, he goes beyond all sur-
" mises, he is above all conjectures, he hath a faculty
" which no creature on earth can ever fathom." Thus
far the unmasker, in his oratorical strain. In what follows, he comes to his closer reasoning, against what I
have said. His words are, " do we not know, that the
" four gospels were writ to, and for believers, as well
" as unbelievers?" Answ. I grant it. Now let us see
your inference ; therefore what these holy historians
recorded, that our Saviour and his apostles said and
preached to unbelievers, was said and preached to believers. The discourse which our Saviour had with the
woman of Samaria, and her townsmen, was addressed to
believers ; because St. John writ his gospel (wherein it
is recorded as a part of our Saviour's history) for believers, as well as unbelievers. St. Peter's preaching to
Cornelius, and St. Paul's preaching at Antioch, at Thessalonica, at Corinth, &c. was not to unbelievers, for
their conversion ; because St. Luke dedicates his history
of the Acts of the apostles to Theophilus, who was a
christian, as the unmasker strenuously proves in this
paragraph. Just as if he should say, that the discourses,
which Cæsar records he had upon several occasions with
the gauls, were not addressed to the gauls alone, but to
the romans also ; because his commentaries were writ
for the romans, as well as others ; or that the sayings
of the antient greeks and romans in Plutarch, were not
spoken by them to their contemporaries only, because
they are recorded by him for the benefit of posterity.

I perused the preachings of our Saviour and his apostles to the unconverted world, to see what they taught
and required to be believed, to make men christians :
and all these I set down, and leave the world to judge
what they contained. The epistles, which were all
written to those who had embraced the faith and were
all christians already, I thought would not so distinctly
show,

show, what were those doctrines which were absolutely
necessary to make men christians; they being not writ
to convert unbelievers, but to build up those who were
already believers, in their most holy faith. This is
plainly expressed in the epistle to the hebrews, chap. v.
11, &c. " Of whom (i. e. Christ) we have many things
" to say, and hard to be uttered, seeing ye are all dull
" of hearing. For when for the time ye ought to be
" teachers, ye have need that one teach you again, which
" be the first principles of the oracles of God; and are
" become such as have need of milk, and not of strong
" meat. For every one that useth milk, is unskilful in
" the word of righteousness; for he is a babe: but
" strong meat belongeth to him that is of full age, even
" those, who by reason of use have their senses exercised,
" to discern both good and bad. Therefore, leaving
" the principles of the doctrine of Christ, let us go on
" unto perfection, not laying again the foundation of
" repentance from dead works, and of faith towards
" God, and of the doctrine of baptism, and of laying on
" of hands, and of the resurrection of the dead, and of
" eternal judgment." Here the apostle shows, what
was his design in writing this epistle, not to teach them
the fundamental doctrines of the christian religion, but
to lead them on to more perfection; that is, to greater
degrees of knowledge, of the wise design, and wonderful
contrivance and carrying on of the gospel, and the evidence of it; which he makes out in this epistle, by
showing its correspondence with the Old Testament,
and particularly with the œconomy of the Mosaical
constitution. Here I might ask the unmasker, Whether those many things which St. Paul tells the hebrews,
he had to say of Christ, (hard to be uttered to them, because they were dull of hearing) had not an " imme-
" diate respect to the occasion, author, way, means, or
" issue of their redemption and salvation?" And therefore, " whether they were such things, without the
" knowledge of which they could not be saved?" as the
unmasker says of such things. p. 23. And the like I
might ask him, concerning those things which the apostle tells the corinthians, 1 epist. chap. iii. 2, that they
                                                    " were

" were not able to bear." For much to the same purpose he speaks to the corinthians, epist. 1. chap. iii, as
in the above-cited places he did to the hebrews : " That
" he, as a wise master-builder, had laid the foundation:"
and that foundation he himself tells us, is, " Jesus the
" Messiah ;" and that there is no other foundation to
be laid. And that in this he laid the foundation of
christianity at Corinth, St. Luke records, Acts xviii. 4,
in these words, " Paul, at Corinth, reasoned in the sy-
" nagogue every sabbath-day, and testified to the jews,
" that Jesus was the Messiah." Upon which foundation, he tells them, there might be a superstructure. But
that, what is built on the foundation, is not the foundation, I think I need not prove. He further tells them,
that he had desired to build upon this foundation ; but
withal says, he had fed them until then " with milk, and
" not with meat ; because they were babes, and had not
" been able to bear it, neither were they yet able."
And therefore this epistle, we see, is almost wholly spent
in reproofs of their miscarriages, and in exhortations and
instructions relating to practice ; and very little said in
it, for the explaining any part of the great mystery of
salvation, contained in the gospel.

By these passages we may see, (were it not evident to
common sense itself, from the nature of things) that the
design of these epistles was not to lay the foundations, or
teach the principles of the christian religion ; they being
writ to those who received them, and were christians
already. The same holds in all the other epistles ; and
therefore the epistles seemed not to me the properest
parts of scripture to give us that foundation, distinct
from all the superstructures built on it ; because in the
epistles, the latter was the thing proposed, rather than
the former. For the main intention of the apostles, in
writing their epistles, could not be to do what was done
already ; to lay down barely the foundations of christianity, to those who were christians already ; but to build
upon it some farther explication of it, which either their
particular circumstances, or a general evidencing of the
truth, wisdom, excellencies, and privileges, &c. of the
gospel required. This was the reason that persuaded me
to

to take the articles of faith, abfolutely neceffary to be received to make a man a chriftian, only from the preachings of our Saviour and his apoftles to the unconverted world, as laid down in the hiftorical part of the New Teftament: and I thought it a good reafon, it being paft doubt, that they in their preachings propofed to the unconverted, all that was neceffary to be believed, to make them chriftians; and alfo, that that faith, upon a profeffion whereof any one was admitted into the church, as a believer, had all that was neceffary in it to make him a chriftian; becaufe, if it wanted any thing neceffary, he had neceffarily not been admitted: unlefs we can fuppofe, that any one was admitted into the chriftian church by our Saviour and his apoftles, who was not yet a chriftian; or pronounced a believer, who yet wanted fomething neceffary to make him a believer, i. e. was a believer and not a believer, at the fame time. But what thofe articles were which had been preached to thofe, to whom the epiftles were writ, and upon the belief whereof they had been admitted into the chriftian church, and became, as they are called, " believers, faints, faithful, " elect," &c. could not be collected out of the epiftles. This, though it were my reafon, and muft be a reafon to every one, who would make this inquiry; and the unmafker quotes the place where I told him it was my reafon; yet he, according to his never-erring illumination, flatly tells me, p. 38, that it was not; and adds, " Here then is want of fincerity," &c. I muft defire him, therefore, to prove what he fays, p. 38, viz.

> XV. That, "by the fame argument, that I would per-
> " fuade, that the fundamentals are not to be fought
> " for in the epiftles, he can prove that they are not
> " to be fought for in the gofpels and in the Acts;
> " becaufe even thefe were writ to thofe that be-
> " lieved."

And next I defire him to prove, what he alfo fays in the fame page, viz.

XVI. That

XVI. That " the epistles being writ to those that
" believed, was not an argument that I did make
" use of."

He tells us, p. 38, that it is the argument whereby I
would persuade : and in the very same page, a few lines
lower, says, " That it is not the argument I did make
" use of." Who, but an errant unmasker, would contradict himself so flatly in the same breath? And yet,
upon that, he raises a complaint of my " want of sin-
" cerity."

For " want of sincerity" in one of us, we need not
go far for an instance. The next paragraph, p. 38—40,
affords us a gross one of it : wherein the unmasker argues strongly, not against any thing I had said, but
against an untruth of his own setting up. Towards the
latter end of the paragraph, p. 40, he has these words :
" It is manifest, that the apostles, in their epistles, taught
" fundamentals; which is contrary to what this gentle-
" man says, that such a thing could not be supposed."
And therefore the unmasker has taken a great deal of
pains to show, that there are fundamental doctrines to
be found in the epistles ; as if I had denied it. And, to
lead the reader into an opinion that I had said so, he set
down these words, " could not be supposed ;" as if they
were my words. And so they are, but not to that purpose. And therefore he did well not to quote the page,
lest the reader, by barely turning to the place, should
have a clear sight of falshood, instead of that sincerity,
which he would make the reader believe, is wanting in
me. My words, p. 153, of " The Reasonableness of
" Christianity," are, " NOR CAN IT BE SUPPOSED, that
" the sending of such fundamentals was the reason of
" the apostles writing to any of them." And a little
lower : " The epistles therefore being all written to those
" that were already believers and christians, the occa-
" sion and end of writing them could not be, to instruct
" them in that which was necessary to make them chris-
" tians." The thing then, that I denied, was not, that
there were any fundamentals in the epistles. For in the
next page I have these express words : " I do not deny, but

" the great doctrines of the christian faith are dropt here
" and there, and scattered up and down in most of
" them." And therefore he might have spared his endeavours, in the next paragraph, to prove, that there
may be fundamentals found in the epistles, until he finds
some body that denies it. And here again, I must repeat my usual question, that with this sincere writer is
so often necessary, viz.

> XVII. Where it is that I say, " That it cannot be
> " supposed, that there are fundamental articles in
> " the epistles?"

If he hopes to shift it off by the word Taught, which
seems fallaciously put in; as if he meant, that there
were some fundamental articles taught, necessary to be
believed to make them christians, in the epistles, which
those whom they were writ to, knew not before: in this
sense I do deny it: and then this will be the

> XVIIIth proposition remaining upon him to prove,
> viz.

> " That there are fundamental articles necessary to be
> " believed to make a man a christian taught in the
> " epistles, which those, whom they were writ to,
> " knew not before."

The former part of his next paragraph, p. 40, runs
thus: " Hear another feigned ground of his omitting
" the epistles, viz. because the fundamental articles are
" here promiscuously, and without distinction, mixed
" with other truths," p. 41. " But who sees not, that
" this is a mere elusion? For on the same account he
" might have forborn to search for fundamental articles
" in the gospels; for they do not lie there together, but
" are dispersed up and down. The doctrinal and histo-
" rical parts are mixed with one another, but he pre-
" tends to sever them. Why then did he not make a
" separation between the doctrines in the epistles, and
" those other matters that are treated of there? He has
        " nothing

" nothing to reply to this, and therefore we muſt again
" look upon what he has ſuggeſted, as a caſt of his ſhuf-
" fling faculty."

The argument contained in theſe words is this: A
man cannot well diſtinguiſh fundamental from non-fundamental doctrines in the epiſtles, where they are promiſcuouſly mixed with non-fundamental doctrines: therefore he cannot well diſtinguiſh fundamental doctrines
from others in the goſpels, and the Acts, where they are
mixed with matters of fact. As if he ſhould ſay, one
cannot well diſtinguiſh a bachelor of divinity from other
divines, where, ſeveral of them ſtand together promiſcuouſly in the ſame habit; therefore one cannot diſtinguiſh a bachelor of divinity from a Billingſgate orator,
where they ſtand together in their diſtinct habits: or
that it is as eaſy to diſtinguiſh fine gold from that of a
little lower allay, where ſeveral pieces of each are mixed
together; as it is to diſtinguiſh pieces of fine gold from
pieces of ſilver, which they are mixed amongſt.

But it ſeems, the unmaſker thinks it as eaſy to diſtinguiſh between fundamental and not fundamental doctrines, in a writing of the ſame author, where they are
promiſcuouſly mixt together, as it is to diſtinguiſh between a fundamental doctrine of faith, and a relation of
a matter of fact, where they are intermixedly reported in
the ſame hiſtory. When he has proved this, the unmaſker will have more reaſon to tax me with eluſion,
ſhuffling, and feigning, in the reaſon I gave for not collecting fundamentals out of the epiſtles. Until then, all
that noiſe muſt ſtand amongſt thoſe ridiculous airs of
triumph and victory which he ſo often gives himſelf,
without the leaſt advantage to his cauſe, or edification
of his reader, though he ſhould a thouſand times ſay,
" That I have nothing to reply."

In the latter part of his paragraph, he ſays, " That
" neceſſary truths, fundamental principles, may be dif-
" tinguiſhed from thoſe that are not ſuch, in the epiſto-
" lary writings, by the nature and importance of them,
" by their immediate reſpect to the author and the means
" of our ſalvation." Anſw. If this be ſo, I deſire him
to give me a definitive collection of fundamentals out of

the

the Epiftles, as I have given one out of the Gofpels and the Acts. If he cannot do that, it is plain, he hath here given a diftinguifhing mark of fundamentals, by which he himfelf cannot diftinguifh them. But yet I am the fhuffler.

The argument in the next paragraph, p. 41, is this :

" Neceffary doctrines of faith, fuch as God abfolutely " demands to be believed for juftification, may be dif-" tinguifhed from rules of holy living, with which they " are mixed in the epiftles ; therefore doctrines of faith " neceffary, and not neceffary to be believed to make a " man a chriftian, may be diftinguifhed, as they ftand " mixed in the epiftles." Which is as good fenfe as to fay, lambs and kids may eafily be diftinguifhed in the fame penn, where they are together, by their diffe-rent natures : therefore the lambs I abfolutely demand of you, as neceffary to fatisfy me, may be diftinguifhed from others in the fame penn, where they are mixed without any diftinction. Doctrines of faith, and pre-cepts of practice, are as diftinguifhable as doing and believing ; and thofe as eafily difcernible one from ano-ther, as thinking and walking : but doctrinal propofi-tions, all of them of divine revelation, are of the fame authority, and of the fame fpecies, in refpect of the neceffity of believing them ; and will be eternally un-diftinguifhable into neceffary, and not neceffary to be believed, until there be fome other way found to diftin-guifh them, than that they are in a book, which is all of divine revelation. Though therefore doctrines of faith, and rules of practice, are very diftinguifhable in the epiftles, yet it does not follow from thence, that fun-damental and not fundamental doctrines, points neceffary and not neceffary to be believed to make men chriftians, are eafily diftinguifhable in the epiftles. Which, there-fore, remains to be proved : and it remains incumbent upon him,

XVIII. " To fet down the marks, whereby the doc-" trines, delivered in the epiftles, may eafily and " exactly

" exactly be diftinguifhed into fundamental, and
" not fundamental articles of faith."

All the reft of that paragraph, containing nothing
againft me, muft be bound up with a great deal of the
like ftuff, which the unmafker has put into his book, to
fhow the world he does not " imitate me in imperti-
" nencies, incoherences, and trifling excurfions," as he
boafts in his firft paragraph. Only I fhall defire the
reader to take the whole paffage concerning this matter,
as it ftands in my " Reafonablenefs of Chriftianity,"
p. 154. " I do not deny but the great doctrines of
" the chriftian faith are dropt here and there, and fcat-
" tered up and down in moft of them. But it is not
" in the epiftles we are to learn what are the funda-
" mental articles of faith, where they are promifcuoufly,
" and without diftinction, mixed with other truths and
" difcourfes, which were (though for edification in-
" deed, yet) only occafional. We fhall find and difcern
" thofe great and neceffary points beft, in the preach-
" ing of our Saviour and his apoftles, to thofe who were
" yet ftrangers and ignorant of the faith, to bring them
" in, and convert them to it." And then let him read
thefe words, which the unmafker has quoted out of
them : " It is not in the epiftles, that we are to learn
" what are the fundamental articles of faith ; they were
" written for the refolving of doubts, and reforming of
" miftakes ;" with his introduction of them in thefe
words : " he commands the reader not to ftir a jot fur-
" ther than the Acts." If I fhould afk him where that
command appears, he muft have recourfe to his old fhift,
that he did not mean as he faid, or elfe ftand convicted
of a malicious untruth. An orator is not bound to fpeak
ftrict truth, though a difputant be. But this unmafker's
writing againft me will excufe him from being of the
latter : and then why may not falfhoods pafs for rhetorical flourifhes, in one who hath been ufed to popular
haranguing ; to which men are not generally fo fevere
as ftrictly to examine them, and expect that they fhould
always be found to contain nothing but precife truth
and ftrict reafoning ? But yet I muft not forget to put

upon

upon his fcore this other propofition of his, which he
has, p. 42, and afk him to fhow,

XIX.   " Where it is that I command my reader not
     " to ftir a jot farther than the Acts?"

In the next two paragraphs, p. 42—46, the unmafker
is at his natural play, of declaiming without proving.
It is pity the Mifhna, out of which he takes his good
breeding, as it told him, that " a well-bred and well-
" taught man anfwers to the firft, in the firft place,"
had not given him this rule too, about order, viz. That
proving fhould go before condemning ; elfe all the fierce
exaggerations ill language can heap up, are but empty
fcurrility.   But it is no wonder that the Jewifh doctors
fhould not provide rules for a chriftian divine, turned
unmafker.   For where a caufe is to be maintained, and
a book to be writ, and arguments are not at hand, yet
fomething muft be found to fill it ; railing in fuch cafes
is much eafier than reafoning, efpecially where a man's
parts lie that way.

The firft of thefe paragraphs, p. 42, he begins thus :
" But let us hear further what this vindicator faith to
" excufe his rejection of the doctrines contained in the
" epiftles, and his putting us off with one article of
" faith."   And then he quotes thefe following words
of mine : " What if the author defigned his treatife, as
" the title fhows, chiefly for thofe who were not yet
" thoroughly and firmly chriftians : purpofing to work
" upon thofe, who either wholly difbelieved, or doubted
" of the truth of the chriftian religion?"

Anfw. This, as he has put it, is a downright falfhood.
For the words he quotes were not ufed by me, " to ex-
" cufe my rejection of the doctrines contained in ' the
" epiftles," or to prove there was but one article ; but
as a reafon why I omitted the mention of fatisfaction.

To demonftrate this, I fhall fet down the whole paffage, as it is, p. 163, 164, of my Vindication, where it
runs thus :
     " But what will become of me that I have not men-
" tioned fatisfaction?

2   " Poffibly

" Possibly this reverend gentleman would have had
" charity enough for a known writer of the brother-
" hood, to have found it by an innuendo in those words
" above quoted, of laying down his life for another.
" But every thing is to be strained here the other way.
" For the author of the " Reasonableness of Christiani-
" ty, &c." is of necessity to be represented as a soci-
" nian; or else his book may be read, and the truths
" in it, which Mr. Edwards likes not, be received;
" and people put upon examining. Thus one, as full
" of happy conjectures and suspicions as this gentle-
" man, might be apt to argue. But what if the author
" designed his treatise, as the title shows, chiefly for
" those who were not yet thoroughly or firmly christians;
" proposing to work on those, who either wholly disbe-
" lieved, or doubted of the truth of the christian re-
" ligion?"

To this he tells me, p. 43, that my " title says no-
" thing for me," i. e. shows not that I designed my
book for those that disbelieved, or doubted of the christian religion.

Answ. I thought that a title that professed the reasonableness of any doctrine, showed it was intended for
those that were not fully satisfied of the reasonableness
of it; unless books are to be writ to convince those of
any thing, who are convinced already. But possibly this
may be the unmasker's way: and if one should judge by
his manner of treating this subject, with declamation
instead of argument, one would think, that he meant it
for no body but those who were of his mind already.
I thought, therefore, " the Reasonableness of Christiani-
" ty, as delivered in the Scripture," a proper title to
signify whom it was chiefly meant for: and, I thank
God, I can with satisfaction say, it has not wanted its
effect upon some of them. But the unmasker proves
for all that, that I could not design it chiefly for dif-
believers or doubters of the christian religion. " For,
" says he, p. 43, how those that wholly disregard and
" disbelieve the scriptures of the New Testament, as
" gentiles, jews, mahometans, and atheists do," (I
crave leave to put in theists, instead of atheists, for a

reason

reason prefently to be mentioned) " are like to attend
" to the Reasonableness of Christianity, as delivered in
" the Scripture, is not to be conceived: and therefore
" we look upon this as all mere sham and sophistry."
Answ. Though the unmasker teaches good breeding
out of the Mischna, yet I thought he had been a minister
of the gospel, and had taught christianity out of the
scripture. Why! good sir, would you teach jews and
mahometans christianity out of the talmud and alcoran;
because they are the books that at present they attend
to, and believe? Or would you, laying by the authority
of all books, preach religion to infidels, in your own
name, and by your own authority, laying aside the scripture? " Is it not to be conceived," no not by a christian
divine, that the way to make unbelievers christians, is
to show them the reasonableness of the religion contained in the scriptures? But it seems the unmasker has
a peculiar way of preaching and propagating christianity
without the scripture; as some men have a peculiar way
of disputing without reason.

In the beginning of this paragraph, p. 43, the unmasker, that is always a fair interpreter of my meaning,
and never fails to know it better than I do, tells me,
That by those that wholly disbelieve, " I must mean
" atheists, turks, jews, and pagans; and by those that
" are not firmly christians, a few weak christians."
But did our unmasker never hear of unbelievers, under
a denomination distinct from that of atheists, turks,
jews, and pagans? Whilst the pulpit and the press have
so often had up the name of theists or deists, has that
name wholly escaped him? It was these I chiefly designed, and I believe, nobody of all that read my Vindication; but the unmasker, mistook me, if he did. But
there at least, p. 165, he might have found the name, as
of a sort of unbelievers not unknown amongst us. But,
whatever he thought, it was convenient, and a sort of
prudence in him (when he would persuade others, that
I had not a design, which I say I had) to lessen as much
as he could, and cover the need of any such design; and
so make it, that I could not intend my book to work
upon those that disbelieved, or did not firmly believe;

　　　　　　　　　　　　　　　　by

by infinuating, there were few or none fuch amongft us. Hence he fays, that by thofe that are not thoroughly and firmly chriftians, " I mean a FEW weak chriftians;" as well, as under thofe who wholly difbelieve, he left the theifts out of my meaning. I am very glad to hear from the unmafker, that there are but few weak chriftians, few that have doubts about the truth of chrif-tianity amongft us. But if there be not a great number of deifts, and that the preventing their increafe be not worth every true chriftian's care and endeavours, thofe who have been fo loud againft them, have been much to blame; and I wifh to God there were no reafon for their complaints. For thefe therefore, I take the liberty to fay, as I did before, that I chiefly defigned my book; and fhall not be afhamed of this fophiftry, as you call it, if it can be fophiftry to allege a matter of fact that I know; until you have arguments to convince me, that you know my intention in publifhing it, better than I do myfelf. And I fhall think it ftill no blameable pru-dence, however you exclaim againft prudence, (as per-haps you have fome reafon) that " I mentioned only
" thofe advantages, that all chriftians are agreed in;
" and that I obferved that command of the apoftle,
" Rom. xiv. 1, " Him that is weak in the faith receive
" ye, but not to doubtful difputations;" without being
" a focinian. I think I did not amifs, that I offered to
" the belief of thofe that ftood off, that, and only that,
" which our Saviour and his apoftles preached for the
" reducing the unconverted world. And would any one
" think, he in earneft went about to perfuade men to be
" chriftians, who fhould ufe that as an argument to re-
" commend the gofpel, which he has obferved men to
" lay hold on as an objection againft it? To urge fuch
" points of controverfy as neceffary articles of faith,
" when we fee our Saviour and the apoftles urged them
" not as neceffary to be believed to make men chriftians,
" is (by our own authority) to add prejudices to pre-
" judices, and to block up our own way to thofe men,
" whom we would have accefs to, and prevail upon."

I have repeated this again out of the 164th page of my Vindication, where there is more to the fame purpofe;

pose; that the reader may see how fully the unmasker has answered it.

Because, I said, " Would any one blame my prudence,
" if I mentioned only those advantages, which all chris-
" tians are agreed in?" the unmasker adds, p. 44, " so-
" cinian christians :" and then, as if the naming of that
had gained him his point, he goes on victoriously thus:
" He has bethought himself better, since he first pub-
" lished his notions, and (as the result of that) he now
" begins to resolve what he writ into prudence. I know
" whence he had this method, (and it is likely he has
" taken more than this from the same hands) viz. from
" the missionary jesuits, that went to preach the gospel
" to the people of China. We are told, that they in-
" structed them in some matters relating to our Saviour;
" they let them know that Jesus was the Messias, the
" person promised to be sent into the world : but they
" concealed his sufferings and death, and they would
" not let them know any thing of his passion and cruci-
" fixion. So our author (their humble imitator) un-
" dertakes to instruct the world in christianity, with an
" omission of its principal articles ; and more especially
" that of the advantage we have by Christ's death, which
" was the prime thing designed in his coming into the
" world. This he calls prudence: so that to hide from
" the people the main articles of the christian religion,
" to disguise the faith of the gospel, to betray christianity
" itself, is, according to this excellent writer, the car-
" dinal virtue of prudence. May we be delivered then,
" say I, from a prudential racovian." And there ends
the rattling for this time ; not to be outdone by any
piece of clock-work in the town. When he is once set
a going, he runs on like an alarum, always in the same
strain of noisy, empty declamation, (wherein every thing
is supposed, and nothing proved) till his own weight has
brought him to the ground : and then, being wound up
with some new topic, takes another run, whether it
makes for or against him, it matters not; he has laid
about him with ill language, let it light where it will,
and the vindicator is paid off.

That I may keep the due distance in our different
ways

ways of writing, I fhall fhow the reader, that I fay not this at random; but that the place affords me occafion to fay fo. He begins this paragraph with thefe words, p. 42, " Let us hear farther, what this vindicator fays " to excufe his rejection of the doctrines contained in " the epiftles." This rejection of the doctrines contained in the epiftles, was the not mentioning the fatisfaction of Chrift, amongft thofe advantages I fhowed that the world received by his coming. This appears by the words he here quotes, as my excufe for that omiffion. In which place, I alfo produced fome paffages in my book, which founded like it, fome words of fcripture that are ufed to prove it; but this will not content him: I am, for all that, a " betrayer of chriftianity, and con- " temner of the epiftles." Why? Becaufe I did not, out of them, name fatisfaction. If you will have the truth of it, fir, there is not any fuch word in any one of the epiftles, or other books of the New Teftament, in my bible, as fatisfying, or fatisfaction made by our Saviour; and fo I could not put it into my " Chriftianity " as delivered in the Scripture." If mine be not a true bible, I defire you to furnifh me with one that is more orthodox; or, if the tranflators have " hid that main " article of the chriftian religion," they are the " be- " trayers of chriftianity, and contemners of the epiftles," who did not put it there; and not I, who did not take a word from thence, which they did not put there. For truly I am not a maker of creeds; nor dare add either to the fcripture, or to the fundamental articles of the chriftian religion.

But you will fay, fatisfaction, though not named in the epiftles, yet may plainly be collected out of them. Anfw. And fo it may out of feveral places in my " Rea- " fonablenefs of Chriftianity," fome whereof, which I took out of the gofpels, I mentioned in my Vindication, ·p. 163, 164, and others of them, which I took out of the epiftles, I fhall point out to you now: as p. 41, I fay, the defign of our Saviour's coming was to be OF- FERED up; and p. 84. I fpeak of the work of our RE- DEMPTION; words, which in the epiftles, are taken to imply fatisfaction. And therefore if that be enough, I

ice

fee not, but I may be free from betraying chriftianity;
but if it be neceffary to name the word Satisfaction, and
he that does not fo, is a betrayer of chriftianity, you will
do well to confider, how you will acquit the holy apoftles from that bold imputation; which if it be extended
as far as it will go, will fcarce come fhort of blafphemy: for I do not remember, that our Saviour has any
where named fatisfaction, or implied it plainer in any
words, than thofe I have quoted from him; and he, I
hope, will efcape the intemperance of your tongue.

You tell me, I had my "prudence from the miffionary
" jefuits in China, who concealed our Saviour's fuffer-
" ings and death, becaufe I undertake to inftruct the
" world in chriftianity, with an omiffion of its principal
" articles." And I pray, fir, from whom did you learn
your prudence, when, taking upon you to teach the fundamental doctrines of chriftianity, in your "Thoughts
" concerning the Caufes of Atheifm," you left out feveral, that you have been pleafed fince to add in your
"Socinianifm unmafked?" Or, if I, as you fay here,
betray chriftianity by this omiffion of this principal article; what do you, who are a profeffed teacher of it, if
you omit any principal article, which your prudence is
fo wary in, that you will not fay you have given us all
that are neceffary to falvation, in that lift you have laft
publifhed? I pray, who acts beft the jefuit, (whofe humble imitator, you fay, I am) you or I? when, pretending
to give a catalogue of fundamentals, you have not reduced them to direct propofitions, but have left fome
of them indefinite, to be collected as every one pleafes:
and inftead of telling us it is a perfect catalogue of fundamentals, plainly fhuffle it off, and tell me, p. 22, "If
" that will not content me, you are fure you can do no-
" thing that will: if I require more, it is folly in you
" to comply with me?" One part of what you here fay,
I own to you, favours not much of the fkill of a jefuit.
You confefs your inability, and I believe it to be perfectly true: that if what you have done already (which
is nothing at all) "will not content me, you are fure,
" you can do nothing that will content me," or any
reafonable man that fhall demand of you a complete
                                                    catalogue

catalogue of fundamentals. But you make it up pretty well, with a confidence becoming one of that order. For he muft have rubbed his forehead hard, who in the fame treatife, where he fo feverely condemns the imperfection of my lift of fundamentals, confeffes that he cannot give a complete catalogue of his own.

You publifh to the world in this 44th, and the next page, that " I hide from the people the main articles of " the chriftian religion ; I difguife the faith of the gof- " pel, betray chriftianity itfelf, and imitate the jefuits " that went to preach the gofpel to the people of China, " by my omiffion of its principal or main articles."

Anfw. I know not how I difguife the faith of the gofpel, &c. in imitation of the jefuits in China ; unlefs taking men off from the inventions of men, and recom- mending to them the reading and ftudy of the holy fcrip- ture, to find what the gofpel is, and requires, be " a dif- " guifing the faith of the gofpel, a betraying of chriftia- " nity, and imitating the jefuits." Befides, fir, if one may afk you, In what fchool did you learn that prudent warinefs and referve, which fo eminently appears, p. 24, of your "Socinianifm unmafked," in thefe words : " Thefe " articles" (meaning thofe which you had before enume- rated as fundamental articles) of faith, " are fuch as muft " IN SOME MEASURE be known and affented to by a " chriftian, fuch as muft GENERALLY be received and " embraced by him ?" You will do well the next time, to fet down, how far your fundamentals muft be known, affented to, and received ; to avoid the fufpicion, that there is a little more of jefuitifm in thefe expreffions, " in fome meafure known and affented to, and gene- " rally received and embraced ;" than what becomes a fincere proteftant preacher of the gofpel. For your fpeaking fo doubtfully of knowing and affenting to thofe, which you give us for fundamental doctrines, which belong (as you fay) to the very effence of chrif- tianity, will hardly efcape being imputed to your want of knowledge, or want of fincerity. And indeed, the word " general," is in familiar ufe with you, and ftands you in good ftead, when you would fay fomething, you

know

know not what; as I shall have occasion to remark to you, when I come to your 91st page.

Further, I do not remember where it was, that I mentioned or undertook to set down all the " principal or " main articles of christianity." To change the terms of the question, from articles necessary to be believed to make a man a christian, into principal or main articles, looks a little jesuitical. But to pass by that: the apostles, when they " went to preach the gospel to peo- " ple," as much strangers to it as the Chinese were, when the Europeans came first amongst them, " Did " they hide from the people the main articles of the " christian religion, disguise the faith of the gospel, and " betray christianity itself?" If they did not, I am sure I have not: for I have not omitted any of the main articles, which they preached to the unbelieving world. Those I have set down, with so much care, not to omit any of them, that you blame me for it more than once, and call it tedious.   However you are pleased to acquit or condemn the apostles in the case, by your supreme determination, I am very indifferent.   If you think fit to condemn them for " disguising or betraying the " christian religion," because they said no more of sa- tisfaction, than I have done, in their preaching at first, to their unbelieving auditors, jews or heathens, to make them, as I think, christians, (for that I am now speaking of) I shall not be sorry to be found in their company, under what censure soever. If you are pleased graciously to take off this your censure from them, for this omis- sion, I shall claim a share in the same indulgence.

But to come to what, perhaps, you will think yourself a little more concerned not to censure, and what the apostles did so long since; for you have given instances of being very apt to make bold with the dead: Pray tell me, does the church of England admit people into the church of Christ at hap-hazard? Or without pro- posing and requiring a profession of all that is necessary to be believed to make a man a christian? If she does not, I desire you to turn to the baptism of those of riper years in our liturgy: where the priest, asking the con-

vert

vert particularly, whether he believes the apoftles creed, which he repeats to him; upon his profeffion that he does, and that he defires to be baptized into that faith, without one word of any other articles, baptizes him; and then declares him a chriftian in thefe words : " We " receive this perʃon into the congregation of Chrift's " flock, and fign him with the fign of the crofs, in to- " ken that he fhall not be afhamed—to CONTINUE " Chrift's faithful foldier and fervant." In all this there is not one word of fatisfaction, no more than in my book, nor fo much neither. And here I afk you, Whether for this omiffion you will pronounce that the church of England difguifes the faith of the gofpel ? However you think fit to treat me, yet methinks you fhould not let yourfelf loofe fo freely againft our firft reformers and the fathers of our church ever fince, as to call them "Betrayers of chriftianity itfelf;" becaufe they think not fo much neceffary to be believed to make a man a chriftian, as you are pleafed to put down in your articles; but omit, as well as I, your " main article of " fatisfaction."

Having thus notably harangued upon the occafion of my faying, " Would any one blame my prudence ?" and thereby made me a " focinian, a jefuit, and a betrayer of " chriftianity itfelf," he has in that anfwered all that fuch a mifcreant as I do, or can fay; and fo paffes by all the reafons I gave for what I did; without any other notice or anfwer, but only denying a matter of fact, which I only can know, and he cannot, viz. my defign in printing my " Reafonablenefs of Chriftianity."

In the next paragraph, p. 45, in anfwer to the words of St. Paul, Rom. xiv. 1, " Him that is weak in the faith " receive ye, but not to doubtful difputations;" which I brought as a reafon, why I mentioned not fatisfaction amongft the benefits received by the coming of our Sa- viour; becaufe, as I tell him in my Vindication, p. 164, " my Reafonablenefs of Chriftianity," as the title fhows, " was defigned chiefly for thofe who were not yet tho- " roughly or firmly chriftians." He replies, and I de- fire him to prove it,

XX. " That

XX. " That I pretend a defign of my book, which
" was never fo much as thought of, until I was
" folicited by my brethren to vindicate it."

All the reft in this paragraph, being either nothing to
this place of the Romans, or what I have anfwered elfewhere, needs no farther anfwer.

The next two paragraphs, p. 46—49, are meant for
an anfwer to fomething I had faid concerning the apoftles creed, upon the occafion of his charging my book
with focinianifm.   They begin thus:

This " author of the new chriftianity" [Anfw. This
new chriftianity is as old as the preaching of our Saviour
and his apoftles, and a little older than the unmafker's
fyftem] " wifely objects, that the apoftles creed hath
" none of thofe articles which I mention," p. 591, &c.
Anfw. If that author wifely objects, the unmafker would
have done well to have replied wifely.   But for a man
wifely to reply, it is in the firft place requifite, that the
objection be truly and fairly fet down in its full force,
and not reprefented fhort, and as will beft ferve the
anfwerer's turn to reply to.   This is neither wife nor
honeft: and this firft part of a wife reply the unmafker
has failed in.   This will appear from my words, and
the occafion of them.   The unmafker had accufed my
book of focinianifm, for omitting fome points, which
he urged as neceffary articles of faith.   To which I
anfwered, That he had done fo only " to give it an ill
" name, not becaufe it was focinian; for he had no
" more reafon to charge it with focinianifm, for the
" omiffions he mentions, than the apoftles creed."
Thefe are my words, which he fhould have either fet
down out of p. 67, which he quotes, or at leaft given
the objection, as I put it, if he had meant to have cleared
it by a fair anfwer.   But he, inftead thereof, contents
himfelf that " I object, that the apoftles creed hath
" none of thofe articles and doctrines which the un-
" mafker mentioned."   Anfw. This at beft is but a
part of my objection, and not to the purpofe which I
there meant, without the reft joined to it; which it has
                                                    pleafed

pleased the unmasker, according to his laudable way, to conceal. My objection, therefore, stands thus :

> That the same articles, for the omission whereof the unmasker charges my book with socinianism, being also omitted in the apostles creed, he has no more reason to charge my book with socinianism, for the omissions mentioned, than he hath to charge the apostles creed with socinianism.

> To this objection of mine, let us now see how he answers, p. 47.

" Nor does any considerate man wonder at it," [i. e. that the apostles creed had none of those articles and doctrines which he had mentioned] " for the creed " is a form of outward profession, which is chiefly to " be made in the public assemblies, when prayers are " put up in the church, and the holy scriptures are " read : then this abridgment of faith is properly used, " or when there is not time or opportunity to make " any enlargement. But we are not to think it expresly " contains in it all the necessary and weighty points, all " the important doctrines of belief; it being only de- " signed to be an abstract."

Answ. Another indispensable requisite in a wise re- ply is, that it should be pertinent. Now what can there be more impertinent, than to confess the matter of fact upon which the objection is grounded ; but instead of destroying the inference drawn from that matter of fact, only amuse the reader with wrong reasons, why that matter of fact was so?

No considerate man, he says, doth wonder, that the articles and doctrines he mentioned, are omitted in the apostles creed : because " that creed is a form of out- " ward profession." Answ. A profession! of what I beseech you? Is it a form to be used for form's sake? I thought it had been a profession of something, even of the christian faith : and if it be so, any considerate man may wonder necessary articles of the christian faith should be left out of it. For how it can be an outward profeffion of the chriftian faith, without containing the chriftian faith, I do not fee ; unlefs a man can out-wardly profefs the chriftian faith in words, that do not contain or exprefs it, i. e. profefs the chriftian faith, when he does not profefs it. But he fays, " It is a pro-" feffion chiefly to be made ufe of in affemblies." Anfw. Do thofe folemn affemblies privilege it from containing the neceffary articles of the chriftian reli-gion? This proves not that it does not, or was not de-figned to contain all the articles neceffary to be believed to make a man a chriftian; unlefs the unmafker can prove that a " form of outward profeffion" of the chrif-tian faith, that contains all fuch neceffary articles, can-not be made ufe of, in the public affemblies. " In the " public affemblies," fays he, " when prayers are put " up by the church, and the holy fcriptures are read, " then this abridgment of faith is properly ufed ; or " when there is not generally time or opportunity to " make an enlargement." Anfw. But that which con-tains not what is abfolutely neceffary to be believed to make a man a chriftian, can no where be properly ufed as a form of outward profeffion of the chriftian faith, and leaft of all, in the folemn public affemblies. All the fenfe I can make of this is, that this abridgment of the chriftian faith, i. e. imperfect collection (as the un-mafker will have it) of fome of the fundamental arti-cles of chriftianity in the apoftles creed, which omits the greateft part of them, is made ufe of as a form of outward profeffion of but part of the chriftian faith in the public affemblies ; when, by reafon of reading of the fcripture and prayers, there is not time or opportunity for a full and perfect profeffion of it.

It is ftrange the chriftian church fhould not find time nor opportunity, in fixteen hundred years, to make, in any of her public affemblies, a profeffion of fo much of her faith, as is neceffary to make a man a chriftian. But pray tell me, has the church any fuch full and complete form of faith, that hath in it all thofe propofitions, you have given us for neceffary articles, (not to fay any thing of thofe which you have referved to yourfelf, in your own breaft, and will not communicate) of which the apoftles

creed

creed is only a fcanty form, a brief imperfect abftract, ufed only to fave time in the crowd of other prefling occafions, that are always in hafte to be difpatched? If fhe has, the unmafker will do well to produce it. If the church has no fuch complete form, befides the apo-ftles creed, any where, of fundamental articles; he will do well to leave talking idly of this abftract, as he goes on to do in the following words:

"But" fays he, "we are not to think that it exprefly "contains in it all the neceffary and weighty points, all "the important doctrines of our belief; it being only "defigned to be an abftract." Anfw. Of what, I be-feech you, is it an abftract? For here the unmafker ftops fhort, and, as one that knows not well what to fay, fpeaks not out what it is an abftract of; but provides himfelf a fubterfuge in the generality of the preceding terms, of "neceffary and weighty points, and impor-"tant doctrines," jumbled together; which can be there of no other ufe, but to cover his ignorance or fo-phiftry. But the queftion being only about neceffary points, to what purpofe are weighty and important doc-trines joined to them; unlefs he will fay, that there is no difference between neceffary and weighty points, fundamental and important doctrines; and if fo, then the diftinction of points into neceffary and not neceffary, will be foolifh and impertinent; and all the doctrines contained in the bible, will be abfolutely neceffary to be explicitly believed by every man to make him a chrif-tian. But taking it for granted, that the diftinction of truths contained in the gofpel, into points abfolutely neceffary, and not abfolutely neceffary, to be believed to make a man a chriftian, is good; I defire the un-mafker to tell us, what the apoftles creed is an abftract of? He will, perhaps, anfwer, that he has told us al-ready in this very page, where he fays, it is an abridg-ment of faith: and he has faid true in words, but faying thofe words by rote, after others, without underftanding them, he has faid fo in a fenfe that is not true. For he fuppofes it an abridgment of faith, by containing only a few of the neceffary articles of faith, and leaving out the far greater part of them; and fo takes a part of a

T 2   thing

thing for an abridgment of it; whereas an abridgment or abſtract of any thing, is the whole in little; and if it be of a ſcience or doctrine, the abridgment conſiſts in the eſſential or neceſſary parts of it contracted into a narrower compaſs than where it lies diffuſed in the ordinary way of delivery, amongſt a great number of tranſitions, explanations, illuſtrations, proofs, reaſonings, corollaries, &c. All which, though they make a part of the diſcourſe, wherein that doctrine is delivered, are left out in the abridgment of it, wherein all the neceſſary parts of it are drawn together into a leſs room. But though an abridgment need to contain none but the eſſential and neceſſary parts, yet all thoſe it ought to contain; or elſe it will not be an abridgment or abſtract of that thing, but an abridgment only of a part of it. I think it could not be ſaid to be an abridgment of the law contained in an act of parliament, wherein any of the things required by that act were omitted; which yet commonly may be reduced into a very narrow compaſs, when ſtripped of all the motives, ends, enacting forms, &c. expreſſed in the act itſelf. If this does not ſatisfy the unmaſker what is properly an abridgment, I ſhall refer him to Mr. Chillingworth, who, I think, will be allowed to underſtand ſenſe, and to ſpeak it properly, at leaſt as well as the unmaſker. And what he ſays happens to be in the very ſame queſtion, between Knot, the jeſuit, and him, that is here between the unmaſker and me: it is but putting the unmaſker in the jeſuit's place, and myſelf (if it may be allowed me, without vanity) in Mr. Chillingworth, the proteſtant's; and Mr. Chillingworth's very words, chap. iv. §. 65, will exactly ſerve for my anſwer: " You trifle affectedly, confounding the " apoſtles belief of the whole religion of Chriſt, as it " comprehends both what we are to do, and what we " are to believe, with that part of it which contains not " duties of obedience, but only the neceſſary articles of " ſimple faith. Now, though the apoſtles belief be, in " the former ſenſe, a larger thing than that which we " call the apoſtles creed; yet, in the latter ſenſe of the " word, the creed (I ſay) is a full comprehenſion of " their belief, which you yourſelf have formerly confeſſed,

" feffed, though fomewhat fearfully and inconfiftently.
" And here again unwillingnefs to fpeak the truth
" makes you fpeak that which is hardly fenfe, and call
it " an abridgment of fome articles of faith." For I
" demand, thofe fome articles, which you fpeak of,
" which are they? Thofe that are out of the creed, or
" thofe that are in it? Thofe that are in it, it compre-
" hends at large, and therefore it is not an abridgment
" of them. Thofe that are out of it, it comprehends
" not at all, and therefore it is not an abridgment of
" them. If you would call it now an abridgment of
" faith; this would be fenfe; and fignify thus much,
" that all the neceffary articles of the chriftian faith are
" comprized in it. For this is the proper duty of
" abridgments, to leave out nothing neceffary." So
that, in Mr. Chillingworth's judgment of an abridgment, it is not fenfe to fay, as you do, p. 47. That
" we are not to think, that the apoftles creed exprefly
" contains in it all the neceffary points of our belief, it
" being only defigned to be an abftract, or an abridg-
" ment of faith:" but on the contrary, we muft conclude, it contains in it all the neceffary articles of faith,
for that very reafon; becaufe it is an abridgment of faith,
as the unmafker calls it. But whether this that Mr.
Chillingworth has given us here, be the nature of an
abridgment or no; this is certain, that the apoftles
creed cannot be a form of profeffion of the chriftian
faith, if any part of the faith neceffary to make a man a
chriftian, be left out of it: and yet fuch a profeffion of
faith would the unmafker have this abridgment of faith
to be. For a little lower, in the 47th page, he fays in
exprefs terms, That " if a man believe no more
" than is, in exprefs terms, in the apoftles creed,
" his faith will not be the faith of a chriftian."
Wherein he does great honour to the primitive church,
and particularly to the church of England. The primitive church admitted converted heathens to baptifm,
upon the faith contained in the apoftles creed: a bare
profeffion of that faith, and no more, was required of
them to be received into the church, and made mem-

bers of Chrift's body. How little different the faith of
the ancient church was, from the faith I have mentioned, may be feen in thefe words of Tertullian:
" Regula fidei una omnino eft, fola, immobilis, irre-
" formabilis, credendi, fcilicet, in unicum Deum omni-
" potentem, mundi conditorem, & filium ejus Jefum
" Chriftum, natum ex virgine Maria, crucifixum fub
" Pontio Pilato, tertia die refufcitatum à mortuis, re-
" ceptum in cœlis, fedentem nunc ad dextram Patris,
" venturum judicare vivos & mortuos, per carnis etiam
" refurrectionem. Hâc lege fidei manente, cætera jam
" difciplinæ & converfationis admittunt novitatem cor-
" rectionis:" Tert. de virg. velan. in principio. This
was the faith, that in Tertullian's time fufficed to make
a chriftian. And the church of England, as I have remarked already, only propofed the articles of the apoftles
creed to the convert to be baptized; and upon his pro-
fefling a belief of them, afks, Whether he will be baptized in this faith; which (if we will believe the
unmafker) " is not the faith of a chriftian." However,
the church, without any more ado, upon the profeffion
of this faith, and no other, baptizes him into it. So
that the ancient church, if the unmafker may be believed, baptized converts into that faith, which " is
" not the faith of a chriftian." And the church of
England, when fhe baptizes any one, makes him not a
chriftian. For he that is baptized only into a faith,
that " is not the faith of a chriftian," I would fain
know how he can thereby be made a chriftian? So that
if the omiffions, which he fo much blames in my book,
make me a Socinian, I fee not how the church of England will efcape that cenfure; fince thofe omiffions are
in that very confeffion of faith which fhe propofes, and
upon a profeffion whereof, fhe baptizes thofe whom fhe
defigns to make chriftians. But it feems that the unmafker (who has made bold to unmafk her too) reafons
right, that the church of England is miftaken, and
makes none but Socinians chriftians; or (as he is pleafed
now to declare) no chriftians at all. Which, if true,
the unmafker had beft look to it, whether he himfelf be
a chriftian, or no; for it is to be feared, he was baptized

tized only into that faith, which he himself confesses
" is not the faith of a christian."

But he brings himself off, in these following words:
" all matters of faith, in some manner, may be reduced
" to this brief platform of belief." Answ. If that be
enough to make him a true and an orthodox christian,
he does not consider whom, in this way, he brings off
with him; for I think he cannot deny, that all matters
of faith, in some manner, may be reduced to that abstract of faith which I have given, as well as to that
brief platform in the apostles creed. So that, for aught
I see, by this rule, we are christians or not christians,
orthodox or not orthodox, equally together.

But yet he says, in the next words: when he calls it an
" abstract, or abbreviature, it is implied, that there are
" more truths to be known and assented to by a christian,
" in order to making him really so, than what we meet
" with here." The quite contrary whereof (as has been
shown) is implied, by its being called an abstract. But
what is that to the purpose? It is not fit abstracts and
abbreviatures should stand in an unmasker's way. They
are sounds men have used for what they pleased; and
why may not the unmasker do so too, and use them in a
sense, that may make the apostles creed be only a
broken scrap of the christian faith? However, in great
condescension, being willing to do the apostles creed
what honour he could, he says, That " all matters of
" faith, in some manner, may be reduced to this brief
" platform of belief." But yet, when it is set in competition with the creed, which he himself is making,
(for it is not yet finished) it is by no means to be allowed
as sufficient to make a man a christian: " There are
" more truths to be known and assented to, in order to
" make a man really a christian." Which, what they
are, the church of England shall know, when this new
reformer thinks fit; and then she may be able to propose to those who are not yet so, a collection of articles of
belief, and baptize them a-new into a faith, which will
really make them christians: but hitherto, if the unmasker may be credited, she has failed in it.

" Yet

" Yet he craves leave to tell me," in the following
words, p. 48, " That the apoftles creed hath more in it
" than I, or my brethren, will fubfcribe to." Were it
not the undoubted privilege of the unmafker to know
me better than I do myfelf, (for he is always telling me
fomething of myfelf, which I did not know) I would,
in my turn, crave leave to tell him, that this is the faith
I was baptized into, no one tittle whereof I have renounced, that I know; and that I heretofore thought,
that gave me title to be a chriftian. But the unmafker
hath otherwife determined : and I know not now where to
find a chriftian. For the belief of the apoftles creed
will not, it feems, make a man one : and what other
belief will, it does not yet pleafe the unmafker to tell us.
But yet, as to the fubfcribing to the apoftles creed, I
muft take leave to fay, however the unmafker may be
right in the faith, he is out in the morals of a chriftian;
it being againft the charity of one, that is really fo, to
pronounce, as he does, peremptorily in a thing that he
cannot know; and to affirm pofitively what I know to
be a downright falfhood. But what others will do, it
is not my talent to determine; that belongs to the unmafker; though, as to all that are my brethren in the
chriftian faith, I may anfwer for them too, that they
will alfo, with me, do that, without which, in that
fenfe, they cannot be my brethren.

Page 49, The unmafker fmartly convinces me of no
fmall blunder, in thefe words : " But was it not judi-
" cioufly faid by this writer, that, " it is well for the
" compilers of the creed, that they lived not in my
" days?" p. 12, " I tell you, friend, it was impoffible
" they fhould; for the learned Ufher and Voffius, and
" others have proved, that that fymbol was drawn up,
" not at once, but that fome articles of it were adjoined
" many years after, far beyond the extent of any man's
" life; and therefore the compilers of the creed could
" not live in my days, nor could I live in theirs." Anfw.
But it feems that, had they lived all together, you could
have lived in their days. " But," fays he, " I let this
" pafs, as one of the blunders of our thoughtful and
" mufing author." Anfw. And I tell you, friend, that
unlefs

unlefs it were to fhow your reading in Ufher and Voffius, you had better have let this blunder of mine alone. Does not the unmafker give here a clear proof, that he is no changeling? Whatever argument he takes in hand, weighty or trivial, material or not material to the thing in queftion, he brings it to the fame fort of fenfe and force. He would fhow me guilty of an abfurdity, in faying, " It is well for the compilers of the creed, that " they lived not in his days." This he proves to be a blunder, becaufe they all lived not in one another's days; therefore it was an abfurdity to fuppofe, they might all live in his days. As if there were any greater abfurdity to bring the compilers, who lived, poffibly, within a few centuries of one another, by a fuppofition, into one time; than it is to bring the unmafker, and any one of them who lived a thoufand years diftant one from another, by a fuppofition, to be contemporaries: for it is by reafon of the compilers living at a diftance one from another, that he proves it impoffible for him to be their contemporary. As if it were not as impoffible in fact, for him who was not born until above a thoufand years after, to live in any of their days, as it is for any one of them to live in either of thofe compilers days, that died before him. The fuppofition of their living together, is as eafy of one as the other, at what diftance foever they lived, and how many foever there were of them. This being fo, I think it had been better for the unmafker to have let alone the blunder, and fhowed (which was his bufinefs) that he does not accufe the compilers of the creed of being all over focinianized, as well as he does me, fince they were as guilty as I, of the omiffion of thofe articles, (viz. " that Chrift is " the word of God : that Chrift was God incarnate : the " eternal and ineffable generation of the Son of God : " that the Son is in the Father, and the Father in the " Son, which expreffes their unity ;" for the omiffion whereof, the unmafker laid focinianifm to my charge. So that it remains ftill upon his fcore to fhow,

XXI. " Why thefe omiffions in the apoftles creed do " not as well make that abftract, as my abridgment of " faith, to be focinian ?"

Page 57.

Page 57, The unmasker " desires the reader to ob-
" serve, that this lank faith of mine is in a manner no
" other than the faith of a turk." And I desire the
reader to observe, that this faith of mine was all that
our Saviour and his apostles preached to the unbelieving world. And this our unmasker cannot deny, as I
think, will appear to any one, who observes what he
says, p. 76, 77, of his Socinianism unmasked. And that
they preached nothing but a " faith, that was in a manner
" no other than the faith of a turk," I think none
amongst christians, but this bold unmasker, will have
the irreverence profanely to say.

He tells us, p. 54, that " the muffelmen" (or, as he
has, for the information of his reader, very pertinently
proved, it should be writ, moslemim ; without which,
perhaps, we should not have known his skill in arabick,
or, in plain English, the mahometans) " believe that
" Christ is a good man, and not above the nature of a
" man, and sent of God to give instruction to the
" world: and my faith," he says, " is of the very same
" scantling." This I shall desire him to prove ; or,
which in other words he insinuates in this and the
neighbouring pages, viz.

XXII. That that faith, which I have affirmed to
be the faith, which is required to make a man
a christian, is no other than what turks believe,
and is contained in the alcoran.

Or, as he expresses it himself, p. 55,

" That a turk, according to me, is a christian ; for I
" make the same faith serve them both."

And particularly to show where it is, I say,

XXIII. That " Christ is not above the nature of a
man," or have made that a necessary article of the
christian faith.

And next, where it is,

XXIV.

XXIV. " That I fpeak as meanly of Chrift's fuffer-
" ing on the crofs, and death, as if there were no
" fuch thing."

For thus he fays of me, p. 54, " I feem to have con-
" fulted the Mahometan bible, which did fay, Chrift
" did not fuffer on the crofs, did not die. For I, and
" my allies, fpeak as meanly of thefe articles, as if there
" were no fuch thing."

To fhow our unmafker's veracity in this cafe, I fhall
trouble my reader with fome paffages out of my " rea-
" fonablenefs of chriftianity," p. 35, " When we
" confider, that he was to fill out the time foretold of
" his miniftry, and after a life illuftrious in miracles
" and good works, attended with humility, meeknefs,
" patience and fuffering, and every way conformable to
" the prophecies of him, fhould be led as a fheep to the
" flaughter, and, with all quiet and fubmiffion, be
" brought to the crofs, though there were no guilt or
" fault found in him." And, p. 42, " contrary to the
" defign of his coming, which was to be offered up a
" lamb, blamelefs and void of offence." And, p. 63,
" laying down his life, both for Jews and Gentiles,"
P. 96, " Given up to contempt, torment, and
death." But, fay what I will, when the unmafker thinks
fit to have it fo, it is fpeaking out of the mahometan
bible, that " Chrift did not fuffer on the crofs, did not
" die; or at leaft, is fpeaking as meanly of thefe articles,
" as if no fuch thing had been."

His next flander is, p. 55, in thefe words: " this
" gentleman prefents the world with a very ill notion
" of faith; for the very devils are capable of all that
" faith, which, he fays, makes a chriftian." It is not
ftrange, that the unmafker fhould mifreprefent the faith,
which, I fay, makes a chriftian; when it feems to be
his whole defign to mifreprefent my meaning every-
where. The frequency of his doing it, I have fhowed
in abundance of inftances, to which I fhall add an eminent one here; which fhows what a fair champion he is
for truth and religion.

Page 104,

Page 104, of my " Reafonablenefs of Chriftianity," I give this account of the faith which makes a chriftian ; that it is " men's entering themfelves in the kingdom " of God ; owning and profeffing themfelves the fub- " jects of Jefus, whom they believe to be the Meffiah, " and receive for their Lord and King : for that was to " be baptized in his name." This fenfe of believing Chrift to be the Meffiah, that is, to take him for our King and Lord, who is to be obeyed, I have expreffed over and over again ; as, p. 110, 111, my words are, " that as " many of them as would believe Jefus the fon of God, " (whom he fent into the world) to be the Meffiah, the " promifed Deliverer, and would receive him for their " king and ruler, fhould have all their paft fins, difo- " bedience and rebellion, forgiven them. And if, for " the future, they lived in fincere obedience to his law, " to the utmoft of their power, the fins of human frailty " for the time to come, as well as thofe of their paft " lives, fhould for his fon's fake, becaufe they gave " themfelves up to him to be his fubjects, be forgiven " them : and fo their faith, which made them to be " baptized into his name, (i. e. inroll themfelves in " the kingdom of Jefus, the Meffiah, and profefs them- " felves his fubjects, and confequently live by the laws " of his kingdom) fhould be accounted to them for " righteoufnefs." Which account of what is neceffary, I clofe with thefe words : " this is the faith, for which " God of his free grace juftifies finful man." And is this the faith of devils ?

To the fame purpofe, p. 113, are thefe words : " the " chief end of his coming was to be a king ; and, as " fuch, to be received by thofe, who would be his fubjects " in the kingdom which he came to erect." And again, p. 112, " only thofe who have believed Jefus to be the " Meffiah, and taken him for their king, with a fincere " endeavour after righteoufnefs in obeying his law, fhall " have their paft fins not imputed to them." And fo again, p. 113, and 120, and in feveral other places ; of which I fhall add but this one more, p. 120, " it is not " enough to believe him to be the Meffiah, unlefs we " obey his laws, and take him to be our king to reign
                                                            " over

" over us." Can the devils thus believe him to be the Messiah? Yet this is that, which, by these and abundance of other places, I have showed to be the meaning of believing him to be the Messiah.

Besides, I have expresly distinguished the faith which makes a christian, from that which the devils have, by proving, that, to the believing Jesus to be the Messiah, must be joined repentance, or else it will not make them true christians: and what this repentance is, may be seen at large in p. 105, &c. some expressions whereof I shall here set down; as, p. 105, " repentance does not " consist in one single act of sorrow, (though that being " first, and leading, gives denomination to the whole) " but in doing works meet for repentance; in a sincere " obedience to the law of Christ, the remainder of our " lives." Again; to distinguish the faith of a christian from that of devils, I say expresly, out of St. Paul's epistle to the galatians, " that which availeth is faith, " but faith working by love; and that faith, without " works, i. e. the works of sincere obedience to the law " and will of Christ, is not sufficient for our justifica- " tion." And, p. 117, " That to inherit eternal life, we must love the Lord our God, " with all our heart, with " all our soul, with all our strength, and with all our " mind." And, p. 121, " Love Christ, in keeping his " commandments."

This, and a great deal more to this purpose, may be seen in my " Reasonableness of Christianity;" particularly, where I answer that objection about the faith of devils, which I handle in p. 102, &c. and therein at large show, wherein the faith of devils comes short of the justifying faith which makes a christian. And yet the good, the sincere, the candid unmasker, with his becoming confidence, tells his readers here, p. 55. " That " I present the world with a very ill notion of faith: for " the very devils are capable of all that faith, which I " say, makes a christian man."

To prevent this calumny, I, in more places than one, distinguished between faith, in a strict sense, as it is a bare assent to any proposition, and that which is called evangelical faith, in a larger sense of the word; which

comprehends

comprehends under it fomething more than a bare fimple affent; as, p. 26, " I mean, this is all that is required " to be believed by thofe who acknowledge but one " eternal, invifible God, the maker of heaven and earth : " for that there is fomething more required to falvation, " befides believing, we fhall fee hereafter." P. 28, " All I fay, that was to be believed for juftification. " For, that this was not all that was required to be " done for juftification, we fhall fee hereafter. P. 51, " Obeying the law of the Meffiah, their King, being no " lefs required, than their believing that Jefus was the " Meffiah, the King and Deliverer, that was promifed " them." P. 102, " As far as their believing could " make them members of Chrift's body." By thefe, and more, the like paffages in my book, my meaning is fo evident, that no-body, but an unmafker, would have faid, that when I fpoke of believing, as a bare fpeculative affent to any propofition, as true, I affirmed that was all that was required of a chriftian for juftification : though that, in the ftrict fenfe of the word, is all that is done in believing. And therefore, I fay, As far as mere believing could make them members of Chrift's body ; plainly fignifying, as much as words can, that the faith, for which they were juftified, included fomething more than a bare affent. This appears, not only from thefe words of mine, p. 104, " St. Paul often, in his " epiftles, puts faith for the whole duty of a chriftian ;" but from my fo often, and almoft every-where, interpreting " believing him to be the Meffiah, by taking " him to be our King;" whereby is meant not a bare idle fpeculation, a bare notional perfuafion of any truth whatfoever, floating in our brains ; but an active principle of life, a faith working by love and obedience. " To make him to be our King," carries with it a right difpofition of the will to honour and obey him, joined to that affent wherewith believers embrace this fundamental truth, that Jefus was the perfon who was by God fent to be their King ; he that was promifed to be their Prince and Saviour.

But, for all this, the unmafker, p. 56, confidently tells his reader, that I fay no fuch thing. His words

are :

are: " But, besides this historical faith, (as it is gene-
" rally called by divines) which is giving credit to
" evangelical truths, as barely revealed, there must be
" something else added to make up the true substantial
" faith of a christian. With the assent of the under-
" standing, must be joined the consent or approbation
" of the will. All those divine truths which the in-
" tellect assents to, must be allowed of by this elective
" power of the soul. True evangelical faith is a hearty
" acceptation of the Messias, as he is offered in the
" gospel. It is a sincere and impartial submission to
" all things required by the evangelical law, which is
" contained in the epistles, as well as the other writings.
" And to this practical assent and choice, there must be
" added, likewise, a firm trust and reliance in the blessed
" author of our salvation. But this late undertaker,
" who attempted to give us a more perfect account,
" than ever was before of christianity, as it is delivered
" in the scriptures, brings us no tidings of any such
" faith belonging to christianity, or discovered to us in
" the scriptures. Which gives us to understand, that
" he verily believes there is no such christian faith; for
" in some of his numerous pages, (especially p. 101,
" &c.) where he speaks so much of belief and faith, he
" might have taken occasion to insert one word about
" his complete faith of the gospel."

Though the places above quoted, out of my " Rea-
" sonableness of Christianity," and the whole tenour, of
the latter part of it, show the falshood of what the unmasker here says; yet I will set down one passage more
out of it; and then ask our unmasker, when he hath
read them, Whether he hath the brow to say again, that
" I bring no tidings of any such faith? " My words are
" Reasonableness of Christianity," p. 129, " Faith in the
" promises of God, relying and acquiescing in his
" word and faithfulness, the Almighty takes well at our
" hands, as a great mark of homage paid by us, poor
" frail creatures, to his goodness and truth, as well as
" to his power and wisdom; and accepts it as an ac-
" knowledgment of his peculiar providence and benig-
" nity to us. And therefore, our Saviour tells us,
" John

" John xii. 44. " He that believes on me, believes
" not on me, but on him that fent me." The works
" of nature fhow his wifdom and power: but it is his
" peculiar care of mankind, moft eminently difcovered
" in his promifes to them, that fhows his bounty and
" goodnefs; and confequently engages their hearts in
" love and affection to him. This oblation of an heart
" fixed with dependence aud affection on him, is the
" moft acceptable tribute we can pay him, the founda-
" tion of true devotion, and life of all religion. What
" a value he puts on this depending on his word, and
" refting fatisfied on his promifes, we have an example
" in Abraham; whofe faith was counted to him for
" righteoufnefs, as we have before remarked out of
" Rom. iv. And his relying firmly on the promife of
" God, without any doubt of its performance, gave him
" the name of the father of the faithful; and gained him
" fo much favour with the Almighty, that he was
" called the friend of God, the higheft and moft glorious
" title that can be beftowed on a creature!"

The great out-cry he makes againft me in his two
next fections, p. 57—60, as if I intended to introduce ignorance and popery, is to be entertained rather
as the noife of a petulant fcold, faying the worft things
fhe could think of, than as the arguing of a man of
fenfe or fincerity. All this mighty accufation is
grounded upon thefe falfhoods: That " I make it my
" great bufinefs to beat men off from divine truths;
" that I cry down all articles of the chriftian faith, but
" one; that I will not fuffer men to look into chrif-
" tianity; that I blaft the epiftolary writings." I fhall
add no more to what I have already faid, about the
epiftles, but thofe few words out of my " Reafonable-
" nefs of Chriftianity, page 154, " The epiftles, re-
" folving doubts, and reforming miftakes, are of great
" advantage to our knowledge and practice." And,
p. 155, 156, " An explicit belief of what God requires
" of thofe, who will enter into, and receive the bene-
" fits of the new covenant, is abfolutely required. The
" other parts of divine revelation are objects of faith,
" and are fo to be received. They are truths, whereof

4   " none

" none, that is once known to be such, [i. e. of divine
" revelation] may, or ought to be disbelieved."

And as for that other saying of his, " That I will
" not suffer men to look into christianity:" I desire to
know where that christianity is locked up, which " I
" will not suffer men to look into." My christianity,
I confess, is contained in the written word of God:
and that I am so far from hindering any one to look into, that I every-where appeal to it, and have quoted so
much of it, that the unmasker complains of being
overlaid with it, and tells me it is tedious. " All di-
" vine revelation, I say, p. 156, requires the obedience
" of faith; and that every one is to receive all the
" parts of it, with a docility and disposition prepared
" to embrace and assent to all truths coming from God;
" and submit his mind to whatever shall appear to him
" to bear that character." I speak, in the same page,
of men's endeavouring to understand it, and of their
interpreting one place by another. This, and the
whole design of my book, shows, that I think it every
christian's duty to read, search, and study the holy
scriptures; and make this their great business: and yet
the good unmasker, in a fit of zeal, displays his throat,
and cries out, p. 59. " Hear, O ye heavens, and give
" ear, O earth; judge whether this be not the way to
" introduce darkness and ignorance into Christendom;
" whether this be not blinding of men's eyes," &c.
for this mighty pathos ends not there. And, all
things considered, I know not whether he had not reason, in his want of arguments, this way to pour out his
concern. For neither the preaching of our Saviour and
his apostles, nor the apostles creed, nor any thing else,
being with him the faith of a christian, i. e. sufficient to
make a christian, but just his set of fundamental articles
(when he himself knows what they be;) in fine, nothing
being christianity but just his system, it is time to cry
out, Help, neighbours! hold fast, friends! Knowledge, religion, christianity is gone, if this be once permitted, that the people should read and understand the
scripture for themselves, as God shall enlighten their
understandings in the use of the means; and not be

forced to depend upon me, and upon my choofing, and my interpretation, for the neceffary points they are to believe to make them chriftians: if I, the great un-mafker, have not the fole power to decree what is, or is not fundamental, and people be not bound to receive it for fuch, faith and the gofpel are given up; darknefs and barbarifm will be brought in upon us by this writer's contrivance. For " he is an underhand factor " for that communion, which cries up ignorance for " the mother of devotion and religion;" i. e. in plain Englifh, for popery. For to this, and nothing elfe, tends all that fputter he makes in the fection before-mentioned.

I do not think there was ever a more thorough-paced declaimer, than our unmafker. He leaves out nothing that he thinks will make an affrighting noife in the ears of his orthodox hearers, though all the blame and cen-fure he pours out upon others light only on himfelf. For let me afk this zealous upholder of light and know-ledge: Does he think it reafonable, that any one, who is not a chriftian, fhould be fuffered to be undifturbed in his parifh? Nay, does he think fit that any fuch fhould live free from the lafh of the magiftrate, or from the perfecution of the ecclefiaftical power? He feems to talk with another air, p. 65. In the next place I afk, Whether any one is a chriftian, who has not the faith of a chriftian? Thirdly, I afk, Whether he has the faith of a chriftian, who does not explicitly believe all the fun-damental articles of chriftianity? And, to conclude I afk him, Whether all thofe that he has fet down, are not fundamental neceffary articles? When the unmafker has fairly anfwered thefe queftions, it will be feen who is for popery, and the ignorance and tyranny that accom-pany it.

The unmafker is for making and impofing articles of faith; but he is for this power in himfelf. He likes not popery (which is nothing but the tyranny and im-pofing upon men's underftandings, faith and con-fciences) in the hands of the old gentleman at Rome: but it would, he thinks, do admirably well in his own hands. And who can blame him for it? Would not

that

that be an excellent way to propagate light and knowledge, by tying up all men to a bundle of articles of
his own culling? Or rather, to the authority of Christ
and his apostles residing in him? For he does not, nor
ever will, give us a full view of fundamentals of his
christianity: but, like the church of Rome, to secure
our dependence, reserves to himself a power of declaring
others, and defining what is matter of faith, as he shall
see occasion.

Now, therefore, veil your bonnets to the unmasker,
all you that have a mind to be christians: break not your
heads about the scriptures, to examine what they require of you: submit your faith implicitly to the unmasker; he will understand and find out the necessary
points for you to believe. Take them, just so many as
he thinks fit to deliver them to you; this is the way to be
knowing christians. But be sure, ask not, Whether
those he is pleased to deliver, be every one of them fundamental, and all the fundamental articles, necessary to
be believed to make a man a christian? Such a capricious
question spoils all, overturns christianity, which is in-
trusted to the unmasker's sole keeping, to be dispensed
out as he thinks fit. If you refuse an implicit faith to
him, he will presently find you have it for the whore of
Babylon; he will smell out popery in it immediately: for he has a very shrewd scent, and you will be
discovered to be an underhand factor for the church of
Rome.

But if the unmasker were such an enemy, as he pretends, to those factors, I wonder he should, in what he
has said concerning the apostles creed, so exactly jump
with Knot the jesuit. If any one doubt of this, I desire
him to look into the fourth chapter of "Knot's charity
"maintained," and there he will see how well our unmasker and that jesuit agree in argument; nay, and expressions too. But yet I do not think him so far guilty,
as to be employed as an underhand factor for popery.
Every body will, I suppose, be ready to pronounce him
so far an innocent, as to clear him from that. The
cunning of his design goes not beyond the laying out
of his preaching oratory, for the setting up his own

system,

fyftem, and making that the fole chriftianity. To that end, he would be glad to have the power of interpreting fcripture, of defining and declaring articles of faith, and impofing them. This, which makes the abfolute power of the pope, he would not, I think, eftablifh at Rome; but it is plain he would have it himfelf if he could get it, for the fupport of the chriftianity of his fyftem. An implicit faith, if he might have the management of it, and the taking fundamentals upon truft from his authority, would be of excellent ufe. Such a power, in his hands, would fpread truth and knowledge in the world, i. e. his own orthodoxy and fet of opinions. But if a man differs, nay, queftions any thing of that, whether it be abfolutely neceffary to make one a chriftian, it is immediately a contrivance to let in popery, and to bring " darknefs and barbarifm into the chriftian world." But I muft tell the innocent unmafker, whether he defigns or no, that if his calling his fyftem the only chriftianity, can bring the world to receive from him articles of faith of his own choofing, as fundamentals neceffary to be believed by all men to make them chriftians, which Chrift and his apoftles did not propofe to all men to make them chriftians; he does only fet up popery in another guife, and lay the foundations of ignorance, darknefs, and barbarifm in the chriftian world; for all the ignorance and blindnefs, that popery introduced, was only upon this foundation. And if he does not fee this, (as there is reafon to excufe his innocence) it would be no hard matter to demonftrate it, if that were at prefent the queftion between us. But there are a great many other propofitions to be proved by him, before we come to that new matter of debate.

But before I quit thefe paragraphs, I muft go on with our unmafker's account, and defire him to fhow, where it is,

XXV. " That I make it my bufinefs to beat men off " from taking notice of any divine truths?"

Next, where it is,

XXVI. That

XXVI. That " I cry down all articles of christian faith but one ?"

Next, how it appears,

XXVII. That " I will not suffer mankind to look " into christianity ?"

Again, where it is,

XXVIII. That " I labour industriously to keep people " in ignorance;" or tell them, that " there is no " necessity of knowing any other doctrines of the " bible ?"

These, and several others of the like strain, particularly concerning one article, and the epistles, (which are his common-places) are to be found in his 59th and 60th pages. And all this out of a presumption, that his system is the only christianity; and that if men were not pressed and persuaded to receive that, just every article of it, upon pain of damnation, christianity would be lost: and not to do this, is to promote ignorance, and contemn the bible. But he fears where no fear is. If his orthodoxy be the truth, and conformable to the scriptures, the laying the foundation only where our Saviour and his apostles have laid it, will not overturn it. And to show him, that it is so, I desire him again to consider what I said in my Vindication, p. 164, 165, which, because I do not remember he any where takes notice of, in his reply, I will here offer again to his consideration : " Convince but men of the mission " of Jesus Christ; make them but see the truth, sim-" plicity, and reasonableness of what he himself hath " taught, and required to be believed by his followers; " and you need not doubt, but being once fully per-" suaded of his doctrine, and the advantages which, all " christians agree, are received by him, such converts " will not lay by the scriptures; but, by a constant " reading and study of them, will get all the light they " can from this divine revelation, and nourish them-

" selves

" felves up in the words of faith and good doctrine, as
" St. Paul fpeaks to Timothy."

If the reading and ftudy of the fcripture were more
preffed than it is, and men were fairly fent to the bible
to find their religion; and not the bible put into their
hands, only to find the opinions of their peculiar fect or
party; Chriftendom would have more chriftians, and
thofe that are, would be more knowing, and more in
the right, than they now are. That which hinders this,
is that felect bundle of doctrines, which it has pleafed
every fect to draw out of the fcriptures, or their own
inventions, with an omiffion (and, as our unmafker
would fay, a contempt) of all the reft. Thefe choice
truths (as the unmafker calls his) are to be the ftanding
orthodoxy of that party, from which none of that
church muft recede, without the forfeiture of their
chriftianity, and the lofs of eternal life. But, whilft the
people keep firm to thefe, they are in the church, and
the way to falvation: which, in effect, what is it but
to encourage ignorance, lazinefs, and neglect of the
fcriptures? For what need they be at the pains of conftantly reading the bible, or perplex their heads with
confidering and weighing what is there delivered; when
believing as the church believes, or faying after, or
not contradicting their domine, or teacher, ferves the
turn?

Further, I defire it may be confidered, what name
that mere mock-fhow, of recommending to men the
ftudy of the fcripture, deferves; if, when they read it,
they muft underftand it juft as he (that would be, and
they are too apt, contrary to the command of Chrift, to
call, their mafter) tells them. If they find any thing
in the word of God, that leads them into opinions he
does not allow; if any thing they meet with in holy
writ, feems to them to thwart, or fhake the received
doctrines, the very propofing of their doubts renders
them fufpected. Reafoning about them, and not ac-
quiefcing in whatever is faid to them, is interpreted
want of due refpect and deference to the authority of
their fpiritual guides; difrepute and cenfures follow:
and if, in purfuance of their own light, they perfift in
　　　　　　　　　　　　　　　　　　　　　　　what

what they think the fcripture teaches them, they are
turned out of the church, delivered to Satan, and no
longer allowed to be chriftians. And is thus a fincere
and rightly directed ftudy of the fcriptures, that men
may underfland and profit thereby, encouraged? This
is the confequence of men's affuming to themfelves a
power of declaring fundamentals, i. e. of fetting up a
chriftianity of their own making. For how elfe can
they turn men of as unblameable lives as others of their
members, out-of the church of Chrift (for fo they count
their communion) for opinions, unlefs thofe opinions
were concluded inconfiftent with chriftianity? Thus
fyftems, the invention of men, are turned into fo many
oppofite gofpels; and nothing is truth in each fect, but
what fuits with them. So that the fcripture ferves but,
like a nofe of wax, to be turned and bent, juft as may
fit the contrary orthodoxies of different focieties. For
it is thefe feveral fyftems, that to each party are the juft
ftandards of truth, and the meaning of the fcripture is to
be meafured only by them. Whoever relinquifhes any
of thofe diftinguifhing points, immediately ceafes to be a
chriftian.

This is the way that the unmafker would have truth
and religion preferved, light and knowledge propagated.
But here too the different fects, giving equal authority
to their own orthodoxies, will be quits with him. For
as far as I can obferve, the fame genius feems to influence them all, even thofe who pretend moft to freedom, the focinians themfelves. For when it is obferved, how pofitive and eager they are in their difputes;
how forward to have their interpretations of fcripture received for authentic, though to others, in feveral
places, they feem very much ftrained; how impatient
they are of contradiction; and with what difrefpect and
roughnefs they often treat their oppofers: may it not be
fufpected, that this fo vifible a warmth in their prefent
circumftances, and zeal for their orthodoxy, would
(had they the power) work in them as it does in others?
They in their turns would, I fear, be ready with their
fet of fundamentals; which they would be as forward to

impofe

impofe on others, as others have been to impofe contrary fundamentals on them.

This is, and always will be, the unavoidable effect of intruding on our Saviour's authority, and requiring more now, as neceffary to be believed to make a man a chriftian, than was at firft required by our Saviour and his apoftles. What elfe can be expected among chriftians, but their tearing, and being torn in pieces, by one another; whilft every fect affumes to itfelf a power of declaring fundamentals, and feverally thus narrow chriftianity to their diftinct fyftems? He that has a mind to fee how fundamentals come to be framed and fafhioned, and upon what motives and confiderations they are often taken up, or laid down, according to the humours, interefts, or defigns of the heads of parties, as if they were things depending on men's pleafure, and to be fuited to their convenience; may find an example worth his notice, in the life of Mr. Baxter, part II. p. 197—205.

Whenever men take upon them to go beyond thofe fundamental articles of chriftianity, which are to be found in the preachings of our Saviour and his apoftles, where will they ftop? Whenever any fet of men will require more, as neceffary to be believed, to make men of their church, i. e. in their fenfe, chriftians, than what our Saviour and his apoftles propofed to thofe whom they made chriftians, and admitted into the church of Chrift; however they may pretend to recommend the fcripture to their people, in effect, no more of it is recommended to them, than juft comports with what the leaders of that fect have refolved chriftianity fhall confift in.

It is no wonder, therefore, there is fo much ignorance amongft chriftians, and fo much vain outcry againft it; whilft almoft every diftinct fociety of chriftians magifterially afcribes orthodoxy to a felect fet of fundamentals, diftinct from thofe propofed in the preaching of our Saviour and his apoftles; which, in no one point, muft be queftioned by any of its communion. By this means their people are never fent to the holy fcriptures, that true fountain of light, but
                                                          hood-

hood-winked : a veil is caft over their eyes, and then they are bid to read their bible. They muft make it all chime to their church's fundamentals, or elfe they were better let it alone. For if they find any thing there againft the received doctrines, though they hold it and exprefs it in the very terms the Holy Ghoft has delivered it in, that will not excufe them. Herefy will be their lot, and they fhall be treated accordingly. And thus we fee how, amongft other good effects, creed-making always has, and always will necelfarily produce and propagate ignorance in the world, however each party blame others for it. And therefore I have often wondered to hear men of feveral churches fo heartily exclaim againft the implicit faith of the church of Rome ; when the fame implicit faith is as much practifed and required in their own, though not fo openly profeffed, and ingenuoufly owned there.

In the next fection, the unmafker queftions the fincerity of mine, and profeffes the greatnefs of his concern for the falvation of men's fouls.'' And tells me of my reflection on him, upon that account, in my Vindication, p. 165. Anfw. I wifh he would, for the right information of the reader, every-where fet down, what he has any thing to fay to, in my book, or my defence of it, and fave me the labour of repeating it. My words in that place are, '' Some men will not bear, that '' any one fhould fpeak of religion, but according to '' the model that they themfelves have made of it. Nay, '' though he propofes it upon the very terms, and in '' the very words, which our Saviour and his apoftles '' preached it in ; yet he fhall not efcape cenfures '' and the fevereft infinuations. To deviate in the leaft, '' or to omit any thing contained in their articles, is '' herefy, under the moft invidious names in fafhion ; '' and it is well if he efcapes being a downright atheift. '' Whether this be the way for teachers to make them- '' felves hearkened to, as men in earneft in religion, '' and really concerned for the falvation of men's fouls, '' I leave them to corfider. What fuccefs it has had, '' towards perfuading men of the truth of chriftianity, '' their own complaints of the prevalency of atheifm, on

'' the

" the one hand, and the number of deifts on the other,
" fufficiently fhow."

I have fet down this paffage at large, both as a confirmation of what I faid but juft now; and alfo to fhow,
that the reflection I there made needed fome other anfwer, than a bare profeffion of his " regard to the fal-
" vation of men's fouls." The affuming an undue authority to his own opinions, and ufing manifeft untruths
in the defence of them, I am fure is no mark, that
the directing men right in the way to falvation is
his chief aim. And I wifh, that the greater liberties
of that fort, which he has again taken in his Socinianifm
unmafked, and which I have fo often laid open, had not
confirmed that reflection. I fhould have been glad,
that any thing in my book had been fairly controverted
and brought to the touch, whether it had, or had not
been confuted. The matter of it would have deferved a
ferious debate (if any had been neceffary) in the words
of fobriety, and the charitable temper of the gofpel, as
I defired in my preface: and that would not have mif-
become the unmafker's function. But it did not confift, it feems, with his defign. Chriftian charity would
not have allowed thofe ill-meant conjectures, and
groundlefs cenfures, which were neceffary to his purpofe: and therefore he took a fhorter courfe, than to
confute my book, and thereby convince me and others.
He makes it his bufinefs to rail at it and the author of
it, that that might be taken for a confutation. For by
what he has hitherto done, arguing feems not to be his
talent. And thus far, who can but allow his wifdom?
But whether it be that " wifdom that is from above;
" firft pure, then peaceable, gentle, eafy to be intreat-
" ed, full of mercy, and good fruits, without partiali-
" ty, and without hypocrify;" I fhall leave to other
readers to judge.

His faying nothing to that other reflection, which
his manner of expreffing himfelf drew from me, would
make one fufpect, it favoured not altogether of the
wifdom of the gofpel; nor fhowed an over-great care
of the falvation of fouls. My words, Vindication, p.
173, are: " I know not how better to fhow my care of
" his

3

" his credit, than by intreating him, that when he takes
" next in hand ſuch a ſubject as this, wherein the ſal-
" vation of ſouls is concerned, he would treat it a
" little more ſeriouſy, and with a little more candour,
" leſt men ſhould find in his writings another cauſe of
" atheiſm, which in this treatiſe he has not thought fit
" to mention. Oſtentation of wit in general, he has
" made a cauſe of atheiſm, p. 28. But the world will
" tell him, that frothy light diſcourſes, concerning the
" ſerious matters of religion, and oſtentation of trifling
" miſbecoming wit, in thoſe who come as ambaſſadors
" from God, under the title of ſucceſſors of the apoſtles,
" in the great commiſſion of the goſpel, are none of the
" leaſt cauſes of atheiſm." But this advice, I am now
ſatisfied, (by his ſecond part of the ſame ſtrain) was
very improper for him; and no more reaſonable, than
if one ſhould adviſe a buffoon to talk gravely, who
has nothing left to draw attention, if he ſhould lay by
his ſcurrility.

The remainder of this fourth chapter, p. 61—67,
being ſpent in ſhowing, why the Socinians are for a few
articles of faith, being a matter that I am not concerned
in; I leave to that forward gentleman to examine, who
examined Mr. Edwards's exceptions againſt the " Rea-
" ſonableneſs of Chriſtianity;" and who, as the un-
" maſker informs me, page 64, was choſen to vindicate
my attempt, &c.

If the unmaſker knows that he was ſo choſen, it is well.
If I had known of ſuch a choice, I ſhould have deſired
that ſome-body ſhould have been choſen to vindicate
my attempt, who had underſtood it better. The unmaſker and examiner are each of them ſo full of themſelves, and their own ſyſtems, that I think they may be
a fit match one for another: and ſo I leave theſe cocks of
the game to try it out in an endleſs battle of wrangling
('till death them part) which of them has made the
true and exact collection of fundamentals; and whoſe
ſyſtem of the two ought to be the prevailing orthodoxy, and be received for ſcripture. Only I warn the
examiner to look to himſelf: for the unmaſker has the
whip hand of him, and gives him to underſtand, p. 65,

that

that if he cannot do it himſelf by the ſtrength of his lungs, the vehemency of his oratory, and endleſs attacks of his repetitions; the eccleſiaſtical power, and the civil magiſtrate's laſh, have, in ſtore, demonſtrative arguments to convince him, that his [the unmaſker's] ſyſtem is the only true chriſtianity.

By the way, I muſt not forget to mind the unmaſker here again, that he hath a very unlucky hand at gueſſing. For whereas he names Socinus, as one from whom I received my platform, and ſays that "Crellius gave me my cue;" it ſo falls out, that they are two authors of whom I never read a page. I ſay not this, as if I thought it a fault if I had; for I think I ſhould have much better ſpent my time in them, than in the writings of our learned unmaſker.

I was ſure there was no offending the unmaſker, without the guilt of atheiſm; only he here, p. 69, very mercifully lays it upon my book, and not upon my deſign. The "tendency of it to irreligion and atheiſm," he has proved in an eloquent harangue, for he is ſuch an orator he cannot ſtir a foot without a ſpeech (made) as he bids us ſuppoſe, by the atheiſtical rabble. And who can deny, but he has choſen a fit employment for himſelf? Where could there be found a better ſpeech-maker for the atheiſtical rabble? But let us hear him: for though he would give the atheiſtical rabble the credit of it, yet it is the unmaſker ſpeaks. And becauſe it is a pity ſuch a pattern of rhetoric and reaſon ſhould be loſt, I have, for my reader's edification, ſet it all down verbatim:

"We are beholden to this worthy adventurer for
"ridding the world of ſo great an incumbrance, viz.
"that huge maſs and unwieldy body of chriſtianity,
"which took up ſo much room. Now we ſee that it
"was this bulk, and not that of mankind, which he had
"an eye to, when he ſo often mentioned this latter.
"This is a phyſician for our turn, indeed; We like this
"chymical operator, that doth not trouble us with a
"parcel of heavy drugs of no value, but contracts it all
"into a few ſpirits, nay doth his buſineſs with a ſingle
"drop. We have been in bondage a long time to
                                          "creeds

" creeds and catechisms, systems and confessions; we
" have been plagued with a tedious bead-roll of articles,
" which our reverend divines have told us, we must
" make the matter of our faith. Yea, so it is, both
" conformists and nonconformists (though disagreeing
" in some other things) have agreed in this, to molest
" and crucify us. But this noble writer (we thank
" him) hath set us free, and eased us, by bringing down
" all the christian faith into one point. We have heard
" some men talk of epistolary composures of the New
" Testament, as if great matters were contained in
" them, as if the great mysteries of christianity (as they
" call them) were unfolded there: but we could never
" make any thing of them; and now we find that this
" writer is partly of our opinion. He tells us, that
" these are letters sent upon occasion; but we are not to
" look for our religion (for now, for this gentleman's
" sake, we begin to talk of religion) in these places.
" We believe it, and we believe that there is no religion
" but in those very chapters and verses, which he has
" set down in his treatise. What need we have any
" other part of the New Testament? That is bible
" enough, if not too much. Happy, thrice happy shall
" this author be perpetually esteemed by us; we will
" chronicle him as our friend and benefactor. It is
" not our way to saint people, otherwise we would
" certainly canonize this gentleman; and when our
" hand is in, his pair of booksellers, for their being so
" beneficial to the world, in publishing so rich a trea-
" sure. It was a blessed day, when this hopeful birth
" saw the light; for hereby all the orthodox creed-
" makers and systematic men are ruined for ever. In
" brief, if we be for any christianity, it shall be
" this author's: for that agrees with us singularly
" well, it being so short, all couched in four words,
" neither more nor less. It is a very fine compendium,
" and we are infinitely obliged to this great reformer
" for it. We are glad at heart, that christianity is
" brought so low by this worthy pen-man; for this is a
" good presage, that it will dwindle into nothing.
" What! but one article, and that so brief too! We
" like

" like fuch a faith, and fuch a religion, becaufe it is
" nearer to none."

He hath no fooner done, but, as it deferved, he cries
out " Euge, fophos! And is not the reader," quoth he,
" fatisfied that fuch language as this hath real truth in
" it? Does not he perceive, that the difcarding all the
" articles but one, makes way for the cafting off that
" too?" Anfw. It is but fuppofing that the reader is a
civil gentleman, and anfwers, Yes, to thefe two
queftions; and then it is demonftration, that by this fpeech
he has irrefragably proved the tendency of my book to
irreligion and atheifm.

I remember Chillingworth fomewhere puts up this
requeft to his adverfary Knot: " Sir, I befeech you,
" when you write again, do us the favour to write
" nothing but fyllogifms. For I find it ftill an ex-
" treme trouble to find out the concealed propofitions,
" which are to connect the parts of your enthymems.
" As now, for example, I profefs to you I have done
" my beft endeavour to find fome glue, or folder, or
" cement, or thread, or any thing to tie the antecedent
" and this confequent together." The unmafker
agrees fo much in a great part of his opinion with that
jefuit, (as I have fhown already) and does fo infinitely
out-do him in fpinning ropes of fand, and a coarfe
thread of inconfiftencies, which runs quite through his
book; that it is with great juftice I put him here in
the jefuit's place, and addrefs the fame requeft to him.

His very next words give me a frefh reafon to do it:
for thus he argues, p. 72, " May we not expect, that
" thofe who deal thus with the creed, i. e. difcard all
" the articles of it but one, will ufe the fame method
" in reducing the ten commandments and the Lord's
" prayer, abbreviate the former into one precept, and
" the latter into one petition?" Anfw. If he will tell
me where this creed he fpeaks of is, it will be much
more eafy to anfwer his demand. Whilft his creed,
which he here fpeaks of, is yet no-where, it is ridiculous
for him to afk queftions about it. The ten commandments, and the Lord's prayer, I know where to find in
exprefs words, fet down by themfelves, with peculiar
marks

marks of distinction. Which is the Lord's prayer, we are plainly taught by this command of our Saviour, Luke xi. 2, " when ye pray, say, Our Father," &c. In the same manner and words, we are taught what we should believe, to make us his disciples, by his command to the apostles what they should preach, Matt. x. 7 " As ye go, preach, saying," (What were they to say? Only this) " The kingdom of heaven is at hand." Or, as St. Luke expresses it, chap. ix. 2, They were sent " to preach the kingdom of God, and to heal the " sick:" which, what it was, we have sufficiently explained. But this creed of the unmasker, which he talks of, where is it? Let him show it us distinctly set out from the rest of the scripture. If he knows where it is, let him produce it, or leave talking of it, until he can. It is not the apostles creed, that is evident: for that creed he has discarded from being the standard of christian faith, and has told the world in words at length, That " if a man believes no more than is in " express terms in the apostles creed, his faith will not " be the faith of a christian." Nay, it is plain, that creed has, in the unmasker's opinion, the same tendency to atheism and irreligion, that my summary has. For the apostles creed, reducing the forty, or, perhaps, the four hundred fundamental articles of his christian creed, to twelve; and leaving out the greatest part of those necessary ones, which he has already, and will hereafter, in good time, give us; does as much dispose men to serve the decalogue, and the Lord's prayer, just so, as my reducing those twelve to two. For so many, at least, he has granted to be in my summary, viz. the article of one God, maker of heaven and earth; and the other, of Jesus the Messiah; though he every-where calls them but one: which, whether it be to show, with what love and regard to truth he continues, and consequently began this controversy; or whether it be to beguile and startle unwary, or confirm prejudiced readers; I shall leave other to judge. It is evident, he thinks his cause would be mightily maimed, if he were forced to leave out the charge of one article; and he would not know what to do for wit or argument, if he should call them

two :

two : for then the whole weight and edge of his strong and sharp reasoning, in his " Thoughts concerning the " causes of atheism," p. 122, would be lost. There you have it in these words : " When the catholic " faith is thus brought down to one single article, it " will soon be reduced to none ; the unit will dwindle " into a cypher" And here again, it makes the whole argument of his atheistical speech, which he winds up with these convincing words : " We are glad to hear " that christianity is brought so low by this worthy pen- " man ; for this is a good presage, that it will dwindle " into nothing.   What ! one article, and that so brief " too ! We like such a faith, and such a religion, be- " cause it is so near none." But I must tell this writer, of equal wit, sense, and modesty, that this religion, which he thus makes a dull farce of, and calls " near none," is that very religion which our Saviour Jesus Christ and his apostles preached, for the conversion and salvation of mankind ; no one article whereof, which they proposed as necessary to be received by unbelievers, to make them christians, is omitted.   And I ask him, Whether it be his errand, as one of our Saviour's ambassadors, to turn it thus into ridicule ? For until he has shown, that they preached otherwise, and more than what the Spirit of truth has recorded of their preaching in their histories, which I have faithfully collected, and set down ; all that he shall say, reflecting upon the plainness and simplicity of their doctrine, however directed against me, will by his atheistical rabble of all kinds, now they are so well entered and instructed in it by him, be all turned upon our Saviour and his apostles.

What tendency this, and all his other trifling, in so serious a cause as this is, has to the propagating of atheism and irreligion in this age, he were best to consider.   This I am sure, the doctrine of but one article (if the author and finisher of our faith, and those he guided by his Spirit, had preached but one article) has no more tendency to atheism, than their doctrine of one God.   But the unmasker every-where talks, as if the strength of our religion lay in the number of its articles;

articles; and would be presently routed, if it had been but a few; and therefore he has mustered up a pretty full band of them, and has a reserve of the Lord knows how many more, which shall be forth-coming upon occasion. But I shall desire to remind this learned divine, who is so afraid of what will become of his religion, if it should propose but one or a few articles, as necessary to be believed to make a man a christian; that the strength and security of our religion lies in the divine authority of those who first promulgated the terms of admittance into the church, and not in the multitude of articles, supposed by some necessary to be believed to make a man a christian: and I would have him remember, when he goes next to make use of this strong argument of " one dwindling into a cypher," that one is as remote as a million from none. And if this be not so, I desire to know whether his way of arguing will not prove pagan polytheism to be more remote from atheism than christianity. He will do well to try the force of his speech in the mouth of an heathen, complaining of the tendency of christianity to atheism, by reducing his great number of gods to but one, which was so near none, and would, therefore, soon be reduced to none.

The unmasker seems to be upon the same topic, where he so pathetically complains of the Socinians, p. 66, in these words; " Is it enough to rob us of our " God, by denying Christ to be so; but must they spoil " us of all the other articles of christian faith but one?" Have a better heart, good sir, for I assure you no-body can rob you of your God, but by your own consent, nor spoil you of any of the articles of your faith. If you look for them, where God has placed them, in the holy scripture, and take them as he has framed and fashioned them there; there you will always find them safe and found. But if they come out of an artificer's shop, and be of human invention, I cannot answer for them: they may, for aught I know, be nothing but an idol of your own setting up, which may be pulled down, should you cry out ever so much, " Great is Diana of the " Ephesians!"

He, who confiders this argument of one and none, as managed by the unmafker, and obferves his pathetical way of reafoning all through his book, muft confefs, that he has got the very philofopher's ftone in difputing. That which would be worthlefs lead in others, he turns into pure gold; his oratory changes its nature, and gives it the noble tincture: fo that what, in plain reafoning, would be nonfenfe, let him but put it into a fpeech, or an exclamation, and there it becomes ftrong argument. Whether this be not fo, I defire mode and figure may decide. And to thofe I fhall defire he would reduce the proofs, which, p. 73, he fays he has given of thefe following propofitions, viz.

XXIX. " That I have corrupted men's minds."

XXX. " That I have depraved the gofpel."

XXXI. " That I have abufed chriftianity."

For all thefe three, p. 73, he affirms of me without proof, and without honefty.

Whether it be from confufion of thought, or unfairnefs of defign; either becaufe he has not clear diftinct notions of what he would fay, or finds it not to his purpofe to fpeak them clearly out, or both together; fo it is, that the unmafker very feldom, but when he rails, delivers himfelf fo that one can certainly tell what he would have.

The queftion is, What is abfolutely neceffary to be believed by every one, to make him a chriftian? It has been clearly made out, from an exact furvey of the hiftory of our Saviour and his apoftles, that the whole aim of all their preaching every-where was, to convince the unbelieving world of thefe two great truths; firft, That there was one, eternal, invifible God, maker of heaven and earth: and next, that Jefus of Nazareth was the Meffiah, the promifed King and Saviour: and that, upon men's believing thefe two articles, they were baptized and admitted into the church, i. e. received as fubjects of Chrift's kingdom, and pronounced
believers.

believers. From whence it unavoidably follows, that thefe two are the only truths neceffary to be believed to make a man a chriftian.

This matter of fact is fo evident from the whole tenour of the four Gofpels and the Acts; and preffes fo hard, that the unmafker, who contends for a great number of other points neceffary to be believed to make a man a chriftian, thinks himfelf concerned to give fome anfwer to it; but, in his ufual way, full of uncertainty and confufion. To clear this matter, he lays down four particulars; the firft is, p. 74, " That the believing " Jefus to be the promifed Meffiah, was the firft ftep " to chriftianity."

The fecond, p. 76, " That though this one propo- " fition, (viz. of Jefus the Meffiah) be mentioned " alone in fome places, yet there is reafon to think, " and be perfuaded, that at the fame time other matters " of faith were propofed."

The third, p. 76, " That though there are feveral " parts and members of the chriftian faith, yet they do " not all occur in any one place of fcripture."

The fourth, p. 78, " That chriftianity was erected by " degrees."

Thefe particulars he tells us, p. 74, " he offers to clear an objection." To fee, therefore, whether they are pertinent or no, we muft examine what the objection is, as he puts it. I think it might have been put in a few words: this I am fure, it ought to have been put very clear and diftinct. But the unmafker has been pleafed to give it us, p. 73, as followeth: " Becaufe I " defigned thefe papers for the fatisfying of the reader's " doubts, about any thing occurring, concerning the " matter before us, and for the eftablifhing of his " wavering mind; I will here (before I pafs to the fe- " cond general head of my difcourfe) anfwer a query, " or objection, which fome, and not without fome " fhow of ground, may be apt to ftart: how comes it " to pafs, they will fay, that this article of faith, viz. " that Jefus is the Meffiah, or Chrift, is fo often re- " peated in the New Teftament? Why is this fometimes " urged, without the mentioning of any other article of

" belief?

" belief? Doth not this plainly fhow, that this is all
" that is required to be believed, as neceffary to make
" a man a chriftian? May we not infer, from the fre-
" quent and fole repetition of this article in feveral
" places of the evangelifts and the Acts, that there is no
" other point of faith of abfolute neceffity; but that
" this alone is fufficient to conftitute a man a true
" member of Chrift?"

By which he fhows, that he is uncertain which way to
put the objection, fo as may be eafieft to get rid of it:
and therefore he has turned it feveral ways, and put
feveral queftions about it.   As firft,

" Why this article of faith," viz. that Jefus is the
Meffiah, " is fo often repeated in the New Teftament?"

His next queftion is, " Why is this fometimes urged
" without the mentioning any other article of belief?"
which fuppofes, that fometimes other articles of belief
are mentioned with it.

The third queftion is, " May we not infer, from the
" frequent and fole repetition of this article, in feveral
" places of the evangelifts and Acts?"

Which laft queftion is in effect, Why is this fo frequently and alone repeated in the evangelifts and the
Acts? i. e. in the preachings of our Saviour and his
apoftles to unbelievers. For of that he muft give an
account, if he will remove the difficulty. Which three,
though put as one, yet are three as diftinct queftions,
and demand a reafon for three as diftinct matters of fact,
as thefe three are, viz. frequently propofed: fometimes
propofed alone; and always propofed alone, in the
preachings of our Saviour and his apoftles: for fo in
truth it was, all through the Gofpels and the Acts, to
the unconverted believers of one God alone.

Thefe three queftions being thus jumbled together in
one objection, let us fee how the four particulars, he
mentions, will account for them.

The firft of them is this: " That believing Jefus to be
" the promifed Meffias," was, fays he, " the firft ftep
" to chriftianity." Let it be fo: What do you infer
from thence? The next words fhow: " therefore this,
                                      " rather

" rather than any other article, was propounded to be
" believed by all thoſe, whom either our Saviour or
" his apoſtles invited to embrace chriſtianity." Let
your premiſes be ever ſo true, and your deduction of this
propoſition be ever ſo regular from them, it is all loſt
labour. This concluſion is not the propoſition you
were to prove. Your queſtions were, " Why this article
" is ſo often propoſed?" And in thoſe frequent repetitions, " Why ſometimes urged alone, and why always
" propoſed alone, viz. to thoſe whom either our Saviour
" or his apoſtles invited to embrace chriſtianity?" And
your anſwer is, Becauſe the believing " Jeſus to be
" the Meſſias, was the firſt ſtep to chriſtianity." This
therefore remains upon you to be proved.

> XXXII. " That, becauſe the believing Jeſus to be
> " the Meſſias is the firſt ſtep to chriſtianity, there-
> " fore this article is frequently propoſed in the
> " New Teſtament, is ſometimes propoſed without
> " the mentioning any other article, and always
> " alone to unbelievers."

And when you have proved this, I ſhall deſire you to
apply it to our preſent controverſy.

His next anſwer to thoſe queſtions is in theſe words,
p. 76, " That though this one propoſition, or article,
" be mentioned alone in ſome places, yet there is reaſon
" to think, and be perſuaded, that at the ſame time
" other matters of faith were propoſed." From whence
it lies upon him to make out this reaſoning, viz.

> XXXIII. " That becauſe there is reaſon to think,
> " and be perſuaded, that at the ſame time that this
> " one article was mentioned alone, (as it was
> " ſometimes) other matters of faith were pro-
> " poſed : therefore this article was often propoſed
> " in the New Teſtament ; ſometimes propoſed
> " alone ; and always propoſed alone, in the preach-
> " ings of our Saviour and his apoſtles to unbe-
> " lievers."

This

This I set down to show the force of his answer to his questions : supposing it to be true, not that I grant it to be true, that where " this one article is mentioned " alone, we have reason to think, and be persuaded, " that at the same time other matters of faith [i. e. ar- " ticles of faith necessary to be believed to make a man " a christian] were proposed :" and I doubt not but to show the contrary.

His third particular, in answer to the question pro- posed in his objection, stands thus, p. 76. " That " though there are several parts and members of the " christian faith, yet they do not all occur in any one " place of the scripture;" which answer lays it upon him to prove,

> XXXIV. That because "the several parts of the mem- > " bers of the christian faith do not all occur in any > " one place of scripture," therefore this article, that > Jesus was the " Messias, was often proposed in the > " New Testament, sometimes proposed alone, and > " always proposed alone," in the preachings of our > Saviour and his apostles, through the history of > the evangelists and the Acts.

The fourth and last particular, which he tells us is th^e main answer to the objection, is in these words' p$_a$ge 7^8,

> " That christianity was erected by degrees."

Which requires him to make out his argument, viz.

> XXXV. " That because christianity was erected by > " degrees, therefore this article," that Jesus was > " the Messias, was often proposed in the new testa- > " ment, sometimes proposed alone, and always > " proposed alone in the preachings of our Saviour > " and his apostles to unbelievers, recorded in the > " history of the evangelists and Acts."

For, as I said before, in these three questions he has put his objection ; to which, he tells us, this is the main answer.

Of

Of thefe four particulars it is, that he fays, p. 74, to
" clear this objection, and to give a full and fatisfactory
" anfwer to all doubts in this affair, I offer thefe en-
" fuing particulars, which will lead the reader to the
" right underftanding of the whole cafe."

How well they have cleared the objection, may be feen
by barely fetting them down as anfwers to the queftions,
wherein he puts the objection.

This is all I have hitherto done; whereby is very
vifible, how well (fuppofing them true) they clear the
objection: and how pertinently they are brought to
anfwer thofe queftions wherein his objection is contained. Perhaps it will be faid, that neither thefe, nor
any thing elfe, can be an appofite anfwer to thofe queftions put fo together. I anfwer, I am of the fame
mind. But if the unmafker, through ignorance or fhuffling, will talk thus confufedly, he muft anfwer for it.
He calls all his three queftions, one objection, over
and over again: and therefore, which of thofe queftions
it does or does not lie in, I fhall not trouble myfelf to
divine; fince I think he himfelf cannot tell: for which-
ever he takes of them, it will involve him in equal difficulties. I now proceed to examine his particulars
themfelves, and the truth contained in them. The firft,
p. 74, ftands thus:

1. " The believing of Jefus to be the promifed
" Meffias was the firft ftep to chriftianity. It was that
" which made way for the embracing of all the other
" articles, a paffage to all the reft." Anfw. If this be,
as he would have it, only the leading article, amongft a
great many other, equally neceffary to be believed, to
make a man a chriftian; this is a reafon why it fhould
be conftantly preached in the firft place: but this is no
reafon why this alone fhould be fo often repeated, and
the other neceffary points not be once mentioned.
For I defire to know what thofe other articles are that,
in the preaching of our Saviour and his apoftles, are repeated or urged befides this?

In the next place, if it be true, that this article, viz.
that Jefus is the Meffiah, was only the firft in order
amongft a great many articles, as neceffary to be be-

lieved; how comes it to pass, that barely upon the proposal and believing of this, men were admitted into the church as believers? The history of the New Testament is full of instances of this, as Acts viii. 5, 12, 13. ix. and in other places.

Though it be true, what the unmasker says here, " That if they did not give credit to this in the first " place, that Jesus of Nazareth was that eminent and " extraordinary person prophesied of long before, and " that he was sent and commissioned by God; there " could be no hope that they would attend to any " other proposals, relating to the christian religion;" yet what he subjoins, " that this is the true reason, " why that article was constantly propounded to be be- " lieved by all that looked towards christianity, and " why it is mentioned so often in the evangelical writ- " ings," is not true. For, first, this supposes that there were other articles joined with it. This he should have first proved, and then given the reason for it; and not, as he does here, suppose what is in question, and then give a reason why it is so; and such a reason that is in-consistent with the matter of fact, that is every-where recorded in holy writ. For, if the true reason why the preaching of this article, " that Jesus was the Messiah," as it is recorded in the history of the New Testament, were only to make way for the other articles, one must needs think, that either our Saviour and his apostles (with reverence be it spoken) were very strange preachers; or, that the evangelists, and author of the Acts, were very strange historians. The first were to instruct the world in a new religion, consisting of a great number of articles, says the unmasker, necessary to be believed to make a man a christian, i. e. a great number of propositions, making a large system, every one whereof is so necessary for a man to understand and believe, that if any one be omitted, he cannot be of that religion. What now did our Saviour and his apostles do? Why, if the unmasker may be believed, they went up and down with danger of their lives, and preached to the world. What did they preach? Even this single proposition to make way for the rest, viz. " This
                                                        " is

" is the eminent man fent from God," to teach you
other things : which amounts to no more but this,
that Jefus was the perfon which was to teach them the
true religion, but that true religion itfelf is not to be
found in all their preaching ; nay, fcarce a word of it.
Can there be any thing more ridiculous than this ? And
yet this was all they preached, if it be true, that this
was all they meant by the preaching every-where,
Jefus to be the Meffiah, and if it were only an introduction, and a making way for the doctrines of the gofpel.
But it is plain, it was called the gofpel itfelf. Let the
unmafker, as a true fucceffor of the apoftles, go and
preach the gofpel, as the apoftles did, to fome part
of the heathen world, where the name of Chrift is not
known : would not he himfelf, and every body think,
he was very foolifhly employed, if he fhould tell them
nothing but this, that Jefus was the perfon promifed
and fent from God to reveal the true religion ; but
fhould teach them nothing of that true religion, but this
preliminary article ? Such the unmafker makes all the
preaching, recorded in the New Teftament, for the converfion of the unbelieving world. He makes the
preaching of our Saviour and his apoftles to be no more
but this, that the great prophet promifed to the world
was come, and that Jefus was he : but what his doctrine
was, that they were filent in, and taught not one article
of it. But the unmafker mifreprefents it : for as to his
accufing the hiftorians, the evangelifts, and writers of the
Acts of the apoftles, for their fhameful omiffion of the
whole doctrine of the chriftian religion, to fave his
hypothefis, as he does under his next head, in thefe
words : "that though this one propofition be mentioned
" alone in fome places, yet there is reafon to think,
" and be perfuaded, that at the fame time other matters
" of faith were propofed ;" I fhall fhow how bold he
makes with thofe infpired hiftorians, when I come to
confider that particular.

How ridiculous, how fenfelefs, this bold unmafker,
and reformer of the hiftory of the New Teftament, makes
the preaching of our Saviour and his apoftles, as it
ftands recorded of them by infallible writers, is vifible.
But

But taking it, as in truth it is there, we shall have a quite other view of it. Our Saviour preached everywhere the kingdom of God; and by his miracles declared himself to be the king of that kingdom. The apostles preached the same, and after his ascension, openly avowed him to be the Prince and Saviour promised: but preached not this as a bare speculative article of simple belief; but that men might receive him for their King, and become his subjects. When they told the world that he was the Christ, it was not as the unmasker will have it: believe this man to be a prophet, and then he will teach you his new religion; which when you have received and embraced all and every article thereof, which are a great number, you will then be christians, if you be not ignorant or incredulous of any of them. But it was, believe this man to be your King sent from God; take him for such, with a resolution to observe the laws he has given you; and you are his subjects, you are christians. For those that truly did so, made themselves his subjects: and to continue so, there was no more required, than a sincere endeavour to know his will in all things, and to obey it. Such a preaching as this, of Jesus to be the Messiah, the King and Deliverer, that God almighty had promised to mankind, and now had effectualy sent, to be their Prince and Ruler, was not a simple preparation to the gospel: but, when received with the obedience of faith, was the very receiving of the gospel, and had all that was requisite to make men christians. And without it be so understood, no-body can clear the preaching of our Saviour and his apostles from that incredible imperfection, or their historians from that unpardonable negligence, and not doing either what they ought, or what they undertook, which our unmasker hath so impiously charged upon them; as will appear yet plainer, in what I have to say to the unmasker's next particular. For, as to the remainder of this paragraph, it contains nothing but his censure and contempt of me, for not being of his mind, for not seeing as he sees, i. e. in effect, not laying that blame which he does, either on the preaching of our Saviour

and

and his apostles, or on the inspired writings of their historians, to make them comply with his system, and the christianity he would make.

The unmasker's second particular, p. 76, tells us, " That though this one proposition or article be men- " tioned alone in some places, yet there is reason to " think and be persuaded, that at the same time other " matters of faith were proposed. For it is confessed " by all intelligent and observing men, that the history " of the scripture is concise; and that in relating matter " of fact, many passages are omitted by the sacred " pen-men. Wherefore, though but this one article " of belief, (because it is a leading one, and makes " way for the rest) be expresly mentioned in some of " the gospels, yet we must not conclude thence, that " no other matter of faith was required to be admitted " of. For things are briefly set down in the evangelical " records, and we must suppose many things which are " not in direct terms related."

Answ. The unmasker here keeps to his usual custom of speaking in doubtful terms. He says, that where this one article, that Jesus is the Messiah, is alone recorded in the preaching of our Saviour and his apostles; " We " have reason to be persuaded, that at the same time " other matters of faith were proposed." If this be to his purpose, by matters of faith, must be meant fundamental articles of faith, absolutely necessary to be believed by every man to make him a christian. That such matters of faith are omitted, in the history of the preaching of our Saviour and his apostles, by the sacred historians; this, he says, " we have reason to be per- " suaded of."

Answ. They need be good reasons to persuade a rational man, that the evangelists, in their history of our Saviour and his apostles, (if they were but ordinarily fair and prudent men) did, in an history published to instruct the world in a new religion, leave out the necessary and fundamental parts of that religion. But let them be considered as inspired writers, under the conduct of the infallible Spirit of God, putting them upon, and directing them in, the writing of this history of the

gofpel : and then it is impoffible for any chriftian, but
the unmafker, to think, that they made any fuch grofs
omiffions, contrary to the defign of their writing, without a demonftration to convince him of it. Now all the
reafon that our unmafker gives, is this : " That it is
" confeffed by all intelligent and obferving men, that
" the hiftory of the fcripture is concife ; and that in
" relating matters of fact, many paffages are omitted
" by the facred pen-men."

Anfw. The unmafker might have fpared the confeffion of intelligent and obferving men, after fo plain a
declaration of St. John himfelf, chap. xx. 31, " Many
" other things did Jefus in the prefence of his difciples,
" which are not written in this book." And again,
xxi. 25, " There are alfo many other things that
" Jefus did, the which if they fhould be written every
" one, I fuppofe the world could not contain the books
" that fhould be written." There needs, therefore, no
opinion of intelligent and obferving men to convince
us, that the hiftory of the gofpel is fo far concife, that a
great many matters of fact are omitted, and a great
many lefs material circumftances, even of thofe that
are fet down. But will any intelligent or obferving
man, any one that bears the name of a chriftian, have
the impudence to fay, that the infpired writers, in the
relation they give us of what Chrift and his apoftles
preached to unbelievers to convert them to the faith,
omitted the fundamental articles, which thofe preachers
propofed to make men chriftians ; and without a belief
of which, they could not be chriftians ?

The unmafker talks after his wonted fafhion ; i. e.
feems to fay fomething, which, when examined, proves
nothing to his purpofe. He tells us, " That in fome
" places," where the article of " Jefus the Meffiah is
" mentioned alone, at the fame time other matters of
" faith were propofed." I afk were thefe other matters of faith all the unmafker's neceffary articles ? If
not, what are thofe other matters of faith to the unmafker's purpofe ? As for example, in St. Peter's fermon,
Acts ii. " Other matters of faith were propofed with
" the article of Jefus the Meffiah." But what does this
make

make for his fundamental articles: were they all proposed with the article of Jesus the Messiah? If not, unbelievers were converted, and brought into the church,
without the unmasker's necessary articles. Three thousand were added to the church by this one sermon. I pass
by, now, St. Luke's not mentioning a syllable of the
greatest part of the unmasker's necessary articles; and
shall consider only, how long that sermon may have
been. It is plain from ver. 15, that it began not until
about nine in the morning; and from ver. 41, that
before night three thousand were converted and baptised. Now I ask the unmasker, Whether so small a
number of hours, as Peter must necessarily employ in
preaching to them, were sufficient to instruct such a
mixed multitude so fully in all those articles, which he
has proposed as necessary to be believed to make a man
a christian; as that every one of those three thousand,
that were that day baptised, did understand, and explicitly believe every one of those his articles, just in
the sense of our unmasker's system? Not to mention
those remaining articles, which the unmasker will not
be able, in twice as many months, to find and declare
to us.

He says, " That in some places," where the article
of " Jesus the Messiah is mentioned alone, at the same
" time other matters of faith were proposed;" Let us
take this to be so at present, yet this helps not the unmasker's case. The fundamental articles, that were
proposed by our Saviour and his apostles, necessary to be
believed to make men christians, are not set down; but
only this single one, of " Jesus the Messiah:" therefore,
will any one dare to say they are omitted every-where
by the evangelists? Did the historians of the gospel
make their relation so concise and short, that giving an
account in so many places of the preaching of our
Saviour and his apostles, for the conversion of the unbelieving world, they did not in any one place, nor in
all of them together, set down the necessary points of
that faith, which their unbelieving hearers were converted to? If they did not, how can their histories be
called the Gospels of Jesus Christ? Or how can they
serve

5

ferve to the end for which they were written? Which
was to publish to the world the doctrine of Jefus Chrift,
that men might be brought into his religion.   Now I
challenge the unmafker to fhow me, not out of any one
place, but out of all the preachings of our Saviour and
his apoftles, recorded in the four Gofpels, and in the
Acts, all thofe propofitions which he has reckoned up
as fundamental articles of faith.   If they are not to be
found there, it is plain, that either they are not articles
of faith, neceffary to be believed to make a man a
chriftian; or elfe, that thofe infpired writers have given
us an account of the gofpel, or chriftian religion, wherein the greateft part of the doctrines, neceffary to be
believed to make a man a chriftian, are wholly
omitted.   Which in fhort is to fay, that the chriftianity,
which is recorded in the Gofpels and the Acts, is not
that chriftianity which is fufficient to make a man a
chriftian.   This (as abfurd and impious as it is) is
what our unmafker charges upon the concifenefs (as he
is pleafed to call it) of the evangelical hiftory.   And
this we muft take upon his word, though thefe infpired
writers tell us the direct contrary: for St. Luke, in his
preface to his gofpel, tells Theophilus, that having a
perfect knowledge of all things, the defign of his writing was to fet them in order, that he might know the
certainty of thofe things that were believed amongft
chriftians.   And his hiftory of the Acts begins thus:
" The former treatife [i. e. his gofpel] have I made,
" O Theophilus, of all that Jefus began to do and to
" teach."   So that, how concife foever the unmafker
will have his hiftory to be, he profeffes it to contain all
that Jefus taught.   Which all muft, in the narroweft
fenfe that can be given it, contain at leaft all things neceffary to make a man a chriftian.   It would elfe be a
very lame and imperfect hiftory of all that Jefus taught,
if the faith contained in it were not fufficient to make a
man a chriftian.   This indeed, as the unmafker hath
been pleafed to term it, would be a very lank faith, a
very lank gofpel.

St. John alfo fays thus, of his hiftory of the gofpel,
chap. xx. 30, 31, " Many other figns truly did Jefus,
in

" in the prefence of his difciples, which are not written
" in this book :" fo far his hiftory is, by his own confeffion, concife. " But thefe," fays he, " are written
" that ye might believe that Jefus is the Meffiah, the
" Son of God ; and that, believing, ye might have life
" through his name." As concife as it was, there
was yet (if the apoftle's word may be taken for it
againft the unmafker's) enough contained in his gofpel,
for the procuring of eternal life, to thofe who believed
it. And, whether it was that one article that he there
fets down, viz. That Jefus was the Meffiah, or that fet
of articles which the unmafker gives us, I fhall leave
to this modern divine to refolve. And, if he thinks
ftill, that all the articles he has fet down in his roll, are
neceffary to be believed to make a man a chriftian, I
muft defire him to fhow them to me in St. John's gofpel,
or elfe to convince the world, that St. John was miftaken,
when he faid, that he had written his gofpel, that men
might believe that " Jefus was the Meffiah, the Son of
" God ; and that, believing, they might have life
" through his name."

So that, granting the hiftory of the fcripture to be fo
concife, as the unmafker would have it, viz. that in
fome places the infallible writers, recording the difcourfes of our Saviour and his apoftles, omitted all the
other fundamental articles propofed by them to be believed to make men chriftians, but this one, that Jefus
was the Meffiah ; yet this will not remove the objection that lies againft his other fundamentals, which are
not to be found in the hiftories of the four evangelifts ;
nay, not to be found in any one of them. If every
one of them contains the gofpel of Jefus Chrift, and
confequently all things neceffary to falvation, whether
this will not be a new ground of accufation againft me,
and give the unmafker a right to charge me with laying
by three of the gofpels with contempt, as well as he did
before charge me with a contempt of the epiftles ; muft
be left to his fovereign authority to determine.

Having fhowed that, allowing all he fays here to be as
he would have it, yet it clears not the objection that
lies againft his fundamentals ; I fhall now examine
what

what truth there is in what he here pretends, viz. that
though the one article, That Jefus is the Meffiah, be
mentioned " alone in fome places, yet we have reafon
" to be perfuaded, from the concifenefs of the" fcripture hiftory, that there were, at the fame time, joined
with it other neceffary articles of faith, in the preaching
of our Saviour and his apoftles.

It is to be obferved, that the unmafker builds upon
this falfe fuppofition, that in fome places, other neceffary articles of faith, joined with that of Jefus the
Meffiah, are by the evangelifts mentioned to be propofed by our Saviour and his apoftles, as neceffary to
be believed to make thofe they preached chriftians.
For his faying, that in fome places, that " one necef-
" fary article is mentioned alone," implies, that in other
places it is not mentioned alone, but joined with other
neceffary articles.   But then it will remain upon him
to fhow,

> XXXVI.   " In what place, either of the Gofpels or
> " of the Acts, other articles of faith are joined
> " with this, and propofed as neceffary to be be-
> " lieved to make men chriftians."

The unmafker, it is probable, will tell us, that the
article of Chrift's refurrection is fometimes joined with
this of the Meffiah, as particularly in that firft fermon
of St. Peter, Acts ii. by which there were three thoufand added to the church at one time.   Anfw.   This
fermon, well confidered, will explain to us both the
preaching of the apoftles; what it was that they propofed to their unbelieving auditors, to make them chriftians;   and alfo the manner of St. Luke's recording
their fermons.   It is true, that here are delivered by St.
Peter many other matters of faith, befides that of Jefus
being the Meffiah: for all that he faid, being of divine
authority, is matter of faith, and may not be difbelieved.   The firft part of his difcourfe is to prove to the
Jews, that what they had obferved of extraordinary at
that time, amongft the difciples, who fpake variety of
tongues, did not proceed from wine, but from the Holy
Ghoft ;

Ghoft; and that this was the pouring out of the Spirit, prophefied of by the prophet Joel. This is all matter of faith, and is written, that it might be believed: but yet I think, that neither the unmafker, nor any body elfe will fay, that this is fuch a neceffary article of faith, that no man could, without an explicit belief of it, be a chriftian; though, being a declaration of the Holy Ghoft by St. Peter, it is fo much a matter of faith, that no-body to whom it is now propofed, can deny it, and be a chriftian. And thus all the fcripture of the New Teftament, given by divine infpiration, is matter of faith, and neceffary to be believed by all chriftians, to whom it is propofed. But yet I do not think any one fo unreafonable as to fay, that every propofition in the New Teftament is a fundamental article of faith, which is required explicitly to be believed to make a man a chriftian.

Here now is a matter of faith joined, in the fame fermon, with this fundamental article, that " Jefus is " the Mefliah;" and reported by the facred hiftorian fo at large, that it takes up a third part of St. Peter's fermon, recorded by St. Luke: and yet it is fuch a matter of faith, as is not contained in the unmafker's catalogue of neceffary articles. I muft afk him then, whether St. Luke were fo concife an hiftorian, that he would fo at large fet down a matter of faith, propofed by St. Peter, that was not neceffary to be believed to make a man a chriftian, and wholly leave out the very mention of all the unmafker's additional neceffary articles, if indeed they were neceffary to be believed to make men chriftians? I know not how any one could charge the hiftorian with greater unfaithfulnefs, or greater folly. But this the unmafker fticks not at, to preferve to himfelf the power of appointing what fhall, and what fhall not, be neceffary articles; and of making his fyftem the chriftianity neceffary, and only neceffary to be received.

The next thing that St. Peter proceeds to, in this his fermon, is, to declare to the unbelieving Jews that Jefus of Nazareth, who had done miracles amongft them, whom they had crucified, and put to death, and whom God had raifed again from the dead, was the Meffiah.

Here indeed our Saviour's crucifixion, death, and refurrection, are mentioned: and if they were no-where elfe recorded, are matters of faith; which, with all the reft of the New Teftament, ought to be believed by every chriftian, to whom it is thus propofed, as a part of divine revelation. But that thefe were not here propofed to the unbelieving Jews, as the fundamental articles, which St. Peter principally aimed at, and endeavoured to convince them of, is evident from hence, that they are made ufe of, as arguments to perfuade them of this fundamental truth, viz. that Jefus was the Meffiah, whom they ought to take for their Lord and Ruler. For whatfoever is brought as an argument, to prove another truth, cannot be thought to be the principal thing aimed at, in that argumentation; though it may have fo ftrong and immediate a connexion with the conclufion, that you cannot deny it, without denying even what is inferred from it, and is therefore the fitter to be an argument to prove it. But that our Saviour's crucifixion, death, and refurrection, were ufed here as arguments to perfuade them into a belief of this fundamental article, that Jefus was the Meffiah, and not as propofitions of a new faith they were to receive, is evident from hence, that St. Peter preached here to thofe who knew the death and crucifixion of Jefus as well as he: and therefore thefe could not be propofed to them, as new articles of faith to be believed; but thofe matters of fact being what the Jews knew already, were a good argument, joined with his refurrection, to convince them of that truth, which he endeavoured to give them a belief of. And therefore he rightly inferred, from thefe facts joined together, this conclufion, the believing whereof would make them chriftians: " Therefore let " all the houfe of Ifrael know affuredly, that God hath " made that fame Jefus, whom ye have crucified, " Lord and Chrift." To the making good this fole propofition, his whole difcourfe tended: this was the fole truth he laboured to convince them of; this the faith he endeavoured to bring them into; which as foon as they had received with repentance, they were by baptiſm admitted into the church, and three thouſand at once were made chriſtians.

Here St. Luke's own confeſſion, without that " of " intelligent and obſerving men," which the un-maſker has recourſe to, might have ſatisfied him again, " that in relating matters of fact, many paſſages " were omitted by the ſacred pen-men." For, ſays St. Luke here, ver. 40, " And with many other words," which are not ſet down.

One would, at firſt ſight, wonder why the unmaſker neglects theſe demonſtrative authorities of the holy pen-men themſelves, where they own their omiſſions, to tell us, that it is " confeſſed by all intelligent and ob-" ſerving men, that in relating matters of fact, many " paſſages are omitted by the ſacred pen-men." St. John, in what he ſays of his goſpel, directly profeſſes large omiſſions, and ſo does St. Luke here. But theſe omiſſions would not ſerve the unmaſker's turn; for they are directly againſt him, and what he would have: and therefore he had reaſon to paſs them by. For St. John, in that paſſage above-cited, chap. xx. 30, 31, tells us, that how much ſoever he had left out of his hiſtory, he had inſerted that which was enough to be believed to eternal life: " but theſe are written, that ye might be-" lieve, and, believing, ye might have life." But this is not all he aſſures us of, viz. that he had recorded all that was neceſſary to be believed to eternal life: but he, in expreſs words, tells us what is that ALL, that is ne-ceſſary to be believed to eternal life; and for the proof of which propoſition alone, he writ all the reſt of his goſpel, viz. that we might believe. What? even this: " That Jeſus is the Chriſt, the Son of God," and that, believing this, we " might have life through his name."

This may ſerve for a key to us, in reading the hiſtory of the New Teſtament; and ſhow us why this article, that Jeſus was the Meſſiah, is no-where omitted, though a great part of the arguments uſed to convince men of it, nay, very often the whole diſcourſe, made to lead men into the belief of it, be intirely omitted.

The Spirit of God directed them every-where to set down the article, which was absolutely necessary to be believed to make men christians; so that that could no ways be doubted of, nor mistaken: but the arguments and evidences, which were to lead men into this faith, would be sufficient, if they were once found any where, though scattered here and there, in those writings, whereof that infallible Spirit was the author. This preserved the decorum used in all histories, and avoided those continual, large, and unnecessary repetitions, which our critical unmasker might have called tedious, with juster reason than he does the repetition of this short proposition, that Jesus is the Messiah; which I set down no oftener in my book, than the Holy Ghost thought fit to insert it in the history of the New Testament, as concise as it is. But this, it seems to our nice unmasker, is "tedious, tedious and offensive." And if a christian, and a successor of the apostles, cannot bear the being so often told, what it was that our Saviour and his apostles every-where preached to the believers of one God, though it be contained in one short proposition; what cause of exception and disgust would it have been to heathen readers, some whereof might, perhaps, have been as critical as the unmasker, if this sacred history had, in every page, been filled with the repeated discourses of the apostles, all of them every-where to the same purpose, viz. to persuade men to believe, that Jesus was the Messiah? It was necessary, even by the laws of history, as often as their preaching any where was mentioned, to tell to what purpose they spoke; which being always to convince men of this one fundamental truth, it is no wonder we find it so often repeated. But the arguments and reasonings with which this one point is urged, are, as they ought to be, in most places, left out. A constant repetition of them had been superfluous, and consequently might justly have been blamed as "tedious." But there is enough recorded abundantly to convince any rational man, any one not wilfully blind, that he is that promised Saviour. And, in this, we have a reason of the omissions in the history of the New Testament; which were no other

than

than such as became prudent, as well as faithful writers. Much less did that concifeness (with which the un-masker would cover his bold censure of the Gospels and the Acts, and, as it seems, lay them by with contempt) make the holy writers omit any thing, in the preaching of our Saviour and his apostles, absolutely necessary to be known and believed to make men christians.

Conformable hereunto, we shall find St. Luke writes his history of the Acts of the apostles. In the begining of it, he sets down at large some of the discourses made to the unbelieving jews. But in most other places, unless it be where there was something particular in the circumstances of the matter, he contents himself to tell to what purpose they spoke; which was every-where only this, that Jesus was the Messiah. Nay, St. Luke, in the first speech of St. Peter, Acts ii, which he thought fit to give us a great part of, yet owns the omission of several things that the apostle said. For, having ex-pressed this fundamental doctrine, that Jesus was the Messiah, and recorded several of the arguments where-with St. Peter urged it, for the conversion of the un-believing jews, his auditors, he adds, ver. 40, " And " with many other words did he testify and exhort, fay- " ing, Save yourselves from this untoward generation." Here he confesses, that he omitted a great deal which St. Peter had said to persuade them, To what? To that which, in other words, he had just said before, ver. 38, " Repent and be baptized every one of you " in the name of Jesus Christ," i. e. Believe Jesus to be the Messiah, take him as such for your Lord and King, and reform your lives by a sincere resolution of obedience to his laws.

Thus we have an account of the omissions in the re-cords of matters of fact in the New Testament. But will the unmasker say, That the preaching of those articles that he has given us, as necessary to be believed to make a man a christian, was part of those matters of fact, which have been omitted in the history of the New Testament? Can any one think, that " the corruption " and degeneracy of human nature, with the true " original of it, (the defection of our first parents) the

" propagation of fin and mortality, our reftoration and
" reconciliation by Chrift's blood, the eminency and
" excellency of his priefthood, the efficacy of his death,
" the full fatisfaction thereby made to divine juftice,
" and his being made an all-fufficient facrifice for fin,
" our juftification by Chrift's righteoufnefs, election,
" adoption," &c. were all propofed, and that too, in
the fenfe of our author's fyftem, by our Saviour and his
apoftles, as fundamental articles of faith, neceffary to be
explicitly believed by every man, to make him a chriftian, in all their difcourfes to unbelievers ; and yet that
the infpired pen-men of thofe hiftories every-where left
the mention of thefe fundamental articles wholly out ?
This would have been to have writ, not a concife, but
an imperfect hiftory of all that Jefus and his apoftles
taught.

What an account would it have been of the gofpel, as
it was firft preached and propagated, if the greateft part
of the neceffary doctrines of it were wholly left out, and
a man could not find, from one end to the other of this
whole hiftory, that religion which is neceffary to be believed to make a man a chriftian ? And yet this is that,
which, under the notion of their being concife, the unmafker would perfuade us to have been done by St. Luke
and the other evangelifts, in their hiftories. And it is
no lefs than what he plainly fays, in his " Thoughts
" concerning the caufes of atheifm," p. 109, where, to
aggravate my fault, in paffing by the epiftles, and to
fhow the neceffity of fearching in them for fundamentals,
he in words blames me ; but in effect condemns the
facred hiftory contained in the Gofpels and the Acts.
" It is moft evident," fays he, " to any thinking man,
" that the author of the Reafonablenefs of Chriftianity,
" purpofely omits the epiftolary writings of the apoftles,
" becaufe they are fraught with other fundamental
" doctrines, befides that one which he mentions. There
" we are inftructed concerning thefe grand heads of
" chriftian divinity." Here, i. e. in the epiftles, fays
he, " there are difcoveries concerning fatisfaction,"
&c. And, in the clofe of his lift of grand heads, as
he calls them, fome whereof I have above fet down out
of

5

of him, he adds, " These are the matters of faith con-
" tained in the epistles." By all which expressions he
plainly signifies, that these, which he calls fundamental
doctrines, are none of those we are instructed in, in the
Gospels and the Acts; that they are not discovered nor
contained in the historical writings of the evangelists:
whereby he confesses, that either our Saviour and his
apostles did not propose them in their preachings to
their unbelieving hearers; or else, that the several
faithful writers of their history, wilfully, i. e. unfaith-
fully, every-where omitted them in the account they
have left us of those preachings; which could scarce
possibly be done by them all, and every-where, without
an actual combination amongst them, to smother the
greatest and most material parts of our Saviour's and his
apostles discourses. For what else did they, if all that
the unmasker has set down in his list be fundamental
doctrines; every one of them absolutely necessary to be
believed to make a man a christian, which our Saviour
and his apostles every-where preached, to make men
christians? but yet St. Luke, and the other evangelists,
by a very guilty and unpardonable concisenes, every-
where omitted them, and throughout their whole
history, never once tell us, they were so much as proposed, much less, that they were those articles which
the apostles laboured to establish and convince men of
every-where, before they admitted them to baptism?
Nay the far greatest part of them, the history they writ
does not any where so much as once mention? How,
after such an imputation as this, the unmasker will
clear himself from laying by the four Gospels and the
Acts with contempt, let him look; if my not collecting
fundamentals out of the epistles had that guilt in it.
For I never denied all the fundamental doctrines to be
there, but only said, that there they were not easy to be
found out, and distinguished from doctrines not fundamental. Whereas our good unmasker charges the
historical books of the New Testament with a total
omission of the far greatest part of those fundamental
doctrines of christianity, which he says, are absolutely
necessary to be believed to make a man a christian.

To

To convince the reader what was absolutely required to be believed to make a man a christian, and thereby clear the holy writers from the unmasker's slander, any one need but look a little farther into the history of the Acts, and observe St. Luke's method in the writing of it. In the beginning, (as we observed before) and in some few other places, he sets down at large the discourses made by the preachers of christianity, to their unbelieving auditors. But in the process of his history, he generally contents himself to relate, what it was their discourses drive at; what was the doctrine they endeavoured to convince their unbelieving hearers of, to make them believers. This, we may observe, is never omitted. This is every-where set down. Thus, Acts v. 42, he tells us, that " daily in the temple, and in " every house, the apostles ceased not to teach, and to " preach JESUS THE MESSIAH." The particulars of their discourses he omits, and the arguments they used to induce men to believe, he omits; but never fails to inform us carefully, what it was the apostles taught and preached, and would have men believe. The account he gives us of St. Paul's preaching at Thessalonica, is this: That " three sabbath-days he REASONED with " the jews out of the scriptures, OPENING and AL- " LEGING, that the Messiah must needs have suffered, " and risen again from the dead; and that Jesus was " the Messiah; Acts xvii. 2, 3. At Corinth, that " he REASONED in the synagogue every sabbath, and " PERSUADED the jews and the greeks, and TESTIFIED " that Jesus was the Messiah;" xviii. 4, 5. That " Apollos mightily convinced the jews, SHOWING BY " THE SCRIPTURES, that Jesus was the Messiah;" xviii. 28.

By these, and the like places, we may be satisfied what it was, that the apostles taught and preached, even this one proposition, That Jesus was the Messiah: for this was the sole proposition they reasoned about; this alone they testified, and they showed out of the scriptures; and of this alone they endeavoured to convince the jews and the greeks that believed one God. So that it is plain from hence, that St. Luke omitted no-

thing,

thing, that the apoſtles taught and preached; none of thoſe doctrines that it was neceſſary to convince unbelievers of, to make them chriſtians; though he, in moſt places, omitted, as was fit, the paſſages of ſcripture which they alleged, and the arguments thoſe inſpired preachers uſed to perſuade men to believe and embrace that doctrine.

Another convincing argument, to ſhow that St. Luke omitted none of thoſe fundamental doctrines, which the apoſtles any where propoſed, as neceſſary to be believed, is from that different account he gives us of their preaching in other places, and to auditors otherwiſe diſpoſed. Where the apoſtles had to do with idolatrous heathens, who were not yet come to the knowledge of the only true God, there, he tells us, they propoſed alſo the article of the one inviſible God, maker of heaven and earth: and this we find recorded in him out of their preaching to the Lyſtrians, Acts xiv. and to the Athenians, Acts xvii. In the latter of which, St. Luke, to convince his reader, that he, out of conciſeneſs, omits none of thoſe fundamental articles, that were any where propoſed by the preachers of the goſpel, as neceſſary to be believed to make men chriſtians, ſets down not only the article of Jeſus the Meſſiah, but that alſo of the one inviſible God, creator of all things; which, if any neceſſary one might, this of all other fundamental articles might, by an author that affected brevity, with the faireſt excuſe, have been omitted, as being implied in that other, of the Meſſiah ordained by God. Indeed in the ſtory of what Paul and Barnabas ſaid at Lyſtra, the article of the Meſſiah is not mentioned. Not that St. Luke omitted that fundamental article, where the apoſtles taught it: but, they having here begun their preaching with that of the one living God, they had not, as appears, time to proceed farther, and propoſe to them what yet remained to make them chriſtians: all that they could do, at that time, was, to hinder the people from ſacrificing to them. And, before we hear any more of their preaching, they were, by the inſtigation of the jews, fallen upon, and Paul ſtoned.

This,

This, by the way, fhows the unmafker's miftake, in his firft particular, p. 74. where he fays, (as he does here again, in the fecond particular, which we are now examining) that " believing Jefus to be the Meffiah is " the firft ftep to chriftianity ; and therefore this, " rather than any other, was propounded to be be- " lieved by all thofe, whom either our Saviour, or the " apoftles, invited to embrace chriftianity." The contrary whereof appears here; where the article of one God is propofed in the firft place, to thofe whofe unbelief made fuch a propofal neceffary. And there- fore, if his reafon (which he ufes again here, p. 76.) were good, viz. That the article of the Meffiah is ex- prefly mentioned alone, " becaufe it is a leading arti- " cle, and makes way for the reft," this reafon would rather conclude for the article of one God ; and that alone fhould be exprefly mentioned, inftead of the other. Since, as he argues for the other, p. 74, " If " they did not believe this, in the firft place," viz. that there was one God, " there could be no hopes " that they would attend unto any other propofal, re- " lating to the chriftian religion." The vanity and falfhood of which reafoning, viz. that " the article of " Jefus the Mefliah was every-where propounded, rather " than any other, becaufe it was the leading article," we fee in the hiftory of St. Paul's preaching to the Athenians. St. Luke mentions more than one article, where more than one was propofed by St. Paul ; though the firft of them was that leading article of one God, which if not received, " in the firft place, there could " be no hope they would attend to the reft."

Something the unmafker would make of this argu- ment, of a leading article, for want of a better, though he knows not what. In his firft particular, p. 74, he makes ufe of it to fhow, why there was but that one article propofed by the firft preachers of the gofpel ; and how well that fucceeds with him, we have feen. For this is demonftration, that if there were but that one propofed by our Saviour and the apoftles, there was but that one neceffary to be believed to make men chriftians ; unlefs he will impioufly fay, that our Saviour

Saviour and the apoftles went about preaching to no purpofe : for if they propofed not all that was neceffary to make men chriftians, it was in vain for them to preach, and others to hear; if when they heard and be-lieved all that was propofed to them, they were not yet chriftians : for if any article was omitted in the pro-pofal, which was neceffary to make a man a chriftian, though they believed all that was propofed to them, they could not yet be chriftians ; unlefs a man can, from an infidel, become a chriftian, without doing what was neceffary to make him a chriftian.

Further, if his argument, of its being a leading arti-cle, proves, that that alone was propofed, it is a con-tradiction to give it as a reafon, why it was fet down alone by the hiftorian, where it was not propofed alone by the preacher, but other neceffary " matters of faith " were propofed with it ;" unlefs it can be true, that this article, of " Jefus is the Meffiah," was propofed alone by our Saviour and his apoftles, becaufe it was a leading article, and was mentioned alone in the hiftory of what they preached, becaufe it was a leading article, though it were not propofed alone, but jointly with other neceffary matters of faith. For this is the ufe he makes here again, p. 76, of his leading article, under his fecond particular, viz. to fhow why the hiftorians mentioned this neceffary article of Jefus the Meffiah alone, in places where the preachers of the gofpel pro-pofed it not alone, but with other neceffary articles. But, in this latter cafe, it has no fhow of a reafon at all. It may be granted as reafonable for the teachers of any religion not to go any farther, where they fee the firft article, which they propofe is rejected ; where the leading truth, on which all the reft depends, is not received. But it can be no reafon at all, for an hiftorian, who writes the hiftory of thefe firft preachers, to fet down only the firft and leading article, and omit all the reft, in inftances where more were not only propofed, but believed and embraced, and upon that the hearers and believers admitted into the church. It is not for hiftorians to put any diftinction between leading, or not leading articles; but, if they will give a true and

ufeful

uſeful account of the religion, whoſe original they are writing, and of the converts made to it, they muſt tell, not one, but all thoſe neceſſary articles, upon aſſent to which, converts were baptized into that religion, and admitted into the church. Whoever ſays otherwiſe, accuſes them of falſifying the ſtory, miſleading the readers, and giving a wrong account of the religion which they pretend to teach the world, and to preſerve and propagate to future ages. This (if it were ſo) no pretence of conciſeneſs could excuſe or palliate.

There is yet remaining one conſideration, which were ſufficient of itſelf to convince us, that it was the ſole article of faith which was preached ; and that if there had been other articles neceſſary to be known and believed by converts, they could not, upon any pretence of conciſeneſs, be ſuppoſed to be omitted : and that is the commiſſions of thoſe, that were ſent to preach the goſpel. Which ſince the ſacred hiſtorians mention, they cannot be ſuppoſed to leave out any of the material and main heads of thoſe commiſſions.

St. Luke records it, chap. iv. 43, that our Saviour ſays of himſelf, " I muſt go into the other towns to " tell the good news of the kingdom ; for (εἰς τᾶτο) " upon this errand am I SENT." This St. Mark calls ſimply preaching, This preaching, what it contained, St. Matthew tells us, chap. iv. 23, " And Jeſus went " about all Galilee, teaching in their ſynagogues, and " preaching the good news of the kingdom, and heal— " ing all manner of ſickneſs and all manner of diſeaſes " among the people." Here we have his commiſſion, or end of his being ſent, and the execution of it ; both terminating in this, that he declared the good news, that the kingdom of the Meſſiah was come ; and gave them to underſtand, by the miracles he did, that he himſelf was he. Nor does St. Matthew ſeem to affect ſuch conciſeneſs, that he would have left it out, if the goſpel had contained any other fundamental parts neceſſary to be believed to make men chriſtians. For he here ſays, " All manner of ſickneſs, and all manner of " diſeaſes," when either of them might have been better
left

3

left out, than any neceffary article of the gofpel, to make
his hiftory concife.

We fee what our Saviour was fent for. In the next
place, let us look into the commiffion he gave the
apoftles, when he fent them to preach the gofpel. We
have it in the tenth of St. Matthew, in thefe words:
" Go not into the way of the Gentiles, and into any
" city of the Samaritans enter ye not. But go rather
" to the loft fheep of the houfe of Ifrael. And as ye
" go, PREACH, SAYING, THE KINGDOM of HEAVEN
" IS AT HAND. Heal the fick, cleanfe the lepers,
" raife the dead, caft out devils: freely have ye re-
" ceived, freely give. Provide neither gold, nor filver,
" nor brafs in your purfes, nor fcrip in your journey;
" neither two coats, neither fhoes, nor yet ftaves, (for
" the workman is worthy of his meat.) And into
" whatfoever city, or town, ye fhall enter, inquire who
" in it is worthy, and there abide until ye go thence.
" And when ye come into any houfe falute it. And
" if the houfe be worthy, let your peace come upon it;
" and if it be not worthy, let your peace return to
" you. And whofoever fhall not receive you, nor
" hear your words; when ye depart out of that houfe,
" or city, fhake off the duft of your feet. Verily I
" fay unto you, it fhall be more tolerable for the land
" of Sodom and Gomorrha, in the day of judgment,
" than for that city. Behold I fend you forth as fheep,
" in the midft of wolves: be ye therefore wife as fer-
" pents, and harmlefs as doves. But beware of men;
" for they will deliver you up to the councils, and they
" will fcourge you in their fynagogues. And ye fhall
" be brought before governors and kings for my fake,
" for a teftimony againft them and the Gentiles. But
" when they deliver you up, take no thought, how or
" what ye fhall fpeak; for it fhall be given you in that
" fame hour, what ye fhall fpeak. For it is not ye
" that fpeak, but the Spirit of your Father, which
" fpeaketh in you. And the brother fhall deliver up
" the brother to death, and the father the child, and
" the children fhall rife up againft the parents, and
" caufe them to be put to death. And ye fhall be hated
" of

" of all men, for my name's fake : but he that en-
" dureth to the end fhall be faved. But when they
" perfecute you in this city, flee ye into another; for veri-
" ly I fay unto you, ye fhall not have gone over the cities
" of Ifrael until the Son of man be come. The difciple
" is not above his mafter, nor the fervant above his lord.
" It is enough for the difciple, that he be as his mafter,
" and the fervant as his lord. If they have called the
" mafter of the houfe Beelzebub, how much more fhall
" they call them of his houfhold ? Fear them not
" therefore ; for there is nothing covered, which fhall
" not be revealed ; and hid, that fhall not be known.
" What I tell you in darknefs, that fpeak ye in light :
" and what ye hear in the ear, that preach ye upon the
" houfe-tops. And fear not them which kill the body,
" but are not able to kill the foul : but rather fear him,
" which is able to deftroy both foul and body in hell.
" Are not two fparrows fold for a farthing ? And one
" of them fhall not fall to the ground without your
" Father. But the very hairs of your head are all num-
" bered. Fear ye not therefore ; ye are of more value
" than many fparrows. Whofoever therefore fhall con-
" fefs me before men, him will I confefs alfo before my
" Father, which is in heaven. But whofoever fhall
" deny me before men, him will I alfo deny before my
" Father, which is in heaven. Think not that I am
" come to fend peace on earth : I came not to fend
" peace, but a fword. For I am come to fet a man at
" variance againft his father, and the daughter againft
" her mother, and the daughter-in-law againft her
" mother-in-law. And a man's foes fhall be they of
" his own houfhold. He that loveth father and mo-
" ther more than me, is not worthy of me : and he that
" loveth fon or daughter more than me, is not worthy
" of me. And he that taketh not his crofs, and fol-
" loweth after me, is not worthy of me. He that
" findeth his life fhall lofe it : and he that lofeth his
" life for my fake, fhall find it. He that receiveth you,
" receiveth me : and he that receiveth me, receiveth
" him that fent me. He that receiveth a prophet in
" the name of a prophet, fhall receive a prophet's re-
" ward; and he that receiveth a righteous man in the
                                        " name

" name of a righteous man, shall receive a righteous
" man's reward. And whosoever shall give to drink
" unto one of these little ones, a cup of cold water
" only, in the name of a disciple, verily I say unto you,
" he shall in no wise lose his reward. And it came to
" pass, when Jesus had made an end of commanding
" his twelve disciples"——

This is the commission our Saviour gave his apostles,
when he sent them abroad to recover and save " the
" lost sheep of the house of Israel." And will any of
the unmasker's intelligent and observing men say, that
the history of the " scripture is so concise, that any
" passages," any essential, any material, nay, any parts
at all of the apostles commission, " are here omitted by
" the sacred penman?" This commission is set down
so at full, and so particularly, that St. Matthew, who
was one of them to whom it was given, seems not to
have left out one word of all that our Saviour gave him
in charge. And it is so large, even to every particular
article of their instructions, that I doubt not, but my
citing so much, " verbatim," out of the sacred text,
will here again be troublesome to the unmasker. But
whether he will venture again to call it tedious, must be
as nature or caution happen to have the better on it.
Can any one, who reads this commission, unless he hath
the brains, as well as the brow of an unmasker, allege,
that the concisenefs of the history of the scripture has
concealed from us those fundamental doctrines, which
our Saviour and his apostles preached; but the sacred
historians thought fit by consent, for unconceivable
reasons, to leave out in the narrative they give us of
those preachings? This passage here, wholly confuteth
that. They could preach nothing but what they were
sent to preach: and that we see is contained in these few
words, " preach, saying, The kingdom of heaven is at
" hand. Heal the sick, cleanse the lepers, raise the
" dead, cast out devils;" i. e. acquaint them, that the
kingdom of the Messiah is come, and let them know,
by the miracles that you do in my name, that I am that
King and Deliverer they expect. If there were any
other necessary articles that were to be believed, for the

faving of the loft fheep they were fent to, can one
think that St. Matthew, who fets down fo minutely
every circumftance of their commiffion, would have
omitted the moft important and material of it? He
was an ear-witnefs, and one that was fent: and fo
(without fuppofing him infpired) could not be mifled
by the fhort account he might receive from others, who
by their own, or others forgetfulnefs, might have dropped thofe other fundamental articles, that the apoftles
were ordered to preach.

The very like account St. Luke gives of our Saviour's
commiffion to the feventy, chap. x. 1—16, " After
" thefe things the Lord appointed other feventy alfo,
" and fent them two and two before his face, into every
" city and place, whither he himfelf would come.
" Therefore faid he unto them, The harveft truly is
" great, but the labourers are few: pray ye therefore
" the Lord of the harveft, that he would fend forth
" labourers into his harveft. Go your ways: behold I
" fend you forth as lambs among wolves. Carry neither
" purfe, nor fcrip, nor fhoes: and falute no man by the
" way. And into whatfoever hou fe ye enter, firft fay,
" Peacebe to this houfe. And if the Son of peace be
" there, your peace fhall reft upon it ; if not, it fhall re-
" turn to you again. And in the fame houfe remain, eat-
" ing and drinking fuch things as they give: for the
" labourer is worthy of his hire. Go not from houfe to
" houfe. And into whatfoever city ye enter, and they
" receive you, eat fuch things as are fet before you.
" And heal the fick that are therein, and SAY UNTO THEM,
" THE KINGDOM OF GOD IS COME NIGH UNTO YOU.
" But into whatfoever city ye enter, and they receive
" you not, go your ways out into the ftreets of the
" fame, and fay, even the very duft of your city, which
" cleaveth on us, we do wipe off againft you ; notwith-
" ftanding, be ye fure of this, that the kingdom of God
" is come nigh unto you. But I fay unto you, that it
" fhall be more tolerable, in that day, for Sodom, than
" for that city. Wo unto thee, Chorazin ! Woe unto
" thee, Bethfaida! For if the mighty works had been
" done in Tyre and Sidon, which have been done in
                                        " you,

" you, they had a great while ago repented ſitting in
" ſackcloth and aſhes. But it ſhall be more tolerable
" for Tyre and Sidon, at the day of judgment, than
" for you. And thou, Capernaum, which art exalted
" to heaven, ſhalt be thruſt down to hell. He that
" heareth you, heareth me : and he that deſpiſeth you,
" deſpiſeth me : and he that deſpiſeth me, deſpiſeth
" him that ſent me."

Our Saviour's commiſſion here to the ſeventy, whom
he ſent to preach, is ſo exactly conformable to that
which he had before given to the twelve apoſtles, that
there needs but this one thing more to be obſerved, to
convince any one that they were ſent to convert their
hearers to this ſole belief, That the kingdom of the
Meſſiah was come, and that Jeſus was the Meſſiah:
and that the hiſtorians of the New Teſtament are not
ſo conciſe in their account of this matter, that they
would have omitted any other neceſſary articles of belief, that had been given to the ſeventy in commiſſion.
That which I mean is, the kingdom of the Meſſiah is
twice mentioned in it to be come, verſe 9, and 11. If
there were other articles given them by our Saviour, to
propoſe to their hearers, St. Luke muſt be very fond of
this one article, when, for conciſeneſs ſake, leaving out
the other fundamental articles, that our Saviour gave
them in charge to preach, he repeats this more than
once.

The unmaſker's third particular, p. 76, begins thus:
" This alſo muſt be thought of, that though there are
" ſeveral parts and members of the chriſtian faith, yet
" they do not all occur in any one place of ſcripture."
Something is in it, (whether owing to his will, or underſtanding, I ſhall not inquire) that the unmaſker always delivers himſelf in doubtful and ambiguous terms.
It had been as eaſy for him to have ſaid, " There are
" ſeveral articles of the chriſtian faith neceſſary to be
" believed to make a man a chriſtian," as to ſay, (as
he does here) " There are ſeveral parts and members
" of the chriſtian faith." But as an evidence of the
clearneſs of his notions, or the fairneſs of his arguing, he
always reſts in generals. There are, I grant, ſeveral

parts and members of the chriftian faith, which do no
more occur in any one place of fcripture, than the whole
New Teftament can be faid to occur in any one place
of fcripture. For every propofition, delivered in the
New Teftament for divine revelation, is " a part and
" member of the chriftian faith." But it is not thofe
" parts and members of the chriftian faith," we are
fpeaking of; but only fuch " parts and members of
" the chriftian faith," as are abfolutely neceffary to be
believed by every man, before he can be a chriftian.
And in that fenfe, I deny his affertion to be true, viz.
that they do not occur in any one place of the fcripture:
for they do all occur in that firft fermon of St. Peter,
Acts ii. 36, by which three thoufand were at that time
brought into the church, and that in thefe words:
" therefore let all the houfe of Ifrael know affuredly,
" that God hath made that fame Jefus, whom you have
" crucified, Lord and Chrift. Repent, and be bap-
" tifed every one of you in the name of Jefus Chrift."
Here is the doctrine of Jefus the Meffiah, the Lord, and
.of repentance, propofed to thofe, who already believe
one God: which, I fay, are all the parts of the chriftian
faith neceffary to be believed to make a man a chriftian.
To fuppofe, as the unmafker does here, that more is required, is to beg, not to prove the queftion.

If he difputes this collection of mine out of that fermon of St. Peter, I will give him a more authentic
collection of the neceffary parts of the chriftian faith,
from an author that he will not queftion. Let him look
into Acts xx. 20, &c. and there he will find St. Paul
faying thus to the elders of Ephefus, whom he was
taking his laft leave of, with an affurance that he fhould
never fee them again: " I have kept back nothing that was
" profitable unto you; but have fhowed you, and have
" taught you publicly, and from houfe to houfe, tefti-
" fying both to the Jews, and alfo the Greeks, re-
" pentance towards God, and faith towards our Lord
" Jefus Chrift." If St. Paul knew what was neceffary to make a chriftian, here it is: here he (if he
knew how to do it, for it is plain from his words he
defigned to do it) has put it together. But there is a

I

greater

greater yet than St. Paul, who has brought all the parts of faith necessary to salvation into one place; I mean our Saviour himself, John xvii. 13, in these words: " This is life eternal, that they might know thee the " only true God, and Jesus Christ, whom thou hast " sent."

But the unmasker goes on: " Therefore, when, in " some places, only one single part of the christian " faith is made mention of, as necessary to be em- " braced in order to salvation, we must be careful not " to take it alone, but to supply it from several other " places, which make mention of other necessary and " indispensable points of belief. I will give the reader " a plain instance of this, Rom. x. 9, " If thou shalt be- " lieve in thine heart, that God hath raised him (i. e. " the Lord Jesus) from the dead, thou shalt be saved." " Here one article of faith, viz. the belief of Christ's " resurrection (because it is of so great importance in " christianity) is only mentioned: but all the rest must " be supposed, because they are mentioned in other " places."

Answ. One would wonder that any one conversant in holy writ, with ever so little attention, much more that an expounder of the scriptures, should so mistake the sense and style of the scripture. Believing Jesus to be the Messiah, with a lively faith, i. e. as I have showed, taking him to be our King, with a sincere submission to the laws of his kingdom, is all that is required to make a man a christian; for this includes repentance too. The believing him therefore to be the Messiah is very often, and with great reason, put both for faith and repentance too; which are sometimes set down singly, where one is put for both, as implying the other; and sometimes they are both mentioned; and then faith, as contradistinguished to repentance, is taken for a simple assent of the mind to this truth, that Jesus is the Messiah. Now this faith is variously expressed in scripture.

There are some particulars in the history of our Saviour, allowed to be so peculiarly appropriated to the Messiah, such incommunicable marks of him, that to

believe

believe them of Jesus of Nazareth, was in effect the same, as to believe him to be the Messiah, and so are put to express it. The principal of these is his resurrection from the dead; which being the great and demonstrative proof of his being the Messiah, it is not at all strange, that the believing his resurrection should be put for believing him to be the Messiah; since the declaring his resurrection, was declaring him to be the Messiah. For thus St. Paul argues, Acts xiii. 32, 33, " We declare unto you good tidings, or we preach the gospel " to you, [for so the word signifies] how that the pro- " mise, that was made unto the fathers, God hath ful- " filled the same unto us their children, in that he hath " raised up Jesus again." The force of which argument lies in this, that, if Jesus was raised from the dead, then he was certainly the Messiah: and thus the promise of the Messiah was fulfilled, in raising Jesus from the dead. The like argument St. Paul useth, 1 Cor. xv. 17. " If Christ be not raised, your faith is vain, you are yet " in your sins;" i. e. if Jesus be not risen from the dead, he is not the Messiah, your believing it is in vain, and you will receive no benefit by that faith. And so, likewise, from the same argument of his resurrection, he at Thessalonica proves him to be the Messiah, Acts xvii. 2, 3, " And Paul, as his manner was, went into the " synagogue, and three sabbath-days reasoned with the " Jews out of the scripures, opening and alleging, " that the Messiah must needs have suffered, and risen " again from the dead; and that this Jesus, whom I " preach unto you, is the Messiah."

The necessary connexion of these two, that if he rose from the dead, he was the Messiah; and if he rose not from the dead, he was not the Messiah; the chief priest and pharisees, that had prosecuted him to death, understood very well: who therefore " came together unto " Pilate, saying, Sir, we remember that that deceiver " said, whilst he was yet alive, After three days I will " rise again. Command therefore, that the sepulchre " be made sure unto the third day, lest his disciples " come by night, and steal him away, and say unto the people, " He is risen from the dead:" " so the last " errour

"errour fhall be worfe than the firft." The errour they here fpeak of, it is plain, was the opinion, that he was the Meffiah. To ftop that belief, which his miracles had procured him amongft the people, they had got him put to death; but if, after that, it fhould be believed, that he rofe again from the dead, this demonftration, that he was the Meffiah, would but eftablifh what they had laboured to deftroy by his death; fince no one, who believed his refurrection, could doubt of his being the Meffiah.

It is not at all therefore to be wondered, that his refurrection, his afcenfion, his rule and dominion, and his coming to judge the quick and the dead, which are chracteriftical marks of the Meffiah, and belong peculiarly to him, fhould fometimes in fcripture be put alone, as fufficient defcriptions of the Meffiah; and the believing them of him put for believing him to be the Meffiah. Thus, Acts x, our Saviour, in Peter's difcourfe to Cornelius, when he brought him the gofpel, is defcribed to be the Meffiah, by his miracles, death, refurrection, dominion, and coming to judge the quick and the dead.

Thefe, (which in my " Reafonablenefs of Chriftiani-" ty," I have upon this ground taken the liberty to call concomitant articles) where they are fet alone for the faith to which falvation is promifed, plainly fignify the believing Jefus to be the Meffiah, that fundamental article, which has the promife of life; and fo give no foundation at all for what the unmafker fays, in thefe words: " Here one article of faith, viz. the belief of " Chrift's refurrection, (becaufe it is of fo great impor-" tance in chriftianity) is only mentioned; but all the " reft muft be fuppofed, becaufe they are mentioned in " other places."

Anfw. If all the reft be of abfolute and indifpenfable neceffity to be believed to make a man a chriftian, all the reft are, every one of them, of equal importance. For things of equal neceffity, to any end, are of equal importance to that end. But here the truth forced its way unawares from the unmafker; Our Saviour's refurrection, for the reafon I have given, is truly of great

Z 3   importance

importance in chriftianity ; fo great, that his being, or not being the Meffiah, ftands or falls with it : fo that thefe two important articles are infeparable, and in effect make but one.   For, fince that time, believe one, and you believe both ; deny one of them, and you can believe neither.   If the unmafker can fhow me any one of the articles in his lift, which is not of this great importance, mentioned alone, with a promife of falvation for believing it, I will grant him to have fome colour for what he fays here.   But where is to be found in the fcripture any fuch expreffion as this : if thou fhalt believe with thy heart " the corruption and degeneracy " of human nature," thou fhalt be faved ? or the like. This place, therefore, out of the Romans, makes not for, but againft his lift of neceffary articles.   One of them, alone, he cannot fhow me any where fet down, with a fuppofition of the reft, as having falvation promifed to it : though it be true, that that one, which alone is abfolutely neceffary to be fuperadded to the belief of one God, is, in divers places, differently expreffed.

That which he fubjoins, as a confequence of what he had faid, is a farther proof of this : " And confequently, " fays he, if we would give an impartial account of our " belief, we muft confult thofe places : and they are " not all together, but difperfed here and there. Where- " fore we muft look them out, and acquaint ourfelves " with the feveral particulars, which make up our be- " lief, and render it intire and confummate."

Anfw; Never was a man conftanter to a loofe way of talking.   The queftion is only about articles neceffary to be believed to make a man a chriftian : and here he talks of the " feveral particulars which make up our " belief, and render it intire and confummate ;" confounding, as he did before, effential and integral parts, which, it feems, he cannot diftinguifh.   Our faith is true and faving, when it is fuch as God, by the new covenant, requires it to be : but it is not intire and confummate, until we explicitly believe all the truths contained in the word of God.   For the whole revelation of truth in the fcripture being the proper and intire object

object of faith, our faith cannot be intire and consummate, until it be adequate to its proper object, which is the whole divine revelation contained in the scripture: and so, to make our faith intire and consummate, we must not look out those places, which, he says, are not altogether. To talk of looking out, and culling of places, is nonsense, where the whole scripture alone can " make up our belief, and render it intire and consum- " mate:" which no one, I think, can hope for, in this frail state of ignorance and errour. To make the unmasker speak sense and to the purpose here, we must understand him thus: " That if we will give an im- " partial account" of the articles, that are necessary to be believed to make a man a christian, " we must con- ". sult those places where they are; for they are not all " together, but dispersed here and there; wherefore we " must look them out," and acquaint ourselves with the several particulars, which make up the fundamental articles of our belief, and will render a catalogue of them intire and consummate. If his supposition be true, I grant his method to be reasonable, and upon that I join issue with him. Let him thus " give an im- " partial account of our belief; let him acquaint us " with the several particulars which make up a " christian's belief, and render it intire and consum- " mate." Until he has done this, let him not talk thus in the air of a method, that will not do: let him not reproach me, as he does, for not taking a course, by which he himself cannot do, what he reviles me for failing in. " But our hasty author," says he, " took " another course, and thereby deceived himself, and " unhappily deceived others." If it be so, I desire the unmasker to take the course he proposes, and thereby undeceive me and others; and " acquaint us with the " several particulars which make up a christian's be- " lief, and render it intire and consummate;" for I am willing to be undeceived: but until he has done that, and shown us by the success of it, that his course is better, he cannot blame us for following that course we have done.

I come now to his fourth and last particular, p. 78, which, he says, " is the main answer to the objection;"

and

and therefore I fhall fet it down in his own words, intire, as it ftands together. " This," fays he, " muft
" be born in our minds, that chriftianity was erected
" by degrees, according to that prediction and promife
" of our Saviour, that " the Spirit fhould teach them
" all things," John xiv. 26. and that " he fhould
" guide them into all truth." John xvi. 13. viz.
" after his departure and afcenfion, when the Holy
" Ghoft was to be fent in a fpecial manner, to en-
" lighten men's minds, and to difcover to them the
" great myfteries of chriftianity. This is to be noted by
" us, as that which gives great light in the prefent cafe.
" The difcovery of the doctrines of the gofpel was
" gradual.   It was by certain fteps, that chriftianity
" climbed to its height.   We are not to think then,
" that all the neceffary doctrines of the chriftian re-
" ligion were clearly publifhed to the world in our
" Saviour's time.   Not but that all that were neceffary
" for that time, were publifhed, but fome which were
" neceffary for the fuceeding one, were not then dif-
" covered, or, at leaft, not fully.   They had ordinarily
" no belief, before Chrift's death and refurrection, of
" thofe fubftantial articles, i. e. that he fhould die and
" rife again : but we read in the Acts, and in the
" epiftles, that thefe were formal articles of faith after-
" wards, and are ever fince neceffary to complete the
" chriftian belief.   So as to other great verities, the
" gofpel increafed by degrees, and was not perfect at
" once. Which furnifhes us with a reafon why moft of the
" choiceft and fublimeft truths of chriftianity are to be
" met with in the epiftles of the apoftles, they being
" fuch doctrines as were not clearly difcovered and
" opened in the Gofpels and the Acts." Thus far the
unmafker.

I thought hitherto, that the covenant of grace in
Chrift Jefus had been but one, immutably the fame :
but our unmafker here makes two, or I know not how
many. For I cannot tell how to conceive, that the
conditions of any covenant fhould be changed, and the
covenant remain the fame ; every change of conditions,
in my apprehenfion, makes a new and another covenant.
We

We are not to think, says the unmasker, " That all the
" neceffary doctrines of the chriftian religion were
" clearly publifhed to the world in our Saviour's time;
" not but that all that were neceffary for that time
" were publifhed : but fome, which were neceffary for
" the fucceeding one, were not then difcovered, or, at
" leaft, not fully." Anfw. The unmasker, conftant
to himfelf, fpeaks here doubtfully, and cannot tell
whether he fhould fay, that the articles neceffary to
fucceeding times, were difcovered in our Saviour's time,
or no; and therefore, that he may provide himfelf a re-
treat, in the doubt he is in, he fays, " They were not
" clearly publifhed; they were not then difcovered,
" or, at leaft, not fully." But we muft defire him to
pull off his mafk, and to that purpofe,

1. I afk him how he can tell, that all the neceffary
doctrines were obfcuredly publifhed, or in part difcovered ? For an obfcure publifhing, a difcovery in part,
is oppofed to, and intimated in, " not clearly publifh-,
" ed, not fully difcovered." And, if a clear and full
difcovery be all that he denies to them, I afk,

XXXVII. " Which thofe fundamental articles are,
    " which were obfcurely publifhed," but not fully
    difcovered in our Saviour's time ?

And next I fhall defire him to tell me,

XXXVIII. Whether there are any articles neceffary
    to be believed to make a man a chriftian, that were
    not difcovered at all in our Saviour's time : and
    which they are ?

If he cannot fhow thefe diftinctly, it is plain he talks
at random about them; but has no clear and diftinct
conception of thofe that were publifhed, or not publifhed, clearly or obfcurely difcovered in our Saviour's
time. It was neceffary for him to fay fomething for
thofe his pretended neceffary articles, which are not
to

to be found any where propofed in the preaching of our Saviour and his apoftles, to their yet unbelieving auditors ; and therefore, he fays, " We are not to think " all the neceffary doctrines of the chriftian religion " were clearly publifhed to the world in our Saviour's " time." But he barely fays it, without giving any reafon, why " we are not to think fo." It is enough that it is neceffary to his hypothefis. He fays, " we are not to think fo," and we are prefently bound not to think fo. Elfe, from another man, that did not ufurp an authority over our thoughts, it would have required fome reafon to make them think, that fomething more was required to make a man a chriftian after, than in our Saviour's time. For, as I take it, it is not a very probable, much lefs a felf-evident propofition, to be received without proof, that there was fomething neceffary for that time to make a man a chriftian, and fomething more, that was neceffary to make a chriftian in the fucceeding time.

However, fince this great mafter fays, " we ought " to think fo," let us in obedience think fo as well as we can ; until he vouchfafes to give us fome reafon to think, that there was more required to be believed to make a man a chriftian, in the fucceeding time, than in our Saviour's. This, inftead of removing, does but increafe the difficulty : for if more were neceffary to be believed to make a man a chriftian after our Saviour's time, than was during his life ; how comes it, that no more was propofed by the apoftles, in their preaching to unbelievers, for the making them chriftians, after our Saviour's death, than there was before ; even this one article, " that he was the Meffiah ?" For I defire the unmafker to fhow me any of thofe articles mentioned in his lift, (except the refurrection and afcenfion of our Saviour, which were intervening matters of fact, evidencing him to be the Meffiah) that were propofed by the apoftles, after our Saviour's time, to their unbelieving hearers, to make them chriftians. This one doctrine, " that Jefus was the Meffiah," was that which was propofed in our Saviour's time to be believed, as neceffary to make a man a chriftian : the fame doctrine

doctrine was, likewise, what was proposed afterwards, in the preaching of the apostles to unbelievers, to make them christians.

I grant, this was more clearly proposed after, than in our Saviour's time: but in both of them it was all that was proposed to the believers of one God, to make them christians. Let him show, that there were any other proposed in, or after our Saviour's time, to be believed, to make unbelievers christians. If he means, by " necessary articles published to the world," the other doctrines contained in the epistles; I grant, they are all of them necessary articles, to be believed by every christian, as far as he understands them. But I deny, that they were proposed to those they were writ to, as necessary to make them christians, for this demonstrative reason; because they were christians already. For example, Many doctrines proving, and explaining, and giving a farther light into the gospel, are published in the epistles to the Corinthians and Thessalonians. These are all of divine authority, and none of them may be disbelieved by any one who is a christian; but yet what was proposed or published to both the Corinthians and Thessalonians, to make them christians, was only this doctrine, " That Jesus was the " Messiah:" as may be seen, Acts xvii, xviii. This, then, was the doctrine necessary to make men christians, in our Saviour's time; and this the only doctrine necessary to make unbelievers christians, after our Saviour's time. The only difference was, that it was more clearly proposed after, than before his ascension: the reason whereof has been sufficiently explained. But any other doctrine but this, proposed clearly or obscurely, in or after our Saviour's time, as necessary to be believed to make unbelievers christians, that remains yet to be shown.

When the unmasker speaks of the doctrines that were necessary for the succeeding time after our Saviour, he is in doubt, whether he should say they were, or were not discovered, in our Saviour's time; and how far they were then discovered: and therefore he says, " Some of them were not then discovered, or at least,

" not

" not fully." We muſt here excuſe the doubtfulneſs of his talking, concerning the diſcovery of his other neceſſary articles. For how could he ſay, they were diſcovered, or not diſcovered, clearly or obſcurely, fully or not fully ; when he does not yet know them all, nor can tell us, what thoſe neceſſary articles are? If he does know them, let him give us a liſt of them, and then we ſhall ſee eaſily, whether they were at all publiſhed or diſcovered in our Saviour's time. If there are ſome of them that were not at all diſcovered in our Saviour's time, let him ſpeak it out, and leave ſhifting: and if ſome of thoſe that were " not neceſſary for our Sa-
" viour's time, but for the ſucceeding one only," were yet diſcovered in our Saviour's time, why were they not neceſſary to be believed in that time? But the truth is, he knows not what theſe doctrines, neceſſary for ſucceeding times, are : and therefore can ſay nothing poſitively about their diſcovery. And for thoſe that he has ſet down, as ſoon as he ſhall name any one of them to be of the number of thoſe, " not neceſſary for our Sa-
" viour's time, but neceſſary for the ſucceeding one," it will preſently appear, either that it was diſcovered in our Saviour's time ; and then it was as neceſſary for his time as the ſucceeding : or elſe, that it was not diſcovered in his time, nor to ſeveral converts after his time, before they were made chriſtians ; and therefore it was no more neceſſary to be believed to make a man a chriſtian in the ſucceeding, than it was in our Saviour's time. However, general poſitions and diſtinctions without a foundation ſerve for ſhow, and to beguile unwary and inattentive readers.

2. Having thus minded him, that the queſtion is about articles of faith, neceſſary to be explicitly and diſtinctly believed to make a man a chriſtian ; I then, in the next place, demand of him to tell me,

XXXIX. Whether or no all the articles, neceſſary now to be diſtinctly and explicitly believed, to make any man a chriſtian, were diſtinctly and explicitly publiſhed or diſcovered in our Saviour's time ?

And

And then I fhall defire to know of him,

XL.　A reafon why they were not.

Thofe that he inftances in, of Chrift's death and re-furrection, will not help him one jot; for they are not new doctrines revealed, new myfteries difcovered; but matters of fact, which happened to our Saviour in their cue time, to complete in him the character and predictions of the Meffiah, and demonftrate him to be the Deliverer promifed. Thefe are recorded of him by the Spirit of God in holy writ, but are no more neceffary to be believed to make a man a chriftian, than any other part of divine revelation, but as far as they have an im-mediate connexion with his being the Meffiah, and can-not be denied without denying him to be the Meffiah; and therefore this article of his refurrection, (which fup-pofes his death) and fuch other propofitions as are con-vertible with his being the Meffiah, are, as they very well may be, put for his being the Meffiah; and, as I have fhowed, propofed to be believed in the place of it.

All that is revealed in fcripture has a confequential necefity of being believed by all thofe, to whom it is propofed; becaufe it is of divine authority, one part as much as another. And, in this fenfe, all the divine truths in the infpired writings are fundamental, and ne-ceffary to be believed. But then this will deftroy our unmafker's felect number of fundamental articles; and " the choiceft and fublimeft truths of chriftianity," which, he tells us, " are to be met with in the Epiftles," will not be more neceffary to be believed than any, which he may think the commoneft or meaneft truths in any of the Epiftles or the Gofpels. Whatfoever part of divine revelation, whether revealed before, or in, or after our Saviour's time; whether it contains (according to the diftinction of our unmafker's nice palate) choice or common, fublime or not fublime truths, is neceffary to be believed by every one to whom it is propofed, as far as he underftands what is propofed. But God, by Jefus Chrift, has entered into a covenant of grace with man-

kind ;

kind; a covenant of faith; inftead of that of works, wherein fome truths are abfolutely neceffary to be explicitly believed by them to make men chriftians; and therefore thofe truths are neceffary to be known and confequently neceffary to be propofed to them to make men chriftians. This is peculiar to them to make men chriftians. For all men, as men, are under a neceffary obligation to believe what God propofes to them to be believed; but there being certain diftinguifhing truths, which belong to the covenant of the gofpel, which if men know not, they cannot be chriftians; and they being, fome of them, fuch as cannot be known without being propofed; thofe, and thofe only, are the neceffary doctrines of chriftianity I fpeak of; without a knowledge of, and affent to which, no man can be a chriftian.

To come therefore to a clear decifion of this controverfy, I defire the unmafker to tell me,

XLI. What thofe doctrines are, which are abfolutely neceffary to be propofed to every man to make him a chriftian?

XLII. 1. Whether they are all the truths of divine revelation contained in the Bible?

For I grant his argument, (which in another place he ufes for fome of them, and truly belongs to them all) viz. that they were revealed and written there, on purpofe to be believed, and that it is indifpenfably neceffary for chriftians to believe them.

XLIII. 2. Or, whether it be only that one article, of Jefus being the Meffiah, which the Hiftory of our Saviour and his apoftles preaching has, with fuch a peculiar diftinction, every-where propofed?

XLIV. 3. Or, whether the doctrines neceffary to be propofed to every one to make him a chriftian, be any fet of truths between the two?

And

And if he fays this latter, then I muft afk him,

XLV. What they are? that we may fee, why thofe, rather than any other, contained in the New Tefta-ment, are neceffary to be propofed to every man to make him a chriftian; and, if they are not every one propofed to him, and affented to by him he cannot be a chriftian.

The unmafker makes a great noife, and hopes to give his unwary, though well-meaning readers, odd thoughts, and ftrong impreffions againft my book, by declaiming againft my lank faith, and my narrowing of chriftianity to one article; which, as he fays, is the next way to reduce it to none. But when it is confidered, it will be found, that it is he that narrows chriftianity. The un-mafker, as if he were arbiter and difpenfer of the oracles of God, takes upon him to fingle out fome texts of fcripture; and, where the words of fcripture will not ferve his turn, to impofe on us his interpretations and deductions, as neceffary articles of faith; which is, in effect, to make them of equal authority with the un-queftionable word of God. And thus, partly in the words of fcripture, and partly in words of his own, he makes a fet of fundamentals, with an exclufion of all the other truths delivered by the Spirit of God, in the Bible; though all the reft be of the fame divine au-thority and original, and ought therefore all equally, as far as they are underftood by every chriftian, to be be-lieved. I tell him, and I defire him to take notice of it, God has no-where given him an authority thus to garble the infpired writings of the holy fcriptures. Every part of it is his word, and ought, every part of it, to be believed by every chriftian man, according as God fhall enable him to underftand it. It ought not to be narrowed to the cut of the unmafker's peculiar fyftem; it is a prefumption of the higheft nature, for him thus to pretend, according to his own fancy, to eftablifh a fet of fundamental articles. This is to diminifh the authority of the word of God, to fet up his own; and create a reverence to his fyftem, from which the feveral

parts

parts of divine revelation are to receive their weight, dignity, and authority. Thofe paffages of holy writ which fuit with that, are fundamental, choice, fublime, and neceffary : the reft of the fcripture (as of no great moment) is not fundamental, is not neceffary to be believed, may be neglected, or muft be tortured, to comply with an analogy of faith of his own making. But though he pretends to a certain fet of fundamentals, yet, to fhow the vanity and impudence of that pretence, he cannot tell us what they are; and therefore in vain contends for a creed he knows not, and is yet no-where. He neither does, and which is more, I tell him, he never can, give us a collection of his fundamentals gathered upon his principles, out of the fcripture, with the rejection of all the reft, as not fundamental. He does not obferve the difference there is between what is neceffary to be believed by every man to make him a chriftian, and what is required to be believed by every chriftian. The firft of thefe is what, by the covenant of the gofpel, is neceffary to be known, and confequently to be propofed to every man, to make him a chriftian : the latter is no lefs than the whole revelation of God, all the divine truths contained in holy fcripture : which every chriftian man is under a neceffity to believe, fo far as it fhall pleafe God, upon his ferious and conftant endeavours, to enlighten his mind to underftand them.

The preaching of our Saviour, and his apoftles, has fufficiently taught us what is neceffary to be propofed to every man, to make him a chriftian. He that believes him to be the promifed Meffiah, takes Jefus for his King, and repenting of his former fins, fincerely refolves to live, for the future, in obedience to his laws, is a fubject of his kingdom, is a chriftian. If he be not, I defire the unmafker to tell me, what more is requifite to make him fo. Until he does that, I reft fatisfied, that this is all that was at firft, and is ftill neceffary to make a man a chriftian.

This, though it be contained in a few words, and thofe not hard to be underftood; though it be in one voluntary act of the mind, relinquifhing all irregular
courfes,

courfes, and fubmitting itfelf to the rule of him, whom God hath fent to be our King, and promifed to be our Saviour; yet it having relation to the race of mankind, from the firft man Adam to the end of the world; it being a contrivance, wherein God has difplayed fo much of his wifdom and goodnefs to the corrupt and loft fons of men; and it being a defign, to which the Almighty had a peculiar regard in the whole conftitution and œconomy of the jews, as well as in the prophecies and hiftory of the Old Teftament; this was a foundation capable of large fuperftructures: 1. In explaining the occafion, neceflity, ufe, and end of his coming. 2. Next in proving him to be the perfon promifed, by a correfpondence of his birth, life, fufferings, death, and refurrection, to all thofe prophecies and types of him, which had given the expectation of fuch a Deliverer; and to thofe defcriptions of him, whereby he might be known, when he did come. 3. In the difcovery of the fort, conftitution, extent, and management of his kingdom. 4. In fhowing from what we are delivered by him, and how that deliverance is wrought out, and what are the confequences of it.

Thefe, and a great many more the like, afford great numbers of truths delivered both in the hiftorical, epiftolary, and prophetical writings of the New Teftament, wherein the myfteries of the gofpel, hidden from former ages, were difcovered; and that more fully, I grant, after the pouring out of the Holy Ghoft upon the apoftles. But could no-body take Chrift for their promifed King, and refolve to obey him, unlefs he underftood all the truths that concerned his kingdom, or, as I may fay, myfteries of ftate of it? The truth of the contrary is manifeft, out of the plain and uniform preaching of the apoftles, after they had received the Holy Ghoft, that was to guide them into all truth. Nay, after the writing of thofe epiftles, wherein were contained the unmafker's fublimeft truths; they everywhere propofed to unbelievers Jefus the Mefliah, to be their King, ordained of God; and to this joined repentance: and this alone they preached for the converfion of their unbelieving hearers. As foon as any one affented to this, he was pronounced a believer; and thefe infpired rulers of the church, thefe infallible preachers of the gofpel, admitted into Chrift's kingdom by baptifm. And this after, long " after our " Saviour's afcenfion, when (as our unmafker expreffes it) " the Holy Ghoft was to be fent in an efpecial manner " to enlighten men's minds, and to difcover to them " the great myfteries of chriftianity," even as long as the apoftles lived : and what others were to do, who afterwards were to preach the gofpel, St. Paul tells us, 1 Cor. iii. 11. " Other foundation can no man lay than " that is laid, even Jefus the Meffiah." Though upon this foundation men might build varioufly things that would, or would not hold the touch, yet however as long as they kept firm to this foundation, they fhould be faved, as appears in the following verfes.

And indeed, if all the doctrines of the gofpel, which are contained in the writings of the apoftles and evangelifts, were neceffary to be underftood, and explicitly believed in the true fenfe of thofe that delivered them, to make a man a chriftian ; I doubt, whether ever any one, even to this day, was a true chriftian ; though I believe the unmafker will not deny, but that, ere this, chriftianity (as he expreffes it) " is by certain fteps " climbed to its height."

But for this the unmafker has found a convenient and wife remedy. It is but for him to have the power to declare, which of the doctrines delivered in holy writ are, and which are not neceffary to be believed, with an additional power to add others of his own, that he cannot find there ; and the bufinefs is done. For unlefs this be allowed him, his fyftem cannot ftand : unlefs his interpretations be received for authentic revelation, we cannot have all the doctrines neceffary for our time ; in truth, we cannot be chriftians. For to this only what he fays, concerning the " gradual difcovery of the doctrines of the gofpel," tends. " We are not to think," fays he, " that all the neceffary doctrines of the " chriftian religion were clearly publifhed to the world " in our Saviour's time : not but that all that were ne-
                                                    " ceffary

" ceffary for that time were publifhed; but fome that
" were neceffary for the fucceeding one, were not then
" difcovered, or, at leaft, not fully."

I muft afk the unmafker a fhort queftion or two; as,
firft,

XLVI. Are not all the doctrines, neceffary for our
time, contained in his fyftem?

Next,

XLVII. Can all the doctrines, neceffary for our
time, be propofed in the exprefs words of the
fcripture?

When he has anfwered thefe two plain queftions, and
(an anfwer to them I fhall expect) the world will then
fee, what he defigns by " doctrines neceffary for our
" Saviour's time, and doctrines neceffary for fucceeding
" times;" whether he means any thing elfe by it, but
the fetting up his fyftem, as the exact ftandard of the
gofpel, and the true and unalterable meafure of chriftianity, in which " it has climbed to its height."

Let not good and fincere chriftians be deceived, nor
perplexed, by this maker of another chriftianity, than
what the infallible Spirit of God has left us in the fcriptures. It is evident from thence, that whoever takes
Jefus the Meffiah for his King, with a refolution to live
by his laws, and does fincerely repent, as often as he
tranfgreffes any of them, is his fubject; all fuch are
chriftians. What they are to know, or believe more,
concerning him and his kingdom, when they are his
fubjects, he has left upon record in the great and facred
code and conftitutions of his kingdom; I mean in the
holy fcriptures. All that is contained therein, as
coming from the God of truth, they are to receive as
truth, and embrace as fuch. But fince it is impoffible
explicitly to believe any propofition of the chriftian
doctrine, but what we underftand, or in any other fenfe,
than we underftand it to have been delivered in; an
explicit belief is, or can be required in no man, of more
than what he underftands of that doctrine. And thus,

whatfoever

whatfoever upon fair endeavours he underftands to be
contained in that doctrine, is neceffary to him to be
believed : nor can he continue a fubject of Chrift upon
other terms.

What he is perfuaded is the meaning of Chrift his
King, in any expreffion he finds in the facred code ;
that, by his allegiance, he is bound to fubmit his mind
to receive for true, or elfe he denies the authority of
Chrift, and refufes to believe him ; nor can be excufed,
by calling any one on earth mafter. And hence it is
evidently impoffible for a chriftian to underftand any
text, in one fenfe, and believe it in another, by whomfoever dictated.

All that is contained in the infpired writings, is all of
divine authority, muft all be allowed for fuch, and received for divine and infallible truth, by every fubject
of Chrift's kingdom, i. e. every chriftian. How comes
then the unmafker to diftinguifh thefe dictates of the
Holy Spirit, into neceffary, and not neceffary truths ?
I defire him to produce his commiffion, whereby he
hath the power given him to tell, which of the divine
truths, contained in the holy fcripture, are of neceffity
to be believed, and which not. Who made him a judge
or divider between them ? Who gave him this power
over the oracles of God, to fet up one and debafe another, at his pleafure ? Some, as he thinks fit, are the
choiceft truths : and what, I befeech him, are the
other ? Who made him a choofer, where no-body can
pick and choofe ? Every propofition there, as far as any
chriftian can underftand it, is indifpenfably neceffary
to be believed : and farther than he does underftand it,
it is impoffible for him to believe it. The laws of
Chrift's kingdom do not require impoffibilities ; for they
are all reafonable, and good.

Some of the truths delivered in the holy writ are very
plain : it is impoffible, I think, to miftake their meaning ; and thofe certainly are all neceffary to be explicitly believed. Others have more difficulty in them,
and are not eafy to be underftood. Is the unmafker appointed Chrift's vicegerent here, or the Holy Ghoft's
interpreter, with authority to pronounce which of thefe

are necessary to be believed, and in what sense, and which not? The obscurity, that is to be found in several passages of the scripture, the difficulties that cover and perplex the meaning of several texts, demand of every christian study, diligence, and attention, in reading and hearing the scriptures; in comparing and examining them; and receiving what light he can from all manner of helps, to understand these books, wherein are contained the words of life. This the unmasker, and every one, is to do for himself; and thereby find out what is necessary for him to believe. But I do not know that the unmasker is to understand and interpret for me, more than I for him. If he has such a power, I desire him to produce it. Until then, I can acknowledge no other infallible, but that guide, which he directs me to himself, here in these words: "according to our Sa-
"viour's promise, the Holy Ghost was to be sent in a
"special manner to enlighten men's minds, and to
"discover to them the great mysteries of chris-
"tianity." For whether by men, he here means those, on whom the Holy Ghost was so eminently poured out, Acts ii. or whether he means by these words, that special assistance of the Holy Ghost, whereby particular men, to the end of the world, are to be led into the truth, by opening their understandings, that they may understand the scriptures, (for he always loves to speak doubtfully and indefinitely) I know no other infallible guide, but the Spirit of God in the scriptures. Nor has God left it in my choice to take any one for such. If he had, I should think the unmasker the unlikeliest to be he, and the last man in the world to be chosen for that guide: and herein I appeal to any sober christian, who hath read what the unmasker has, with so little truth and decency, (for it is not always men's fault if they have not sense) writ upon this question, whether he would not be of the same mind?

But yet, as very an unmasker as he is, he will be extremely apt to call you names, nay, to declare you no christian; and boldly affirm, you have no christianity, if you will not swallow it just as it is of his cooking. You must take it just as he has been pleased to dole it;

no more, nor no lefs, than what is in his fyftem.   He
hath put himfelf into the throne of Chrift, and pretends
to tell you which are, and which are not the indifpenfable laws of his kingdom: which parts of his divine revelation you muft neceffarily know, underftand,
and believe, and in what fenfe; and which you need not
trouble your head about, but may pafs by, as not neceffary to be believed.   He will tell you, that fome of
his neceffary articles are myfteries, and yet (as he does,
p. 115, of his " Thoughts concerning the caufes of
" atheifm") that they are eafy to be underftood by any
man, when explained to him.   In anfwer to that, I
demanded of him, " Who was to explain them?   The
" papifts, I told him, would explain fome of them
" one way, and the reformed another; the remonftrants
" and anti-remonftrants give them different fenfes; and
" probably the trinitarians and unitarians will profefs,
" that they underftand not each other's explications."
But to this, in his reply, he has not vouchfafed to give
me any anfwer; which yet I expect, and I will tell him
why: becaufe, as there are different explainers, there
will be different fundamentals.   And therefore unlefs
he can fhow his authority to be the fole explainer of fundamentals, he will in vain make fuch a pother about his
fundamentals.   Another explainer, of as good authority as he, will fet up others againft them.   And what
then fhall we be the better for all this ftir and noife of
fundamentals?   All the effect of it will be juft the fame
it has been thefe thoufand years and upwards; fchifms,
feparations, contentions, animofities, quarrels, blood
and butchery, and all that train of mifchiefs, which
have fo long haraffed and defamed chriftianity, and are
fo contrary to the doctrine, fpirit, and end of the gofpel; and which muft ftill continue as long as any fuch
unmafker fhall take upon him to be the difpenfer and
dictator to others of fundamentals; and peremptorily to
define which parts of divine revelation are neceffary to
be believed, and which chriftians may with fafety dif-
penfe with, and not believe.

To conclude, what was fufficient to make a man a
chriftian in our Saviour's time, is fufficient ftill, viz. the
taking

taking him for our King and Lord, ordained fo by God. What was neceffary to be believed by all chriftians in our Saviour's time, as an indifpenfable duty, which they owed to their lord and mafter, was the believing all divine revelation, as far as every one could underftand it : and juft fo it is ftill, neither more nor lefs. This being fo, the unmafker may make what ufe he pleafes of his notion, " that chriftianity was erected by de-" grees," it will no way (in that fenfe, in which it is true) turn to the advantage of his felect, fundamental, neceffary doctrines.

The next chapter has nothing in it but his great bug-bear, whereby he hopes to fright people from reading my book, by crying out, Socinianifm, Socinianifm! Whereas I challenge him again, to fhow one word of focinianifm in it. But, however, it is worth while to write a book to prove me a focinian. Truly, I did not think myfelf fo confiderable, that the world need be troubled about me, whether I were a follower of Socinus, Arminius, Calvin, or any other leader of a fect among chriftians. A chriftian I am fure I am, becaufe I be-lieve " Jefus to be the Meffiah," the King and Saviour promifed, and fent by God : and, as a fubject of his kingdom, I take the rule of my faith and life from his will, declared and left upon record in the infpired writings of the apoftles and evangelifts in the New Teftament; which I endeavour to the utmoft of my power, as is my duty, to underftand in their true fenfe and meaning. To lead me into their true meaning, I know (as I have above declared) no infallible guide, but the fame Holy Spirit, from whom thefe writings at firft came. If the unmafker knows any other infallible interpreter of fcripture, I defire him to direct me to him : until then, I fhall think it according to my mafter's rule, not to be called, nor to call any man on earth, Mafter. No man, I think, has a right to pre-fcribe to me my faith, or magifterially to impofe his interpretations or opinions on me : nor is it material to any one what mine are, any farther than they carry their own evidence with them. If this, which I think makes me of no fect, entitles me to the name of a papift, or a focinian, becaufe the unmafker thinks thefe the worft and moft invidious he can give me: and labours to fix them on me for no other reafon, but becaufe I will not take him for my mafter on earth, and his fyftem for my gofpel: I fhall leave him to recommend himfelf to the world by this fkill, who, no doubt, will have reafon to thank him for the rarenefs and fubtilty of his difcovery. For I think, I am the firft man that ever was found to be at the fame time a focinian, and a factor for Rome. But what is too hard for fuch an unmafker? I muft be what he thinks fit; when he pleafes, a papift; and when he pleafes, a focinian; and when he pleafes, a mahometan: and probably, when he has confidered a little better, an atheift; for I hardly efcaped it, when he writ laft. My book, he fays, had a tendency to it; and if he can but go on, as he has done hitherto, from furmifes to certainties, by that time he writes next, his difcovery will be advanced, and he will certainly find me an atheift. Only one thing I dare affure him of, that he fhall never find, that I treat the things of God or religion fo, as if I made only a trade or a jeft of them. But let us now fee, how at prefent he proves me a focinian.

His firft argument is, my not anfwering for my leaving out Matth. xxviii. 19, and John i. 1, page 82, of his Socinianifm unmafked. This he takes to be a confeffion, that I am a focinian. I hope he means fairly, and that if it be fo on my fide, it muft be taken for a ftanding rule between us, that where any thing is not anfwered, it muft be taken for granted. And upon that fcore I muft defire him to remember fome paffages of my Vindication, which I have already, and others, which I fhall mind him of hereafter, which he paffed over in filence, and had nothing to fay to; which therefore, by his own rule, I fhall defire the reader to obferve, that he has granted.

This being premifed, I muft tell the unmafker, that I perceive he reads my book with the fame underftanding that he writes his own. If he had done otherwife, he might have feen, that I had given him a reafon for my omiffion of thofe two, and other " plain and obvious
                                                    " paffages,

" passages, and famous testimonies in the evangelists,"
as he calls them ; where I say, p. 166, " That if I have
" left out out none of those passages or testimonies,
" which contain what our Saviour and his apostles
" preached and required assent to, to make men be-
" lievers, I shall think my omissions (let them be what
" they will) no faults in the present case. Whatever
" doctrines Mr. Edwards would have to be believed,
" to make a man a christian, he will be sure to find
" them in those preachings, and famous testimonies,
" of our Saviour and his apostles, I have quoted. And
" if they are not there, he may rest satisfied, that they
" were not proposed, by our Saviour and his apostles,
" as necessary to be believed to make men Christ's dis-
" ciples." . From which words, any one, but an unmasker, could have understood my answer to be, that
all that was necessary to be believed to make men
christians, might be found in what our Saviour and his
apostles proposed to unbelievers for their conversion :
but the two passages above-mentioned, as well as a
great many others in the evangelists, being none of
those, I had no reason to take notice of them. But the
unmasker having, out of his good pleasure, put it once
upon me, as he does in his " Thoughts of the causes of
" atheism," p. 107, that I was an " epitomizer of the
" evangelical writings," though every one may see I
make not that my business ; yet it is no matter for
that, I must be always accountable to that fancy of his.
But when he has proved,

> XLVIII. That this is not as just a reason for my
> omitting them, as several other obvious passages
> and famous testimonies in the evangelists, which I
> there mention, for whose omission he does not
> blame me ;

I will undertake to give him another reason, which I
know not whether he were not better let alone.
    The next proof of my being a socinian, is, that I take
the Son of God to be an expression used to signify the
Messiah. Slichtingius and Socinus understood it so ;
                                                    and

and therefore I am, the unmasker says, a socinian. Just as good an argument, as that I believe Jesus to be a prophet, and so do the mahometans; therefore I am a mahometan: or thus, the unmasker holds, that the apostles creed does not contain all things necessary to salvation; and so says Knot the jesuit; therefore the unmasker is a papist. Let me turn the tables, and by the same argument I am orthodox again. For two orthodox, pious, and very eminent prelates of our church, whom, when I follow authorities, I shall prefer to Slichtingius and Socinus, understand it as I do; and therefore I am orthodox. Nay, it so falls out, that if it were of force either way, the argument would weigh most on this side; since I am not wholly a stranger to the writings of those two orthodox bishops; but I never read a page in either of those socinians. The never sufficiently admired and valued archbishop Tillotson's words, which I quoted, the unmasker says, " do not " necessarily import any such thing." I know no words that necessarily import any thing to a caviller. But he was known to have such clear thoughts, and so clear a style, so far from having any thing doubtful or fallacious in what he said, that I shall only set down his words as they are in his sermon of sincerity, p. 2, to show his meaning: " Nathanael," says he, " being " satisfied, that he [our Saviour,] was the Messiah, he " presently owned him for such, calling him THE SON " OF GOD, and the King of Israel."

The words of the other eminent prelate, the bishop of Ely, whom our church is still happy in, are these: " To " be the Son of God, and to be Christ, being but " different expressions of the same thing:" witness, p. 14. And p. 10, " It is the very same thing to believe, " that Jesus is the Christ," and to believe, " that Jesus " is the Son of God, express it how you please." " This " alone is the faith which can regenerate a man, and " put a divine Spirit into him, that it makes him a " conqueror over the world, as Jesus was." Of this the unmasker says, that this reverend author, " speaking " only in a general way, represents these two as the " same thing," viz. that Jesus is the Christ, and that

Jesus

Jefus is the Son of God, becaufe thefe expreffions are applied to the fame perfon, and becaufe they are both comprehended in one general name, viz. Jefus. Anfw. The queftion is, Whether thefe two expreffions, " the " Son of God," and " the Meffiah," in the learned bifhop's opinion, fignify the fame thing? If his opinion had been afked in the point, I know not how he could have declared it more clearly. For he fays, they are " Expreffions of the fame thing;" and that it is the very fame thing to believe " that Jefus is the Mef- " fiah," and to believe, " that he is the Son of God;" which cannot be fo, if Meffiah and Son of God have different fignifications: for then they will make two diftinct propofitions in different fenfes, which it can be no more the fame thing to believe, than it is the fame thing to believe, that Mr. Edwards is a notable preacher, and a notable railer; or than it is to believe one truth, and all truths. For by the fame reafon, that it is the fame thing to believe two diftinct truths, it will be the fame thing to believe two thoufand diftinct truths, and confequently all truths. The unmafker, that he might feem to fay fomething, fays, that " the " reverend author reprefents thefe as the fame thing." Anfw. The unmafker never fails, like Midas, to turn every thing he touches into his own metal. The learned bifhop fays, very directly and plainly, that " to be " the Son of God, and to be the Meffiah, are expreffions " of the fame thing:" and the unmafker fays, he " reprefents thefe expreffions as one thing:" for it is of expreffions that both the bifhop and he fpeak. Now, expreffions can be one thing, but one of thefe two ways: either in found, and fo thefe two expreffions are not one; or in fignification, and fo they are. And then the unmafker fays, but in other words, what the bifhop had faid before, viz. That thefe two, " to be the Son " of God, and to be the Meffiah, are expreffions of the " fame thing." Only the unmafker has put in the word reprefents, to amufe his reader, as if he had faid fomething; and fo indeed he does, after his fafhion, i. e. obfcurely and fallacioufly; which, when it comes to be examined, is but the fame thing under fhow of a

difference;

difference; or elfe, if it has a different meaning, it is demonftratively falfe. But fo it be obfcure enough to deceive a willing reader, who will not be at the pains to examine what he fays, it ferves his turn.

But yet, as if he had faid fomething of weight, he gives reafons for putting " reprefents thefe two ex-" preffions as one thing," inftead of faying " thefe two " are but different expreffions of the fame thing."

The firft of his reafons is, Becaufe the reverend author is here " fpeaking only in a general way." Anfw. What does the unmafker mean by a general way? The learned bifhop fpeaks of two particular expreffions ap-plied to our Saviour. But was his difcourfe ever fo general, how could that alter the plain fignification of his words, viz. that thofe two are but " different ex-" preffions of the fame thing?"

Secondly, " Becaufe thefe expreffions are applied to the fame perfon." Anfw. A very demonftrative rea-fon, is it not? that therefore they cannot be different expreffions of the fame thing!

Thirdly, " And becaufe they are both comprehended " in one general name, viz. Jefus." Anfw. It requires fome fkill to put fo many falfhoods in fo few words; for neither both, nor either of thefe expreffions are com-prehended in the name, Jefus; and that Jefus, the name of a particular perfon, fhould be a general name, is a difcovery referved to be found out by this new logician. However, general, is a learned word, which when a man of learning has ufed twice, as a reafon of the fame thing, he is covered with generals. He need not trouble him-felf any farther about fenfe; he may fafely talk what ftuff he pleafes, without the leaft fufpicion of his reader.

Having thus ftrongly proved juft nothing, he pro-ceeds and tells us, p. 91, " Yet it does not follow " thence, but that if we will fpeak ftrictly and clofely, " we muft be forced to confefs, they are of different " fignifications." By which words (if his words have any fignification) he plainly allows, that the bifhop meant as he fays, that thefe two are but " different ex-" preffions of the fame thing:" but withal tells him, that, if he will " fpeak clofely and ftrictly," he muft

fay,

fay, " they are of different fignifications." My concernment in the cafe being only, that in the paffage
alleged, the reverend author faid, that the Son of God,
and the Mefliah, were " different expreffions of the
" fame thing," I have no more to demand after thefe
words of the unmafker; he has in them granted all I
would have: and I fhall not meddle with his " fpeaking
" clofely and ftrictly," but fhall leave it to the decifive
authority of this fuperlative critic to determine whether this learned bifhop, or any one living, befides himfelf, can underftand the phrafes of the New Teftament,
and " fpeak ftrictly and clofely" concerning them.
Perhaps, his being yet alive, may preferve this eminent
prelate from the malicious driveling of this unmafker's
pen, which has befpattered the afhes of two of the fame
order, who were no mean ornaments of the Englifh
church; and if they had been now alive, no-body will
doubt but the unmafker would have treated them after
another fafhion.

But let me afk the unmafker, whether if either of
thefe pious prelates, whofe words I have above quoted,
did underftand that phrafe of the Son of God to ftand
for the Mefliah; (which they might do without holding
any one focinian tenet) he will dare to pronounce him a
focinian? This is fo ridiculous an inference, that I
could not but laugh at it. But withal tell him, Vindic.
p. 172. " That if the fenfe, wherein I underftand thofe
" texts, be a miftake, I fhall be beholden to him to fet
" me right: but they are not popular authorities, or
" frightful names, whereby I judge of truth or falf-
" hood." To which I fubjoin thefe words: " You
" will now, no doubt, applaud your conjectures; the
" point is gained, and I am openly a focinian; fince
" I will not difown, that I think the Son of God was
" a phrafe, that, among the jews, in our Saviour's
" time, was ufed for the Mefliah, though the focinians
" underftood it in the fame fenfe. And therefore I
" muft certainly be of their perfuafion in every thing
" elfe. I admire the acutenefs, force, and fairnefs of
" your reafoning; and fo I leave you to triumph in
" your conjectures." Nor has he failed my expectation:
" for

" for here, p. 91, of his Socinianifm unmafked, he,
" upon this, erects his comb, and crows moft mightily.
" We may," fays he, " from hence, as well as other
" reafons, pronounce him the fame with thofe gentle-
" men (i. e. as he is pleafed to call them, my good
" patrons and friends, the racovians;) which you may
" perceive he is very apprehenfive of, and thinks, that
" this will be reckoned a good evidence of his being,
" what he denied himfelf to be before." " The point is
" gained, faith he, and I am openly a focinian." " He
" never uttered truer words in his life, and they are the
" confutation of all his pretences to the contrary. This
" truth, which unwarily dropped from his pen, confirms
" what I have laid to his charge." Now you have
fung your fong of triumph, it is fit you fhould gain your
victory, by fhowing,

> XLIX. How my underftanding the Son of God to
> be a phrafe ufed amongft the jews, in our Saviour's
> time, to fignify the Meffiah, proves me to be a
> focinian?

Or, if you think you have proved it already, I defire
you to put your proof into a fyllogifm: for I confefs
myfelf fo dull, as not to fee any fuch conclufion deduci-
ble from my underftanding that phrafe as I do, even
when you have proved that I am miftaken in it.

The places, which in the New Teftament fhow, that
the Son of God ftands for the Meffiah, are fo many
and fo clear, that I imagine no-body that ever confidered and compared them together, could doubt of their
meaning, unlefs he were an unmafker. Several of them
I have collected and fet down in my " Reafonablenefs
of Chriftianity," p. 17, 18, 19, 21, 28, 52.

Firft, John the Baptift, John i. 20, when the jews
fent to know who he was, confeffed he himfelf was not
the Meffiah. But of Jefus he fays, ver. 34, after having
feveral ways, in the foregoing verfes, declared him to
be the Meffiah: " And I faw and bare record, that this
" is the SON OF GOD." And again, chap. iii. 26—
36, he declaring Jefus to be, and himfelf not to be the
Meffiah,

Messiah, he does it in these synonymous terms, of the Messiah, and the Son of God; as appears by comparing ver. 28, 35, 36.

Nathanael owns him to be the Messiah, in these words, John i. 50, "Thou art the SON OF GOD, thou art the "King of Israel:" which our Saviour, in the next verse, calls believing; a term, all through the history of our Saviour, used for owning Jesus to be the Messiah. And for confirming that faith of his, that he was the Messiah, our Saviour further adds, that he should see greater things, i. e. should see him do greater miracles, to evidence that he was the Messiah.

Luke iv. 41, "And devils also came out of many, "crying, Thou art the Messiah, the Son of God; and "he, rebuking them, suffered them not to speak." And so again, St. Mark tells us, chap. iii. 11, 12, "That unclean spirits, when they saw him, fell down "before him, and cried, saying, Thou art the Son of "God. And he strictly charged them, that they should "not make him known." In both these places, which relate to different times, and different occasions, the devils declare Jesus to be the Son of God. It is certain, whatever they meant by it, they used a phrase of a known signification in that country: and what may we reasonably think they designed to make known to the people by it? Can we imagine these unclean spirits were promoters of the gospel, and had a mind to acknowledge and publish to the people the deity of our Saviour, which the unmasker would have to be the signification of the Son of God? Who can entertain such a thought? No, they were no friends to our Saviour: and therefore desired to spread a belief of him, that he was the Messiah, that so he might, by the envy of the scribes and pharisees, be disturbed in his ministry, and be cut off before he had completed it. And therefore we see, our Saviour in both places forbids them to make him known; as he did his disciples themselves, for the same reason. For when St. Peter, Matt. xvi. 16, had owned Jesus to be the Messiah, in these words: "Thou art the "Messiah, the Son of the living God;" it follows, ver. 20, "Then charged he his disciples, that they should

"tell

" tell no man that he was Jesus the Messiah :" just as he had forbid the devils to make him known, i. e. to be the Messiah.   Besides, these words here of St. Peter, can be taken in no other sense, but barely to signify, that Jesus was the Messiah, to make them a proper answer to our Saviour's question.   His first question here to his disciples, ver. 13, is, " Whom do men say, that I, the "Son of man," am ? The question is not, Of what original do you think the Messiah, when he comes, will be ? For then this question would have been as it is, Matt. xxii. 42, " What think ye of the Messiah, whose Son is he ?" if he had inquired about the common opinion, concerning the nature and descent of the Messiah.   But this question is concerning himself: Whom, of all the extraordinary persons known to the jews, or mentioned in their sacred writings, the people thought him to be ? That this was the meaning of his question, is evident from the answer the apostles gave to it, and his further demand, ver. 14, 15, " They said, Some say thou art John the Baptist, some Elias, and others Jeremias, or one of the prophets.   He saith unto them, But whom say ye that I am ? The people take me, some for one of the prophets or extraordinary messengers from God, and some for another : But which of them do you take me to be ? " Simon Peter answered and said, Thou art the " Messiah, the Son of the living God." In all which discourse, it is evident there was not the least inquiry made by our Saviour concerning the person, nature, or qualifications of the Messiah ; but whether the people or his apostles thought him, i. e. Jesus of Nazareth, to be the Messiah.   To which St. Peter gave him a direct and plain answer in the foregoing words, declaring their belief of him to be the Messiah : which is all that, with any manner of congruity, could be made the sense of St. Peter's answer.   This alone of itself were enough to justify my interpretation of St. Peter's words, without the authority of St. Mark and St. Luke, both whose words confirm it. For St. Mark, chap. viii. 29, renders it, " Thou art the Messiah ;" and St. Luke, chap. ix. 20, " The Messiah of God." To the like question, " Who " art thou ?" John the Baptist gives a like answer,

John

John i. 19, 20, " I am not the Chrift." By which anfwer, as well as by the foregoing verfes, it is plain, nothing was underftood to be meant by that queftion, but, Which of the extraordinary perfons, promifed to, or expected by, the jews art thou?

John xi. 27, the phrafe of the Son of God is made ufe of by Martha; and that it was ufed by her to fignify the Meffiah, and nothing elfe, is evident out of the context. Martha tells our Saviour, that if he had been there, before her brother died, he, by that divine power which he had manifefted in fo many miracles which he had done, could have faved his life; and that now, if our Saviour would afk it of God, he might obtain the reftoration of his life. Jefus tells her, he fhall rife again: which words, Martha taking to mean, at the general refurrection, at the laft day; Jefus thereupon takes occafion to intimate to her, that he was the Meffiah, by telling her, that he was " the refurrection " and the life;" i. e. that the life, which mankind fhould receive at the general refurrection, was by and through him. This was a defcription of the Meffiah, it being a received opinion among the jews, that when the Meffiah came, the juft fhould rife, and live with him for ever. And having made this declaration of himfelf to be the Meffiah, he afks Martha, " Believeft " thou this?" What? Not whofe fon the Meffiah fhould be; but whether he himfelf was the Meffiah, by whom believers fhould have eternal life at the laft day. And to this fhe gives this direct and appofite anfwer: " Yea, Lord, I believe that thou art the Chrift, the Son " of God, which fhould come into the world." The queftion was only, Whether fhe was perfuaded, that thofe, who believed in him, fhould be raifed to eternal life; that was in effect, " Whether he was the Meffiah?" And to this fhe anfwers, Yea, Lord, I believe this of thee: and then fhe explains what was contained in that faith of her's; even this, that he was the Meffiah, that was promifed to come, by whom alone men were to receive eternal life.

What the jews alfo underftood by the Son of God, is likewife clear from that paffage at the latter end of

Luke xxii.   They having taken our Saviour, and being
very defirous to get a confeffion from his own mouth,
that he was the Meffiah, that they might be from
thence able to raife a formal and prevalent accufation
againft him before Pilate; the only thing the council
afked him, was, Whether he was the Meffiah? v. 67.
To which he anfwers fo, in the following words, that
he lets them fee he underftood, that the defign of their
queftion was to entrap him, and not to believe in him,
whatever he fhould declare of himfelf.   But yet he tells
them, " Hereafter fhall the Son of man fit on the right
" hand of the power of God :" Words that, to the jews
plainly enough owned him to be the Meffiah; but yet
fuch as could not have any force againft him with Pilate.
He having confeffed fo much, they hope to draw yet a
clearer confeffion from him.   " Then faid they all,
" Art thou then the Son of God ? And he faid unto them,
" Ye fay that I am.   And they faid, What need we
" any further witnefs ? For we ourfelves have heard of
" his own mouth."   Can any one think, that the doctrine of his deity (which is that which the unmafker
accufes me for waving) was that which the jews defigned to accufe our Saviour of, before Pilate; or that
they needed witneffes for? Common fenfe, as well as the
current of the whole hiftory, fhows the contrary.   No,
it was to accufe him, that he owned himfelf to be the
Meffiah, and thereby claimed a title to be King of the
Jews. The Son of God was fo known a name amongft the
jews, to ftand for the Meffiah; that having got that from
his mouth, they thought they had proof enough for
treafon againft him.   This carries with it a clear and
eafy meaning.   But if the Son of God be to be taken,
as the unmafker would have it, for a declaration of his
deity, I defire him to make common and coherent
fenfe of it.

    I fhall add one confideration more to fhow that the
Son of God was a form of fpeech then ufed among the
jews, to fignify the Meffiah, from the perfons that ufed
it, viz. John the Baptift, Nathanael, St. Peter, Martha,
the Sanhedrim, and the centurion, Matt. xxvii. 54.
Here are jews, heathens, friends, enemies, men, women,
                                                believers

believers and unbelievers, all indifferently use this phrase of the Son of God, and apply it to Jesus. The question between the unmasker and me, is, Whether it was used by these several persons, as an appellation of the Messiah, or (as the unmasker would have it) in a quite different sense: as such an application of divinity to our Saviour, that he that shall deny that to be the meaning of it in the minds of these speakers, denies the divinity of Jesus Christ. For if they did speak it without that meaning, it is plain it was a phrase known to have another meaning; or else they had talked unintelligible jargon. Now I will ask the unmasker, " Whether he " thinks, that the eternal generation, or, as the un- " masker calls it, filiation of Jesus the Son of God, " was a doctrine that had entered into the thoughts of " all the persons above-mentioned, even of the Roman " centurion, and the soldiers that were with him watching " Jesus?" If he says he does, I suppose he thinks so only for this time, and for this occasion: and then it will lie upon him to give the world convincing reasons for his opinion, that they may think so too; or if he does not think so, he must give up his argument, and allow that this phrase, in these places, does not necessarily import the deity of our Saviour, and the doctrine of his eternal generation: and so a man may take it to be an expression standing for the Messiah, without being a socinian, any more than he himself is one.

" There is one place, the unmasker tells us, p. 87, " that confutes all the surmises about the identity of " these terms. It is, says he, that famous confession " of faith which the Ethiopian eunuch made, when " Philip told him, he might be baptized, if he be- " lieved. This, without doubt, was said, according to " that apprehension, which he had of Christ, from " Philip's instructing him; for he said he preached " unto him Jesus, ver. 35. He had acquainted him, " that Jesus was the Christ, the anointed of God, and " also, that he was the Son of God; which includes " in it, that he was God. And accordingly, this noble " proselyte gives this account of his faith, in order to " his being baptized, in order to his being admitted a

" member

" member of Chrift's church:"   " I believe that Jefus
" is the Son of God:" or you may read it according to
" the Greek, I believe the Son of God to be Jefus
" Chrift." Where there are thefe two diftinct propofitions :

" 1ft, That Jefus is the Chrift, the Meffiah.
" 2dly, That he is not only the Meffiah, but the Son
" of God."

The unmafker is every-where fteadily the fame
fubtle arguer. Whether he has proved that the Son of
God, in this confeffion of the eunuch, fignifies what he
would have, we fhall examine by and by. This at leaft
is demonftration, that this paffage of his overturns his
principles ; and reduces his long lift of fundamentals to
two propofitions, the belief whereof is fufficient to
make a man a chriftian. " This noble profelyte, fays
" the unmafker, gives this account of his faith, in order
" to his being baptized, in order to his being admitted
" a member of Chrift's church." And what is that
faith, according to the unmafker? he tells you, " there
" are in it thefe two diftinct propofitions, viz. I be-
" lieve, 1ft, That Jefus is the Chrift, the Meffiah:
" 2dly, That he is not only the Meffiah, but the Son of
" God." If this famous confeffion, containing but
thefe two articles, were enough to his being baptized ;
if this faith were fufficient to make this noble profelyte
a chriftian ; what is become of all thofe other articles
of the unmafker's fyftem, without the belief whereof,
he, in other places, tells us, a man cannot be a chriftian ?
If he had here told us, that " Philip had not time nor
" opportunity," during his fhort ftay with the eunuch,
to explain to him all the unmafker's fyftem, and make
him underftand all his fundamentals ; he had had reafon
on his fide : and he might have urged it as a reafon why
Philip taught him no more. But neverthelefs he had,
by allowing the eunuch's confeffion of faith fufficient
for his admittance as a member of Chrift's church,
given up his other fundamentals, as neceffary to be believed to make a man a chriftian ; even that of the Holy
Trinity ; and he has at laft reduced his neceffary articles
to thefe two, viz. " That Jefus is the Meffiah ;" and
                                        that

that " Jesus is the Son of God." So that, after his ridiculous calling mine a lank faith, I desire him to consider what he will now call his own. Mine is next to none, because, as he says, it is but one article. If that reasoning be good, his is not far from none; it consists but in two articles, which is next to one, and very little more remote from none than one is. If any one had but as much wit as the unmasker, and could be but as smart upon the number two, as he has been upon an unit, here were a brave opportunity for him to lay out his parts ; and he might make vehement complaints against one, that has thus " cramped our faith, cor-
" rupted men's minds, depraved the gospel, and
" abused christianity." But if it should fall out, as I think it will, that the unmasker's two articles should prove to be but one ; he has saved another that labour, and he stands painted to himself with his own charcoal.

The unmasker would have the Son of God, in the confession of the eunuch, to signify something different from the Messiah : and his reason is, because else it would be an absurd tautology. Ans. There are many exegetical expressions put together in scripture, which, though they signify the same thing, yet are not absurd tautologies. The unmasker here inverts the proposition, and would have it to signify thus : " The Son of God
" is Jesus the Messiah ;" which is a proposition so different from what the apostles proposed, every-where else, that he ought to have given a reason why, when, every-where else, they made the proposition to be, of something affirmed of Jesus of Nazareth, the eunuch should make the affirmation to be of something concerning the Son of God : as if the eunuch knew very well, what the Son of God signified, viz. as the un-masker tells us here, that it included or signified God ; and that Philip (who, we read, at Samaria preached τὸν Χριςὸν, the Messiah, i. e. instructed them who the Messiah was) had here taken pains only to instruct him, that this God was Jesus the Messiah, and to bring him to assent to that proposition. Whether this be natural to conceive, I leave to the reader.

The

The tautology, on which the unmasker builds his whole objection, will be quite removed if we take Chrift here for a proper name, in which way it is ufed by the evangelifts and apoftles in other places, and particularly by St. Luke, in Acts ii. 38. iii. 6, 20. iv. 10. xxiv. 24, &c. In two of thefe places it cannot, with any good fenfe, be taken otherwife; for, if it be not in Acts iii. 6, and iv. 10, ufed as a proper name, we muft read thofe places thus, " Jefus the Meffiah of Naza-" reth." And I think it plain in thofe others cited, as well as in feveral other places of the New Teftament, that the word Chrift is ufed as a proper name. We may eafily conceive, that long before the Acts were writ, the name of Chrift was grown, by a familiar ufe, to denote the perfon of our Saviour, as much as Jefus. This is fo manifeft, that it gave a name to his followers ; who, as St. Luke tells us, xi. 26, were called chriftians ; and that, if chronologifts miftake not, twenty years before St. Luke writ his hiftory of the apoftles : and this fo generally, that Agrippa, a Jew, ufes it, Acts xxvi. 28. And that Chrift, as the proper name of our Saviour, was got as far as Rome, before St. Luke writ the Acts, appears out of Suetonius, l. 5. and by that name he is called in Tacitus, Ann. l. 15. It is no wonder then, that St. Luke, in writing this hiftory, fhould fometimes fet it down alone, fometimes joined with that of Jefus, as a proper name ; which is much eafier to conceive he did here, than that Philip propofed more to the eunuch to be believed to make him a chriftian, than what, in other places, was propofed for the converfion of others, or than what he himfelf propofed at Samaria.

His 7th chapter is, to prove, that I am a focinian, becaufe I omitted Chrift's fatisfaction. That matter having been anfwered, p. 265, where it came properly under confideration, I fhall only obferve here, that the great ftrefs of his argument lies as it did before, not upon my total omiffion of it out of my book, but on this, that " I have no fuch thing in the place where the " advantages of Chrift's coming are purpofely treated " of;" from whence he will have this to be an un-avoidable inference, viz. " That I was of opinion, that

Chrift

" Christ came not to satisfy for us." The reason of my omission of it in that place, I told him, was because my book was chiefly designed for deists ; and therefore I mentioned only those advantages, which all christians must agree in ; and, in omitting of that, complied with the apostle's rule, Rom. xiv. To this he tells me flatly, that was not the design of my book. Whether the un-masker knows with what design I published it, better than myself, must be left to the reader to judge : for as for his veracity in what he knows, or knows not, he has given so many instances of it, that I may safely refer that to any body. One instance more of it may be found in this very chapter, where he says, " I pretend
" indeed, pag. 163, that, in another place of my book,
" I mention Christ's restoring all mankind from the
" state of death, and restoring them to life : and his
" laying down his life for another, as our Saviour pro-
" fesses he did. These few words this vindicator has
" picked up in his book since he wrote it. This is all,
" through his whole treatise, that he hath dropped con-
" cerning that advantage of Christ's incarnation ; i. e.
" Christ's satisfaction." Answ. But that this is not all that I have dropped through my whole treatise, con-cerning that advantage, may appear by those places above-mentioned, p. 163, where I say, that the design of Christ's coming was to be offered up, and speak of the work of redemption ; which are expressions taken to imply our Saviour's satisfaction. But the unmasker thinking I should have quoted them, if there had been any more, besides those mentioned in my vindication, upon that presumption sticks not boldly to affirm, that there were no more ; and so goes on with the veracity of an unmasker. If affirming would do it, nothing could be wanting in his cause, that might be for his purpose. Whether he be as good at proving, this con-sequence (among other propositions, which remain upon him to be proved) will try, viz.

L. That if the satisfaction of Christ be not mentioned
    in the place where the advantages of Christ's
    coming are purposely treated of, then I am of opi-
    nion, that Christ came not to satisfy for us :

Which

Which is all the argument of his 7th chapter.

His laſt chapter, as his firſt, begins with a commendation of himſelf; particularly, it boaſts his freedom from bigotiſm, dogmatizing, cenſorioufnefs, and uncharitablenefs. I think he hath drawn himſelf ſo well with his own pen, that I ſhall need refer the reader only to what he himſelf has wrote in this controverſy, for his character.

In the next paragraph, p. 104, he tells me, " I laugh " at orthodoxy." Anſw. There is nothing that I think deſerves a more ſerious eſteem than right opinion, (as the word ſignifies) if taken up with the ſenfe and love of truth. But this way of becoming orthodox has always modeſty accompanying it, and a fair acknowledgment of fallibility in ourſelves, as well as a ſuppoſition of errour in others. On the other ſide there is nothing more ridiculous, than for any man, or company of men, to aſſume the title of orthodoxy to their own ſet of opinions, as if infallibility were annexed to their ſyſtems, and thoſe were to be the ſtanding meaſure of truth to all the world; from whence they erect to themſelves a power to cenfure and condemn others, for differing at all from the tenets they have pitched upon. The conſideration of human frailty ought to check this vanity: but ſince it does not, but that, with a ſort of allowance, it ſhows itſelf in almoſt all religious ſocieties, the playing the trick round ſufficiently turns it into ridicule. For each ſociety having an equal right to a good opinion of themſelves, a man by paſſing but a river, or a hill, loſes that orthodoxy in one company, which puffed him up with ſuch aſſurance and inſolence in another; and is there, with equal juſtice, himſelf expoſed to the like cenfures of errour and hereſy, which he was ſo forward to lay on others at home. When it ſhall appear, that infallibility is intailed upon one ſet of men of any denomination, or truth confined to any ſpot of ground, the name and uſe of orthodoxy, as now it is in faſhion every-where, will in that one place be reaſonable. Until then, this ridiculous cant will be a foundation too weak to ſuſtain that uſurpation that is raiſed upon it. It is not that I do not think every one ſhould be per-

ſuaded

ſuaded of the truth of thoſe opinions he profeſſes. It is
that I contend for; and it is that which I fear the great
ſticklers for orthodoxy often fail in. For we ſee generally that numbers of them exactly jump in a whole
large collection of doctrines, conſiſting of abundance of
particulars; as if their notions were, by one common
ſtamp, printed on their minds, even to the leaſt linea-
ment. This is very hard, if not impoſſible, to be conceived of thoſe who take up their opinions only from
conviction. But, how fully ſoever I am perſuaded of
the truth of what I hold, I am in common juſtice to
allow the ſame ſincerity to him that differs from me;
and ſo we are upon equal terms. This perſuaſion of
truth on each ſide, inveſts neither of us with a right to
cenſure or condemn the other. I have no more reaſon
to treat him ill for differing from me, than he has to
treat me ill for the ſame cauſe. Pity him, I may; inform him fairly, I ought: but contemn, malign, revile,
or any otherwiſe prejudice him for not thinking juſt as I
do, that I ought not. My orthodoxy gives me no more
authority over him, than his (for every one is orthodox
to himſelf) gives him over me. When the word orthodoxy (which in effect ſignifies no more but the opinions
of my party) is made uſe of as a pretence to domineer,
(as ordinarily it is) it is, and always will be, ridiculous.

He ſays, " I hate, even with a deadly hatred, all cate-
" chiſms and confeſſions, all ſyſtems and models." I
do not remember, that I have once mentioned the word
catechiſm, either in my Reaſonableneſs of Chriſtianity,
or Vindication; but he knows " I hate them deadly,"
and I know I do not. And as for ſyſtems and models,
all that I ſay of them, in the pages he quotes to prove
my hatred of them, is only this, viz. in my Vindication, p.
164, 165, " Some had rather you ſhould write booty, and
" croſs your own deſign of removing men's prejudices to
" chriſtianity, than leave out one tittle of what they
" put into their ſyſtems.—Some men will not bear it,
" that any one ſhould ſpeak of religion, but according
" to the model that they themſelves have made of it."
In neither of which places do I ſpeak againſt ſyſtems or
models, but the ill uſe that ſome men make of them.

He

He tells me also in the same place, p. 104, that I deride mysteries. But for this he hath quoted neither words nor place: and where he does not do that, I have reason, from the frequent liberties he takes to impute to me what no-where appears in my books, to desire the reader to take what he says not to be true. For did he mean fairly, he might, by quoting my words, put all such matters of fact out of doubt; and not force me, so often as he does, to demand where it is: as I do now here again,

LI. Where it is that I deride mysteries?

His next words, p. 104, are very remarkable: they are, "O how he [the vindicator] grins at the spirit of
" creed-making! p. 169, Vindic. The very thoughts
" of which do so haunt him, so plague and torment him,
" that he cannot rest until it be conjured down. And
" here, by the way, seeing I have mentioned his ran-
" cour against systematic books and writings, I might
" represent the misery that is coming upon all book-
" sellers, if this gentleman and his correspondence go
" on successfully. Here is an effectual plot to under-
" mine Stationers-hall; for all systems and bodies of
" divinity, philosophy, &c. must be cashiered: what-
" soever looks like system must not be bought or sold.
" This will fall heavy on the gentlemen of St. Paul's
" church-yard, and other places." Here the politic
unmasker seems to threaten me with the posse of Paul's
church-yard, because my book might lessen their gain in
the sale of theological systems. I remember that " De-
" metrius the shrine-maker, which brought no small
" gain to the craftsmen, whom he called together, with
" the workmen of like occupation, and said to this
" purpose: Sirs, ye know, that by this craft we have
" our wealth: moreover ye see and hear, that this Paul
" hath persuaded, and turned away much people, saying
" that they be no gods that are made with hands; so
" that this our craft is in danger to be set at nought.
" And when they heard these sayings, they were full of
" wrath, and cried out, saying, Great is Diana of the
                                    " Ephesians."

" Ephesians." Have you, sir, who are so good at speech-making, as a worthy successor of the silver-smith, regulating your zeal for the truth, and your writing divinity by the profit it will bring, made a speech to this purpose to the craftsmen, and told them, that I say, articles of faith, and creeds, and systems in religion, cannot be made by men's hands or fancies; but must be just such, and no other than what God hath given us in the scriptures? And are they ready to cry out to your content, " Great is Diana of the Ephesians?" If you have well warmed them with your oratory, it is to be hoped they will heartily join with you, and bestir themselves, and choose you for their champion, to prevent the misery, you tell them, is coming upon them, in the loss of the sale of systems and bodies of divinity: for, as for philosophy, which you name too, I think you went a little too far; nothing of that kind, as I remember, hath been so much as mentioned. But, however, some sort of orators, when their hands are in, omit nothing, true or false, that may move those they would work upon. Is not this a worthy employment, and becoming a preacher of the gospel, to be a solicitor for Stationers-hall? And make the gain of the gentlemen of Paul's church-yard, a consideration for or against any book writ concerning religion? This, if it were ever thought on before, nobody but an unmasker, who lays all open, was ever so foolish as to publish. But here you have an account of his zeal: the views of gain are to measure the truths of divinity. Had his zeal, as he pretends in the next paragraph, no other aims, but the " defence of the gospel;" it is probable this controversy would have been managed after another fashion.

Whether what he says in the next, p. 105, to excuse his so often pretending to " know my heart and " thoughts," will satisfy the reader; I shall not trouble myself. By his so often doing it again, in his Socinianism unmasked, I see he cannot write without it. And so I leave it to the judgment of the readers, whether he can be allowed to know other men's thoughts, who, on many occasions, seems not well to know his own. The railing in the remainder of this chapter I shall pass by,

as

as I have done a great deal of the fame ftrain in his book : only to fhow how well he underſtands or repreſents my fenſe, I ſhall ſet down my words, as they are in the pages he quotes, and his inferences from them.

Vindication, p. 171.

I know not but it may be true that the anti-trini-tarians and racovians un-derſtand thoſe places as I do ; but it is more than I know, that they do ſo. I took not my fenſe of thoſe texts from thoſe writers, but from the ſcripture itſelf, giving light to its own meaning, by one place compared with another. What, in this way, appears to me its true meaning, I ſhall not decline, becauſe I am told, that it is ſo un-derſtood by the racovians, whom I never yet read ; nor embrace the contrary, though the generality of

Socinianiſm Unmaſked, p. 108.

" The profeſſed divines " of England you muſt " know, are but a pitiful " ſort of folks with this " great racovian rabbi. " He tells us plainly, that " he is not mindful of what " the generality of divines " declare for, p. 171. He " labours ſo concernedly " to ingratiate himſelf with " the mob, the multitude " (which he ſo often talks " of) that he has no regard " to theſe. The generality of " the rabble are more con-" ſiderable with him than " the generality of divines."

divines I more converſe with, ſhould declare for it. If the ſenſe wherein I underſtand thoſe texts be a miſtake, I ſhall be beholden to you, if you will ſet me right. But they are not popular authorities, or frightful names, whereby I judge of truth or falſhood.

He tells me here of the generality of divines. If he had ſaid of the church of England, I could have under-ſtood him : but he ſays, " The profeſſed divines of Eng-" land ;" and there being ſeveral ſorts of divines in England, who, I think, do not every-where agree in their interpretations of ſcripture ; which of them is it I muſt have regard to, where they differ ? If he cannot tell me that, he complains here of me for a fault, which he himſelf knows not how to mend.

Vindication,

Vindication, p. 169.

The lift of materials for his creed, (for the articles are not yet formed) Mr. Edwards clofes, p. 111, with thefe words: " Thefe are " the matters of faith con- " tained in the epiftles; and " they are effential and in- " tegral parts of the gofpel " itfelf."

Socinianifm Unmafked, p. 109.

" This author, as de- " mure and grave as he " would fometimes feem " to be, can fcoff at the " matters of faith con- " tained in the apoftles " epiftles, p. 169."

What! juft thefe, neither more nor lefs? If you are fure of it, pray let us have them fpeedily, for the reconciling of differences in the chriftian church, which has been fo cruelly torn about the articles of the chriftian faith, to the great reproach of chriftian charity, and fcandal of our true religion.

Does the vindicator here " fcoff at the matters of " faith contained in the epiftles?" or fhow the vain pretences of the unmafker: who undertakes to give us, out of the epiftles, a collection of fundamentals, without being able to fay, whether thofe he fets down be all or no?

Vindication, p. 176.

I hope you do not think, how contemptibly foever you fpeak of the venerable mob, as you are pleafed to dignify them, p. 117, that the bulk of mankind, or, in your phrafe, the rabble, are not

Socinianifm Unmafked, p. 110.

" To coax the mob, " he profanely brings in " that place of fcripture; " Have any of the rulers " believed in him?"

concerned in religion; or ought not to underftand it, in order to their falvation. I remember the pharifees treated the common people with contempt; and faid, " Have any of the rulers, or of the pharifees, believed " in him? But this people who know not the law, are " curfed." But yet thefe, who in the cenfure of the pharifees, were curfed, were fome of the poor, or, if you pleafe to have it fo, the mob, to whom the gofpel

was

was preached by our Saviour, as he tells John's difciples, Matt. xi. 5.

Where the profanenefs of this is, I do not fee; unlefs fome unknown facrednefs of the unmafker's perfon make it profanenefs to fhow, that he, like the pharifees of old, has a great contempt for the common people, i. e. the far greater part of mankind; as if they and their falvation were below the regard of this elevated rabbi. But this, of profanenefs, may be well born from him, fince in the next words my mentioning another part of his carriage is no lefs than irreligion.

Vindication, p. 173.	Socinianifm Unmafked,
He prefers what I fay to him myfelf, to what is offered to him, from the word of God, and makes me this compliment, that I begin to mend about the clofe, i. e. when I leave off quoting of fcripture, and the dull work	p. 110. "Ridiculoufly and ir- "religioufly he pretends," that I prefer what he faith to me to what is offered to me from the word of God, p. 173.

was done "of going through the hiftory of the Evange- "lifts and the Acts," which he computes, p. 105, to take up three quarters of my book.

The matter of fact is as I relate it, and fo is beyond pretence; and for this I refer the reader to the 105th and 114th pages of his "Thoughts concerning the "caufes of atheifm." But had I miftaken, I know not how he could have called it, irreligioufly. Make the worft of it that can be, how comes it to be irreligious? What is there divine in an unmafker, that one cannot pretend, (true or falfe) that he prefers what I fay, to what is offered him from the word of God, without doing it irreligioufly? Does the very affuming the power to define articles, and determine who are, and who are not chriftians, by a creed not yet made, erect an unmafker prefently into God's throne, and beftow on him the title of Dominus Deufque nofter, whereby offences againft him come to be irreligious acts? I have

mif-

mifreprefented his meaning ; let it be fo : Where is the
irreligion of it ? Thus it is : the power of making a religion for others, (and thofe that make creeds do that)
being once got into any one's fancy, muft at laft make
all oppofitions to thofe creeds and creed-makers irreligion. Thus we fee, in procefs of time, it did in the
church of Rome : but it was in length of time, and by
gentle degrees. The unmafker, it feems, cannot ftay,
is in hafte, and at one jump leaps into the chair. He
has given us yet but a piece of his creed, and yet that's
enough to fet him above the ftate of human miftakes or
frailties ; and to mention any fuch thing in him, is to do
irreligioufly.

"We may further fee," fays the unmafker, p. 110,
"how counterfeit the vindicator's gravity is, whilft he
"condemns frothy and light difcourfes," p.173.Vindic.
And "yet, in many pages together, moft irreverently
treats a great part of the apoftolical writings, and throws
afide the main articles of religion, as unneceffary." Anfwer in my Vindic. p. 170, you may remember thefe
words : "I require you to publifh to the world thofe
"paffages, which fhow my contempt of the epiftles."
Why do you not (efpecially having been fo called upon
to do it) fet down thofe words, wherein "I moft ir-
"reverently treat a great part of the apoftolical writ-
"ings ?" At leaft, why do you not quote thofe many
pages wherein I do it ? This looks a little fufpicioufly,
that you cannot : and the more becaufe you have, in this
very page, not been fparing to quote places which you
thought to your purpofe. I muft take leave, therefore,
(if it may be done without irreligion) to affure the reader, that this is another of your many miftakes in matters of fact, for which you have not fo much as the excufe of inadvertency : for, as he fees, you have been
minded of it before. But an unmafker, fay what you
will to him, will be an unmafker ftill.

He clofes what he has to fay to me, in his Socinianifm
unmafked, as if he were in the pulpit, with an ufe of
exhortation. The falfe infinuations it is filled with
make the conclufion of a piece with the introduction.
As he fets out, fo he ends, and therein fhows wherein

he

he places his ftrength. A cuftom of making bold with truth is fo feldom curable in a grown man, and the unmafker fhows fo little fenfe of fhame, where it is charged upon him, beyond a poffibility of clearing himfelf, that no-body is to trouble themfelves any farther about that part of his eftablifhed character. Letting therefore that alone to nature and cuftom, two fure guides, I fhall only intreat him, to prevent his taking railing for argument, (which I fear he too often does) that upon his entrance, every-where, upon any new argument, he would fet it down in fyllogifm ; and when he has done that (that I may know what is to be anfwered) let him then give vent, as he pleafes, to his noble vein of wit and oratory.

The lifting a man's felf up in his own opinion, has had the credit, in former ages, to be thought the loweft degradation that human nature could well fink itfelf to. Hence, fays the wife man, Prov. xxvi. 5, " Anfwer a " fool according to his folly, left he be wife in his own " conceit :" hereby fhowing, that felf-conceitednefs is a degree beneath ordinary folly. And therefore he there provides a fence againft it, to keep even fools from finking yet lower, by falling into it. Whether what was not fo in Solomon's days be now, by length of time, in ours, grown into a mark of wifdom and parts, and an evidence of great performances, I fhall not inquire. Mr. Edwards, who goes beyond all that ever I yet met with, in the commendation of his own, beft knows why he fo extols what he has done in this controverfy. For fear the praifes he has not been fparing of, in his Socinianifm unmafked, fhould not fufficiently trumpet out his worth, or might be forgotten ; he, in a new piece, intitled, " the Socinian creed," proclaims again his mighty deeds, and the victory he has eftablifhed to himfelf by them, in thefe words: " But he and " his friends (the one-article men) feem to have made " fatisfaction, by their profound filence lately, whereby " they acknowledge to the world, that they have nothing " to fay in reply to what I laid to their charge, and fully " proved againft them, &c." Socinian creed, p. 128. This frefh teftimony of no ordinary conceit, which Mr.

Edwards

Edwards hath, of the excellency and strength of his reasoning, in his Socinianism unmasked, I leave with him
and his friends, to be considered of at their leisure : and,
if they think I have misapplied the term of conceited-
ness, to so wise, understanding, and every way accomplished a disputant, (if we may believe himself) I will
teach them a way how he, or any body else, may fully
convince me of it. There remains on his score, marked
in this reply of mine, several propositions to be proved
by him. If he can find but arguments to prove them,
that will bear the setting down in form, and will so
publish them, I will allow myself to be mistaken. Nay,
which is more, if he, or any body, in the 112 pages of
his Socinianism unmasked, can find but ten arguments
that will bear the test of syllogism, the true touchstone
of right arguing ; I will grant, that that treatise deserves
all those commendations he has bestowed upon it, though
it be made up more of his own panegyric, than a confutation of me.

In his socinian creed, (for a creed-maker he will be ;
and whether he has been as lucky for the socinians as
for the orthodox, I know not) p. 120, he begins with
me, and that with the same conquering hand and skill,
which can never fail of victory ; if a man has but wit
enough to know what proposition he is able to confute,
and then make that his adversary's tenet. But the repetitions of his old song concerning one article, the
epistles, &c. which occur here again, I shall only set
down, that none of these excellent things may be lost,
whereby this acute and unanswerable writer has so well
deserved his own commendations : viz. " That I say,
" there is but one single article of the christian truth
" necessary to be believed and assented to by us, p. 121.
" That I slight the christian principles, curtail the arti-
" cles of our faith, and ravish christianity itself from
" him, p. 123. And that I turn the epistles of the
" apostles into waste paper," p. 127.

These and the like slanders I have already given an
answer to, in my reply to his former book. Only one
new one here I cannot pass over in silence, because of the
remarkable profaneness which seems to me to be in it ;

which, I think, deferves public notice. In my 'Reafonablenefs of Chriftianity," I have laid together thofe paffages of our Saviour's life, which feemed to me moft eminently to fhow his wifdom, in that conduct of himfelf, with that referve and caution which was neceffary to preferve him, and carry him through the appointed time of his miniftry. Some have thought I had herein done confiderable fervice to the chriftian religion, by removing thofe objections which fome were apt to make from our Saviour's carriage, not rightly underftood. This creed-maker tells me, p. 127, "That "I make our Saviour a coward:" a word not to be applied to the Saviour of the world by a pious or difcrete chriftian, upon any pretence, without great neceffity, and fure grounds! If he had fet down my words, and quoted the page, (which was the leaft could have been done to excufe fuch a phrafe) we fhould then have feen which of us two this impious and irreligious epithet, given to the holy Jefus, has for its author. In the mean time, I leave it with him, to be accounted for, by his piety, to thofe, who by his example fhall be encouraged to entertain fo vile a thought, or ufe fo profane an expreffion of the Captain of our falvation, who freely gave himfelf up to death for us.

He alfo fays in the fame page, 127, "That I every- "where ftrike at fyftems, the defign of which is to "eftablifh one of my own, or to fofter fcepticifm, by "beating down all others."

For clear reafon, or good fenfe, I do not think our creed-maker ever had his fellow. In the immediately preceding words of the fame fentence he charges me with "a great antipathy againft fyftems;" and, before he comes to the end of it, finds out my defign to be the "eftablifhing one of my own." So that this, "my antipathy againft fyftems" makes me in love with one. "My defign, he fays, is to eftablifh a fyftem of "my own, or to fofter fcepticifm, in beating down all "others." Let my book, if he pleafes, be my fyftem of chriftianity. Now is it in me any more foftering fcepticifm to fay my fyftem is true, and others not, than it is in the creed-maker to fay fo of all other fyftems but

but his own? For I hope he does not allow any fyftem of chriftianity to be true, that differs from his, any more than I do.

But I have fpoken againft all fyftems. Anfw. And always fhall, fo far as they are fet up by particular men, or parties, as the juft meafure of every man's faith; wherein every thing that is contained, is required and impofed to be believed to make a man a chriftian: fuch an opinion and ufe of fyftems I fhall always be againft, until the creed-maker fhall tell me, amongft the variety of them, which alone is to be received and refted in, in the abfence of his creed; which is not yet finifhed, and, I fear, will not, as long as I live. That every man fhould receive from others, or make to himfelf fuch a fyftem of chriftianity, as he found moft conformable to the word of God, according to the beft of his underftanding, is what I never fpoke againft: but think it every one's duty to labour for, and to take all opportunities, as long as he lives, by ftudying the fcriptures every day, to perfect.

But this, I fear, will not go eafily down with our author; for then he cannot be a creed-maker for others: a thing he fhows himfelf very forward to be; how able to perform it, we fhall fee when his creed is made. In the mean time, talking loudly and at random, about fundamentals, without knowing what is fo, may ftand him in fome ftead.

This being all that is new, which I think myfelf concerned in, in this focinian creed, I pafs on to his Poftfcript. In the firft page whereof, I find thefe words: " I found that the manager of the Reafonablenefs of " chriftianity had prevailed with a gentleman to make " a fermon upon my refutation of that treatife, and the " vindication of it." Such a piece of impertinency, as this, might have been born from a fair adverfary: but the fample Mr. Edwards has given of himfelf, in his Socinianifm unmafked, perfuades me this ought to be bound up with what he fays of me in his introduction to that book, in thefe words: " Among others, they " thought and made choice of a gentleman, who, they " knew, would be extraordinary ufeful to them. And

" he

" he, it is probable, was as forward to be made ufe of
" by them, and prefently accepted of the office that was
" affigned him :" and more there to the fame purpofe.
All which I know to be utterly falfe.

It is a pity that one who relies fo intirely upon it,
fhould have no better an invention. The focinians fet
the author of the " Reafonablenefs of chriftianity,"
&c. on work to write that book ; by which difcovery
the world being (as Mr. Edwards fays) let into the project, that book is confounded, baffled, blown off, and
by this fkilful artifice there is an end of it. Mr. Bold
preaches and publifhes a fermon without this irrefragable gentleman's good leave and liking. What now
muft be done to difcredit it, and keep it from being
read ? Why, Mr. Bold too was fet on work, by " the
" manager of the Reafonablenefs of Chriftianity," &c.
In your whole ftorehoufe of ftratagems, you that are fo
great a conqueror, have you but this one way to deftroy
a book, which you fet your mightinefs againft, but to
tell the world it was a job of journey-work for fomebody you do not like? Some other would have done
better in this new cafe, had your happy invention been
ready with it : for you are not fo bafhful or referved,
but that you may be allowed to be as great a wit as he
who profeffed himfelf " ready at any time to fay a good
" or a new thing, if he could but think of it." But in
good earneft, fir, if one fhould afk you, Do you think
no books contain truth in them, which were undertaken
by the procuration of a bookfeller? I defire you to be a
little tender in the point, not knowing how far it may
reach. Ay, but fuch bookfellers live not at the lower
end of Pater-nofter-row, but in Paul's church-yard,
and are the managers of other-guife books, than " the
" Reafonablenefs of Chriftianity." And therefore you
very rightly fubjoin, " Indeed it was a great mafter-
" piece of procuration, and we can't but think that
" man muft fpeak truth, and defend it very impartially
" and fubftantially, who is thus brought on to under-
" take the caufe." And fo Mr. Bold's fermon is found
to have neither truth nor fenfe in it, becaufe it was
printed by a bookfeller at the lower end of Pater-nofter-
row ;

row; for that, I dare say, is all you know of the matter. But that is hint enough for a happy diviner, to be
fure of the reft, and with confidence to report that for
certain matter of fact, which had never any being but in
the fore-cafting fide of his politic brain.

But whatever were the reafons that moved Mr. B———
to preach that fermon, of which I know nothing ; this
I am fure, it fhows only the weaknefs and malice (I will
not fay, and ill breeding, for that concerns not one of
Mr: Edwards's pitch) of any one who excepts againft
it, to take notice of any thing more than what the author
has publifhed. Therein alone confifts the errour, if
there be any ; and that alone thofe meddle with, who
write for the fake of truth. But poor cavillers have other
purpofes, and therefore muft ufe other fhifts, and make
a buftle about fomething befides the argument, to prejudice and beguile unwary readers.

The only exception the creed-maker makes to Mr.
Bold's fermon, is the contradiction he imputes to him,
in faying : " That there is but one point or article
" neceffary to be believed for the making a man a chri-
" ftian : and that there are many points befides this,
" which Jefus Chrift hath taught and revealed, which
" every fincere chriftian is indifpenfably obliged to en-
" deavour to underftand :" and " that there are parti-
" cular points and articles, which being known to be
" revealed by Chrift, chriftians muft indifpenfably af-
" fent to." And where, now, is there any thing like
a contradiction in this ? Let it be granted, for example, that the creed-maker's fet of articles, (let their
number be what they will, when he has found them all
out) are neceffary to be believed, for the making a man a
chriftian. Is there any contradiction in it to fay, there
are many points befides thefe, which Jefus Chrift hath
taught and revealed, which every fincere chriftian is indifpenfably obliged to endeavour to underftand ? If this
be not fo, it is but for any one to be perfect in Mr.
Edwards's creed, and then he may lay by the bible, and
from thenceforth he is abfolutely difpenfed with from
ftudying or underftanding any thing more of the fcripture,

But

But Mr. Edwards's supremacy is not yet so far established, that he will dare to say, that christians are
not obliged to endeavour to understand any other points
revealed in the scripture, but what are contained in his
creed.   He cannot yet well discard all the rest of the
scripture, because he has yet need of it for the complet-
ing of his creed, which is like to secure the bible to us
for some time yet.   For I will be answerable for it,
he will not be quickly able to resolve what texts of the
scripture do, and what do not, contain points necessary
to be believed.   So that I am apt to imagine, that the
creed-maker, upon second thoughts, will allow that
saying, that there is but one, or there are but twelve,
or there are but as many as he shall set down, (when
he has resolved which they shall be) necessary to the
making a man a christian; and the saying, there are
other points besides, contained in the scripture, which
every sincere christian is indispensably obliged to endeavour to understand, and must believe, when he knows
them to be revealed by Jesus Christ, are two propositions that may consist together without a contradiction.

Every christian is to partake of that bread, and that
cup, which is the communion of the body and blood
of Christ.   And is not every sincere christian indispensably obliged to endeavour to understand these
words of our Saviour's institution, " This is my body,
and this is my blood?"   And if, upon his serious endeavour to do it, he understands them in a literal sense,
that Christ meant, that that was really his body and
blood, and nothing else; must he not necessarily believe
that the bread and wine, in the Lord's supper, is
changed really into his body and blood, though he
doth not know how?   Or, if having his mind set
otherwise, he understands the bread and wine to be
really the body and blood of Christ, without ceasing to
be the true bread and wine: or else, if he understands
them, that the body and blood of Christ are verily and
indeed given and received, in the sacrament, in a spiritual manner: or, lastly, if he understands our Saviour to
mean, by those words, the bread and wine to be only a
representation

representation of his body and blood; in which way foever of these four, a christian understands these words of our Saviour to be meant by him, is he not obliged in that sense to believe them to be true, and assent to them? Or can he be a christian, and understand these words to be meant by our Saviour, in one sense, and deny his assent to them as true, in that sense? Would not this be to deny our Saviour's veracity, and consequently his being the Messiah, sent from God? And yet this is put upon a christian, where he understands the scripture in one sense, and is required to believe it in another. From all which it is evident, that to say there is one, or any number of articles necessary to be known and believed to make a man a christian, and that there are others contained in the scripture, which a man is obliged to endeavour to understand, and obliged also to assent to, as he does understand them, is no contradiction.

To believe Jesus to be the Messiah, and to take him to be his Lord and King, let us suppose to be that only which is necessary to make a man a christian: may it not yet be necessary for him, being a christian, to study the doctrine and law of this his Lord and King, and believe that all that he delivered is true? Is there any contradiction in holding of this? But this creed-maker, to make sure work, and not to fail of a contradiction in Mr. Bold's words, mis-repeats them, p. 241, and quite contrary, both to what they are in the sermon, and what they are, as set down by the creed-maker himself, in the immediately preceding page. Mr. Bold says, " There " are other points that Jesus Christ hath taught and " revealed, which every sincere christian is indispensa-" bly obliged to understand; and which being known " to be revealed by Christ, he must indispensably assent " to. From which the creed-maker argues thus; p. " 240, Now if there be other points, and particular " articles, and those many, which a sincere christian is " obliged, and that necessarily and indispensably, to un-" derstand, believe and assent to; then this writer hath, " in effect, yielded to that proposition I maintained, " viz. that the belief of one article is not sufficient to

C c 4   " make

" make a man a chriſtian; and conſequently he runs
" counter to the propoſition he had laid down."

Is there no difference, I beſeech you, between being
" indiſpenſably obliged to endeavour to underſtand, and
" being indiſpenſably obliged to underſtand any point?"
It is the firſt of theſe Mr. Bold ſays, and it is the latter
of theſe you argue from, and ſo conclude nothing againſt
him: nor can you to your purpoſe. For until Mr.
Bold ſays (which he is far from ſaying) that every ſincere chriſtian is neceſſarily and indiſpenſably obliged to
underſtand all thoſe texts of ſcripture, from whence you
ſhould have drawn your neceſſary articles, (when you
have perfected your creed) in the ſame ſenſe that you
do; you can conclude nothing againſt what he had ſaid,
concerning that one article, or any thing that looks like
running counter to it. For it may be enough to con-
ſtitute a man a chriſtian, and one of Chriſt's ſubjects,
to take Jeſus to be the Meſſiah, his appointed King,
and yet, without a contradiction, ſo that it may be his
indiſpenſable duty, as a ſubject of that kingdom, to endeavour to underſtand all the dictates of his ſovereign,
and to aſſent to the truth of them, as far as he underſtands them.

But that which the good creed-maker aims at, without which all his neceſſary articles fall, is, that it ſhould
be granted him, that every ſincere chriſtian was neceſſarily and indiſpenſably obliged to underſtand all thoſe
parts of divine revelation, from whence he pretends to
draw his articles, in their true meaning, i. e. juſt as
he does. But his infallibility is not yet ſo eſtabliſhed,
but that there will need ſome proof of that propoſition.
And when he has proved, that every ſincere chriſtian is
neceſſarily and indiſpenſably obliged to underſtand thoſe
texts in their true meaning; and that his interpretation of them is that true meaning; I ſhall then aſk
him, Whether " every ſincere chriſtian is not as ne-
" ceſſarily and indiſpenſably obliged" to underſtand
other texts of ſcripture in their true meaning, though
they have no place in his ſyſtem?

For example, To make uſe of the inſtance above-
mentioned, is not every ſincere chriſtian neceſſarily
and

and indifpenfably obliged to endeavour to underftand
thefe words of our Saviour, " This is my body, and
" this is my blood," that he may know what he receives
in the facrament? Does he ceafe to be a chriftian, who
happens not to underftand them juft as the creed-maker
does? Or may not the old gentleman at Rome (who
has fomewhat the ancienter title to infallibility) make
tranfubftantiation a fundamental article neceffary to be
believed there, as well as the creed-maker here make his
fenfe of any difputed text of fcripture a fundamental article neceffary to be believed?

Let us fuppofe Mr. Bold had faid, that inftead of one
point, the right knowledge of the creed-maker's one
hundred points (when he has refolved on them) doth
conftitute and make a perfon a chriftian; yet there are
many other points Jefus Chrift hath taught and revealed, which every fincere chriftian is indifpenfably obliged
to endeavour to underftand, and to make a due ufe of;
for this, I think, the creed-maker will not deny. From
whence, in the creed-maker's words, I will thus argue :
" Now if there be other points, and particular articles,
" and thófe many, which a fincere chriftian is obliged,
" and that neceffarily and indifpenfably, to underftand,
" and believe, and affent to; then this writer doth, in
" effect, yield to that propofition which I maintained,
" viz. That the belief of thofe one hundred articles
" is not fufficient to make a man a chriftian :" for this
is that which I maintain, that upon this ground the
belief of the articles, which he has fet down in his lift,
are not fufficient to make a man a chriftian; and that
upon Mr. Bold's reafon, which the creed-maker infifts
on againft one article, viz. becaufe there are many other
points Jefus Chrift hath taught and revealed, which
every fincere chriftian is as neceffarily and indifpenfably obliged to endeavour to underftand, and make a due
ufe of.

But this creed-maker is cautious, beyond any of his
predeceffors : He will not be fo caught by his own argument; and therefore is very fhy to give you the precife articles that every fincere chriftian is neceffarily and
indifpenfably obliged to underftand and give his affent
to.

to. Something he is fure there is, that he is indifpenfably obliged to underftand and affent to, to make him a
chriftian ; but what that is he cannot yet tell. So that
whether he be a chriftian or no, he does not know ; and
what other people will think of him, from his treating
of the ferious things of chriftianity, in fo trifling and
fcandalous a way, muft be left to them.

In the next paragraph, p. 242, the creed-maker tells
us, Mr. Bold goes on to confute himfelf, in faying, " A
" true chriftian muft affent unto this, that Chrift Jefus
" is God." But this is juft fuch another confutation of
himfelf as the before-mentioned, i. e. as much as a
falfhood, fubftituted by another man, can be a confutation of a man's felf, who has fpoken truth all of a-piece.
For the creed-maker, according to his fure way of
baffling his opponents, fo as to leave them nothing to
anfwer, hath here, as he did before, changed Mr. Bold's
words, which in the 35th page, quoted by the creed-
maker, ftand thus : " When a true chriftian under-
" ftands, that Chrift Jefus hath taught, that he is God,
" he muft affent unto it :" which is true, and conformable to what he had faid before, that every fincere
chriftian muft endeavour to underftand the points taught
and revealed by Jefus Chrift ; which being known to be
revealed by him, he muft affent unto.

The like piece of honefty the creed-maker fhows in
the next paragraph, p. 243, where he charges Mr.
Bold with faying, " That a true chriftian is as much
" obliged to believe, that the Holy Spirit is God, as
" to believe that Jefus is the Chrift," p. 40. In which
place, Mr. Bold's words are : " When a true chriftian
" underftands, that Chrift Jefus hath given this ac-
" count of the Holy Spirit, viz. that he is God ; he
" is as much obliged to believe it, as he is to believe,
" that Jefus is the Chrift :" which is an inconteftæ-
ble truth, but fuch an one as the creed-maker himfelf
faw would do him no fervice ; and therefore he mangles
it, and leaves out half to ferve his turn. But he that
fhould give a teftimony in the flight affairs of men, and
their temporal concerns, before a court of judicature, as
the creed-maker does here, and almoft every-where, in
the

the great affairs of religion, and the everlafting concern of fouls, before all mankind, would lofe his ears for it. What, therefore, this worthy gentleman alleges out of Mr. Bold, as a contradiction to himfelf, being only the creed-maker's contradiction to truth, and clear matter of fact, needs no other anfwer.

The reft of what he calls " Reflections on Mr. Bold's " fermon" being nothing but either rude and mifbecoming language of him; or pitiful childifh application to him, to change his perfuafion at the creed-maker's entreaty, and give up the truth he hath owned, in courtefy to this doughty combatant ; fhows the ability of the man. Leave off begging the queftion, and fupercilioufly prefuming, that you are in the right; and, inftead of that, fhow by argument : and I dare anfwer for Mr. Bold, you will have him, and I promife you, with him, one convert more. But arguing is not, it feems, this notable difputant's way. If boafting of himfelf, and contemning of others, falfe quotations, and feigned matters of fact, which the reader neither can know, nor is the queftion concerned in, if he did know, will not do ; there is an end of him : he has fhown his excellency in fcurrilous declamation ; and there you have the whole of this unanfwerable writer. And for this, I appeal to his own writings in this controverfy, if any judicious reader can have the patience to look them over.

In the beginning of his " Reflections on Mr. Bold's " fermon," he confidently tells the world, " that he " had found that the manager of the Reafonablenefs of " Chriftianity had prevailed on Mr. Bold to preach a " fermon upon his Reflections, &c." And adds, " And " we cannot but think, that that man muft fpeak the " truth, and defend it very impartially and fubftan- " tially, who is thus brought on to undertake the " caufe." And at the latter end he addreffes himfelf to Mr. Bold, as one that is drawn off, to be an under journeyman-worker in focinianifm. In his gracious allowance, " Mr. Bold is, feemingly, a man of fome " relifh of religion and piety," p. 244. He is forced alfo to own him to be a man of fobriety and temper,

p. 245.

p. 245. A very good rife, to give him out to the world, in the very next words, as a man of a profligate confcience : for fo he muft be, who can be drawn off to preach, or write for focinianifm, when he thinks it a moft dangerous errour ; who can " diffemble with himfelf, " and choke his inward perfuafions," (as the creed-maker infinuates that Mr. Bold does, in the fame addrefs to him, p. 248.) and write contrary to his light. Had the creed-maker had reafon to think in earneft, that Mr. Bold was going off to focinianifm, he might have reafoned with him fairly, as with a man running into a dangerous errour ; or if he had certainly known, that he was by any bye-ends prevailed on to undertake a caufe contrary to his confcience, he might have fome reafon to tell the world, as he does, p. 239, " That we " cannot think he fhould fpeak truth, who is thus " brought to undertake the caufe." If he does not certainly know, that " Mr. Bold was THUS brought to undertake the caufe," he could not have fhown a more villainous and unchriftian mind, than in publifhing fuch a character of a minifter of the gofpel, and a worthy man, upon no other grounds, but becaufe it might be fubfervient to his ends. He is engaged in a controverfy, that by argument he cannot maintain ; nor knew any other way, from the beginning, to attack the book he pretends to write againft, but by crying out focinianifm ; a name he knows in great difgrace with all other fects of chriftians, and therefore fufficient to deter all thofe who approve and condemn books by hearfay, without examining their truth themfelves, from perufing a treatife, to which he could affix that imputation. Mr. Bold's name, (who is publickly known to be no focinian) he forefees, will wipe off that falfe imputation, with a great many of thofe who are led by names more than things. This feems exceedingly to trouble him, and he labours, might and main, to get Mr. Bold to quit a book as focinian, which Mr. Bold knows is not focinian, becaufe he has read and confidered it.

But though our creed-maker be mightily concerned, that Mr. B——d fhould not appear in the defence of it ; yet this concern cannot raife him one jot above that
honefty,

honesty, skill, and good breeding, which appears towards others. He manages this matter with Mr. B---d, as he has done the rest of the controversy; just in the same strain of invention, civility, wit, and good sense. He tells him, besides what I have above set down, " That he is drawn off to debase himself, and the post, " i. e. the ministry he is in, p. 245. That he hath said " very ill things, to the lessening and impairing, yea, " to the defaming of that knowledge and belief of our " Saviour, and of the articles of christianity, which are " necessarily required of us, p. 245. That the devout " and pious," (whereby he means himself: for one, and none, is his own beloved wit and argument) " observ- " ing that Mr. Bold is come to the necessity of but ONE " article of faith, they expect that he may in time hold " that NONE is necessary, p. 248. That if he writes " again in the same strain, he will write rather like a " Turkish spy, than a christian preacher; and that he " is a backslider, and sailing to Racovia with a side " wind:" than which, what can there be more scur- rilous, or more malicious? And yet at the same time that he outrages him thus, beyond not only what christian charity, but common civility, would allow in an ingenuous adversary, he makes some awkward attempts to soothe him with some ill-timed commendations; and would have his undervaluing Mr. Bold's animad- versions pass for a compliment to him; because he, for that reason, pretends not to believe so crude and shal- low a thing (as he is pleased to call it) to be his. A notable contrivance to gain the greater liberty of rail- ing at him under another name, when Mr. B—d's, it seems, is too well known to serve him so well to that purpose. Besides, it is of good use to fill up three or four pages of his Reflections; a great convenience to a writer, who knows all the ways of baffling his oppo- nents, but argument; and who always makes a great deal of stir about matters foreign to his subject; which, whether they are granted or denied, make nothing at all to the truth of the question on either side. For what is it to the shallowness or depth of the animadversions, who writ them? Or to the truth or falshood of Mr.

B---d's

B---d's defence of the " Reasonablenefs of Chriftianity," whether a layman, or a churchman, a focinian, or
one of the church of England, anfwered the creed-
maker as well as he? Yet this is urged as a matter of
great weight; but yet, in reality, it amounts to no more
but this, that a man of any denomination, who wifhes
well to the peace of chriftianity, and has obferved the
horrible effects the chriftian religion has felt from the
impofitions of men, in matters of faith, may have reafon
to defend a book, wherein the fimplicity of the gofpel,
and the doctrine propofed by our Saviour and his
apoftles, for the converfion of unbelievers, is made out,
though there be not one word of the diftinguifhing
tenets of his fect in it. But that all thofe, who, under
any name, are for impofing their own orthodoxy, as
neceffary to be believed, and perfecuting thofe who
diffent from them, fhould be all againft it, is not perhaps very ftrange.

One thing more I muft obferve of the creed-maker
on this occafion : in his focinian creed, chap. vi. the
author of the " Reafonablenefs of Chriftianity, &c."
and his book, muft be judged of, by the characters and
writings of thofe who entertain or commend his notions. " A profeffed unitarian has defended it ;" therefore he is a focinian. The author of A letter to the
deifts fpeaks well of it ; therefore he is a deift. Another, as an abetter of the Reafonablenefs of Chriftianity, he mentions, p. 125, whofe letters I have never
feen: and his opinions too are, I fuppofe, fet down
there as belonging to me. Whatever is bad in the
tenets or writings of thefe men, infects me. But the
mifchief is, Mr. Bold's orthodoxy will do me no good :
but becaufe he has defended my book againft Mr.
Edwards, all my faults are become his, and he has a
mighty load of accufations laid upon him. Thus contrary caufes ferve fo good a natured, fo charitable, and
candid a writer as the creed-maker, to the fame purpofe of cenfure and railing. But I fhall defire him to
figure to himfelf the lovelinefs of that creature, which
turns every thing into venom. What others are, or
hold, who have expreffed favourable thoughts of my
8   book,

book, I think myfelf not concerned in. What opinions others have publifhed, make thofe in my book neither true nor falfe; and he that, for the fake of truth, would confute the errours in it, fhould fhow their falfhood and weaknefs, as they are: but they who write for other ends than truth, are always bufy with other matters; and where they can do nothing by reafon and argument, hope to prevail with fome by borrowed prejudices and party.

Taking therefore the Animadverfions, as well as the fermon, to be his, whofe name they bear, I fhall leave to Mr. B—d himfelf to take what notice he thinks fit of the little fenfe, as well as great impudence, of putting his name in print to what is not his, or taking it away from what he hath fet it to, whether it belongs to his bookfeller or anfwerer. Only I cannot pafs by the palpable falfifying of Mr. B—d's words, in the beginning of his epiftle to the reader, without mention. Mr. B—d's words are: " whereby I came to be furnifhed " with a truer and more juft notion of the main defign " of that TREATISE." And the good creed-maker fets them down thus: " The main defign of MY OWN " TREATISE OR SERMON :" a fure way for fuch a champion for truth to fecure to himfelf the laurel or the whetftone!

This irrefiftible difputant, (who filences all that come in his way, fo that thofe that would cannot anfwer him) to make good the mighty encomiums he has given himfelf, ought (one would think) to clear all as he goes, and leave nothing by the way unanfwered, for fear he fhould fall into the number of thofe poor baffled wretches, whom he with fo much fcorn reproaches, that they would anfwer, if they could.

Mr. B—D begins his Animadverfions with this remark, that our creed-maker had faid, That " I give it " over and over again in thefe formal words, viz. That " nothing is required to be believed by any chriftian " man but this, " That Jefus is the Meffiah." To which Mr. B---d replies, p. 4. in thefe words: " Though I " have read over the Reafonablenefs of Chriftianity, &c. " with fome attention, I have not obferved thofe
formal

" formal words in any part of that book, nor any
" words that are capable of that conftruction; provided
" they be confidered with the relation they have to, and
" the manifeft dependence they have on, what goes be-
" fore, or what follows after them."

BUT TO THIS Mr. Edwards ANSWERS NOT.

Whether it was becaufe he would not, or becaufe he
could not, let the reader judge. But this is down upon
his fcore already, and it is expected he fhould anfwer to
it, or elfe confefs that he cannot. And that there may
be a fair decifion of this difpute, I expect the fame
ufage from him, that he fhould fet down any propofition
of his I have not anfwered to, and call on me for an anfwer, if I can; and if I cannot, I promife him to own it
in print.

The creed-maker had faid, " That it is moft evident
" to any thinking and confiderate perfon, that I purpofely
" omit the epiftolary writings of the apoftles becaufe
" they are fraught with other fundamental doctrines,
" befides that which I mention."

To this Mr. B---d anfwers, p. 5. That if by " funda-
" mental articles, Mr. Edwards means here, all the
" propofitions delivered in the epiftles, concerning juft
" thofe particular heads, he [Mr. Edwards] had here
" mentioned; it lies upon him to prove, that Jefus
" Chrift hath made it neceffary, that every perfon muft
" have an explicit knowledge and belief of all thofe,
" before he can be a chriftian."

BUT TO THIS Mr. Edwards ANSWERS NOT.

And yet, without an anfwer to it, all his talk about
fundamentals, and thofe which he pretended to fet
down in that place, under the name of fundamentals,
will fignify nothing in the prefent cafe; wherein, by
fundamentals, were meant fuch propofitions which
every perfon muft neceffarily have an explicit knowledge and belief of, before he can be a chriftian.

Mr. B---d, in the fame place, p. 6, 7, very truly and
pertinently adds, " That it did not pertain to [my]
" undertaking to inquire what doctrines, either in the
" Epiftles, or the Evangelifts and the Acts, were of
" greateft moment to be underftood by them who are
" chriftians;

" chriftians; but what was neceffary to be known and
" believed to a perfon's being a chriftian. For there
" are many important doctrines, both in the Gofpels,
" and in the Acts, befides this, " That Jefus is the
" Meffiah." But how many foever the doctrines be,
" which are taught in the epiftles, if there be no doc-
" trine befides this, " That Jefus is the Meffiah,"
" taught there as neceffary to be believed to make a
" man a chriftian; all the doctrines taught there will
" not make any thing againft what this author has
" afferted, nor againft the method he hath obferved:
" efpecially, confidering we have an account, in the
" Acts of the apoftles, of what thofe perfons, by whom
" the epiftles were writ, did teach, as neceffary to be
" believed to people's being chriftians."

This, and what Mr. B---d fubjoins, " That it was
" not my defign to give an abftract of any of the in-
" fpired books," is fo true, and has fo clear reafon in
it, that any, but this writer, would have thought himfelf concerned to have anfwered fomething to it.

BUT TO THIS Mr. Edwards ANSWERS NOT.

It not being, it feems, a creed-maker's bufinefs to
convince men's underftanding by reafon; but to impofe on their belief by authority; or, where that is
wanting, by falfhood and bawling. And to fuch Mr.
Bold obferves well, p. 8, " That if I had given the like
" account of the epiftles, that would have been as little
" fatisfactory as what I have done already, to thofe who
" are refolved not to diftinguifh " betwixt what is ne-
" ceffary to be believed to make a man a chriftian, and
" thofe articles which are to be believed by thofe who
" are chriftians," as they can attain to know that Chrift
" hath taught them."

This diftinction the creed-maker, no-where that I
remember, takes any notice of; unlefs it be p. 255,
where he has fomething relating hereunto, which we
fhall confider, when we come to that place. I fhall
now go on to fhow what Mr. Bold has faid, to which he
anfwers not.

Mr. BOLD farther tells him, p. 10, that if he will
prove any thing in oppofition to the Reafonablenefs of

Chriftianity, &c. it muft be this: "That Jefus Chrift
" and his apoftles have taught, that the belief of fome
" one article, or certain number of articles diftinct
" from this, " That Jefus is the Mefliah," either as ex-
" clufive of, or in conjunction with, the belief of this
" article, doth conftitute and make a perfon a chrif-
" tian: but that the belief of this, that Jefus is the
" Mefliah alone, doth not make a man a chriftian."

But to this Mr. Edwards IRREFRAGABLY AN-
SWERS NOTHING.

Mr. Bold alfo, p. 10, charges him with his falfly
accufing me in thefe words: " He pretends to contend
" for one fingle article, with the exclufion of all the reft,
" for this reafon; becaufe all men ought to underftand
" their religion." And again, where he fays, I am at
this, viz. " That we muft not have any point of doc-
" trine in our religion, that the mob doth not, at the
" very firft naming of it, perfectly underftand and
" agree to;" Mr. Bold has quoted my exprefs words
to the contrary.

But to this this unanfwerable gentleman AN-
SWERS NOTHING.

But if he be fuch a mighty difputant, that nothing
can ftand in his way; I fhall expect his direct anfwer to
it among thofe other propofitions which I have fet down
to his fcore, and I require him to prove, if he can.

The creed-maker fpends above four pages of his Reflections, in a great ftir who is the author of thofe animadverfions he is reflecting on. To which I tell him,
it matters not to a lover of truth, or a confuter of errours,
who was the author; but what they contain. He who
makes fuch a deal of do about that which is nothing
to the queftion, fhows he has but little mind to the argument; that his hopes are more in the recommendation of names, and prejudice of parties, than in the
ftrength of his reafons, and the goodnefs of his caufe.
A lover of truth follows that, whoever be for or againft
it; and can fuffer himfelf to pafs by no argument of his
adverfary, without taking notice of it, either in allowing
its force, or giving it a fair anfwer. Were the creed-
maker capable of giving fuch an evidence as this of his
                                                              love

love of truth, he would not have paffed over the twenty firft pages of Mr. Bold's Animadverfions in filence. The fallhoods that are therein charged upon him, would have required an anfwer of him, if he could have given any; and I tell him, he muft give an anfwer, or confefs the falfhoods.

In his 255th page, he comes to take notice of thefe words of Mr. Bold, in the 21ft page of his Animadver-fions, viz. " That a convert to chriftianity, or a chrif-
" tian, muft neceffarily believe as many articles as he
" fhall attain to know, that Chrift Jefus hath taught."
" Which, fays the creed-maker, wholly invalidates
" what he had faid before, in thefe words," viz. " That
" Jefus Chrift and his apoftles did not teach any thing
" as neceffary to be believed to make a man a chriftian,
" but only this one propofition, That Jefus of Naza-
" reth was the Meffiah." The reafon he gives to fhow that the former of thefe propofitions (in Mr. Bold) in-validates the latter, and that the animadverter contra-dicts himfelf, ftands thus : " For, fays he, if a chriftian
" muft give affent to all the articles taught by our
" Saviour in the gofpel, and that neceffarily ; then all
" thofe propofitions reckoned up in my late difcourfe,
" being taught by Chrift, or his apoftles, are neceffary
" to be believed." Anf. And what, I befeech you, be-comes of the reft of the propofitions taught by Chrift, or his apoftles, which you have not reckoned up in your late difcourfe? Are not they neceffary to be believed,
" if a chriftian muft give an affent to ALL the articles
" taught by our Saviour and his apoftles ?"

Sir, if you will argue right from that antecedent, it muft ftand thus : " If a chriftian muft give an affent to
" ALL the articles taught by our Saviour and his
" apoftles, and that neceffarily ;" then all the propo-fitions in the New Teftament, taught by Chrift, or his apoftles, are neceffary to be believed. This confe-quence I grant to be true, and neceffarily to follow from that antecedent, and pray make your beft of it : but withal remember, that it puts an utter end to your felect number of fundamentals, and makes all the truths de-

livered

livered in the New Teſtament neceſſary to be explicitly
believed by every chriſtian.

But, Sir, I muſt take notice to you, that if it be uncertain, whether he that writ the Animadverſions, be
the ſame perſon that preached the ſermon, yet it is very
viſible, that it is the very ſame perſon that reflects on
both; becauſe he here again uſes the ſame trick, in anſwering in the Animadverſions the ſame thing that had
been ſaid in the ſermon, viz. by pretending to argue
from words as Mr. Bold's, when Mr. Bold has ſaid no
ſuch thing. The propoſition you argue from here is
this: " If a chriſtian muſt give his aſſent to all the ar-
" ticles taught by our Saviour, and that neceſſarily."
But Mr. Bold ſays no ſuch thing. His words, as ſet
down by yourſelf, are: " A chriſtian muſt neceſſarily"
" believe as many articles as he ſhall attain to know
" that Chriſt Jeſus hath taught." And is there no difference between " ALL that Chriſt Jeſus hath taught,
" and AS MANY as any one ſhall attain to know that
" Chriſt Jeſus hath taught?" There is ſo great a difference between theſe two, that one can ſcarce think
even ſuch a creed-maker could miſtake it. For one of
them admits all thoſe to be chriſtians, who, taking Jeſus
for the Meſſiah, their Lord and King, ſincerely apply
themſelves to underſtand and obey his doctrine and law,
and to believe all that they underſtand to be taught by
him: the other ſhuts out, if not all mankind, yet nine
hundred ninety-nine of a thouſand, of thoſe who profeſs
themſelves chriſtians, from being really ſo. For he
ſpeaks within compaſs, who ſays there is not one of a
thouſand, if there be any one man at all, who explicitly
knows and believes all that our Saviour and his apoſtles
taught, i. e. all that is delivered in the New Teſtament,
in the true ſenſe that it is there intended. For if giving
aſſent to it, in any ſenſe, will ſerve the turn, our creed-
maker can have no exception againſt Socinians, Papiſts,
Lutherans, or any other, who, acknowledging the
ſcripture to be the word of God, do yet oppoſe his
ſyſtem.

But the creed-maker goes on, p. 255, and endeavours
to prove that what is neceſſary to be believed by every
chriſtian,

christian, is necessary to be believed to make a man a
christian, in these words: " But he will say, the belief
" of those propositions makes not a man a christian.
" Then, I say, they are not necessary and indispensable;
" for what is absolutely necessary in christianity, is ab-
" solutely requisite to make a man a christian."

Ignorance, or something worse, makes our creed-
maker always speak doubtfully or obscurely, whenever he
pretends to argue; for here " absolutely necessary in
" christianity," either signifies nothing, but absolutely
necessary to make a man a christian; and then it is
proving the same proposition, by the same proposition:
or else has a very obscure and doubtful signification.
For, if I ask him, Whether it be absolutely necessary in
christianity, to obey every one of our Saviour's commands, What will he answer me? If he answers, No; I
ask him, Which of our Saviour's commands is it not,
in christianity, absolutely necessary to obey? If he answers, YES; then I tell him, by this rule, there are no
christians; because there is no one that does in all things
obey all our Saviour's commands, and therein fails to
perform what is absolutely necessary in christianity; and
so, by his rule, is no christian. If he answers, Sincere
endeavour to obey, is all that is absolutely necessary;
I reply, And so sincere endeavour to understand, is all
that is absolutely necessary: neither perfect obedience,
nor perfect understanding, is absolutely necessary in
christianity.

But his proposition, being put in terms clear, and not
loose and fallacious, should stand thus, viz. " What is
" absolutely necessary to every christian, is absolutely
" requisite to make a man a christian." But then I
deny, that he can infer from Mr. Bold's words, that
those propositions (i. e. which he has set down as fundamental, or necessary to be believed) are absolutely necessary to be believed by every christian. For that
indispensable necessity Mr. Bold speaks of, is not abso-
lute, but conditional. His words are, " A christian
" must believe as many articles, as he shall attain to
" know that Jesus Christ hath taught." So that he
places the indispensable necessity of believing, upon the

condition

condition of attaining to know that Chrift taught fo. An endeavour to know what Jefus Chrift taught, Mr. B—d fays truly, is abfolutely neceffary to every one who is a chriftian; and to believe what he has attained to know that Jefus Chrift taught, that alfo, he fays, is abfolutely neceffary to every chriftian. But all this granted, (as true it is) it ftill remains (and eternally will remain) to be proved from this, (which is all that Mr. Bold fays) that fomething elfe is abfolutely required to make a man a chriftian, befides the unfeigned taking Jefus to be the Meffiah, his King, and Lord; and accordingly, a fincere refolution to obey and believe all that he commanded and taught.

The gaoler, Acts xvi. 30, in anfwer to his queftion, " What he fhould do to be faved?" was anfwered, " That he fhould believe in the Lord Jefus Chrift." And the text fays, that the gaoler " took them the " fame hour of the night and wafhed their ftripes, and " was baptized, he and all his, ftraightway." Now, I will afk our creed-maker, whether St. Paul, in fpeaking to him the word of the Lord, propofed and explained to him all thofe propofitions and fundamental heads of doctrine, which our creed-maker has fet down as neceffary to be believed to make a man a chriftian? Let it be confidered the gaoler was a heathen, and one that feems to have no more fenfe of religion or humanity, than thofe of that calling ufe to have: for he had let them alone under the pain of their ftripes, without any remedy, or fo much as the eafe of wafhing them, from the day before, until after his converfion; which was not until after midnight. And can any one think, that between his afking what he fhould do to be faved, and his being baptized, which, the text fays, was the fame hour, and ftraightway; there was time enough for St. Paul and Silas, to explain to him all the creed-maker's articles, and make fuch a man as that, and all his houfe, underftand the creed-maker's whole fyftem; efpecially, fince we hear nothing of it in the converfion of thefe, or any others, who were brought into the faith, in the whole hiftory of the preaching of our Saviour and the apoftles? Now let me afk the creed-maker, whether
the

the gaoler was not a chriftian, when he was baptized ;
and whether, if he had then immediately died, he had
not been faved, without the belief of any one article
more, than what Paul and Silas had then taught him ?
Whence it follows, that what was then propofed to him
to be believed, (which appears to be nothing, but that
Jefus was the Meffiah) was all that was abfolutely neceffary to be believed to make him a chriftian ; though
this hinders not, but that afterwards it might be neceffary for him, indifpenfably neceffary, to believe
other articles, when he attained to the knowledge that
Chrift had taught them. And the reafon of it is plain :
becaufe the knowing that Chrift hath taught any
thing, and the not receiving it for true (which is
believing it) is inconfiftent with the believing him
to be the Meffiah, fent from God to enlighten and
fave the world. Every word of divine revelation is
abfolutely and indifpenfably neceffary to be believed by
every chriftian, as foon as he comes to know it to
be taught by our Saviour, or his apoftles, or to be
of divine revelation. But yet this is far enough from
making it abfolutely neceffary to every chriftian, to
know every text in the fcripture, much lefs to underftand every text in the fcripture ; and leaft of all, to
underftand it as the creed-maker is pleafed to put his
fenfe upon it.

This the good creed-maker either will not, or cannot
underftand : but gives us a lift of articles culled out of
the fcripture by his own authority, and tells us, thofe
are abfolutely neceffary to be believed by every one, to
make him a chriftian. For what is of abfolute neceffity in chriftianity, as thofe, he fays, are, he tells us, is
abfolutely requifite to make a man a chriftian. But
when he is afked, Whether thefe are all the articles of
abfolute neceffity to be believed to make a man a chriftian ? this worthy divine, that takes upon himfelf to
be a fucceffor of the apoftles, cannot tell. And yet,
having taken upon himfelf alfo to be a creed-maker, he
muft fuffer himfelf to be called upon for it again and again,
until he tells us what is of abfolute neceffity to be believed
to make a man a chriftian, or confefs that he cannot.

In the mean time, I take the liberty to fay, that every

pro-

propofition delivered in the New Teftament by our Saviour, or his apoftles, and fo received by any chriftian as of divine revelation, is of as abfolute neceffity to be affented to by him, in the fenfe he underftands it to be taught by them, as any one of thofe propofitions enumerated by the creed-maker: and if he thinks otherwife, I fhall defire him to prove it. The reafon whereof is this, that in divine revelation, the ground of faith being the only authority of the propofer: where that is the fame, there is no difference in the obligation or meafure of believing. Whatever the Meffiah, that came from God, taught, is equally to be believed by every one who receives him as the Meffiah, as foon as he underftands what it was he taught. There is no fuch thing as garbling his doctrine, and making one part of it more neceffary to be believed than another, when it is underftood. His faying is, and muft be, of unqueftionable authority to all that receive him as their heavenly King; and carries with it an equal obligation of affent to all that he fays as true. But fince no-body can explicitly affent to any propofition of our Saviour's as true, but in the fenfe he underftands our Saviour to have fpoken it in; the fame authority of the Meffiah, his King, obliges every one abfolutely and indifpenfably to believe every part of the New Teftament in that fenfe he underftands it; for elfe he rejects the authority of the deliverer, if he refufes his affent to it in that fenfe which he is perfuaded it was delivered in. But the taking him for the Meffiah, his King and Lord, laying upon every one who is his fubject, an obligation to endeavour to know his will in all things; every true chriftian is under an abfolute and indifpenfable neceffity, by being his fubject, to ftudy the fcriptures with an unprejudiced mind, according to that meafure of time, opportunity, and helps which he has; that in thefe facred writings, he may find what his Lord and Mafter hath by himfelf, or by the mouths of his apoftles, required of him, either to be believed or done.

The creed-maker, in the following page, 256, hath thefe words: "It is worth the reader's obferving, "that notwithstanding I had in twelve pages together "(viz.

" (viz. from the eighth to the twentieth) proved, that
" several propositions are neceffary to be believed by
" us, in order to our being chriftians; yet this fham-
" animadverter attends not to any one of the particulars
" which I had mentioned, nor offers any thing againft
" them; but only, in a lumping way, dooms them all
" in thofe magifterial words : " I do not fee any proof
" he produces," p. 21. " This is his wonderful way
" of confuting me, by pretending that he cannot fee
" any proof in what I allege : and all the world muft
" be led by his eyes."

Anfw. " It is worth the reader's obferving," that
the creed-maker does not reply to what Mr. Bold has
faid to him, as we have already feen, and fhall fee more
as we go on; and therefore he has little reafon to complain of him, for not having anfwered enough.   Mr.
Bold did well to leave that which was an infignificant
lump, fo as it was, together ; for it is no wonderful
thing not to fee any proof, where there is no proof.
There is indeed, in thofe pages the creed-maker mentions, much confidence, much affertion, a great many
queftions afked, and a great deal faid after his fafhion :
but for a proof, I deny there is any one.   And if what
I have faid in another place already, does not convince him of it, I challenge him, with all his eyes, and
thofe of the world to boot, to find out, in thofe twelve
renowned pages, one proof.   Let him fet down the
propofition, and his proof of its being abfolutely and
indifpenfably neceffary to be believed to make a man a
chriftian; and I too will join with him in his teftimo-
nial of himfelf, that he is irrefragable.   But I muft tell
him before-hand, talking a great deal loofely will not
do it.

Mr. Bold and I fay we cannot fee any proof in thofe
twelve pages : the way to make us fee, or to convince
the world that we are blind, is to fingle out one proof
out of that wood of words there, which you feem to
take for arguments, and fet it down in a fyllogifm,
which is the fair trial of a proof or no proof.   You
have, indeed, a fyllogifm in the 23d page ; but that
is not in thofe twelve pages you mention.   Befides, I
have

have fhowed in another place, what that proves; to which I refer you.

In anfwer to the creed-maker's queftion, about his other fundamentals found in the epiftles: " Why did " the apoftles write thefe doctrines? Was it not, " that thofe they writ to, might give their affent to " them?" Mr. Bold, p. 22, replies: " But then it may " be afked again, Were not thofe perfons chriftians " to whom the apoftles thefe doctrines, and whom " they required to affent to them? Yes, verily. And " if fo, What was it that made them chriftians before " their affent to thefe doctrines was required? If it " were any thing befides their believing Jefus to be " the Meffiah, it ought to be inftanced in, and made out."

BUT TO THIS Mr. Edwards ANSWERS NOT.

The next thing in controverfy between Mr. Bold and the creed-maker, (for I follow Mr. B—d's order) is about a matter of fact, viz. Whether the creed-maker has proved, " that Jefus Chrift and his apoftles have " taught, that no man can be a chriftian, or fhall be " faved, unlefs he has an explicit knowledge of all " thofe things, which have an immediate refpect to " the occafion, author, way, means and iffue of our " falvation, and which are neceffary for the knowing " the true nature and defign of it?" This, Mr. Bold, p. 24, tells him, " he has not done." To this the creed-maker replies, p. 258.

" And yet the reader may fatisfy himfelf, that this is " the very thing that I had been proving juft before, " and indeed, all along in the foregoing chapter." Anfw. There have been thofe who have been feven years proving a thing, which at laft they could not do; and I give you feven years to prove this propofition, which you fhould there have proved; and I muft add to your fcore here, viz.

LII. That Jefus Chrift, or his apoftles, have taught, that no man can be a chriftian, or can be faved, unlefs he hath an explicit knowledge of all thefe things which have an immediate refpect to the occa- fion, author, way, means and iffue of our falvation, and

which

which are neceffary for our knowing the true nature
and defign of it.

Nor muft the poor excufe, of faying, It was not
neceffary " to add any farther medium, and proceed
" to another fyllogifm, becaufe you had fecured that
" propofition before ;" go for payment. If you had
fecured it, as you fay, it had been quite as eafy, and
much for your credit, to have produced the proof
whereby you had fecured it, than to fay you had done
it ; and there-upon to reproach Mr. Bold with heed-
leffnefs ; and to tell the world, that " he cares not
" what he faith." The rule of fair difpute is, indifpenfably to prove, where any thing is denied. To
evade this is fhuffling : and he that, inftead of it, anfwers with ill language, in my country, is called a foul-
mouthed wrangler.

To the creed-maker's exception to my demand,
about the actual belief of all his fundamentals in his
new creed, Mr. Bold afks, p. 24, " Whether a man
" can believe particular propofitions, and not actually
" believe them ?"

BUT TO THIS Mr. Edwards ANSWERS NOT.

Mr. Bold, p. 25, farther acknowledges the creed-
maker's fundamental propofitions to " be in the bible ;
" and that they are for this purpofe there, that they
" might be believed :" and fo, he faith, " is every other
" propofition which is taught in our bibles." But afks,
" How will it thence follow, that no man can be a
" chriftian, until he particularly know, and actually af-
" fent to every propofition in our bibles ?"

BUT TO THIS Mr. Edwards ANSWERS NOT.

From p. 26. to 30. Mr. Bold fhows, that the creed-
maker's reply concerning my not gathering of fundamentals out of the epiftles is nothing to the purpofe :
and this he demonftratively proves.

AND TO THIS Mr. Edwards ANSWERS NOT.

The creed-maker had falfly faid, That " I bring no
" tidings of an evangelical faith:" and thence very
readily and charitably infers : " Which gives us to
" underftand, that he verily believes there is no fuch
" chriftian

" chriſtian faith." To this Mr. Bold thus ſoftly replies, p. 31, " I think Mr. Edwards is much miſta-
" ken, both in his aſſertion and inference:" and to
ſhow that he could not ſo infer, adds: " If the author
" of the Reaſonableneſs of Chriſtianity, &c. had not
" brought any tidings of ſuch a faith, I think it could
" not be thence juſtly inferred, that he verily believes
" there is no ſuch chriſtian faith: becauſe his inquiry
" and ſearch was not concerning chriſtian faith, conſi-
" dered ſubjectively but objectively; what the articles
" be, which muſt be believed to make a man a chriſtian;
" and not, with what ſort of faith theſe articles are to be
" believed."

To this the creed-maker anſwers indeed; but it is
ſomething as much worſe than nothing, as falſhood is
worſe than ſilence. His words are, p. 258, " It may
" be queſtioned, from what he [the animadverter] hath
" the confidence to ſay, p. 31, viz. There is no in-
" quiry in the Reaſonableneſs of Chriſtianity, con-
" cerning faith ſubjectively conſidered, but only ob-
" jectively," &c. And thus having ſet down Mr.
B—d's words, otherwiſe than they are; for Mr. Bold
does not ſay, there is no inquiry, i. e. no mention, (for
ſo the creed-maker explains inquiries here. For to
convince Mr. Bold that there is an inquiry, i. e. mention, of ſubjective faith, he alleges, that ſubjective
faith is ſpoken of in the 296th and 297th pages of my
book.) But Mr. Bold ſays not, that faith, conſidered
ſubjectively, is not ſpoken of any where in the Reaſonableneſs of Chriſtianity, &c. but " that the au-
" thor's inquiry and ſearch (i. e. the author's ſearch, or
" deſign of his ſearch) was not concerning chriſtian
" faith conſidered ſubjectively." And thus the creed-
maker, impoſing on his reader, by perverting Mr. Bold's
ſenſe, from what was the intention of my inquiry and
ſearch, to what I had ſaid in it, he goes on, after his
ſcurrilous faſhion, to inſult, in theſe words which follow:
" I ſay, it may be gueſſed from this, what a liberty this
" writer takes, to aſſert what he pleaſes." Anſw. " To
" aſſert what one pleaſes," without truth and without
certainty, is the worſt character can be given a writer;
and

and with falfhood to charge it another, is no mean flander and injury to a man's neighbour. And yet to thefe
fhameful arts muft he be driven, who finding his
ftrength of managing a caufe to lie only in fiction and
falfhood, has no other but the dull Billingfgate way of
covering it, by endeavouring to divert the reader's obfervation and cenfure from himfelf, by a confident repeated imputation of that to his adverfary, which he
himfelf is fo frequent in the commiffion of. And of
this the inftances I have given, are a fufficient proof;
in which I have been at the pains to fet down the words
on both fides, and the pages where they are to be found,
for the reader's full fatisfaction.

The caufe in debate between us is of great weight,
and concerns every chriftian. That any evidence in the
propofal, or defence of it, can be fufficient to conquer
all men's prejudices, is vanity to imagine. But this,
I think, I may juftly demand of every reader, that fince
there are great and vifible falfhoods on one fide or the
other (for the accufations of this kind are pofitive and
frequent) he would examine on which fide they are: and
upon that I will venture the caufe in any reader's judgment, who will but be at the pains of turning to the
pages marked out to him; and as for him that will not do
that, I care not much what he fays.

The creed-maker's following words, p. 258, have
the natural mark of their author. They are thefe:
" How can this animadverter come off with peremp-
" torily declaring, that fubjective faith is not inquired
" into, in the treatife of the Reafonablenefs of Chri-
" ftianity, &c. when in another place, p. 35. and 36,
" he avers, That chriftian faith and chriftianity, confi-
" dered fubjectively, are the fame?" Anfw. In which
words there are two manifeft untruths: the one is,
" That Mr. Bold peremptorily declares, that fubjec-
" tive faith is not inquired into, i. e. fpoken of, in the
" Reafonablenefs of Chriftianity," &c. Whereas Mr.
Bold fays in that place, p. 31, " If he [i. e. the au-
" thor] had not faid one word concerning faith fub-
" jectively confidered." The creed-maker's other untruth is his faying, " That the animadverter avers, p.

" 35, 36, that chriſtian faith and chriſtianity, confi-
" dered ſubjectively, are the ſame." Whereas it is evident, that Mr. Bold, arguing againſt theſe words of the
creed-maker, (" The belief of Jeſus being the Meſſiah,
" was one of the firſt and leading acts of chriſtian
" faith") ſpeaks in that place of an act of faith, as
theſe words of his demonſtrate: " Now, I appre-
" hend that chriſtian faith and chriſtianity, confidered
" ſubjectively, (and an ACT of chriſtian faith, I think,
" cannot be underſtood in any other ſenſe) are the
" very ſame." I muſt therefore deſire him to ſet
down the words wherein the animadverter peremptorily
declares,

LIII. That ſubjective faith is not inquired into, or
    ſpoken of, in the treatiſe of the Reaſonableneſs of
    Chriſtianity, &c.

And next, to produce the words wherein the animad-
    verter avers,

LIV. That chriſtian faith and chriſtianity, confidered
    ſubjectively, are the ſame.

To the creed-maker's ſaying, " That the author of
" the Reaſonableneſs of Chriſtianity, &c. brings us no
" tidings of evangelical faith belonging to chriſtianity,"
Mr. Bold replies: That I have done it in all thoſe
pages where I ſpeak of taking and accepting Jeſus to be
our King and Ruler; and particularly he ſets down my
words out of pages 119, &c.
    BUT TO THIS Mr. Edwards ANSWERS NOT.
    The creed-maker ſays, p. 59. of his Socinianiſm un-
maſked, that the author of the Reaſonableneſs of Chriſtianity " tells men again and again, that a chriſtian
" man, or member of Chriſt, needs not know or be-
" lieve any more than that one individual point." To
which Mr. Bold thus replies, p. 33, " If any man will
" ſhow me thoſe words in any part of the Reaſonable-
" neſs, &c. I ſhall ſuſpect I was not awake all the
" time I was reading that book: and I am as certain
                                                " as

" as one awake can be, that there are several passages
" in that book directly contrary to these words. And
" there are some expressions in the Vindication of the
" Reasonableness, &c. one would think, if Mr. Edwards
" had observed them, they would have prevented that
" mistake."

But to this Mr. Edwards answers not.

Mr. Bold, p. 34, takes notice, that the creed-maker
had not put the query, or objection, right, which, he
says, " Some, and not without some show of ground, may
" be apt to start : and therefore Mr. Bold puts the query
" right, viz. " Why did Jesus Christ, and his apostles,
" require assent to, and belief of, this one article alone,
" viz. That Jesus is the Messiah, to constitute and make
" a man a christian, or true member of Christ, (as it is
" abundantly evident they did, from the Reasonableness
" of Christianity) if the belief of more articles is ab-
" solutely necessary to make and constitute a man a
" christian ?"

But to this Mr. Edwards answers not.

And therefore I put the objection, or query, to him
again, in Mr. Bold's words, and expect an answer to
it, viz.

LV. Why did Jesus Christ, and his apostles, require
assent to and belief of this one article alone, viz.
That Jesus is the Messiah, to make a man a christian, (as it is abundantly evident they did, from all
their preaching, recorded throughout all the whole
history of the Evangelists and the Acts) if the belief
of more articles be absolutely necessary to make a
man a christian ?

The creed-maker having made believing Jesus to be
the Messiah, only one of the first and leading acts of
christian faith; Mr. Bold, p. 35, rightly tells him,
That " christian faith must be the belief of something
" or other : and if it be the belief of any thing besides
" this, that Jesus is the Christ, or Messiah, that other
" thing should be specified; and it should be made ap-
" pear, that the belief that Jesus is the Messiah, without
the

" the belief of that other propofition, is not chriftian faith."

BUT TO THIS Mr. Edwards ANSWERS NOT.

Mr. B—d, in the four following pages, 36—39, has excellently explained the difference between that faith which conftitutes a man a chriftian, and that faith whereby one that is a chriftian, believes the doctrines taught by our Saviour ; and the ground of that difference : and therein has fully overturned this propofition, " That believing Jefus to be the Meffiah, is but a ftep, " or the firft ftep to chriftianity."

BUT TO THIS Mr. Edwards ANSWERS NOT.

To the creed-maker's fuppofing that other matters of faith were propofed with this, that Jefus is the Meffiah; Mr. Bold replies, That this fhould be proved, viz. that other articles were propofed, as requifite to be believed to make men chriftians.   And, p. 40, he gives a reafon why he is of another mind, viz. " Becaufe there is no- " thing but this recorded, which was infifted on for that " purpofe."

BUT TO THIS Mr. Edwards ANSWERS NOT.

Mr. Bold, p. 42, fhows that Rom. x. 9, which the creed-maker brought againft it, confirms the affertion of the author of the Reafonablenefs, &c. concerning the faith that makes a man a chriftian.

BUT TO THIS Mr. Edwards ANSWERS NOT.

The creed-maker fays, p. 78, " This is the main " anfwer to the objection, (or query above propofed) viz. " That chriftianity was erected by degrees."   This Mr. Bold, p. 43, proves to be nothing to the purpofe, by this reafon, viz. " Becaufe what makes one man a " chriftian, or ever did make any man a chriftian, will " at any time, to the end of the world, make another " man a chriftian :" and afks, " Will not that make a " chriftian now, which made the apoftles themfelves " chriftians ?"

BUT TO THIS Mr. Edwards ANSWERS NOT.

In anfwer to his fixth chapter, Mr. Bold, p. 45, tells him, " It was not my bufinefs to difcourfe of the " Trinity, or any other particular doctrines, propofed " to be believed by them who are chriftians ; and that " it is no fair and juft ground to accufe a man, with " rejecting the doctrines of the Trinity, and that Jefus

" is

" is God, because he does not interpret some parti-
" cular texts to the same purpose others do."

BUT TO THIS Mr. Edwards ANSWERS NOT.

Indeed he takes notice of these words of Mr. Bold,
in this•paragraph, viz. " Hence Mr. Edwards takes oc-
" casion to write many pages about these terms [viz.
" Messiah and Son of God]; but I do not perceive that
" he pretends to offer any proof, that these were not
" synonymous terms amongst the jews at that time,
" which is the point he should have proved, if he de-
" signed to invalidate what this author says about that
" matter." To this the creed-maker replies, p. 257.
" The animadverter doth not so much as offer one
" syllable to disprove what I delivered, and closely
" urged on that head." Answ. What need any answer
to disprove, where there is no proof brought, that reaches
the proposition in question? If there had been any such
proof, the producing of it, in short, had been a more
convincing argument to the reader, than so much bragging of what has been done. For here are more words
spent, (for I have not set them all down) than would
have served to have expressed the proof of this proposition, viz. that the terms above-mentioned were not
synonymous amongst the Jews, if there had been any
proof of it. But having already examined what the
creed-maker brags he has closely urged, I shall say no
more of it here.

To the creedmaker's making me a socinian, in his
eighth chapter, for not naming Christ's satisfaction
among the advantages and benefits of Christ's coming
into the world; Mr Bold replies, " 1. That it is no
" proof, because I promised not to name every one of
" them. And the mention of some is no denial of
" others." 2. He replies, That " satisfaction is not
" so strictly to be termed an advantage, as the effects
" and fruits of it are; and that the doctrine of satis-
" faction instructs us in the way how Christ did, by di-
" vine appointment, obtain those advantages for us."
And this was an answer that deserved some reply from
the creed-maker.

BUT TO THIS HE ANSWERS NOT.

Mr. Bold fays right, that this is a doctrine that is of mighty importance for a chriftian to be well acquainted with. And I will add to it, that it is very hard for a chriftian, who reads the fcripture with attention, and an unprejudiced mind, to deny the fatisfaction of Chrift: but it being a term not ufed by the Holy Ghoft in the fcripture, and very varioufly explained by thofe that do ufe it, and very much ftumbled at by thofe I was there fpeaking to, who were fuch, as I there fay, "Who will "not take a bleffing, unlefs they be inftructed what "need they had of it, and why it was beftowed upon "them;" I left it, with the other difputed doctrines of chriftianity, to be looked into, (to fee what it was Chrift had taught concerning it) by thofe who were chriftians, and believed Jefus to be the Saviour promifed, and fent from God. And to thofe who yet doubted that he was fo, and made this objection, "What need was there of a Saviour?" I thought it moft reafonable to offer fuch particulars only as were agreed on by all chriftians, and were capable of no difpute, but muft be acknowledged by every body to be needful. This, though the words above-quoted out of the Reafonablenefs of Chriftianity, &c. p. 129, fhow to be my defign; yet the creed-maker plainly gives me the lye, and tells me it was not my defign. "All the "world are faithlefs, falfe, treacherous, hypocritical "ftrainers upon their reafon and confcience, diffem- "blers, journeymen, mercenary hirelings, except Mr. "Edwards:" I mean, all the world that oppofes him. And muft not one think he is mightily beholden to the excellency and readinefs of his own nature, who is no fooner engaged in controverfy, but he immediately finds out in his adverfaries thefe arts of equivocation, lying and effrontery, in managing of it? Reafon and learning, and acquired improvements, might elfe have let him gone on with others, in the dull and ordinary way of fair arguing; wherein, poffibly, he might have done no great feats. Muft not a rich and fertile foil within, and a prompt genius, wherein a man may readily fpy the propenfities of bafe and corrupt nature, be acknow- ledged to be an excellent qualification for a difputant,

to

to help him to the quick difcovery and laying open of
the faults of his opponents; which a mind otherwife
difpofed would not fo much as fufpect? But Mr. Bold,
without this, could not have been fo foon found out to
be a journeyman, a diffembler, an hired mercenary, and
ftored with all thofe good qualities, wherein he hath his
full fhare with me. But why would he then venture
upon Mr. Edwards, who is fo very quick-fighted in
thefe matters, and knows fo well what villainous man is
capable of?

I fhould not here, in this my Vindication, have given
the reader fo much of Mr. Bold's reafoning, which,
though clear and ftrong, yet has more beauty and force,
as it ftands in the whole piece in his book; nor fhould I
have fo often repeated this remark upon each paffage,
viz. " To this Mr. Edwards anfwers not;" had it not
been the fhorteft and propereft comment could be made
on that triumphant paragraph of his, which begins in
the 128th page of his Socinian creed; wherein, among
a great deal of no fmall ftrutting, are thefe words : " By
" their profound filence they acknowledge they have
" nothing to reply." He that defires to fee more of
the fame noble ftrain, may have recourfe to that eminent
place. Befides, it was fit the reader fhould have this
one tafte more of the creed-maker's genius, who, paffing by in filence all thefe clear and appofite replies of
Mr. Bold, loudly complains of him, p. 259, " That
" where he [Mr. Bold] finds fomething that he dares
" not object againft, he fhifts it off." And again, p.
260, " That he does not make any offer at reafon;
" there is not the leaft fhadow of an argument---As if
" he were only hired to fay fomething againft me, [the
" creed-maker] though not at all to the purpofe: and
" truly, any man may difcern a MERCENARY ftroke all
" along;" with a great deal more to the fame purpofe.
For fuch language as this, mixed with fcurrility, neither
fit to be fpoken by, nor of, a minifter of the gofpel,
make up the remainder of his poftfcript. But to prevent this for the future; I demand of him, that if in
either of his treatifes, there be any thing againft what I
have faid, in my Reafonablenefs of Chriftianity, which

he thinks not fully anfwered, he will fet down the propofition in direct words, and note the page of his book
where it is to be found: and I promife him to anfwer it.
For as for his railing, and other ftuff befides the matter,
I fhall hereafter no more trouble myfelf to take notice of
it.   And fo much for Mr. Edwards.

THERE is another gentleman, and of another fort
        of make, parts and breeding, who, (as it feems,
afhamed of Mr. Edwards's way of handling controverfies in religion) has had fomething to fay of my " Rea-
" fonablenefs of Chriftianity, &c." and fo has made it
neceffary for me to fay a word to him, before I let thofe
papers go out of my hand.   It is the author of " the
" Occafional paper," numb. 1.   The fecond, third, and
fourth pages of that paper, gave me great hopes to meet
with a man, who would examine all the miftakes which
came abroad in print, with that temper and indifferency,
that might fet an exact pattern for controverfy, to thofe
who would approve themfelves to be fincere contenders
for truth and knowledge, and nothing elfe, in the difputes
they engaged in.   Making him allowance for the miftakes that felf-indulgence is apt to impofe upon human
frailty, I am apt to believe he thought his performance
had been fuch: but I crave leave to obferve, that good
and candid men are often mifled, from a fair unbiaffed
purfuit of truth, by an over-great zeal for fomething,
that they, upon wrong grounds, take to be fo; and that
it is not fo eafy to be a fair and unprejudiced champion
for truth, as fome, who profefs it, think it to be.   To
acquaint him with the occafion of this remark, I muft
defire him to read and confider his nineteenth page; and
then to tell me,

    1. Whether he knows, that the doctrine propofed in
the " Reafonablenefs of Chriftianity, &c." was borrowed, as he fays, from Hobbes's Leviathan? For I
tell him, I borrowed it only from the writers of the four
Gofpels and the Acts; and did not know thofe words,
he quoted out of the Leviathan, were there, or any thing
like them.   Nor do I know yet, any farther than as I
believe them to be there, from his quotation.

                                        2. Whether

2. Whether affirming, as he does pofitively, this, which he could not know to be true, and is in itfelf perfectly falfe, were meant to increafe or leffen the credit of the author of the " Reafonablenefs of Chriftianity, &c." in the opinion of the world? Or is confonant with his own rule, p. 3, " of putting candid conftructions on " what adverfaries fay?" Or with what follows, in thefe words? " The more divine the caufe is, ftill the " greater fhould be the caution. The very difcourfing " about Almighty God, or our holy religion, fhould " compofe our paffions, and infpire us with candour " and love. It is very indecent to handle fuch fub- " jects, in a manner that betrays rancour and fpite. " Thefe are fiends that ought to vanifh, and fhould " never mix, either with a fearch after truth, or the de- " fence of religion."

3. Whether the propofitions which he has, out of my book, inferted into his nineteenth page, and fays, " are " confonant to the words of the Leviathan," were thofe of all my book, which were likelieft to give the reader a true and fair notion of the doctrine contained in it? If they were not, I muft defire him to remember and beware of his fiends. Not but that he will find thofe propofitions there to be true. But that neither he nor others may miftake my book, this is that, in fhort, which it fays:

1. That there is a faith that makes men chriftians.

2. That this faith is the believing " Jefus of Nazareth to be the Meffiah."

3. That the believing Jefus to be the Meffiah includes in it a receiving him for our Lord and King, promifed and fent from God: and fo lays upon all his fubjects an abfolute and indifpenfable neceffity of affenting to all that they can attain the knowledge that he taught; and of a fincere obedience to all that he commanded.

This, whether it be the doctrine of the Leviathan, I know not. This appears to me out of the New Teftament, from whence (as I told him in the preface) I took it to be the doctrine of our Saviour and his apoftles; and I would not willingly be miftaken in it. If therefore

fore

fore there be any other faith befides this, abfolutely re-quifite to make a man a chriftian, I fhall here again de-fire this gentleman to inform me what it is; i. e. to fet downall thofe propofitions which are fo indifpenfably to be believed, (for it is of fimple believing I perceive the controverfy runs) that no man can be a believer, i. e. a chriftian, without an actual knowledge of, and an ex-plicit affent to, them. If he fhall do this with that candour and fairnefs he declares to be neceffary in fuch matters, I fhall own myfelf obliged to him: for I am in earneft, and I would not be miftaken in it.

If he fhall decline it, I, and the world too, muft con-clude, that upon a review of my doctrine, he is con-vinced of the truth of it, and is fatisfied, that I am in the right. For it is impoffible to think, that a man of that fairnefs and candour, which he folemnly prefaces his difcourfe with, fhould continue to condemn the ac-count I have given of the faith which I am perfuaded makes a chriftian; and yet he himfelf will not tell me, (when I earneftly demand it of him, as defirous to be rid of my errour, if it be one) what is that more, which is abfolutely required to be believed by every one, be-fore he can be a believer, i. e. what is indifpenfably ne-ceffary to be known, and explicitly believed, to make a man a chriftian.

Another thing which I muft defire this author to ex-amine, by thofe his own rules, is, what he fays of me, p. 30, where he makes me to have a prejudice againft the miniftry of the gofpel, and their office, from what I have faid in my Reafonablenefs, &c. p. 135, 136, con-cerning the priefts of the world, in our Saviour's time: which he calls bitter reflections.

If he will tell me what is fo bitter, in any one of thofe paffages which he has fet down, that is not true, or ought not to be faid there, and give me the reafon why he is offended at it; I promife him to make what reparation he fhall think fit, to the memory of thofe priefts, whom he, with fo much good-nature, patronizes, near feventeen hundred years after they have been out of the world; and is fo tenderly concerned for their repu-tation, that he excepts againft that, as faid againft them,
which

which was not. For one of the three places he fets down, was not fpoken of priefts. But his making my mentioning the faults of the priefts of old, in our Saviour's time, to be an " expofing the office of the " minifters of the gofpel now, and a vilifying thofe " who are employed in it;" I muft defire him to ex-amine, by his own rules of love and candour; and to tell me, " Whether I have not reafon, here again, to mind " him of his FIENDS, and to advife him to beware of " them?" And to fhow him why I think I have, I crave leave to afk him thefe queftions:

1. Whether I do not all along plainly, and in exprefs words, fpeak of the priefts of the world, preceding, and in our Saviour's time? Nor can my argument bear any other fenfe.

2. Whether all I have faid of them be not true?

3. Whether the reprefenting truly the carriage of the jewifh, and more efpecially of the heathen priefts, in our Saviour's time, as my argument required, can expofe the office of the minifters of the gofpel now? Or ought to have fuch an interpretation put upon it?

4. Whether what he fays of the " air and language I " ufe, reaching farther," carry any thing elfe in it, but a declaration, that he thinks fome men's carriage now, hath fome affinity with what I have truly faid, of the priefts of the world, before chriftianity; and that there-fore the faults of thofe fhould have been let alone, or touched more gently, for fear fome fhould think thefe now concerned in it?

5. Whether, in truth, this be not to accufe them, with a defign to draw the envy of it on me? Whether out of good-will to them, or to me, or both, let him look. This I am fure, I have fpoke of none but the priefts before chriftianity, both jewifh and heathen! And for thofe of the jews, what our Saviour has pro-nounced of them, juftifies my reflections from being bitter; and that the idolatrous heathen priefts were better than they, I believe our author will not fay: and if he were preaching againft them, as oppofing the mi-nifters of the gofpel, I fuppofe he will give as ill a character of them. But if any one extends my words

farther, than to thofe they were fpoke of, I afk whether that agrees with his rules of love and candour?

I fhall impatiently expect from this author of the occafional paper, an anfwer to thefe queftions; and hope to find them fuch as becomes that temper, and love of truth, which he profeffes. I long to meet with a man, who, laying afide party, and intereft, and prejudice, appears in controverfy fo as to make good the character of a champion of truth for truth's fake; a character not fo hard to be known whom it belongs to, as to be deferved. Whoever is truly fuch an one, his oppofition to me will be an obligation. For he that propofes to himfelf the convincing me of an errour, only for truth's fake, cannot, I know, mix any rancour, or fpite, or ill-will, with it. He will keep himfelf at a diftance from thofe FIENDS, and be as ready to hear, as offer reafon. And two fo difpofed can hardly mifs truth between them, in a fair inquiry after it; at leaft, they will not loofe good-breeding, and efpecially charity, a virtue much more neceffary than the attaining of the knowledge of obfcure truths, that are not eafy to be found; and probably, therefore, not neceffary to be known.

The unbiaffed defign of the writer, purely to defend and propagate truth, feems to me to be that alone which legitimates controverfies. I am fure it plainly diftinguifhes fuch from all others, in their fuccefs and ufefulnefs. If a man, as a fincere friend to the perfon, and to the truth, labours to bring another out of errour, there can be nothing more beautiful, nor more beneficial. If party, paffion, or vanity direct his pen, and have a hand in the controverfy; there can be nothing more unbecoming, more prejudicial, nor more odious. What thoughts I fhall have of a man that fhall, as a chriftian, go about to inform me what is neceffary to be believed to make a man a chriftian, I have declared, in the preface to my " Reafonablenefs of Chriftianity, " &c." nor do I find myfelf yet altered. He that, in print, finds fault with my imperfect difcovery of that, wherein the faith, which makes a man a chriftian, confifts, and will not tell me what more is required, will do well to fatisfy the world what they ought to think of him.

8

INDEX.

I N D E X

INDEX.

INDEX.

INDEX.

INDEX.

INDEX.

KEY TEXTS

Classic Works in the History of Ideas

Also Available in this series:

ARISTOTELIANISM
John Leofric Stocks
ISBN 1 85506 222 4 : 1925 Edition : 174pp : £12.99/$19.95

CHURCHES IN THE MODERN STATE
J. N. Figgis
ISBN 1 85506 543 6 : 1913 Edition : 276pp : £13.99/$19.95

DESCARTES
Anthony Kenny
ISBN 1 85506 236 4 : 1968 Edition : 256pp : £9.99/$14.95

DESCARTES'S RULES FOR THE DIRECTION OF THE MIND
Harold H. Joachim (Edited by Errol E. Harris)
ISBN 1 85506 517 7 : 1957 Edition : 124pp : £9.99/$15.95

AN ESSAY ON PHILOSOPHICAL METHOD
R. G. Collingwood
ISBN 1 85506 392 1 : 1933 Edition : 240pp : £14.99/$24.95

FOUR DISSERTATIONS
David Hume
New Introduction by John Immerwahr
ISBN 1 85506 393 X : 1757 Edition : 258pp : £14.99/$24.95

FRANCIS HUTCHESON
William Robert Scott
ISBN 1 85506 169 4 : 1900 Edition : 318pp : £14.99/$28.95

A HISTORY OF POLITICAL THOUGHT IN THE
ENGLISH REVOLUTION
Perez Zagorin
ISBN 1 85506 544 4 : 1954 Edition : 215pp : £12.99/$19.95

HUMAN NATURE, OR THE FUNDAMENTAL ELEMENTS OF POLICY
bound with
DE CORPORE POLITICO
Thomas Hobbes
New Introduction by G.A.J. Rogers
ISBN 1 85506 351 4 : 1840 Edition : 228pp : £14.99/$24.95

THE HUNTING OF LEVIATHAN
Samuel Mintz
ISBN 1 85506 481 2 : 1962 Edition : 200pp : £14.99/$24.95

AN INTRODUCTION TO THE PHILOSOPHY OF HISTORY
W. H. Walsh
ISBN 1 85506 170 8 : 1961 Edition : 176pp : £12.99/$19.95

LOCKE AND THE WAY OF IDEAS
John W. Yolton
ISBN 1 85506 226 7 : 1956 Edition : 248pp : £15.99/$28.95

OF THE CONDUCT OF THE UNDERSTANDING
John Locke
New Introduction by John Yolton
ISBN 1 85506 225 9 : 1706 Edition : 160pp : £12.99/$19.95

ON THE AESTHETIC EDUCATION OF MAN, IN A SERIES OF LETTERS
Friedrich Schiller (Translated by Reginald Snell)
ISBN 1 85506 322 0 : 1954 Edition : 150pp : £14.99/$26.95

OUTLINES OF THE HISTORY OF GREEK PHILOSOPHY
Eduard Zeller
ISBN 1 85506 545 2 : 1931 Edition : 340pp : £14.99/$19.95

PHILOSOPHICAL STUDIES
J. McT. E. McTaggart (Edited with an original introduction by S. V. Keeling)
New Introduction by Gerald Rochelle
ISBN 1 85506 479 0 : 1934 Edition : 300pp : £12.99/$19.95

THE PHILOSOPHY OF HEGEL
G. R. G. Mure
ISBN 1 85506 237 2 : 1965 Edition : 224pp : £12.99
[Not available in the USA]

THE PHILOSOPHY OF KANT
John Kemp
ISBN 1 85506 238 0 : 1968 Edition : 138pp : £9.99
[Not available in the USA]

PHILOSOPHY AND LOGICAL SYNTAX
Rudolf Carnap
ISBN 1 85506 428 6 : 1935 Edition : 99pp : £12.99/$14.95

THE PHILOSOPHY OF NIETZSCHE
Abraham Wolf
ISBN 1 85506 353 0 : 1915 Edition : 120pp : £9.99/$14.95

THE PHILOSOPHY OF RELIGION 1875–1980
Alan P. F. Sell
ISBN 1 85506 482 0 : 1988 Edition : 260pp : £12.99/$19.95

PLATO'S PROGRESS
Gilbert Ryle
ISBN 1 85506 321 2 : 1966 Edition : 320pp : £16.99/$29.95

POLITICAL THEORIES OF THE MIDDLE AGE
Otto Gierke (Translated with an introduction by F. W. Maitland)
ISBN 1 85506 478 2 : 1900 Edition : 278pp : £12.99/$19.95

RATIONALISM
John Cottingham
ISBN 1 85506 524 X : 1984 Edition : 187pp : £12.99/$22.95

THE REASONABLENESS OF CHRISTIANITY
John Locke
New Introduction by Victor Nuovo
ISBN 1 85506 522 3 : 1794 Edition : 440pp : £17.99/$29.95

RELIGION AND PHILOSOPHY
R. G. Collingwood
ISBN 1 85506 317 4 : 1916 Edition : 238pp : £14.99/$24.95

SCHOPENHAUER
Patrick Gardiner
ISBN 1 85506 525 8 : 1963 Edition : 315pp : £14.99/$24.95

SCIENCE AND METHOD
Henri Poincaré
ISBN 1 85506 431 6 : 1914 Edition : 288pp : £14.99/$24.95

SIX SECULAR PHILOSOPHERS
Lewis White Beck
ISBN 1 85506 518 5 : 1960 Edition : 126pp : £9.99/$15.95

SOME DOGMAS OF RELIGION
J. McT. E. McTaggart
New Introduction by Gerald Rochelle
ISBN 1 85506 519 3 : 1930 Edition : 299pp : £13.99/$24.95

THOMAS HOBBES
A. E. Taylor
ISBN 1 85506 523 1 : 1908 Edition : 136pp : £9.99/$14.95

THE UNCONSCIOUS. A CONCEPTUAL ANALYSIS
Alasdair MacIntyre
ISBN 1 85506 520 7 : 1958 Edition : 109pp : £11.99/$19.95

THE UNITY OF SCIENCE
Rudolf Carnap
ISBN 1 85506 391 3 : 1934 Edition : 102pp : £9.99/$14.95

UK Office
11 Great George Street, Bristol BS1 5RR
Tel. (0117) 929 1377, Fax (0117) 922 1918

USA Office
Books International, P.O. Box 605, Herndon, Virginia 22070, USA
Tel. 1-703-435-7064, Fax 1-703-689-0660

6981